A Critical Approach to Human Growth and Development

# A CRITICAL APPROACH TO HUMAN GROWTH AND DEVELOPMENT

## A Textbook for Social Work Students and Practitioners

Paula Nicolson

*Emeritus Professor of Health and Social Care*
*University of London*
*(Royal Holloway)*

First published 2014 by
PALGRAVE MACMILLAN

Palgrave Macmillan in the UK is an imprint of Macmillan Publishers Limited,
registered in England, company number 785998, of Houndmills, Basingstoke,
Hampshire RG21 6XS.

Palgrave Macmillan in the US is a division of St Martin's Press LLC,
175 Fifth Avenue, New York, NY 10010.

Palgrave Macmillan is the global academic imprint of the above companies
and has companies and representatives throughout the world.

Palgrave® and Macmillan® are registered trademarks in the United States,
the United Kingdom, Europe and other countries

ISBN: 978-0-230-24902-8

This book is printed on paper suitable for recycling and made from fully
managed and sustained forest sources. Logging, pulping and manufacturing
processes are expected to conform to the environmental regulations of the
country of origin.

A catalogue record for this book is available from the British Library.

A catalog record for this book is available from the Library of Congress.

Printed in China

# CONTENTS

# ACKNOWLEDGEMENTS

I have been teaching undergraduate and graduate social workers, psychologists, sociologists and medical students for more than 35 years. I have enjoyed teaching you all and am grateful for the knowledge and experience of working with so many who went on to become successful social workers, psychologists, managers, doctors, academics and other professionals. I continue, now in a freelance capacity, to teach social workers studying advanced practice at master's level, as well as consulting to social work organizations. Without involvement in such diverse areas of organizational life I doubt I could have undertaken the challenge of this book.

Equally, colleagues, researchers and doctoral students, too many to list you all, have made a difference to how I have understood the subject matter of human growth and development (HGD). They include Bipasha Ahmed, Rinku Alam, Rowan Bayne, Gary Bellamy, Jan Burns, Toni Bifulco, the late Precilla Choi, Kathy Doherty, Rebekah Fox, Merryn Gott, Yael Ilan-Clarke, Sharon Hinchliff, Christine Horrocks, Marsha Koletsi, Sian Lewis, Paula Lokman, the late Barrie Newman, Marie Reid, Brian Roberts, Owen Rossan, Emma Rowland, Graham Smith, Jonathan Smith, Vicki Smith, Paula Reavey, Alison Thomas, Sue Thorpe, Jill Tunaley, Jane Ussher, Sue Wilkinson and Anna Williams.

More recently, colleagues, teachers and friends from my training as an organizational consultant at the Tavistock and Portman NHS Foundation Trust, particularly Helen Shaw, Andrew Briggs, Haddy Davis, Angela Eden, Sebastian Green, Catherine Hartley, Ben Neal, Chris Ramsden and Stuart Stevenson, have made a difference to my thinking about the intra-psychic context of HGD. Also, I must not forget my colleagues and friends from the Department of Social Work at Royal Holloway, University of London including Anna Gupta, Kristin Heffernan, Liz Hudson, Frank Keating and Alix Walton.

As ever, I acknowledge the patience and support of Derry Nicolson, Kate Nicolson, Darren Annon, Malachi and Azriel Annon-Nicolson.

I am also indebted to Catherine Gray of Palgrave who persuaded me to take on this project and whose patience, helpful comments and support have ensured that this book emerged into the light of day.

Thanks to all of you.

Paula Nicolson, December 2013

# WHAT TO EXPECT

Theories of human growth and development (HGD) and their application to practice are fundamental to professional social work. My intention with this book is to provide a key resource for social work students, lecturers and practitioners, one which makes sense of the many ideas emanating from the disciplines of psychology, biology and sociology, in particular, that are encompassed by the term HGD. My approach is designed to prepare students to develop a critical approach to this field of knowledge. I hope qualified and experienced practitioners might also be able to use this book for reference purposes, and that it will prove an aid to workplace supervision and mentoring.

Social work takes place in complex, rapidly changing conditions and is a highly stressful, although potentially equally rewarding, profession. More than ever before, social work practice operates in partnerships with other agencies and professional groups, all requiring the ability to engage in complex negotiations about priorities surrounding practice.

This book offers an applied-evidence base from a critical standpoint for social work practitioners, combining a tool kit with the academic knowledge and critical skills to aid decision-making as part of a developmental reflective-relational practice. For social workers and related professionals, understanding HGD is part of the core knowledge base that informs decisions about best practice for effectively supporting service users. Without a strong grasp of HGD it would be impossible to exercise the degree of decision-making necessary for working in complex situations with vulnerable or older adults, people with mental health problems, or in child protection cases.

Working with and alongside people requires us to think, *What is going on here and why?* at the point of every interaction. It is the capacity to handle different kinds of knowledge – emotional, analytical and so on – wisely at a number of levels that shapes the authority we employ as professionals when we make decisions about other people's lives. Some social workers are naturally better at making intuitive sense of other people's behaviour than others. But we can all sharpen our intuitive and analytical skills to ensure we provide well-informed assessments and make compassionate as well as effective decisions.

The book is divided into two parts. In the Introduction, I explain the book's analytical and organizational framework. Part I then provides contextual background on some of the major themes and theories of HGD. Here I also introduce the idea of a reflective-relational approach to practice. Part II employs a material-discursive-intra-psychic (MDI) approach, which takes account of the physical, social and emotional elements of HGD, to the key developmental stages of the lifespan, exploring each theoretically with up-to-date research examples and practice-based illustrations.

## Part I: Theories of HGD and how to think about them critically

Chapters 1 to 3 explore the origins of the nature/nurture debate, which has proved one of the richest, and most contested, areas of debate in psychology and other social and human sciences. I ask whether nature (in the form of our bodies) or nurture (in the form of our social relationships) has the more influential role in shaping our lives and identities. In these three chapters I outline some of the key theories within psychology, psychobiology and sociology that address this question and then introduce a critical dimension to experts' claims about the brain (neuroscience) and the relative importance of the environment.

Chapter 4 draws upon the concept of the lifespan (sometimes discussed elsewhere as the life-course or life-cycle) as an organizing device for understanding developmental change. This chapter specifically identifies some of the key issues represented by each stage of life, based loosely on Erikson's 'eight ages' which I shall describe in more detail below and also explains the interdisciplinary MDI model more fully.

In Chapter 5, the key concepts around attachment, separation and loss are explored, with particular emphasis on some of the classic experiments, theory and clinical observations that have underpinned a century of theoretical development. While this particular chapter focuses on early life, the concepts linked to attachment theory will be revisited in Part II in relation to adolescence and adulthood.

Chapter 6 proposes a *reflective-relational* approach towards evidence-based practice. This perspective on practice brings together critical thinking about your developing knowledge of the lifespan using the MDI approach to theory with an awareness of your self and how you relate to other people. Reflective-relational practice, therefore, builds upon your growing understanding of developmental stage, background, behaviour, social context and emotional reactions of service users and practitioners. With this framework in mind, you have the tools to recognize how (and when) to apply theory to practice in a reflective-relational way.

## Part II: The lifespan: a material-discursive-intra-psychic approach to theory and practice

Part II concentrates on theories that are most relevant to each stage of growth and development, again using a material-discursive-intra-psychic framework as a means of analysis.

In Chapter 7, Infancy and early childhood, we explore the early days, weeks and months of life, up until around the age of five when most children in the Western world will start nursery and/or school. We look at the evidence from cognitive developmental studies (Piaget, 1990) and neuropsychology (Meltzoff and Decety, 2003), and identify links between these perspectives and the work of Erikson (1959/1980) and other more socially disposed developmental theorists, particularly Melanie Klein (1975), John Bowlby (1988) and Donald Winnicott (1965).

Chapter 8, considering Older Childhood, foregrounds life outside the home from nursery school onwards and features the child's increasing ability to make relationships and develop expectations of consistency (or the opposite, depending on experience). The theories identified in preceding chapters are also linked into descriptions of this stage alongside attachment theory and Erikson's work which are used to demonstrate the range of possible emotional, biological and social outcomes for each child, and indeed every one of us. Development of thinking, too, is particularly important at this stage of life, and we look at this again in the social and biological context.

Adolescence, discussed in Chapter 9, is pivotal, because adolescence is for many either a turning point or the stage of life where future possibilities are fixed. It has particular importance in considerations of inequalities in health, education and employment potential. The chapter also explores sexuality and its crucial role in the development and failure of relationships.

Chapter 10, Young Adulthood, describes the stage at which the normal expectation is for a person to become independent of their family of origin, spend time with and be influenced by their own friends and perhaps move towards a serious intimate relationship and (possibly) parenthood. There are many pitfalls and risks to such expectations and these are considered in the context of twenty-first century Western societies. There is evidence that three generations of family remain living in the same household (which may not, of course, be so unusual in other parts of the world) and an *unexpected* increased dependency at both ends of the lifespan, which impacts particularly on those entering adulthood.

Chapter 11 examines Midlife, during which time a person may feel their life is either settling down or falling apart. We consider what theories might be drawn upon to understand and help support someone in the latter category because they are more likely to have contact with social workers and other health care professionals.

Older age, the subject of Chapter 12, is a stage of life that has changed greatly since the 1990s. Women and men are living longer on average, but health inequalities have become intensified. There are also large differences in income for older people. Thus health, well-being, emotional and economic certainty and uncertainty face this group – particularly in the face of the economic fallout from the global recession of 2008.

Finally, in Chapter 13, I draw together the experience of HGD, assessing the value of using both lifespan and MDI frameworks.

All chapters provide information about theory and practice to support decisions that social workers make in their day-to-day work.

## Using the book

At the start of each chapter I list three learning objectives to help you to think about and evaluate the content quickly. At the end of each chapter, there is a summary that picks up on these objectives and an annotated further reading list.

In most chapters, I introduce case examples in which HGD issues are appropriate and an MDI approach to the analysis and subsequent decision-making is likely to support best practice.

Also, at key stages of the chapters, to draw your attention to a theory/practice matter I have introduced Pause and Reflect boxes, again intended to bring together the ideas from theory and practice.

In what follows there is a small cast of characters, all of whom are based on real people, although important identifying details have been altered. They have all had contact with social workers in different types of agency, including and mostly with myself or people I have mentored, consulted or coached. Although potential identifying information has been changed, the challenges these people faced were real for them and will resonate with the experiences of many other people. Each case study demonstrates how complex growth and development can be, and how social workers might be charged to make and support decisions at various stages of life.

Although the book is geared primarily to students on qualifying social work programmes in the UK, research from North America, Australia and elsewhere features strongly across all the studies that informs HGD, and some of it is described here.

I use the female and male genders randomly, and hopefully evenly, when talking about the individual in preference to s/he.

Enjoy the book!

# INTRODUCTION: WHAT IS SO IMPORTANT ABOUT HGD?

## What do we mean by human growth and development (HGD)?

Growing and developing are common to us all, but each one of us experiences these processes and their outcomes differently. As part of being human we make choices and decisions about how to live our own lives, but we also have our opportunities constrained or enhanced by biological (perhaps genetic) factors, our own and others' beliefs about what is important and what is possible, our emotional needs and the social and economic resources available to us.

Over time, our bodies change in size and shape and our physical, mental and emotional capabilities also develop and change. Newborn infants, for instance, are able to grasp and suck but unable to stand or hold on to anything. By the time they are two years old, it is likely that they will also be able to speak and scribble, run and jump. As time goes on, many of us develop increased capacities for complex physical tasks (tying shoe laces, dancing or playing football).

However, we also age. Aging and development are parallel processes with some widespread misunderstandings held about both of them. So for instance, although many of us may feel less physically agile when we reach thirty than we were at eighteen, we have to acknowledge significant exceptions. David Beckham, the famous footballer, did not retire from top class football until he was nearly forty, showing how risky it is to make sweeping assumptions about age alongside capacity.

It has been suggested by some that we are also less *mentally* agile once we leave our twenties than we may have been in our teens. Many children, for instance, demonstrate abilities with technologies that their parents and grandparents may be slower to grasp. Although we can learn to use new technologies, perhaps for the first time, in middle age, there are reasons that some of us find them harder to master than it appears to be for those brought up with them as part of their early life. The same is superficially true of learning a foreign language. Early exposure to more than one language, including the need to respond in more than one

1

language, not only ensures fluency but also appears to increase our ability to learn yet more languages when we are older. It is about training the brain.

But we need to think about this more clearly, and from an informed, evidence-based position. Are we less mentally agile as we age or are there fewer *opportunities* to learn new ways of thinking and behaving? For example, many women don't develop their abilities to multi-task (a good measure of mental agility) until they have juggled family relationships, managing children and their careers – frequently after reaching their thirties.

More concentrated, deeper thinking is also likely to be connected with growing older (and as the saying goes, wiser). Many of the same adults who find computer games difficult to master will be able to solve complex problems involved with managing other forms of information technology or perhaps those problems entailed with managing groups of people.

So, although there are commonly held beliefs indicating that we begin to deteriorate mentally at twenty-one or thereabouts, that is clearly a simplistic view. Certainly there is a common lifespan during which we become older, our bodies become less contained, our sight and hearing become weaker and so on. Many people suffer memory loss in old age, sometimes to a very debilitating degree. But the lifespan is a complex process and we do more than simply live. Along with the physical and sensual changes that appear as deteriorations, we *grow* and *change* intellectually and emotionally. We frequently hear people say (and perhaps echo their sentiment), *'if only I knew then what I know now'*. How often do parents try to make sure their children understand the mistakes they are so obviously making – misusing drugs, having unprotected sex, not doing their homework? Looking back from the point of view of experience, many years of observations, reflection and putting our thoughts and feelings together, we can anticipate what hazards might befall children in ways that perhaps we were unable to do for ourselves when we were young.

Older adults too have choices and take risks. Relationships grow and change – they may fail, leaving people lonely and vulnerable. Frequently older people make new kinds of relationships that are fulfilling in different ways from those they sustained when they were younger. Responsibilities and expectations change with growth and aging. With these our identities change and cries from the heart of *'how* could *I have done that?'* vie for prominence with *'how did I* manage *that?"* as we become older.

## Adopting a critical perspective to HGD

So much has been written over recent years under the label of HGD that it is easy to assume a shared understanding of what these concepts of *growth* and *development* mean. It is one of the first rules of critical thinking that you should not take ideas or beliefs for granted, no matter how popular or widespread they are. Seemingly basic questions can prove important if we stop to ask them:

- Can we assume there are normal pathways to HGD, and if so how might we know?
- Do different experiences impact on individuals in different ways, and how might we find out if this is the case?
- If there *are* normal pathways of HGD, how might we explain and evaluate our individual differences?

This book seeks to explore some of the theories scholars and researchers have come up with in pursuit of answers to such questions, with a view to providing students with the analytical tools to assess the relative value of what can often seem to be conflicting accounts. I question the status of the evidence or knowledge-claims presented by experts – about attachment, for instance. How might we decide what are facts and what are favoured ideas, concepts and hypotheses that expert researchers and theorists put into the public domain? Once a particular set of ideas has been discussed in scientific journals and the media, they become very influential but what resources can we draw on to assess the real contribution of a theory or a piece of research evidence?

There is often a general bias, or preferred view of the world, among all academics who articulate claims to knowledge – whether theoretical or research-based. Those writers who take on a more sociological or contextual approach (focusing on inequalities, for instance) frequently neglect some of the more biological perspectives on HGD. They might dismiss psychology as overly *individualistic* (focusing solely on individual experiences rather than identifying a trend or characteristic of a group), as *reductionist* (ignoring the context in which growth and development occur and focusing on the most basic observable fact – citing a genetic cause of behaviour for example) or as *determinist* (assuming a particular measure in early childhood will prescribe all future achievement). These terms are important for considering the role of research evidence and how it informs practice. We will return to them in Chapters 1 to 3.

Despite these challenges to psychology as a discipline, the evidence that an understanding of individual or family/group psychology can make an important contribution to addressing certain problems holds fast.

On the other hand, neuropsychologists (also known as cognitive neuroscientists and sometimes brain scientists) might tend to belittle arguments that human beings are anything beyond biology. For example, in their eyes emotion is a learned physiological pattern that becomes seared into a neural pathway in the brain that is consequently triggered when external events provide appropriate stimulation.

By taking a critical standpoint, we can interrogate their different theoretical positions and consider alternative viewpoints. This gives us the scope to grasp a more multidimensional view of the issue under consideration. For social workers, this means considering problems and their potential solutions in the round, rather than relying on first assumptions.

## Taking these ideas forward

What might you expect from reading on? The book is based on two complementary explanatory frameworks.

Firstly, I use the concept of the *lifespan*, drawn from Erik Erikson's (1950/1963) influential psychosocial model of human development, to underline and describe the processes of growth and development in a psychological, biological and cultural context. The lifespan, discussed in more detail in Chapter 4, provides a particularly clear and helpful framework for describing, understanding and explaining our experiences of growing older. It allows for a full exploration of the complex nature of human relationships and how our bodies develop at every stage of life. Given the diverse and often challenging nature of social work, Erik Erikson's model offers a versatile and inclusive framework for thinking about human behaviour.

Secondly, I develop a more in-depth and detailed account through a *material-discursive-intra-psychic* perspective, which I have developed in order to explore HGD in depth. The material-discursive-intra-psychic perspective (MDI) is developed throughout the book, also beginning with a detailed account in Chapter 4. It provides the book's critical lens. Psychologists began to think about how to link biological and social contexts and the place of language in explaining the biological and social world in the 1990s. This was done particularly around issues of gender, sexuality and the female body (Ussher, 1997) and health (Yardley, 1996) in what became known as the material-discursive and/or the bio-psychosocial models. More recently, Jane Ussher and colleagues have developed this work in relation to women's reproductive bodies (Ussher, 2003; Ussher et al., 2002), linking unconscious and emotional elements in a paradigm they have termed a material-discursive-intra-psychic perspective

I have used these ideas to develop a more comprehensive material-discursive-intra-psychic model drawing additionally on the work of sociologist, Anthony Giddens, who has used different levels of consciousness, including the unconscious, in his analysis of the structure of society (Giddens, 1986/2003, 1991). Giddens also considered Erikson's approach to the lifespan particularly useful as a framework for his ideas about living in society.

## BOX 0.1

**The material-discursive-intra-psychic (MDI) model**

You will read more about the MDI model in Chapter 4, but I want to explain now a little more of what I have included within this approach:

- *'Material'* refers to the biological and social elements of our lives which have a physical, bodily or economic reality or impact for each one of us. It refers, in other words, to our bodies, brains (as opposed to minds), physical needs and material circumstances (housing, diet, income, etc.), as well as our social and intimate relationships. When it is appropriate in this book, and it often seems to be, I draw a distinction between bio-material and socio-material contexts; that is, the biological and societal contexts which impact on HGD.
- The *'discursive'* relates to the way we talk and think about the world and our experiences of being part of it. Our words and ideas inform how we behave as powerfully as our material environment does, so that through talking and thinking we construct a view of the world and our experience of our selves, other people and the organizations and social institutions which make up part of the social fabric. The discursive dimension of HGD operates on different levels, from talking about research findings to commonly held popular beliefs that inhabit our everyday thinking. It works at the level of language (e.g. what words we choose) and at the level of narrative (i.e. the stories we use to explore the world and our experience of it). As we shall see, it is particularly valuable for thinking critically about the role of *power* in understanding how we make sense of experience.
- The *'intra-psychic'* focuses on our interior lives, particularly the emotional and unconscious aspects of experience and relating to others. We are sometimes aware of our emotional reactions to people and events and sometimes we cannot understand our own responses. At other times we are even unaware that we are reacting in a particular way to things. This may be because some very early, perhaps preverbal (i.e. things that happened to us before we had the words to understand them) feelings and experiences have been brought up to the surface by a contemporary situation or relationship.

A model of HGD that takes account of all these frameworks (see Box 0.1) is particularly relevant to a discipline and practice such as social work where life-changing decisions are made and depend upon social workers' judgments.

The MDI model allows us to see that HGD takes place at the interface between psychology, biology and sociology. In other words, while our sense of who we are and our capacity to reflect is psychological, the opportunities for this reflection are essentially dictated by our biological capacity to do so and the social context in which we have been brought up and currently live. While for academic purposes, psychology, sociology and biology are seen as distinct disciplines, when it comes to addressing people's real-life problems, it makes better sense for us to think in cross-disciplinary ways. The MDI model brings the strands together, offering a critical stance to psychology, informed by biology, sociology and – in particular – social constructionist ideas.

While there is no chance of an all-embracing fully integrated model that can be pulled out to suit every situation, taking an MDI approach will go some way to reminding us that:

- there are different theoretical perspectives and that in any situation there may be alternative approaches to draw upon in decision-making;
- there are fashions in research and knowledge so that while evolutionary and genetic approaches, for example, might be identified as advanced knowledge in 2013, it may well be that older, less favoured perspectives could shed light on the particular situation facing a practitioner and her service users;
- the linking of three ideas – material-discursive-intra-psychic – represents the sliding scale from which it is possible to link knowledge that might at first appear to be contradictory (more on this in Chapter 4).

To introduce this two-pronged approach to HGD – lifespan and MDI – it might be helpful to unpack some of the key ideas developed later in the book.

As I've explained, the book adopts a critical standpoint. This means that, for each theory, attitude or idea put forward by experts or scientists about any aspect of being human, there are possibilities for seeing things in a *different* way. The diverse examples of intelligence, beauty and child rearing help us to see how this might be the case.

Thus, intelligence (which is difficult to define anyway) has been described by some scientific experts as innate, meaning that we are born with a specific capacity for being intelligent which cannot be fundamentally improved, however stimulating and supportive the environment might be. However, there is an equally strong argument, also presented by experts, that if an infant is surrounded by adults who respond positively and stimulate him, by playing classical music, talking to him, helping him touch things around him and so on, then his capacity for intelligence will grow.

As we shall see in Chapter 1, the meaning of intelligence and how to measure it has been disputed. In the late nineteenth century, psychologists developed what they presented as reliable and valid intelligence tests. This meant that the questions and answers to be used in these tests had been pretested on large populations across different age groups and a calculation was developed to show the level of a person's intelligence. This is known as the IQ score (Intelligence Quotient). The average score for each age group was calculated as 100 so that scoring above or below that meant exceptionally high or low levels of intelligence. However, in the 1930s Piaget questioned the use of correct answers in this way and suggested that it was more important to ask why someone got the answer wrong or right in order to gain an understanding of what constituted intelligence. Even more important, perhaps, is consideration of *emotional* intelligence (Howe, 2008, 2010; Morrison, 2007).

If someone has no sense of another person's mood, needs, intentions and feelings, how can they engage intelligently with others (Ingram, 2012)? We look at emotional intelligence as part of Chapter 5, focusing on reflective-relational practice.

The second example – the concept of beauty – varies across cultures and generations. In Western societies in the early twenty-first century the thin ideal dominates popular views about female beauty (Harrison, 2003; Malson, 1998) but, as we see in later chapters looking particularly at adolescence, adherence to this can lead to serious eating disorders and health risks. Researchers, though, have shown that different ethnic groups do not necessarily share the values incorporated in the thin ideal, so that ethnicity may be protective against eating disorders for some young people whose culture has not supported an internalization of this view of beauty (Warren et al., 2005). This example has wider relevance in social work for the importance of our awareness of cultural diversity in considering what is viewed as good or bad, right or wrong.

The third example – child rearing practices – can again be shown to have varied across generations and cultures. In most cases, experts have proposed ideas and practices that have either been discredited or superseded (Bronfenbrenner and Condry, 1970). Such ideas include advice to mothers on whether an infant should be fed on demand or at set intervals (Spock, 1946) and what they themselves can eat and drink or feed to their babies (Fox et al., 2009). They also include views on whether smacking or other forms of corporal punishment are acceptable (and effective!) in dealing with children's bad behaviour or whether they can be construed as a form of child abuse (Erlanger, 1974; Larzelere, 2000).

Questioning issues such as these should become second nature to students in the course of reading this book.

Social workers, and other similar professional groups, need to have a clear sense of what happens throughout the lifespan. In applied terms, this might mean having a working understanding of many situations. For example, what are the boundaries of normal behaviour for a teenage man? How should a new mother be responding to her baby in order for the baby to thrive? How long is it appropriate for an elderly man to grieve for his late wife? When should a baby be expected to start crawling?

As social work students or practitioners thinking about HGD, you need to cultivate a sense of what is known and understood about relationships and interactions across the stages of the lifespan. This will come from reading about the research evidence and thinking about the conclusions that have been drawn from it. Also, you need to be aware that the lifespan is not simply a linear model from birth to death. On one level, of course, as we get older there is no going back, as we saw in the discussion of development and aging. Indeed, some theorists have been tempted to relate age to stage as irrefutable facts – that at a particular age a person will be expected to behave (emotionally, socially and physically) in a particular and typical way. This would suggest that adolescents, for example, experiment with independence from their parents and try out new kinds of relationships, and this behaviour is driven by the biological impact of puberty and the social impact of the ending of their school years.

However, each one of us lives in relation to other people. We are all also emotionally volatile and under certain pressures and tensions we might return emotionally to characteristics more reminiscent of an earlier life stage than the one we have reached. Older people might find themselves crying when they are lonely or others in midlife might scream with frustration – both responses being more commonly associated with infancy and childhood.

Relationship breakdowns, illness and a whole range of day-to-day dilemmas also bring people into conflict with how they might be expected to be according to a linear lifespan. A ten-year-old girl might be a carer to her father who is suffering from multiple sclerosis, and therefore substitute the carefree life of a typical ten-year-old for a sense of responsibility for another's welfare. A man in his thirties might return home to his parents, looking for material and emotional comfort, after being made redundant.

To practise social work effectively from an evidence base then it is important to understand that we all have a memory and the ability to be reflective and *think* about who we are and how we fit in. To be reflective means to have an *identity* or a sense of selfhood and (perhaps) maintain a degree of consistency about who we are and how we manage the world around us. We can think about how we behave and what we might do to improve our well-being and that of others. We can reflect on our role in the family, social group, organization and society. Furthermore, we can be relational and hold in mind that we are all individuals living in relationships.

Social workers are involved with people at all stages of development from infancy to older age. Mostly, the people they work with have problems, or are perceived to have problems, in dealing with crucial elements of their lives. For example, they might be coping with poverty and social exclusion and the related problems of poor housing, health and nutrition. Social workers are frequently concerned with supporting the emotionally vulnerable, whether in regard to child care, substance and alcohol abuse, disabilities or psychiatric problems.

To be effective, a social worker has to have a working knowledge of themselves and others. Some of this is acquired from reading a book such as this one, or assimilating information from supervision or tutorials. However, that is only the beginning. The confident and competent professional also has to *learn from their experience*, making links between the theory, and their own experiences of practice and life. As Eileen Munro, in her review of child protection, for example, makes abundantly clear, social work involves *working with uncertainty.* You cannot know what is really going on in families or how long any improvements and other chang-es might last. While Munro (2011) focused specifically on child protection services, the same reality holds true for those working with users of mental health services or other vulnerable adults. Social workers work with uncertain human situations and have responsibility for managing the risk of an unfavourable outcome.

Understanding the different theories of HGD helps us to make some sense of people's vulnerabilities and decisions about intervention. Social workers need an awareness of the variety of difficulties that people might face, and the possibilities for problems across each of the different stages in the human lifespan. Conse-quently social workers require a deep and wide knowledge of HGD.

To summarize, social work is about working professionally and ethically with people who are vulnerable, and this mostly needs to be done in cooperation with other professional agencies and organizations who also work with these groups of people. Working with others (service users or professional partners) means that a core knowledge base and skill set focuses on what makes people *behave* in the way they do – on their own behalf, to members of their family and others in the community. Accordingly, social workers need to be observant and to make sense of their observations in the context of that person's life-circumstances while also understanding where they themselves are located personally, socially, politically and professionally. While there is no infallible check list that provides the answers to human behaviour and relationships, the knowledge bases derived from psychol-ogy, biology and sociology enable the reflective, ethical and informed social worker to make the best possible judgments and to take the best possible decisions (Fook, 2002; Nicolson et al., 2006; Ruch, 2005).

Most social workers in the UK work for the local authority but various agen-cies in the voluntary sector also employ qualified social workers. In the UK, social work activity is loosely divided into child protection and family support (children's services) or working with vulnerable adults, particularly those with mental health problems, mental or physical disability and the vulnerable elderly. Vulnerability for all these groups of people is likely to mean that they have low incomes and possibly poor quality accommodation, poor health status and quality of life.

Social workers engage in partnerships with other professionals such as teach-ers, health visitors, psychologists, psychiatrists, nurses and occupational thera-pists. This demands a great deal of understanding about other people and the ability to attend to oneself in that context.

HGD is a core part of social work training internationally and, albeit sometimes under different headings, it always has been. It is clear why this should be the case. Without understanding and knowledge of emotional and social life it would be im-possible to assess and support service users, work alongside others and it would also be impossible to care for oneself.

# I

# THEORIES OF HGD AND HOW TO THINK ABOUT THEM CRITICALLY

# 1

# NATURE VERSUS NURTURE: A MATTER OF CHOICE?

**LEARNING OBJECTIVES**

- To recognize the concept of *nature* and its place in the nature/nurture debate.
- To recognize the concept of *nurture* and its place in the nature/nurture debate.
- To distinguish between the contributions to HGD by each of the core disciplines: psychology, biology and sociology.

## Introduction

This chapter introduces the nature/nurture debate, suggesting why it is important to understand its role in explaining human growth and development. The nature/nurture debate is in fact one of the key issues in HGD, with the nature side focusing upon the extent to which our biological make-up, including genetic inheritance (that is what we have inherited biologically from our parents and grandparents) which sets up our future lives, versus the nurture side which focuses on the extent to which we are the product of our upbringing and environment. In other words, how pre-programmed are our life chances and well-being through the course of our growth and development?

I have chosen the nature/nurture debate as an entry point into the field of HGD to demonstrate the range of perspectives available in this lively and contested field. It is also a good starting point for identifying where different theories might be located on a spectrum of thinking. The first three chapters of this book will also enable you to begin to think critically about theory and research related to nature/nurture and HGD and how this thinking might link to your professional judgments.

In this chapter I explore the historical background to the ideas about what makes us human. Then in Chapter 2 I focus on those biologically-based theories that take nature as the most influential means of determining our life experiences (physical, intellectual and emotional). In Chapter 3 I investigate the work of the scientists who consider that nurture (or the social and physical environment) carries greater weight in determining who we might become. It is important to keep in mind as you read about these ideas that being human for all of us involves a mixture of influences as we progress through the lifespan (see Table 1.1).

**Table 1.1** *Different accounts of HGD and key researchers*

| Biological psychology | Social/behavioural psychology | Psychoanalytic psychology | Sociology |
|---|---|---|---|
| Evolutionary psychology (Buss; Cosmides; Hrdy; Campbell; Dunbar; Richards) | Behaviourism (Watson; Skinner) | Psychoanalysis (Freud; Erikson; Klein; Winnicott) | Symbolic interactionism (Mead; Goffman) |
| Cognitive-development (Piaget) | Social learning (Bandura) | Attachment (Bowlby) | Ecological systems theory (Bronfenbrenner) |
| Cognitive neuroscience (Schore; Baron-Cohen) | Social psychology (Milgram) | | Socialization (Bernstein) |

## Background to the debate

Explanations of how much our lives are influenced by biology and how much by social context are not new. Plato and Descartes, philosophers who were thinking and writing some centuries earlier than ours, proposed that many human characteristics are in-born and therefore impossible to influence in any major way. In other words, for these scholars, *biology* is *destiny*.

Other thinkers, such as the eighteenth century philosopher John Locke and the twentieth century psychologist B.F. Skinner (whose work on behaviourism we examine in Chapter 3), have argued for the *tabula rasa* (blank slate) as the blueprint for HGD. That is, they claimed that any newborn human baby can be made to develop mental and emotional capacities (such as intelligence or kindness) if you provide a suitable environment. So, for instance, some parents believe that if you play classical music to a baby, read to them even before they have developed their language skills and give them complex toys then that baby will grow to be intellectually able. The opposite is also expected to be true, and in Chapter 3 you will see the results of studies where anxiety and aggression were employed artificially and shown to have a deleterious impact on the child's development. As you will also read, the ethics of much of this work would have been condemned by contemporary psychologists.

The nature/nurture debate in the nineteenth century was influenced strongly by the work of Francis Galton. He talked about heredity versus environment but also coined the phrase *nature versus nurture* for the benefit of the non-scientific wider audience (Galton, 1869). Galton's controversial thesis proposed that genius was inherited, and for this he cited people of note in his own family, including himself and his cousin Charles Darwin, whose work was particularly famous at the time. His concerns focused on the people he identified as 'less intelligent' who in his opinion had more children than those he perceived to be more 'talented'. Galton argued that this resulted in a long-term detriment to human society because he believed that nature was hereditary. He proposed that these large numbers of less talented people would soon outnumber the more talented ones and called for the manipulation of the human gene pool to prevent those deemed to be less intelligent from having children (or at least not having too many children).

These ideas were couched in the science of *eugenics,* which basically supports the need to improve the genetic composition of a group of people or a nation by making the case for inherited capabilities and personalities. Eugenicists argue that, if you make sure that only those with desirable characteristics are supported to have larger families, the population as a whole would be better than if choices about having children (how many and with whom) were left up to individuals. There are of course major ethical issues arising from such a perspective.

Despite Galton's prominent position as a scientist and writer, this work was divisive from the outset. Eugenics fell completely into disrepute in the early twentieth century when it became associated with Adolf Hitler's mass extermination of Jewish people, homosexuals, disabled people and other minorities in line with the Nazi ideology of racial purification. Tribal and religious partisan conflicts which have led to genocide, such as those between Bosnian Muslims and Serbs, Tutsis and Hutus in Rwanda and Sunni and Shia Muslims in some parts of Africa and the Middle East have been referred to as 'ethnic cleansing'. However, these struggles (bloody as they inevitably are) are not to be confused with eugenics-based mass extermination. Ethnic cleansing is based on the political desire to gain control over territory and resources and remove (by force and fear) a group with a background of different ethnicicty or beliefs.

Hitler's appalling policy finally consigned eugenics to the scientific scrapheap, but it also in effect delayed *objective* studies of genetics until the late twentieth and early twenty-first century.

It is the recent developments in evolutionary sciences – the mapping of the human genome and the widespread use of DNA which contains the genetic code that is more or less unique to each of us as individuals – coupled with our abilities to scan brain images that has meant the nature/nurture debate has returned, reinvigorated. It now represents one of the most important contemporary dialogues among biologists, psychologists, social scientists, theologians and philosophers.

### What is meant by nature and nurture?

Nature is the biological basis of HGD that mostly refers to hereditary characteristics. These might be inconsequential, such as 'she inherited blue eyes from her father' or 'he has his mother's nose'. However, nature might also be used to justify or predict life chances by indicating that intelligence, personality, sexual orientation, obesity, mental and physical health status or criminality are inherited characteristics. Such a position could have implications for the way that decisions are made and (scarce) resources allocated in health and social care as well as for education, housing and welfare benefits.

For example, an extreme version of this argument might be that criminality can be predicted on the basis of whether a child's parents or relatives have a criminal record. The consequences of such a view might involve deciding not to allocate resources to establish whether the child has special educational needs on grounds that they are likely to end up in a young offenders' institution regardless of what support they are given at school.

Social workers make judgments every day about what levels of independence or support are needed by people who are struggling against adversity. Understanding the role of biology and genetics in HGD is a vital part of the social worker's knowledge-mix but by no means the only consideration.

Nurture refers to the immediate family context we are born into. Did an individual experience 'good enough parenting'? This phrase is the paediatrician and psychoanalyst Donald Winnicott's famous standard for child care. We will be talking a little more about his work in later chapters, but for now we will explain briefly his belief that there was no point in anyone expecting or aspiring to be a perfect parent. More importantly, there was no point in anyone berating themselves for failing to live up to that ideal. What the parent needed to know was that love and attention to the infant or young child's physical, social and emotional needs only had to be as good as that person was able to provide (Winnicott, 1965). Other aspects of nurture would indicate whether a family had enough money to provide a healthy diet for the children, and whether the family and their children had access to good education, housing and health care.

Nurture implies the influence of culture and social context. Nurture includes the influence of our religious or cultural background, our ethnic identity, family background, interpersonal influence and social class. The influence of nurture will vary over the lifespan because people do experience transitions – for example, social class and income mobility, changes in religious beliefs or new realizations

## PAUSE AND REFLECT

**Francis Galton**

Francis Galton claimed that he came from a family of geniuses. Think about your own family tree.

Whether or not you were raised by your biological parents, how far do you feel you take after the family you grew up with?

Have you tried to trace your ancestry online or through archives? If you have, what motivated you? What have you found out about yourself through doing this?

Draw a family tree and trace any characteristics you believe you share with some or all of your family members. What does it tell you about your own case of nature versus nurture?

Some of you will, of course, have more direct information about your immediate ancestors than others will. However, it is an interesting exercise for everyone.

about their sexuality – all of these can profoundly influence how they think, social-ize and behave.

Most experts are likely to take a perspective on HGD that involves the *interaction* between nature and nurture. However, it is important from the start of your studies to maintain an awareness of the tension between nature and nurture for the fol-lowing reasons.

- *Theories of HGD tend to give precedence to one or other of these dimensions.* Thus the popular accounts of gendered behaviour by evolutionary psychologists rely almost exclusively on nature, focusing on what they call 'mating behaviours' and sexual attraction, while discursive psychology tends towards the nurture end of the spectrum in that it concerns itself with the development of shared meanings which have evolved via language.
- *To maintain a healthy scepticism or critical awareness* of theories of HGD overall, and particularly, as discussed below, to hold on to the *politics of evidence.*
- *To evaluate the (often implicit) theories you apply to your own beliefs and formula-tions of social work practices.* For example you might consider whether youth offenders are born or made. Taking a nature-based approach – assuming they are born to offend – might remove blame from the family. However, this implies a reliance on *biological determinism* (a belief that biology is destiny) and *reduc-tionism* (that biology is the core of human nature and in the end our motivation and experience all boil down to biology). Alternatively, taking a nurture-based approach might imply that family and culture are implicated in young people's transgressions. This may lead to thinking about *human agency* (motivation, in-dependence, selfhood and responsibility) and what this might mean for an indi-vidual's life experience.

## What influences people's lives across the lifespan?

Considering the way we grow and develop requires an acknowledgement of various factors.

- The complex nature of the lifespan in that children do not exist in isolation from adults, nor older people from younger ones, and becoming a parent or grand-parent has implications for all the generations involved.
- The vast array of influences on each one of us as we develop across the lifespan – genes, bodies, context and our own minds.
- The perplexing mysteries to which no-one has definitive answers – either as researchers or as practitioners.

Perhaps a more pertinent set of questions revolves around a different end of the spectrum – why those of us from fairly peaceful, supportive and ordinary

## PAUSE AND REFLECT

**The life of Susan Boyle**

How do we explain the life of Susan Boyle, who became famous in 2009 for competing in a British television talent show? Her first recorded album became a best seller around the world and she later performed for the Queen's Diamond Jubilee Pageant.

Boyle, whose Irish immigrant father was a coal miner, suffered an oxygen debt during birth and was identified as simple-minded. However, her singing voice has enabled her to become an international star of huge acclaim. She came from Glasgow in Scotland, one of the most socially and economically deprived areas of Europe, but was able to demonstrate her talent and thrive despite her start in life.

Exceptions who defy the odds and rise from what would normally be assessed as poor life chances to stardom, such as Boyle, provide heart-warming inspirations. While their lives have resisted what might have been predicted for them, it is important to remember that they do still remain exceptional cases.

backgrounds have the capacity to behave as bullies, violent abusers or even murderers? Think about examples that abound in everyday life: the step-father who subjected the young child in his care to violence, starvation and neglect; the man who punched and kicked his wife every time he felt frustration in his life; the man who murdered his ex-partner and children, or the woman who poisoned her frail mother for whose care she was responsible.

## How do we account for extreme behaviour?

The behaviour of Huda Ben Amer, someone described as an ordinary Libyan woman, was an example of extreme behaviour that appeared beyond the bounds of normal explanation. She was among the crowd watching a public hanging of a young man who had questioned the actions of the government during the early years of the Gaddafi regime. As everyone else watched horrified while the victim flailed around at the end of the rope, Ben Amer walked across to the gallows, yanked his legs down and broke his neck. This, of course, hastened his death and may be interpreted as an act of kindness. However, she might have made the decision to cut him down, and perhaps taken the watching crowd with her. It is most likely that she was making the point that the man should die, a supposition that is supported by her subsequent emergence as a rich and influential member of the Gaddafi regime, the more because, during the 2011 uprising, she fled for her life and her house was burned down. Was there something in her genes that made her so cruel in support of self-interest? Had she been treated badly when she was a child? She was not conforming to the actions of those around her as most people would do, but there may have been a reference group such as the powerful dictator and his close supporters who influenced her. Did she somehow see the young man in question as less of a human being than she was because he was branded as a traitor and vulnerable?

From examination of the various case histories of Nazis, terrorists and the ordinary people who took part in experiments such as those directed by Stanley Milgram (Milgram, 1963) there is rarely anything that stands out as cruel and violent in their backgrounds, or even evidence that they were excluded from society for any reason while growing up.

### Are bullies and murderers born or made?

Milgram's studies (Milgram, 1963; Slater et al., 2006) have become well known through their replication in the popular media, but we will summarize them here.

Milgram ran a series of experiments (each with slightly different conditions) in which naïve participants thought they were taking part in a learning experiment. A member of the experimental team acted as the learner and the participant was instructed by another team member to give electric shocks every time the learner made a mistake. In reality, no shocks were administered.

Even though the learner called out to say they had a heart condition and begged the person to stop giving him shocks, at least two-thirds of the participants continued to shock him until he was eventually silent. They were, several claimed, only following orders. However, when they were debriefed some people became upset and repentant about what they had done. Some remained disturbed by what they had learned about themselves for years.

Slater and colleagues (Slater et al., 2006) simulated the Milgram experiments on a computer with the participants knowing full well that they were not really giving electric shocks. Following the style of the original experiments, the participants were invited to administer a series of word association memory tests to the (female) virtual human representing the learner. When she gave an incorrect answer, the participants were instructed to administer an electric shock to her, increasing the voltage each time. She responded with increasing discomfort and protests, eventually demanding termination of the experiment.

Of the 34 participants, 23 saw and heard the virtual human and 11 communicated with her only through a text interface. Their results showed that, in spite of the fact that all participants knew for sure that neither the stranger nor the shocks were real, the participants who saw and heard her dismay and protests tended to respond to the situation at the subjective (self-report), behavioural (how they behaved at the time and afterwards) and physiological (measures of hormonal and neurological activity) levels as if the situation had been real. As one of the participants noted – she had to keep reminding herself that this was a virtual reality and that no one was really being hurt.

**PAUSE AND REFLECT**

**Can experiments tell us about real life?**

Research findings and observations of human behaviour outside of the laboratory suggest that many adults who abuse children, their intimate partners or vulnerable adults know what they are doing because they receive feedback when their victims cry, beg, scream and demonstrate serious pain and distress, and the research also shows that we are all able to recognize these responses for what they are. It also suggests that some people feel guilt and remorse while others want to pass the blame onto those who were giving the orders.

Every day social workers meet people from a variety of backgrounds who are perpetrators and victims of violence and abuse – the abandoned boy, the simple girl and the cruel and selfish parent or carer. Social workers are expected to assess the risks that people like these might cause harm to themselves or to others (Dube et al., 2001; Joffe, 1999; Slack et al., 2004). Mostly it is possible to make some predictions about the ways people will live their lives and also how they will treat and be treated by others, but only after engaging with HGD theories.

What are the implications of this experimental evidence for formulating your practice with perpetrators of abuse?

Are the perpetrators in the studies naturally cruel or might there be another explanation for their behaviour?

## Assessing risk using the nature/nurture debate

Think about the following example in which the police and local authorities were blamed by neighbours and the press for the death of David Askew. He was a 64-year-old man with learning difficulties, nicknamed 'Dopey Dave', who lived in Greater Manchester with his mother (89 years old) and brother (aged 67). He was constantly bullied and abused by a group of local teenagers, with one child in the group as young as eight. Over several years, these young people's behaviour involved breaking his front gate, interfering with his mother's mobility scooter and verbally abusing him and his family on a daily basis. Apparently, on the day of his death, he went out to stop the young people from interfering with his mother's scooter and died of a heart attack. The group did not show any empathy towards the man or his family.

The thoughtless and prolonged cruelty allegedly perpetrated by these young people, including a young child, is shocking when the details are presented in a real-life case but, after looking at the psychological evidence about human behaviour, it should not be a surprise. It also may have little to do with the background of the young people themselves. It is, however, likely (from Slater's work which we looked at above) that they had a keen idea of what they were doing and knew they were inflicting harm. It is also likely that the young people were indeed disturbed about what they had done, but wanted to keep up a certain hard appearance.

These are not the only examples of vulnerable adults with learning difficulties being tormented by people who were fully able to understand what they were doing to another human being. Such events are relatively frequent, although they don't always have such a dramatic climax.

## PAUSE AND REFLECT

**What we (don't) always see and do about risk**

Were the young people who tormented David Askew different from others in that they were genetically predisposed to cruelty, or did the circumstances tempt them into this behaviour?

Why didn't the neighbours and police respond supportively? Both groups appeared to show concern but it would seem that no-one put a great deal of effort into coming to Mr Askew's aid. Does this say something about human beings in general or just the circumstances surrounding this case?

Why are so many people in similar situations prepared to turn a blind eye to such vicious and damaging behaviour in others: the neighbour who did not call a social worker or the police when they heard violence and screaming through the wall; the sibling who knew their father was sexually abusing their sister or the father who avoided noticing the way his wife was neglecting their child?

How do we balance our feelings and our objective knowledge? We realize that some people do not intend harm but nonetheless cause it.

Some people who cause harm to others are in need of a great deal of support themselves. Others seem not to care about what they have done. How much harm can be attributed to innate cruelties and how much to the way people were brought up and the cruelties inflicted upon them?

How much of what happens can be attributed to the situation itself – the opportunity to cause harm?

These are all practical questions about the roles of nature and nurture in HGD.

As a social work practitioner you are frequently expected to be involved in decision-making about risk management and you need to use your understanding of HGD and the evidence about nature/nurture in a clear way. There is no easy answer and no set formula, but the following issues are worth bearing in mind.

As was clear from the experimental evidence, everyone and anyone can behave in a thoughtless and even cruel manner. The vulnerability of an individual needs to be set against the benefits of independent living for them and their family. In the case described above, a great deal of responsibility was placed on the head of Mr Askew to look after his mother, and his anxiety about doing this may well have contributed to his assiduous complaints to and about the local children. The influence of the peer and social groups is likely to influence extreme behaviours, whereas any one individual may not behave in irresponsible or cruel ways.

Stanley Milgram's work is part of a tradition in social psychology that has focused on how we respond to the *presence of others*. Sometimes, simply being in a room with someone can change our behaviour for better or worse. Some early experiments demonstrated that being with others in a group can influence how you make decisions, even if you know that the group decision is inaccurate. One example is Asch's (1940) experiment in which he asked people to compare the lengths of lines. However this kind of behaviour is particularly troubling if you consider how you might be influenced to make a decision about intervention in a case.

This general phenomenon is called *co-presence* and is part of a group of theories about *social facilitation* (Zajonc, 1965). We might become more productive if we sense that another person is competing with us in completing a task, or alternatively we might decide that we don't need to work as hard because the other person (or people) can do the work for us. This is known as *diffusion of responsibility.*

However, it appears that when there are a number of possible helpers, for example witnesses to a mugging or a road traffic accident, then each witness might take the view that someone else will help. The *bystander effect*, which has its origins in the concept of diffusion of responsibility, is particularly relevant for understanding some of the behaviours described in the Askew case. Violence or verbally abusive, bullying behaviour of the group of young people might be ignored or even tacitly supported because of a reluctance to intervene, possibly because of fears for your own safety (Chekroun and Brauer, 2002). The term 'bystander apathy' was made famous by the Kitty Genovese murder in New York. She was murdered outside a block of flats in New York City in full view of the occupants, but no-one assisted her despite cries for help. This case, originally discussed by Darley and Latane (1968), has become the core of many studies and questions about the human condition (Grofman, 1974). One of many on-line references to the ongoing debates about the Genovese case and its implications is: www.trutv.com/library/crime/serial_killers/predators/kitty_genovese/1.html, but if you type 'Kitty Genovese' into a search engine you will find others, including pictures, which give you a sense of the entire scenario.

### Good Samaritans?

The other side of the bystander apathy coin comes to the fore in the following somewhat apocryphal story from Bernard Hare about an event in 1982 that he claims profoundly changed the way he saw life. He was a student living away from home when his father told him that his mother was in hospital and would not survive the night. He went to the station and bought a ticket but realized he would miss his connection at Peterborough. On hearing his story, the train conductor decided to hold up the connection so that Bernard made it in time to his dying mother's bedside. In response to Hare asking the conductor what he could do in return, the conductor told him to do good deeds to others in distress. Hare says he has done what he could ever since then – a clear case (perhaps) of the influence of nurture.

But this event happened in adulthood and was part of a particularly stressful and poignant set of events. How might the details of the context impact upon us in a profound way that changes our behaviour?

There is, in short, no one truth about what makes all and each of us human, nor has any one expert or group of experts provided the definitive answer to what makes people take part in life in the way they do. The way the processes behind HGD are understood by social workers, scientists, popular commentators and politicians has changed over time and depends upon the politics of science.

### How do we know what we know?

There are *fashions* in how and what type of research is funded, and it may be that such fashions often result in different types of knowledge and understanding. There continues to be a struggle between the hard sciences of cognitive and neuro-psychology and the softer social sciences including psychology, sociology, geography, anthropology and so on – with the latter facing accusations of being out of date or too costly to promote. The Academy of Social Sciences has been running a campaign to demonstrate to the UK Government the continuing effectiveness of the social sciences. Its publications can be accessed on its website (www.acss.org.uk/). This is a useful website for students to look at generally to clarify the role of the different social sciences in providing evidence about the relationship between well-being and policy.

One example of research that is radically different from the traditional approach is the use of qualitative research methods, a practice that has become increasingly common among social scientists as well as those in social work research. Qualitative research provides a different *order* of information about human behaviour from that provided by experimental methods or survey data (Hollway and Jefferson, 2003; Shaw and Gould, 2001). Frequently, the knowledge derived from these different types of study is complementary. Sometimes, however, different pathways to discovery raise questions about what is really going on because they may appear to be contradictory (Greene and Caracelli, 1997). When this is the case it is usually the dominant paradigm – the model of knowledge and approach to research which uses a form of *measurement* – that takes precedence by being seen as the true evidence. But this does not mean that statistically-based research provides better knowledge. It is more that it reflects the research and cultural values of contemporary Western, patriarchal, industrial societies.

One example of contradictory evidence has come from my own work: a study of postnatal depression in which I used in-depth interviews and qualitative data methods of analysis. The traditional quantitative-based studies all suggested that postnatal depression was an atypical depression caused by the essential features of women's reproductive bodies. Women are subject to their raging hormones at various periods in their lives, none more so than following childbirth. The implication drawn from the hormonal evidence was that women's biology was faulty. Through using a different methodology and coming at the problem from a different standpoint – looking at the context of women's lives after childbirth and getting their views of how they felt –I saw a different picture. I discovered that in a great many cases depression was the consequence of physical stresses such as tiredness and psychological trauma, loss and change, and the challenges of forming new patterns of family dynamics (Nicolson, 1998). This was very much against the dominant paradigm, or model, at the time.

Different *epistemological* positions, that is different theories of knowledge, of this kind result in different knowledge-claims, and there is a growing critique about whether knowledge (or evidence) is objective, or whether what counts as the most important knowledge is the knowledge of the powerful (rather than an ultimate truth as it might be presented) (Foucault, 1970; Webb, 2010).

---

**PAUSE AND REFLECT**

**Explaining 'facts'?**

What is the importance of understanding epistemology or different theories of knowledge?
  How do we identify the epistemological underpinnings of research evidence? To do this we always need to think about the ways in which facts are communicated.
  We also need to consider whether another explanation might fit the facts.
  It is important to be aware that there is no consensus on what counts as social work knowledge (Aymer and Okitikpi, 2000). This is highlighted in an article contrasting service users' and social workers' knowledge about anti-oppressive practice and suggesting that sometimes experts take over. So perhaps when social workers identify what anti-oppressive practice means, this might in fact be oppressive as it removes the opportunity from service users to define what they see as anti-oppressive and oppressive in social work practice (Beresford, 2000).

---

There are new technologies, such as MRI (magnetic resonance imaging) scanners, and scientific discoveries, such as the mapping of the human genome, which influence what kind of knowledge provides the most common explanations for HGD. Every popular media presentation of a psychological or health issue now seems to be explained as being hard wired into the genes. We still cannot make this statement without qualification, although many commentators seem to do so.

That is not to devalue progress in science. We can map the brain. We can test for genetic inheritance and how this relates to health concerns. But the best scientists will make the point that environment still plays a vital part in the outcome of how a particular genetic make-up will be influenced by the social context.

### Who is mad here? Nature versus nurture in thinking about mental health

The nature/nurture debate has long been influential in the treatment of mental illness, beginning with the development of medical expertise by nineteenth century psychiatrists and later in the work of the anti-psychiatrists in the mid-twentieth century. The ways in which nature and nurture have been applied in making life-changing decisions about people's mental health, and how it should be treated, have become and remain highly contested.

Over the intervening years, emerging theories have taken one side or the other and the proof that this question remains unresolved may be seen in the 2013 resurgence of some key questions.

Is schizophrenia an objective, clinical, biological and genetic phenomenon? Is it therefore an illness that demands medication rather than talking treatment? Or is

NATURE VERSUS NURTURE: A MATTER OF CHOICE?     25

it the outcome of dysfunctional family dynamics? Or is it in fact a manufactured catch-all category for conditions we don't understand? This debate has been alive in contemporary psychology and psychiatry for at least forty years – and seems to be no closer to resolution (Bentall, 2006; Boyle, 2007).

Let us review the ongoing questions of 'what is mental illness?' and 'how is it caused?'. What follows will give you an insight into both the nature/nurture debate and the role of critical thinking within it.

In the 1960s and 1970s, the concept of the dysfunctional family and family therapy were popular among those working in mental health (Bhui and Dinos, 2011; Laing and Esterson, 1970). The 1990s heralded a plethora of biological explanations including the influence of food and/or genes on mental health (Addington and Rapoport, 2009; Bhui and Dinos, 2011). Starting in the 2000s, family dysfunction has again been proposed as an explanation, although the cost and cost-effectiveness of clinical work involving some types of talking cure keeps such theories at bay (Andrews et al., 2000; Double, 2002; Leader, 2009).

In the late 1950s and early 1960s, the anti-psychiatrist R.D. Laing, and later some of his close colleagues, produced observable clinical evidence that many people who were diagnosed as schizophrenic were not mad – it was the system that was insane (Laing, 1959). Later they cited detailed evidence based on close observation of the damaging influence of dysfunctional families upon vulnerable members, making them go mad (Laing and Esterson, 1970).

These ideas were new and exciting at the time and supported the anti-establishment critical thinking that led to many innovations in practice around mental health issues. Until relatively recently, these ideas were (almost) never investigated or taken seriously because of the twenty-first century's technological advances that had, it is claimed, proved that schizophrenia is an organic disease. However, not only do several prominent psychiatrists remain sceptical (Double, 2002; Kendall, 2011) but some psychiatrists and clinical psychologists actively dispute this claim.

I want to illustrate this more thoroughly using Trevor Pateman's (1972) reading of one of the original case studies in *Sanity, Madness and the Family* (Laing and Esterson, 1970) . Pateman focuses on the 'Abbotts' (the fictional name given to one of the families) and their daughter Maya who had been diagnosed as schizophrenic:

Consider the following passage from Laing and Esterson's commentary on this case:

'An idea of reference that she [the daughter] had was that something she could not fathom was going on between her parents, seemingly about her ... Indeed there was. When they were all interviewed together, her mother and father kept exchanging with each other a constant series of nods, winks, gestures, knowing smiles, so obvious to the observer that he commented on them after twenty minutes of the first such interview. They continued, however, unabated and denied ... The consequences, so it seems to us, of this failure by her parents to acknowledge the validity of similar comments by Maya, was that Maya could not know when she was perceiving or when she was imagining things to be going on between her parents. These open yet unavowed nonverbal exchanges between father and mother were in fact quite public and perfectly obvious. Much of what could be taken to be paranoid about Maya arose because she mistrusted her own mistrust. She could not really believe that what she thought she saw going on was going on.' (website version, p. 90)

Pateman goes on to say:

My own reading of this runs as follows. We learn to tell right from wrong mainly from our parents. They are our chief moral authorities, from whom we learn not simply a list of particular rights and wrongs, but general rules of right and wrong (ethical principles) and, importantly, criteria for telling right from wrong where no general rule obviously applies or where it is a case of making an exception to a general rule. Of course, all of this, no doubt, goes on unconsciously ... Maya's parents consistently deny the truth of her statements and thereby undermine any developing mastery of epistemological criteria and/or her perceptions themselves. She is thus disabled from achieving a cognitive mastery of the world.

Pateman's account here is doubly interesting in the context of the nature/ nurture debate. Firstly, he provides a brief snapshot of the points that Laing and Esterson were making about each family they described and discussed. They were arguing that it is not always the diagnosed person who is mad but that sometimes a person cannot cope with the family or other system they are living in, particularly when there appears to be a difference between what is claimed to be going on and what the person perceives.

The second salient point here is that parents' and children's behaviours are inherently linked. Parents have power over their children *consciously* in that they can reward or punish behaviours; but also *unconsciously* in that parents (or primary care-givers) become part of the mental life of any growing infant and child in that we all hear our parents' views so know whether or not we are transgressing them. We will look further into this process from different standpoints in later chapters.

It is also interesting to see something of a recent resurgence in understanding mental illness from a social/cultural/interpersonal perspective, particularly in the cases of depression (Leader, 2009) and schizophrenia. Despite the various ways and different levels at which our development has been influenced by biology, society, community and family, there remains within the psychic lives of us all a primitive (un)conscious awareness of the influence of the important adults in our early life. This is of course very difficult to prove indisputably, and much of the evidence comes either from psychoanalytic psychotherapy practitioners or from detailed observational studies of adults and infants. Early relationships and the ways in which we are treated, nevertheless, do provide us with our first and most important sense of how we are positioned in the social world (see Chapter 5, where the focus is on attachment, and Chapter 7 about infancy and early childhood, where I discuss this more fully).

## Nature and nurture explained?

We need to think about what it means to be human at every stage of life, and making sense of the relationships between nature and nurture helps us to begin grasping the key ideas that scientists and scholars have proposed and developed. In what follows, continuing from the discussions above, the different theories of develop-mental and biological psychology and socialization will be described. Each one of them makes a significant contribution to our general understanding of both nature and nurture and how they impact upon HGD. You will decide for yourself how the evidence each offers will persuade you of their case. What you need to consider is what influences the balance in either direction of each of the theories.

It important then to recognize, firstly, that these areas of knowledge are all connected and they all borrow and develop concepts from each other. Secondly, as a practitioner it is important to be able to use elements (or pick and mix in an informed way) from all of these perspectives when assessing risk or planning interventions. You therefore need to ask yourself as you read on which types of explanation make the most sense and why we are still debating issues of nature versus nurture in the twenty-first century.

---

**CHAPTER SUMMARY**

In this chapter you have been introduced to the concepts of both nature and nurture. You have also reviewed the background to the debate between the two and the various disciplinary perspectives on HGD from psychology, biology and sociology that feed into it.

The chapter explored some forms of extreme behaviour, including obedience to authority, cruelty and kindness to strangers, identifying experimental and real-life evidence of both. It also raised questions of research ethics and research fashions and how consideration of these helps you to develop a

*critical approach* to what is seen as knowledge and evidence of HGD.

A case study questioning the nature of *madness* and how to recognize who is mad was presented, along with researcher descriptions of a family scenario in which dysfunctional interactions were discussed in relation to the potential impact such communication might have upon vulnerable people.

In the following two chapters these perspectives will be developed to deepen your understanding.

**FURTHER READING**

On family relationships:

Laing, R. D., and Esterson, A. (1970) *Sanity, Madness and the Family*. Harmondsworth: Penguin.

Reading Laing and Esterson's descriptions of family interactions and relationships is fascinating in itself, but, in the context of thinking critically about mental health and family relationships, it provides important insights.

On research methods:

Milgram, S. (1963) Behavioural study of obedience. *Journal of Abnormal and Social Psychology, 67*, 371–378.

Milgram's work is endlessly absorbing and makes you wonder how you might have acted in the situations described. It is also worth thinking as you read this about the *ethics* of this research.

# 2

# BIOLOGICALLY-BASED PSYCHOLOGICAL THEORIES OF HGD

**LEARNING OBJECTIVES**

- To explore the nature side of the debate.
- To explore what is meant by the term *reductionist*.
- To learn to recognize the biologically-based psychological theories.

## Introduction

As we learned in Chapter 1, theories based on both nature and nurture are used to explain different aspects of HGD. You will also have understood that different academic disciplines such as psychology and biology use different methods to collect evidence for their knowledge. It is also important to bear in mind, as you saw in the previous chapter, that each of these disciplines has distinct approaches within it. In this chapter we are focusing upon the psychological theories that are biologically-based.

Biologically-based theories from psychology focus upon the individual and in particular emphasize the biological basis of thought and behaviour. This means that the brain, or mind, is described as containing biological elements influenced by hormones (which act as chemical messengers between the brain and the body) and genes (through which characteristics such as eye colour, body shape, intelligence and sometimes diseases) are passed across generations.

Psychology traditionally claims to be both the science of behaviour and the science of mind. But, as we shall see, it is by no means a unified discipline, with internal debates much like the ones around nature and nurture. Contemporary academic psychology specifically takes pride, as a science, on being logical (one idea leading to the next in a clear progression), rational (totally able to be explained without emotional interference) and objective (similarly independent of any emotion or biased thinking). Psychology in the broadest sense, though, claims that it is able to make predictions from its scientific evidence base about how we *think* and *behave* under certain *conditions*. These conditions included psycho-socio-biological ones such as gender, age, ethnicity, personality and intelligence. In other words, there is acknowledgement across most perspectives in psychology that, although, say, a genetic explanation might be favoured, everything is influenced by social and physical context. For instance a young man might be taller and biologically better able to develop strong muscles than his sister. However, if she trains to be an athlete while he prefers to be a couch potato, then she will grow up with greater physical strength than he has.

The various approaches to psychology and HGD outlined in both this chapter and in Chapter 3 reflect the diversity and contradictions within the discipline, and the ways in which psychology, biology and sociology both crisscross and diverge when considering some basic ideas. The intention here is to draw out the parts of these approaches that will enhance social workers' understanding of HGD and support practice.

### Biology versus psychology?

How much do we know about what influences HGD above all from nature or nurture? The nature/nurture debate is often seen as a biology versus sociology/psychology debate but, increasingly, as we learn more about cognitive neuroscience and genetics, the boundaries have become blurred.

As we see in Chapter 5, human *attachment* in infancy for example, with its echoes throughout life, is strongly influenced by both social/environmental and biological factors and has both psychological and biological outcomes. Failure to experience warmth and emotional nourishment in infancy not only leads to feelings of isolation and rejection but we can see that deprivation of a good attachment experience influences hormonal and neurological messages to the developing brain (Schore, 2001).

### The case for nature

Biologically-based psychology argues the case for nature having greater influence than nurture as follows:

- Each of us is born with hard-wiring that holds genetic instructions governing both general human developmental processes as well as unique individual ones.
- These include, for example, gender and explain differences in gender roles, behaviours and power relations between men and women throughout the lifespan.
- Differences (for example in personalities and behaviours) between the sexes are considered to be inevitable and the result of sex hormones which impact upon the brain before and shortly after birth (Baron-Cohen 2004; Knickmeyer et al. 2005).
- This does not mean that there is no overlap in skills (because we all have individual patterns of DNA) but, on the whole, women's and men's psychological differences are biologically-based.

The environment is taken to have some influence upon the genetic programme, particularly basic influences such as the nurturing of an infant by an adult, the provision of adequate food and warmth or intellectual stimulation without which the baby would fail to thrive and die or become seriously ill (Bifulco et al., 2003).

Although such provisions are fundamental to ensuring that babies thrive and survive, the detail of the environmental context in which this happens is unique to each individual. However, the position proposed by biologically-influenced psychologists is that the genetic code underpins behaviour and other factors such as intelligence and personality, and as such it is predominant in the future life chances of every one of us (Kanazawa, 2010).

Expanding on this view, the mind is a set of information-processing modules designed by natural selection to solve adaptive problems faced by our hunter-gatherer ancestors. That means that biologically-based characteristics might be bred into a society because there is a biological imperative to mate with someone who is likely to produce offspring that will survive to maturity. One example might be that some African tribes are tall and lean because their survival depends on being able to hunt fast-moving animals living on the plains. Over centuries long-limbed women and men have been seen as more attractive, preferred partners and gradually families have passed on genes that are likely to produce these characteristics.

As we shall see below, this way of thinking about the brain, mind and behaviour is changing the manner in which evolutionary psychologists have approached old topics, such as sexual behaviour, while opening up new ones such as child abuse, suggesting that this might occur if the child is not (or suspected not to be) the offspring of the male abuser (Buss, 2000; Cosmides and Tooby, 1994). Taking an evolutionary perspective to sexual behaviour, for instance, places priority on reproductive fitness or the power of a man's attraction towards a woman, and vice versa, because each believes that will produce the children most likely to survive and adapt.

### Cognitive developmental psychology

Cognition is about thinking and reasoning. Intellectual and cognitive development provides the evidence about how thinking evolves and develops over the lifespan. The most famous cognitive-developmental theories emerged from the work of Jean Piaget, the Swiss biologist whose work was not translated into English (and therefore not widely available to North American or British scholars) until the 1960s (Piaget, 1990; Rayner, 1986). This work, which came as a refreshing change to the measurement culture that had been core to the discipline, still represents a landmark in our understanding of HGD. This is particularly true for making sense of the development of *reasoning* and later, via the work of Lawrence Kohlberg, of *moral reasoning* (Kohlberg, 1969). For a discussion of Kohlberg's work, see Chapter 8.

Piaget's work was particularly important because it represented a radical departure from the research methods used at the time to test intelligence and other characteristics. The use of the intelligence test in the early twentieth century meant that children and adults were given scores for their responses to a series of questions that required closed answers and were either right or wrong. However, Piaget was interested in how children *thought* about the answers they gave. He believed this information provided more insight into cognitive development, regardless of whether the answer was correct or not. Piaget then developed tasks which tapped into the way children thought about a problem and then identified the ways in which they chose their response. This was rich, complex data from which he concluded that, at certain stages of development, a child might have neither the biologically-based mental structures nor the social and material experience to make sense of certain problems.

Piaget's work involved consideration of biological and psychological development but he also paid attention to the role of the emotional and material context. While he showed clearly through his studies with young children that the human capability to think and reason unfolded as the biological brain developed with age (between birth and about ten years of age), there was still an important ingredient to HGD that needed to be remembered: *opportunities* for growth and development provided by the environment are essential for in-born capacities to develop to their full potential.

Piaget demonstrated that we make sense of the world from infancy onwards via a process of *adaptation*, taking in information from the environment which provides clues as to what is outside of us (*assimilation*) and, as a consequence, we gradually change the evidence we employ to understand or to *accommodate* to that environment. Take a look at Tables 2.1 and 2.2 in which Piaget's theory is outlined. This explains the processes through which the developmental changes take place, followed by his identification of the age at which a child is most likely to be able to operate certain capacities. His work makes it clear that the infant/child actively engages with the environment, showing that we have an agentic quality – we are not simply passive cyphers, we are biologically driven to explore our world.

Looking more technically at Piaget's theory, we see that Table 2.1 outlines four *propositions* which identify the strategies that infants and young children employ to engage with and explore their environment. These develop gradually from the basic biological survival/reflex instincts which involve an exploration of the infant's environment through sucking, grasping and so on in Proposition 1.

As a result of this primitive exploration, the infant will assimilate information – take in and make sense of it – to increase the sophistication of their strategies. It is this that Piaget proposes as the beginning of thinking. These strategies are then accommodated into the infant's *schema* (a kind of multidimensional map) of themselves in the physical and biological world.

**Table 2.1** *Piaget's theory of cognitive development*

| Proposition 1 | Every child is born with strategies for interacting with the environment, which is the beginning of thinking.<br>The newborn infant can follow basic rules to explore the world using in-born skills such as sucking, grasping, seeing, hearing and touching. |
|---|---|
| Proposition 2 | Changes in the basic strategies evolve as the child assimilates experiences and accommodates them into the original strategies. To do this, the child has to have an interaction with the social and physical environment.<br>The child uses these primitive strategies for rudimentary thinking – grasping in different ways, touching and looking at differently shaped and textured objects and gradually develops these skills into means of exploring the world around her. |
| Proposition 3 | As the child grows she develops a set of 'theories' about how to negotiate the world based on the level of understanding she has reached.<br>The child tries out different methods of using her increasing skills and begins to realize that some objects are constant and can be classified, and that things can be added to and taken away. |
| Proposition 4 | Biological maturation and experience become part of the child's construction of reality as she grows and matures.<br>The child develops this through exploration and experimentation with the environment. |

**Table 2.2** *Piaget's stages of development*

| Age | Stage | |
|---|---|---|
| 0–2 | Sensorimotor | The infant begins to interact with the world, primarily through the senses and by actions with objects. The infant cannot hold an image of the object in her mind at this stage, suggesting there is no active memory. |
| 2–6 | Preooperational | The child is able to represent object to herself internally, but still focuses on its external qualities such as touch or colour. The child thinks that when she is not with someone or in a particular place they do not exist. This is an ego-centric way of thinking of the world. |
| 6–12 | Concrete operations | Abstract thought develops rapidly so the child is able to work out complex problems without the presence of objects. Also the child is able to understand continuity and that things happen that she cannot actually see. For example, she knows that her friends, parents and teachers exist when they are not there with her. |
| 12+ | Formal operations | There is increased sophistication in the level of abstract thought so that the young person can work out complex abstract problems and communicate them to others. |

Table 2.2 shows how Piaget constructed a pathway or *trajectory* of developmental stages, based on his theories of adaptation and assimilation, to make the point that an infant/child has to be biologically equipped to move from one stage to the next. As you see from the tables, it is not until the child is over the age of twelve that he can engage in complex abstract thought.

Piaget's work has been subjected to a great deal of criticism, both from the conservative researchers, who considered it to be a radical critique of intelligence testing (Dale, 1970), and from the radical and Marxist thinkers of the 1970s, who found it too much in favour of establishment views (Broughton, 1981). However, his work remains pivotal in opening up ideas about the complexities of *reasoning* that had been overlooked in the traditional measurement of intelligence (Carpendale, 2000). Piaget's work also has cross-cultural validity, meaning that the same theory can be demonstrated to work across different kinds of societies and cultures (Furby, 1971), and his theories have also contributed to thinking about e-learning as a form of education in schools (Ravenscroft, 2001).

## Brains, hormones and evolution

During the 1970s and 1980s, study of the biological bases of thought and behaviour were challenged because they were considered to be reductionist and, to some extent, marginal in that they failed to take social contexts into account. The term *reductionist* in the context of psychology or biology refers to the approach whereby the emotion or behaviour is *reduced* to its basic elements such as biological, hormonal or neurological processes.

Recent discoveries in cognitive neuroscience, genetics and evolutionary psychology, however, have altered the face of psychology as an academic discipline. According to some, it has changed for the better (Duchaine et al., 2001; Shore, 1997; Swain et al., 2007) but others take the opposite view (Canter, 2012; Marks, 2012; Velmans, 2012). Much of the new research is exciting because we can see (literally through the use of brain scans and analysis of DNA) how our biology can shape our lives. However, what some of the enthusiasts ignore is that, while biology *can* shape our lives, it is by no means the only influence, and perhaps not even the most important one.

### Brain versus mind?

One of the preoccupations in both recent and contemporary psychology has been the location and conceptualization of the human mind. In the eighteenth century, the word 'psychology' referred to the philosophical discipline focused on the study of spiritual being, the self, the soul, core, essence, nature, mind, psyche.

However, since its origins as an academic discipline and experimental science from the nineteenth century onwards, psychology has been bedevilled by the puzzle posed by Cartesian dualism, a term you will hear regularly if you take an interest in brain science. According to the seventeenth-century philospher, Descartes, there is a conceptual separation of the mind (the thinking thing) from the body (the feeling thing).

In Cartesian science, the mind is physically located in, and is part of, the *material matter* of the brain. That is all. Everything psychological or emotional  should and could be explained by psychobiology (and now *is* because of technological developments). This is an excellent example of reductionist psychology. This perspective has been intensified, particularly the ability to use imaging techniques to map the brain and identify different locations for specific functions such as reading and writing, pleasure, anxiety – all of which can now be more closely related to behaviour. But what of our sense of being in the world and having a mind and body of our own – our consciousness?

### Consciousness

Consciousness refers to our sense of self-awareness, including our ability to reflect on our self and our environment. Thus, all of us reading this book have access to a state of consciousness. Something happens when we are conscious that does not happen when we are not conscious, and that is also the case when we are conscious and not conscious of *something* (Velmans, 2012). We can manage and manipulate our consciousness through specific drugs (such as LSD), meditation and hypnosis – all intentionally induced. But how often have you driven on a motorway or walked to work and suddenly realized that you have no awareness of your journey? What happens as you drift off to sleep and you are in a state of semi-consciousness? And of course you might write brilliant notes during a lecture while not having any awareness of what the lecturer was saying!

These may all appear to be examples from personal experiences based (you think) upon something to do with you yourself. But are you simply experiencing what an expert might refer to as *a brain-induced reflex action to an internal or external stimulus* (Revonsuo, 2001)? The brain is an organ just like your stomach – and if you feel stressed your stomach is likely to tighten up as a reflex. You don't deliberately or even consciously tighten your stomach – it tightens itself. Ask yourself now whether brains (and thus minds) are simply the equivalent of a robot or a machine? Is the mind simply a set of neural connections?

Unsurprisingly, the analysis and explanations of consciousness have been the stuff of psychological and philosophical study (and of course part of the nature/nurture debate) for generations (Blackmore, 2012). Debates surround questions about the relationship between the mechanics of the brain versus something more spiritual or cultural about the processes of consciousness. Evidence can be used to support any of these viewpoints, or at least different nuances in the theory of consciousness (Blackmore, 2006).

### Evolutionary psychology

Evolutionary psychology, as you saw in the introduction to this chapter, attempts to discover and understand the design of the human mind. Evolutionary psychology is an approach which applies knowledge and principles from evolutionary biology to research on the structure of the human mind. Duchaine and colleagues, for example, describe the human brain as a set of computational machines, designed by natural selection to solve the adaptive problems faced by our hunter-gather ancestors. It is a *way of thinking* about psychology that can be applied to any topic within it (Duchaine et al., 2001).

This approach to understanding behaviour focuses upon the brain as a biological organ which, as with any other organ such as the heart, has adapted over centuries to maximize the chances of survival of the species. Graham Richards has argued that evolutionary psychology might have been a richer approach to psychology if it hadn't veered further towards neuroscience than to understanding human evolution per se. He proposed that evolutionary psychology took this direction largely because of the general interest in sex differences and gender relations (Richards, 2003). His view has been borne out by researchers' choices of study topics, particularly prevalent being mating behaviours (Buss et al., 1992; Schmitt et al., 2001) including rape. Contrary to feminist beliefs that rape is a form of domination and control of women by men, some evolutionary psychology researchers have related it to psychological adaptation to sex and gender, suggesting that men's brains are subject to high degrees of sexual arousal that may lead to coercion. Furthermore, young men's brains and the brains of men of low socio-economic status are likely to be adapted to being more sexually coercive (Archer and Vaughan, 2001; Thornhill and Thornhill, 1992). Needless to say, this research was subjected to criticism for being misogynist, that is representing a hatred of women (Burr, 2001; Segal, 2001). There were also warnings about the extrapolation of theoretical models directly from animal research because there is a great deal of evidence to indicate sexual coercion among some animals and birds (Archer and Vaughan, 2001).

## PAUSE AND REFLECT

Consider the quality of the evidence about the different ways in which young women and young men mature physically, and particularly about the evidence proposed by evolutionary psychologists on the differential adaptation in the gendered image that leads to behavioural differences. We will ask you to think about this again when you consider the bio-material context of puberty and adolescent development in Chapter 9.

Evolutionary psychologists more broadly have moved beyond studies of mating behaviour and focused on the related topic of 'parental investment' (Bjorklund et al., 2002). They suggest that, in *families*, women have greater parental investment than men because women can only produce one child every year and men can produce numerous children provided they gain access to women. This implies that men would naturally have serial families and many women would be left as lone parents. Thus, women marry (mate with or partner) men who have the greatest resources – physical, financial, political. The more attractive the woman, the more

**PAUSE AND REFLECT**

Why might the parental investment model have important implications for theorizing gender inequalities?

How might it be (mis)applied to make the case for women's lack of achievement of high office in the public sphere?

likely she is to attract a man with resources who can support her investment in producing children with the best possible genetic endowment. Men have sexual relationships with as many women as they can in order to maximize their reproductive potential, and the more powerful the man the more likely he is to gain access to the most women, and indeed women of his choice.

Evolutionary psychology is particularly relevant to social work because it claims knowledge of relationships, sexual behaviour and family life, including child abuse, neglect and domestic violence (Daly and Wilson, 1996; Peters et al., 2002).

The basis for evolutionary psychology is Darwinian *sexual selection* – that individuals who happen to have genetically influenced characteristics that give them advantage (e.g. good looks, intelligence) are likely to produce more offspring who will survive. In other words, this is a theory of the 'survival of the fittest'. The reader needs to judge for themselves the extent to which the same model of behaviour might translate to the human family, and perhaps note with interest Darwin's cousin Francis Galton's worries about the large size of some less desirable families which we noted in Chapter 1.

Other researchers and writers, such as Graham Richards (1987, 2003) and Robin Dunbar (Dunbar et al., 1999), have concerned themselves more with the development of social behaviour and cultural values, including beliefs and superstition, or like Nigel Nicholson, the management of organizations (Nicholson, 2000). Others, such as Sarah Blaffer Hrdy (1997, 2003), an evolutionary biologist, have challenged the lack of thinking by some evolutionary psychologists that has perpetuated the dichotomy of the conceptual separation between the sexes based on an uncritical view of Darwin's ideas about sexual selection and reproduction.

The final example in our review of evolutionary psychology is the work of Anne Campbell, whose ideas focus upon the evolutionary basis of the typically overlooked background to female competitiveness and aggression (Campbell, 2004). Female aggressiveness, she suggests, is based on the need to escalate competition for male partners by the use of physical violence when a high quality male partner is difficult to come by, for whatever reason. The unpleasant image of women pulling out each other's hair when one of them has tried to take a partner from the other, seen in some television soap operas, springs to mind. Campbell also noted that men and women describe their aggressive behaviours in different ways, thus assigning them with different meanings (Driscoll et al., 2006). An aggressive or competitive woman is also likely to be understood by others as less feminine and out of control than a man acting in a similar vein. So, for instance, the woman who has too much to drink at the office party and becomes raucous may well be more concerned later about how she behaved than the man who had exhibited similar behaviour. And the witnesses to her behaviour might also draw conclusions about her that are more negative than those they would draw about a man whose behaviour was the same.

## Cognitive neuroscience

Cognitive neuroscience, which takes a Cartesian position towards the mind (i.e. that the mind is physically located in the brain and is nothing but a product of its own biology) has found a new lease of life of late. Evolutionary psychology, the study of behavioural genetics and the relevant technology, particularly around MRI (magnetic resonance imaging), have enabled researchers to identify more information about the brain's neural pathways, including the evolutionary features of different areas of the brain. We now see some parts of the brain as primitive, with basic reflex functions originating from early human development.

The aim of cognitive neuroscience is to map different areas of the brain and explain how each underpins different brain functions such as *memory* or *language*. While recent advances in neuroscience suggest that it is a new area of psychological knowledge, the study of the relationship between the brain and behaviour was, in fact, one of the founding elements of the discipline as it emerged during the nineteenth century. In the twenty-first century, the areas of the brain that relate to certain functions, such as pain, memory, happiness and emotion, can be seen to light up on a MRI scanner when they are stimulated. These patterns are consistent; under the same conditions there is the same picture on the scanner each time. But what is the significance of discovering which part of the brain controls particular functions?

Even though some theorists and scientists appear to take an extreme position on either side of the nature/nurture debate, there is always some degree of overlap and shared assumptions. For example, psychoanalytic theories, frequently pilloried for not having a scientific experimental basis, have always shared common ground with the biological/nature point of view. Psychoanalysts and brain scientists are concerned about parts of the brain and mind that pre-exist birth and help or hinder adaptation and development.

The debate about the value of knowledge based on using this new technology focuses upon how far we can think of the brain and mind as being essentially *biological* and how far the biological is overridden by the *social*. Schwartz and his colleagues (Schwartz et al., 2005), for example, summarize these issues as the assumption that neuropsychology will ultimately explain all psychologically-described behaviour. They assume that not only aspects of human behaviour that are related clearly to brain activity (e.g. pain, fight/flight anxiety and safety responses) but, akin to the Cartesian position, also intrinsic experiential content (i.e. what we experience), such as *feeling, knowing, effort* and similar mental properties, may be similarly reduced to brain activity.

Social scientists have been relatively slow to challenge this position for many reasons. In part, this can be attributed to the need to preserve thinking about important overlaps between social science and cognitive neuroscience knowledge, including consciousness, psychological development, evolutionary psychology, attachment behaviours, unconscious processes that can be identified by brain imaging, and how some emotion-related behaviour can be changed and those changes monitored in the brain (Cozolino, 2006; Dunbar, 2003; Shore, 1997; Swain et al., 2007). In this and later chapters of this book, several of these issues will be explored in more depth which will make the arguments and counter-arguments posed by the scientists working from different perspectives more of a live topic for you.

There have, of course, been challenges to this reductionist cognitive neuroscience position (Gannon, 2002; Rose and Rose, 2001) which have focused particularly on the role of evolutionary psychology (Richards, 2003), including an expression of regret that evolutionary psychology moved towards a narrow link with neuroscience rather than considering *palaepsychology*, the study of our ancestors, which looks at the characteristics and processes of human evolution in a broader sense, and in a more interdisciplinary way.

Most recently, social scientists have launched a vibrant critique on what they call the 'biologizing' of social science, offering alternative positions to genetics, cognitive neuroscience and evolutionary psychology (Canter, 2012; Marks, 2012; Richards, 1987; Velmans, 2012). David Canter suggests that the discourses of biological explanations of the mind have become so powerful that this kind of thinking has become a faith. He argues that, while it makes perfect sense to accept that genetics play an important role in individual differences in appearance, health and abilities, we need also to consider that biology is not the whole story. As he says, 'evolutionary explanations do not hold the secret to all aspects of human actions and experience. Furthermore, it is important to evaluate biological explanations from many aspects of modern civilization' (Canter, 2012: 101).

In this book, the MDI approach identifies ways in which biology, psychology and sociology might helpfully overlap to provide a plausible and effective explanation for human development. Taking the material, discursive and the intra-psychic into account in this way provides a critical evaluation of each of these perspectives so that biological reductionist or radical social explanations are avoided and the result is a more dynamic and fluid take on the human condition.

## CHAPTER SUMMARY

In this chapter we looked at biological psychology approaches to understanding HGD. We introduced the idea of Cartesian dualism which suggests that the mind is nothing more than the impulses and reflexes of the physical matter of the brain. We thus examined the case for biology over more social explanations of being human, reviewing cognitive development theory through the work of Piaget, evolutionary psychology and cognitive neuroscience and recent ideas about the mapping of the brain. A critical view of each of these approaches was proposed, and we focused on the criticism that some of these approaches were *reductionist*

This multidisciplinary work on HGD has contributed to the richness of our knowledge, but has also divided academic opinion about the strength and value of some theories over others. As you will have noticed, some social scientists have challenged cognitive neuroscientists and evolutionary psychologists for excessive biologization of the brain/mind questions. There are polarized opinions on both sides of the debate, and you will see in the next chapter that the classic theories (such as behaviourism and psychoanalysis) overlap these polarized divides. The main source of contention at present has come about because of the ways in which brain functions and genetic influences can now be 'mapped'. Therefore some scientists claim that human beings can be reduced to the physical matter of the brain while others argue that the mind comprises the interactions between the individual, brain, body, family, society and the genetic and cultural opportunities for learning.

## FURTHER READING

To understand some of the debates in evolutionary psychology, particularly about gender roles the following are accessible and to the point:

Anne Campbell (2002) *A Mind of Her Own*. Oxford: Oxford University Press.
Hrdy, S.B. (2003) The Optimal Number of Fathers. In S.J. Scher and F. Rauscher (eds), *Evolutionary Psychology* (pp. 111–133). Norwell, MA: Kluwer Academic Publishers.

For the debates on consciousness:

Blackmore, S. (2006) *Conversations on Consciousness: What the best minds think about the brain*. Oxford: Oxford University Press.

# 3

# SOCIAL PSYCHOLOGY AND SOCIOLOGICAL THEORIES OF HGD

## Introduction

As we develop the nature/nurture debate in the wake of Chapters 1 and 2, it is time to focus more directly on the nurture side of the coin. Nurture – the influence of the social context on HGD – includes the role and influence of the family, family values and culture, material wealth, physical environment, peer groups and social institutions such as education and religion. As with biology and theories about the influence of nature, the nurture argument is complex and diverse in its use of evidence.

You were introduced to social psychology in Chapter 1 when you read about Milgram's work on obedience, studies of bystander apathy and diffusion of responsibility. You will have noticed that these studies included explanations of the role of power and influence between human beings in different types of situation. These types of situation, such as making decisions that differ from those your boss demands or from those of the group, are relatively easily translated into real life, as we saw in Chapter 1.

Behaviourist approaches – which focus on how the environment influences our learning – and psychoanalytic ideas – which involve the role of the unconscious in our emotions and behaviours – also embody social aspects of psychology. As you will see, they take rather different perspectives on HGD from each other, although they share common features too, particularly the inclusion of biology within the framework of their theories. The differences are that, while behaviourists consider that the brain and mind to be *blank slates* at the start of life, psychoanalysts believe that we are born with an already formed and active unconscious. Both approaches, therefore, hold a theory of the brain as key to the root of their thinking.

Sociology is different again. Having its roots in anthropology and social psychology, it is the study of groups and society/societies. Its topics still overlap with both social psychology and anthropology, but, as you will now be aware, for psychology the focus of attention is the individual, often in some relation to others, while anthropology mostly focuses on social practices in primitive cultures.

Sociological approaches to HGD, as with all of the theories discussed so far, have been subject to changes in fashion, both internally to the discipline and in its contribution to social work (Ferguson, 2001; Houston, 2001; Webb, 2010). Marxist sociology emphasized the struggle between ordinary people and the relative few who held the wealth, while sociological theories of socialization, community and education also examined social class but took a less partial interest, concentrating on how we come to take on and transmit social values from our own family and class. There was a focus on language, education and literature as a means of transmitting culture as you will see below. However, all of these approaches to studying society, which were prominent during the 1960s and 1970s, have become virtually obsolete within the social work curriculum, even though they still render some important insights that contribute to the challenges of nature/nurture debates.

The work of Foucault (Webb, 2010), particularly his analysis of the relationship between power and knowledge and his ideas about criminality, mental health and sexuality, has risen to prominence and ripped into the previously prominent psychoanalytic, Marxist and socialization perspectives in social work theory. Particularly interesting to HGD is Foucault's proposition that *truth* is contingent upon a specific historical period.

Foucault's book *The Order of Things* (2002b) marked the beginning of his (and sociologists in general) thinking about discourse (using language to structure a sense of your place and the way the world appears around you), knowledge and power and, in particular, how he considers the role of discourse over time to regulate belief and behaviour. This means that what counts as, for example, good practice in social work depends on the prominent discourses of the period. Therefore, in the 1950s when social work was in the hands of the lady almoner, usually a middle-class, semi-professional woman who was available in hospitals or charitable agencies to help out those in short-term need of money or practical support, service users were seen to be socially and emotionally inadequate individuals and families. They were recognized to be in need of good works for which they were expected to be grateful.

By contrast, discourses becoming prominent in the 1990s and 2000s saw service users as socially excluded (the idea of which was not explained so much by individuals' problems but by the way society was structured). Their experiences were, therefore, understood via a socio-economic analysis of social inequalities (i.e. what was going wrong in the distribution of wealth) rather than an individualistic one. So thinking in the 1990s and 2000s was about society looking at itself and wondering why not everyone benefited by the creation of wealth. This changed towards to the end of the first decade of the twenty-first century when people who received benefits became demonized in the dominant discourse and the term 'benefit' became associated with 'scrounger'.

Models of disability, for example, are subject to different discourses on disability and the dominance of different ones has changed over time. The medical model of disability which underpinned thinking in the 1970s and 1980s identifies disabled people *themselves* as having difficulties with their lives because of an illness, accident or genetic condition that has left them less able than their peers. They were the problem.

The social model of disability, by contrast, has described disabled people as excluded from society because of *social expectations* of what a person should be able to do physically (Oliver, 1992). Oliver argued that disability was not a fixed condition (and therefore not a function of physical impairment as the medical model suggests) but a product of society. It is *socially constructed* through the use of discourse. The London 2012 Paralympic Games confirmed this point admirably, when we all saw people with a range of apparent physical and mental disabilities show themselves to be highly accomplished athletes. They proved themselves in certain contexts to be far more physically able than those not identified as disabled.

For the rest of the chapter I shall look at different approaches to HGD which take a social perspective, but remember that they may be very different from each other in the extent to which biology and/or society are drawn upon.

I now want to examine the roots of sociological thinking a little more and begin by looking at symbolic interactionism and phenomenology which explore the ways in which language is used to communicate and transmit social values. I then look at socialization, the process by which values are transmitted across generations at home and in organizations.

## Symbolic interactionist and phenomenological sociology

As long ago as the turn of the nineteenth to the twentieth century, Charles Cooley (1902/1930/2009), developed the idea of the 'looking glass self'. This approach suggested that we gain our sense of identity and selfhood by *reflecting upon the way others react to us*, thereby gradually making sense of who we think others think we are. It sounds complicated when described like this, but consider how you started thinking about yourself. Perhaps proud parents would tell you that you were good or clever or beautiful. Maybe you were told the opposite. You were popular at school and therefore came to think of yourself as someone other people wanted to be with. Or the opposite. Actually, for most of us our experience is in between these extremes and we learn, through being reflected in others' reactions, some of our strengths and weaknesses.

Richard Jenkins, in his book on social identity, explored the relationship we all experience between a sense of self or personhood, which provides us with an identity and a sense of who we are as an individual, and a *social identity*, which is how we as an individual can experience ourselves in the social world (Jenkins, 2002). As with the experience of socialization, the use (and understanding) of language is a key element of this process of *self-consciousness*, the sense that we are actually in the world and there is continuity which is the essence of human social development.

### PAUSE AND REFLECT

How frequently do you experience a sense that you are talking to yourself?

You might be trying to encourage yourself by saying you are just as good as the other students on your course. You might be trying to understand why you acted in a particular way or you might be trying to work out what someone who is important to you – a friend or a tutor – has made of something you did.

This form of internal communication is an important tool for self-understanding and the development of a sense of self as a member of a community and society. It is called reflection or *reflexivity* – the capacity to reflect on yourself.

As we shall also see from Chapter 4 onwards, being self-aware and being able to *reflect* on who we are and what we do in relation to others are crucial skills in social work practice.

Symbolic interactionism has this type of interaction central to its understanding of human social development. It is a sociological theory that identifies the significance of language (or symbols which convey language) as a means of communication with others and with one's self, hence the rather daunting title of this area of study. It was derived from the works of George Herbert Mead (1934/1967), Charles Cooley (1902/1930/2009) and Herbert Blumer (1969). Jenkins suggests the need for contemporary sociology to rehabilitate this work, including the work of Irving Goffman (1961) which we shall see below, if we are to make sense of social development. Anthony Giddens, whose ideas are important for MDI theory and whose work is developed in Chapter 4, likewise proposes the continuing importance of these writers for making sense of our relationship with the societies we inhabit (1986/2003, 1991)

Mead particularly emphasized the development of the relationship between the individual and the social world via a continual process of *reflexivity* (being able to think of ourselves and our behaviour from a position of objectivity). In order to do this we have to think about society, or the social world, through the symbolization of a 'generalized other'. In other words, we have an idea in our minds of what other people are like and how they might judge us and we might judge them. We cannot, of course, know for sure anything about others, particularly those we do not know or have not met. Even so, through our experience of being with others from the start of life (parents, siblings, carers), as Cooley proposed, survival and getting a sense of who we are comes from *symbolizing* that other person/people in our mind and reacting as we think they would want or expect us to.

Thus human behaviour does not unfold towards a predestined end but is an active *constructing* process whereby we endeavour to make sense of the social and physical worlds in which we live through reflecting on experience of self and others (Meltzer et al., 1980). We then build a sense of what the world is like in our minds and act towards it according to how we have constructed it. We are not only active agents but we are reflexive ones in that we make sense of who we are through *interaction with our self*.

Antony Giddens has also argued that the self is not a passive entity, determined only by external influence, but that the self also makes a contribution to the social context. This means that we as individuals shape the world we live in as well as experience the impact of the social context upon our own lives and experiences. In other words, we are reflexive and *agentic* beings.

The concept of agency refers to autonomy and being influential over, and giving meaning to, our actions. Reflexivity is the ability to think about one's self. Both concepts are central to the critical thinking promoted in this book.

The concept of reflexivity will be explored in more depth below as being intrinsic to effective practice skills.

### Goffman and the example of the Asylum

Irving Goffman's (1961) classic set of essays on the moral career of a mental patient is an example of symbolic interactionist sociology that demonstrates the ways in which the individual is influenced by and influences the social context. Unusually for the time period, the researcher, Goffman, took a job in the institution in order to conduct his studies, claiming that he had to experience participation in the institution to really understand what life was like. This was in direct contrast to the kind of objective approach to research that would have given inmates a psychological test on admission and after treatment to examine outcome and change. Goffman identified the regime of the asylum as rigid and a total institution that prevented its boundaries from being breached by new ideas or ways of being.

The early experience of the new patient was one in which they were influenced to define themselves according to the norms of the institution (i.e. that they were mental patients and insane). They were thus systematically stripped of an individual identity and became part of a mass identity of *inmates*. The customs of the mental hospital as an institution then became more important to them than their own view of themselves.

**PAUSE AND REFLECT**

**Conformity and the (mad) system?**

The film and novel *One Flew Over the Cuckoo's Nest* demonstrates what happens to people who do not accept the norms of an institution. In this story the humiliated, depressed and conforming long-term patients are briefly awakened to what is happening to them by a rebellious new patient, McMurphy, who leads a bid for a mass escape. The institution responded by making some concessions to the patients but the rebel himself was punished and ultimately controlled by a forced lobotomy. (This is an outmoded and discredited operation for schizophrenia in which nerves that linked the front and back parts of the brain were severed. The effect was to dull the ability to think or to experience emotion.) The patients, including McMurphy, then settled down to dull, emotionless and depressing lives. The staff felt able to carry on with what they were doing – handing out medicines, keeping the patients occupied – but the sparks of adventure and fun had disappeared.

## Socialization

Sociologists have given a great deal of attention to understanding socialization, and particularly the role of language: how it happens, when we are most likely to be influenced, who influences us and how cultural change occurs. Socialization is the *process* that occurs in families, schools, neighbourhoods, peer groups and wider cultural institutions that makes each of us aware of behavioural values and norms as we grow up (Leyendecker et al., 2002; Miller and Harwood, 2001). It has proved to be a useful mechanism for understanding HGD, initially offering insights into childrearing and education (Bernstein and Henderson, 1969) and social aspects of developmental psychology such as learning to play with others (Bereczkei and Csanaky, 2001; Miller and Harwood, 2001; E. Newson and Newson, 1965; J. Newson and Newson, 2007) and has since developed to look more broadly at different cultural norms and values in multi-ethnic and multicultural societies (Parke and Buriel, 2007) .

This type of approach explored how cultures are *transmitted* from generation to generation making us able to work and live with other people through understanding what boundaries may not be transgressed and what is considered to be acceptable and desirable behaviour (Arnett, 1995; Belsky et al., 1991).

Socialization as a concept is most frequently used now, in the twenty-first century, to consider socialization within the educational process for school and university students or in organizational cultures (Allen, 2006; Weidman et al., 2001). So, for example, you begin your education and training as people interested in social work but, through being informed about social work practice, the legal system, ethics and values, you will either take this knowledge to heart, consequently becoming socialized into the social work culture, or you might reject these ideas and values and recognize that you will not fit into the professional world of social work.

Basil Bernstein and his colleagues working at the Institute of Education in London in the 1960s were interested in social mobility, particularly why working class children found it difficult to become middle class. The education system thought it was offering opportunities for most children and young people to aspire to better-paid and perhaps less hazardous jobs than their parents' generation. By hazardous I mean both physically hazardous, such as working with machinery and being at risk of injury, and in the sense that employment was patchy, e,g. London dockworkers never knew from day to day whether they had work.

In the 1960s, for example, school friends eventually drifted apart because some left school early for unskilled work and others went on to train for a profession or attend university.

With this in mind, Bernstein's classic work in the 1960s and 1970s explored the key processes of socialization for young children among their families and at school. Bernstein studied the way language is used to communicate a range of ideas, beliefs and values between people. He began to identify that, although children had friendships across class backgrounds, there were important differences between the ways the children interacted in their own homes. Middle-class professional parents had books in the house, read broadsheet newspapers, read stories and talked to their children, often using abstract concepts and perhaps talking about political decisions or the economy, or even gossiping in a way that brought in some kind of theory of why people did what they did. On the other hand, working-class children mostly lived in families where there was far less discussion of ideas in abstract terms. Language was used to communicate in the here and now and describe more concrete ideas.

What intrigued Bernstein was the way that the middle-class children seemed able to use a different language style (or linguistic code as he called it) to communicate with parents and teachers while also being equally comfortable using the same language style as their working class friends to communicate with them. These different linguistic codes were eventually called 'elaborate' for the discussion of abstract ideas and 'restricted' referring to the way the working-class children communicated. The processes of infant/child socialization then are primarily

## PAUSE AND REFLECT

**Linguistic code or professional jargon?**

You might think of linguistic codes as equivalent to professional jargon – a shorthand means of communicating among similar groups.

- Might your professional jargon exclude some service users and other professional groups?

- How far do you think you have become socialized into understanding the social rules about relationships as a professional social worker?
- Have you developed an understanding of the language and language rules of a professional social worker?

about understanding the rules of social relationships and developing complex linguistic codes for understanding these rules (Bernstein, 1964).

Despite the importance of Bernstein's work at the time, having read Chapter 1 in
particular it will be no surprise to you that this kind of thinking – analyzing working
and middle class as separate cultures – fell out of fashion.

## Ecological systems approaches

In this section, I explore the ways in which ideas about society have been seen as
a system and how the relationship between the social system and the developing
individual serve to influence socialization and the transmission of social values as
part of HGD. Especially in its early phases, and to a great extent throughout the
lifespan, human development takes place through processes of progressively more
complex, shared interaction between an active, evolving bio-psychological human
organism (body and mind) and the persons, objects and symbols in its immediate
external environment (Bronfenbrenner, 1999: 5).

The work of Uri Bronfenbrenner and the development of his *bio-ecological*
model have perhaps had the most direct influence on child-care policy in the
United States, and some of this work migrated to the UK (Bronfenbrenner and
Morris, 2007). Indeed, it has been claimed that the ecosystems perspective has
become the most influential approach for understanding the relationship between the person and the social environment in social work theory and practice
(Kondrat, 2002).

Bronfenbrenner's *Ecological Systems Theory* (1999) takes for granted that growth
and development reflect the influence of several environmental systems, of which
he identified five. *Ecomaps* that make use of this theory may be used as diagnostic
tools and complement genograms. In Chapters 6 to 9 I use ecomaps and genograms to explore real-life examples

The five environmental systems are as follows:

- *Micro system* – the setting in which the individual lives. These contexts include
  the person's family, peers, school and neighbourhood. It is in the micro system
  that the most direct interactions with social agents take place, with parents,
  peers and teachers, for example. The individual is not a passive recipient of experiences in these settings, but someone who helps to construct the settings.
- *Meso system* – refers to relations between microsystems or connections between
  contexts. Examples are the relation of family experiences to school experiences,
  school experiences to out-of-school experiences, and family experiences to peer
  experiences.
- *Exo system* – involves links between a social setting in which the individual does
  not have an active role and the individual's immediate context. For example,

a child's experience at home may be influenced by a mother's experiences at work. The mother might receive a promotion that requires more travel, which might increase conflict with her partner and change patterns of interaction with the child.

- *Macro system* – describes the culture in which individuals live. Cultural contexts include developing and industrialized countries, socio-economic status, poverty and ethnicity.
- *Chrono system* – the patterning of environmental events and transitions over the lifespan, as well as socio-historical circumstances. Taking divorce as an example of a transition,  researchers have found that its negative effects on children often peak in the first year after the divorce. By two years after the divorce, family interaction is less chaotic and more stable.

As we have seen in this chapter and Chapter 1, HGD is highly complex and this model provides a useful means of making sense of how the individual both acts upon and is influenced by the different levels of systems that comprise society and culture. What is missing here are the details of the individual's bio-material and intra-psychic life. It is through these that the MDI perspective provides added value, both to the nature/nurture debate and related theories and to the social/ sociological approaches outlined in this chapter.

## Social psychological or nurture theories of HGD

While the nurture-based theories from biologically-based psychology, which we discussed in Chapter 2, did focus on the influence of the environment, this did not necessarily mean that they took account of the environment as social in the sense of relationships between people. Likewise, the nurture approaches do not necessarily take interactions between people as central to their perspective. Behaviourist ideas (or learning theory) identify HGD through the nurture-lens but do not involve equal engagement between the developing person and adults. Behaviourism looks like the extreme opposite to the nature position because it argues that all personality, thinking and behaviour are the products of *learning* brought about through social and physical environmental factors. This view, known as *classical behaviourism*, was developed during the 1920s and 1930s and includes the work of John Watson (2009) on *classical conditioning* and the variation by B.F. Skinner called *operant conditioning* (DiLillo and Peterson, 2001; Skinner, 1938, 1971/2002; Staddon and Cerutti, 2003). Much of the work underpinning these early theories (as with evolutionary psychology) was conducted with animals or birds, such as the famous dogs that Pavlov made to salivate on the expectation of food rather than the presentation of food itself (Rescorla, 1988) and the pigeons who pressed bars in order to receive food from Skinner.

**Table 3.1** Behaviourism

| Classical conditioning | This type of learning involves two stages:<br>• The first is the 'pairing' of an instinctive or natural behaviour towards the external environment, such as salivating (the *unconditioned reflex*) when smelling food (the *unconditioned stimulus*)<br>• The second stage is the occurrence of salivation as a response to hearing plates rattle (the conditioned reflex) |
|---|---|
| Operant conditioning | This involves a behaviour that is already taking place (such as learning to read) and the intrinsic reward (*positive reinforcement*) when the child has achieved the task.<br>• Positive reinforcement: pleasant consequences to a random behaviour<br>• Negative reinforcement: unpleasant consequences<br>• Punishment: deprivation or pain at a behaviour |

Behaviourist perspectives per se are no longer favoured as a *full* explanation of development although, clearly, learning – and learning through the carrot and stick approach – still has a key role to play in how we think and behave. Developments from Skinner's work, for instance, play their part in helping parents to change certain behaviours in their children such as toilet training (Berkowitz and Graziano, 1972). Children who come to use their potty are often helped to do so by being rewarded each time they urinate or defecate into it rather than soil a nappy. At first this may be a random event because the parent has placed the child on the potty in expectation of a bowel movement. Eventually the child learns that reward will follow potty use and then using the potty will become rewarding in its own right. However, the direct *training* of children has now been largely discredited and replaced by more sophisticated use of similar methods for bringing about pro-social behaviours, such as reasoning with the child, explaining what they have done that they should not have, followed by sending them to the 'naughty step' (Burney and Gelsthorpe, 2008).

What is interesting for us, perhaps, is how behaviourist perspectives have become revitalized via the examination of brain behaviour. Learning is now associated with brain function and biochemical make-up so that these early approaches to the psychology of learning have come full circle (Pomerleau, 1981).

Behaviourist approaches to psychology have remained in the foreground in some clinical work, such as treating panic disorders and phobias (Davey, 1992) and helping people to stop smoking or understand why they smoke (Kenny and Markou, 2005). Another example is, cognitive behavioural therapy (CBT) which involves learning to respond *differently* to feelings, emotions and fears. Its clinical use for treating depression and anxiety in particular has achieved immense popularity across the world because it is cheap and reasonably effective, at least in the medium term (Lewis et al., 2002; Scott et al., 2006). CBT is mostly done one-to-one and may be a useful technique for some service users (such as agoraphobic or

## PAUSE AND REFLECT

**'Little Albert'**

To get a clear idea of what the early behaviourists in particular believed I want to describe the case of 'Little Albert' and its significance within the origins of developmental behavioural psychology

In 1920, John Watson, the American psychologist hailed by many as the father of behaviourism, conducted an experiment to demonstrate how human beings can be conditioned in a counter-logical way. He wished to show that we can be taught to go against what we now think of as instincts and which Watson argued did not actually exist. He chose for his subject an eleven-month old boy – Little Albert. Previously very little effort had been made to study babies and children directly, which is perhaps another reason why Watson's work has become so infamous.

The goal of the experiment was to show how principles of classical conditioning could be applied to condition (or teach) fear of a white rat into 'Little Albert'.

The experiments Watson used involved banging a loud gong while presenting the white rat to the baby. The *gong* (rather than the rat) made the baby upset and cry. He had no knowledge at this stage of his life about rats and whether or not he would like them.

Eventually the white rat was presented to the child without the sound of the gong, but the baby continued to demonstrate symptoms of distress. Thus, Watson argued, Albert had learned or been conditioned to be frightened of white rats. Watson's idea was that we are born as a blank slate and so we can be taught and learn to love, hate, desire or fear whatever the environment throws at us. While no social scientist would take this position in contemporary academic life, the work of Watson and others has made important contributions to understanding *some* of the ways in which we learn to adapt to our social and physical (the material) context.

How would you assess the Little Albert experiment:

- The ethics?
- The research design?
- The value of the results?
- What do you think Albert would have been like as an adult?
- How much do you think the conditioning he experienced would have a long-term impact on his personality?

depressed people) for between thirty and forty-five minutes per session and takes place over a time-limited set of sessions.

However there is an ongoing tension between cognitive neuroscience developments and how they may or may not support some of the theories held by behaviourists. Skinner weighed into this debate, rejecting such links, particularly arguing that some cognitive neuroscientists have confused the identification of feelings and states of mind with behaviour (1985). This tension, as you will have noticed from the criticisms by Canter (2012) and others discussed in Chapter 2, has not been resolved, but for now it has to be the focus of further reading. Behaviourism *research* remains high profile in studies of education, particularly teaching competencies (Hyland, 2006) and in relation to behaviour change. Furthermore, social learning theory has developed to show that methods of conditioning and learning from behaviourist ideas can be adapted to take account of what happens *between* human beings not just *to* them.

## Social learning theory and observational learning approaches to explaining violence: nature *and* nurture

The development of the social learning model was the work of Albert Bandura (Bandura, 1973, 1977) who developed what is now known as *social learning theory*. Building from classical and operant conditioning, Bandura and colleagues pro-posed that learning can occur through watching people behave in particular ways. In other words, children *observe* and *model* behaviours of others who are usually significant and influential adults. The behaviours become part of the child's own behavioural repertoire. This is particularly important when examining ways in which children have been influenced by their parents' behaviours, especially when considering the replication of disadvantage, violence and poor parenting practices (Fox et al., 1995).

### *The BoBo doll: studies of aggression*

Bandura's most quoted work to illustrate social learning theory was the BoBo doll experiments (Bandura, 1973). He made a film of a female student beating up a BoBo doll (an inflatable doll with a weight in the bottom to make it bob back up if knocked down). The woman punched the doll, kicked it, sat on it, hit it with a little hammer while shouting aggressively. Bandura showed his film to groups of chil-dren in kindergartens who were then let out to play in an area where there was a BoBo doll. Several of them beat, kicked and hit the doll with the hammers. Thus they modelled the behaviour of the woman in the film. But, interestingly, not all of them did so.

Bandura made the point that in his study the children had not received any direct reward (as there would be with classical or operant conditioning) but many still exhibited quite marked behaviour towards a doll they had not attacked in this way before. He called the process of copying someone else's behaviour *observational learning or modelling*.

The phases of observational or social learning are:

1. **Attention**. If you are going to learn anything, you have to be paying attention. You need to be alert and interested. Some of the things that influence attention involve characteristics of the model. If the model is colourful and dramatic, for example, we pay more attention. If the model is attractive or prestigious, or appears to be particularly competent, you will pay more attention. And if the model seems more like yourself, you pay more attention.
2. **Retention.** You must be able to remember *what* you have paid attention to. This is where imagery and language come in. You store what you have seen the mod-el doing in the form of mental images or verbal descriptions. When so stored,

you can later bring up the image or description and reproduce it with your own behaviour.

3. **Reproduction.** You have to be able to *translate* the images or descriptions into actual behavior. So you have to have the ability to reproduce the behaviour in the first place. In other words, if you don't have the motor skills to run fast or drive a racing car you are not going to be able to reproduce that type of behaviour. If a young child sees someone being kind to a cat then that is possible for him to reproduce.

4. **Motivation**. For a number of possible reasons you are going to have to be motivated to want to model the behaviour. Therefore you need to see some benefit, even it is simply that something looks like fun or because you want to be like the person who is being observed.

Interest in the BoBo doll effect has persisted, particularly in relation to parental aggression (Baumrind, 1966; Burney and Gelsthorpe, 2008; Guerney, 2001) and corporal punishment (Conrade and Ho, 2001). It could also be used to consider domestic violence between intimate couples and violence to children (Ferguson, 2009).

## Psychodynamic theories of HGD

Psychodynamic theories present a cross-over group of approaches to understanding nature and nurture but it seems that, although this group of theories take the biological basis of the unconscious and conscious mind very seriously, they may actually fit better into the nurture side of the debate. You can judge for yourselves.

Psychoanalytic or psychodynamic theories of HGD have a complex history with social work (Pearson et al., 1988). Psychodynamic, also called psychoanalytic, psychology, has its origins in the late nineteenth century with Sigmund Freud as its founding father. Freud focused mostly upon his explanation of the role of the *unconscious* in HGD. Unconscious processes, he proposed, had a profound influence on behaviour, personality, relationships and emotion with the unconscious present from the start of life and always integral to everyday conscious activities.

Following Freud, the psychoanalytic movement became and remains influential across the world, particularly, but not only, the Western industrialized developed parts. Although it has moved in and out of fashion in social work, it has never completely been replaced and contemporary issues including reflective practice and relation-based social work (Ruch et al., 2010) owe much to psychoanalytic or psychodynamic ideas. Matters of attachment, separation and loss also owe a great deal to psychodynamic theory (see Chapter 5 for a fuller discussion and detailed examples).

Freud considered that there are three basic structures of personality serving what he called the gratification of the instincts. These are the *id, ego* and *superego*.

The *id* is the original source of personality and contains everything that an individual inherits, the instinctual drives and the pleasure-seeking impulses. Like a young child, the id can be seen to operate according to the pleasure principle, avoiding pain and obtaining pleasure, regardless of external considerations. This basic push for gratification remains part of the personality, but with the qualification as we gain experience that gratification can often be achieved better by a more considered approach to the external world.

By planning and negotiating, the child gradually transfers energy from the id to the *ego*. This is the second structure to develop and mediates between the demands of the id and the realities of life. The ego also mediates between the id and the superego, known colloquially as the conscience. The *superego*, which enables individuals to decide between right and wrong, is the third structure to develop.

The ego is the mainly conscious part of the mind, and the id and superego are unconscious. These parts of the personality are seen as being in conflict, and the result of this conflict is *anxiety*. Most people experience anxiety, which can often be directly handled by the ego.

### Defence mechanisms

Sometimes there is too much anxiety to be handled by the ego, and individuals resort to 'defence mechanisms', Freud's term for unconscious strategies for reducing anxiety. Because these mechanisms are unconscious they involve some self-deception, but they are quite normal and part of everyone's experience. The defences can take the form of denial, repression, rationalization, projection and displacement. So, for instance, someone might repress the feelings surrounding the break-up of their relationship by insisting to themselves that nothing has gone wrong (denial). Alternatively, he may rationalize that he never loved his partner anyway, and a break-up would be the sensible solution. Projecting the anxiety would mean experiencing the partner as uncaring and unworthy of love, when in fact the person fears those particular qualities reside in themselves. Finally, anxiety about the break-up could be displaced by having arguments at work or being irritable with the children, and thus focusing attention on these problems, and away from the source of the anxiety.

## Psychosexual development

In the course of development a child goes through a series of what Freud called 'psychosexual stages'. The ego and superego develop at this time. Also, the goals of gratification change according to the focus of the libido, which centres upon a

*Table 3.2* Psychosexual development

| Age | Stage |
|---|---|
| 0–1 year | **Oral stage**: the mouth is the focus of libidinal pleasure and stimulation and the main task is feeding and weaning |
| 2–3 years | **Anal stage**: the anus is the focus of pleasure and stimulation with toilet training as the main task |
| 4–5 years | **Phallic stage**: the genitals are the focus of pleasure and stimulation; here the Oedipal situation occurs |
| 6–12 years | **Latency stage**: sexual energy is replaced by intellectual and other forms of energy |
| 13–18 years | **Genital stage**: the focus is on genital sexuality and the development of sexual relationships |

particular part of the body (called the erogenous zone) at each stage. These are the mouth, the anus and the genitals.

Freud proposed five stages of development (see Table 3.2).

Between the age of 0 and 1 year, the infant goes through the oral stage, when the libidinal focus is on the mouth, tongue and lips. The major source of pleasure surrounds this area, and attachment to the mother is related to her being a source of oral pleasure.

The anal stage occurs between the ages of 2 and 3 years. During this stage, the baby is sensitive to the anal region of his body, which corresponds to the parents' efforts in toilet training. If toilet training becomes fraught, which it often does, Freud considered that a child might suffer to some extent for the rest of his life.

The phallic stage takes place between the ages of 4 and 5. It is characterized by a shift away from the anal region towards the genital erogenous zone. At this stage both boys and girls may begin quite naturally to masturbate.

Freud considered that an important event occurs during the phallic stage, which he called the Oedipal conflict. Freud himself put more emphasis on the events related to boys' development than to that of girls, but he believed that parallel occurrences, took place for girls. He suggested that the boy becomes intuitively aware of his mother's sexuality, and at about the age of 4 begins to have a (sort of) sexual attraction to his mother, regarding his father as a sexual rival. He sees his father as having the ultimate power to castrate him as a punishment and thus the boy is caught between desire for his mother and fear of his father's power to achieve his revenge. The result of this conflict is anxiety, to which he responds with a process Freud calls 'identification'. Thus he tries to make himself as much like his father as possible so that he takes on some of his father's powers too.

The related process which, according to psychoanalytic theory, occurs for girls is not described very well by Freud. He merely asserts that the girl sees her mother as a rival for her father's sexual attentions, although he argues that she will not fear her mother's power so much as the boy fears his father's – perhaps because she assumes she has already been castrated. This means her anxiety is weaker and so is her identification. Freud proposed that all this happens at an unconscious level.

Between the ages of 6 and 12, Freud says that children go through a period of latency without any major developmental changes. During these years the child's friends are almost exclusively of the same sex and there is further development of the defence mechanisms, particularly those of denial (for instance, the child says that he is not tired when he is clearly unable to keep awake!) and repression, in which unacceptable thoughts and feelings, particularly those about sexuality, are forced out of consciousness.

Between the ages of 13 and 18, and beyond, the adolescent's psychosexual stage corresponds with hormonal and biological changes, with the focus of interest on the genitals. The child is now interested in people of the other sex and, according to Freud, with mature heterosexual love being the maturational goal.

Freud's work is a major attempt to explain human development, human relationships and emotions and explore the different ways in which we are (apparently) irrational.

Freud's studies of developmental psychology led him to believe that structural re-organization of the personality occurs at certain crucial points in development, and that these stages are universal features in the development of all human beings. Children want their wishes to be fulfilled immediately and flare up in anger if they are frustrated. They also show strong sexual passion. He considered that during socialization anti-social impulses were brought under control so that a process of internalization through which children moved from external behavioural controls (rewards and punishments) to internal self-controls occurred. This transition linked with children's feelings towards their parents. Parental pressure towards socialization makes children angry and the thought of expressing this anger arouses their anxiety, partly because they might lose their parents if they were to express their anger too fervently. Children therefore repress their anger and turn it in on themselves. This is the foundation of 'guilt' – a powerful motivating force in development. The internalization of the parents' (and thus society's) rules is embodied in the *superego* which is a harsh, punitive and inflexible psychological mechanism.

## *Psychosocial development*

I only want to flag up Erikson's work here as it belongs among psychoanalytic theories of HGD. However, the detail is discussed in Chapter 4 because his work is particularly important in the development of ideas in this book.

Erik Erikson's (1963) model of the life cycle (frequently called 'Eight Ages of Man') explores change through a series of *crises* that move people from one stage of psychosocial development to the next. Successfully overcoming these crises equips an individual with the skills and knowledge to cope with the demands of the next stage of life. Central to his theory is the negotiation of a viable *identity* that enables the individual to progress towards forming mature intimate relationships. Erikson believed that, provided a person is aware and reconciled to the strengths they have gained through the challenges throughout their life, they will be able to face old age and death without fear.

## CHAPTER SUMMARY

This chapter has explored the social psychological and sociologically-focused (or nurture-based) approaches to explain HGD. Here the theories related to language as a means of explaining, and thus constructing, reality were introduced, along with ideas about the fluid nature of some concepts. The relationship between self and society was also introduced, particularly in the context of conversations with the subjective and objective senses of selfhood.

These ideas will be particularly important in subsequent chapters for building the discursive into the MDI model of HGD.

Reading this chapter should therefore have helped you to be aware of the range of social psychological, sociological and systems-based theories available to explain HGD.

It will also have helped you to understand the interface(s) between the different theories described above and to begin to look critically at what are presented as scientific facts.

## FURTHER READING

For ideas on how mostly social approaches to psychology are applied to social work you will find this book engaging and easy to read:

Nicolson, P., Bayne, R. and Owen, J. (2006) *Applied Psychology for Social Workers*. Basingstoke: Palgrave.

The following will provide detailed and somewhat specialist background to sociological theories of HGD but are well worth considering for an essay or dissertation:

Bronfenbrenner, U. and Morris, P.A. (2007) *The Bioecological Model of Human Development*: Hoboken, NJ: John Wiley & Sons, Inc.
Giddens, A. (1986/2003) *The Constitution of Society: Outline of the theory of structuration*. Berkeley and Los Angeles: University of Calfornia Press.
Giddens, A. (1991) *Modernity and Self-identity: Self and society in the late modern age*. San Francisco: Stanford University Press.

Goffman, I. (1961) *Asylums: Essays on the social situation of mental patients and other inmates*. New York: Doubleday Anchor.
Jenkins, R. (2002) *Social Identity*. London: Routledge.
Parke, R.D. and Buriel, R. (2007). Socialization in the Family: Ethnic and ecological perspectives. *Handbook of Child Psychology*: Hoboken, NJ: John Wiley & Sons, Inc.

For theories and application of psychoanalytic ideas to social work which are accessible:

Bower, M. (2005). *Psychoanalytic Theory for Social Work Practice*. London: Routledge.
Smith, V., Collard, P., Nicolson, P. and Bayne, R. (2012). *Key Concepts in Counselling and Psychotherapy: A Critical A–Z Guide to Theory*. Milton Keynes: McGraw-Hill/ Open University Press.

# 4

# THE LIFESPAN: INTERDISCIPLINARY AND CRITICAL PERSPECTIVES

**LEARNING OBJECTIVES**

- To understand the concept of the lifespan.
- To show how we play a part in the management of our own lives.
- To introduce and develop an understanding of a material-discursive-intra-psychic (MDI) approach to HGD in order to review the different elements of our lives.

## Introduction

Understanding the idea of a *lifespan* draws upon *interdisciplinary* approaches to exploring HGD, taking elements from biology, social and biological psychology and sociology. Chapters 1 to 3 stressed the conflicts and meeting points between these disciplines across the nature/nurture debates. In this chapter the concept of the *lifespan* and how it relates to all stages of HGD theory is outlined and developed, together with a more detailed account of the material-discursive-intra-psychic (MDI) perspective and how this type of critical thinking helps us to start relating theory to social work practice. I hope it might also be a good starting point to encourage future social work researchers.

The lifespan approach, particularly as proposed by the psychoanalyst and anthropologist Erik Erikson, focuses on his psychosocial theory of development, which was outlined very briefly at the end of the previous chapter. The theory is particularly relevant to thinking about practice because it describes HGD by drawing attention to the ways in which each individual lifespan is:

- *dependent* on other people, i.e. we are all psychologically, biologically and socially *relational* in that we are unable to survive without others;
- *social* and can never exist outside a culture or social context because it is this that gives us a sense of how to relate;
- *reflective*, i.e. that each one of us makes sense of who we are by recalling our past experiences and anticipating future ones and by thinking about ourselves in the context of our present;
- *imperfect*, i.e. that even those with happy childhoods grow older with some insecurities and anxieties arising from unfulfilled needs and/or frightening

situations, although, equally, each of us will have some *strengths* to draw upon regardless of our early life experiences;

• employs both *conscious and unconscious* processes to bind our sense of identity together, i.e. things which we know about because we can remember about them and things we 'know' about which are beneath the surface of our identity and consciousness but nonetheless have an impact on our ways of being with others and seeing the world(s) around us.

What is particularly useful for practitioners using Erikson's model is the sliding scale between positive and negative outcomes at each stage of the lifespan. This means that the model can be adapted as a first-step basic tool kit for assessment and decision-making. So decision-making about the age/stage experience of a service user becomes further improved by adopting the framework of the MDI perspective. Therefore a practitioner who has achieved an informed and effective grasp of the model will be able to make a decision about well-being for any person within any life stage.

Linked to this model of the lifespan, then, it should be becoming clear from your reading so far how the MDI approach meshes and complements critical thinking about HGD. You will learn even more about how these ideas are interlinked by reading on.

## The lifespan approach: development versus aging?

By now you should be familiar with the terminology used in the study of HGD. You may also be aware of how terminology is influenced by different academic traditions (such as the contrasting approaches of biological psychology and social psychology) because each has specific ways of looking at the subject area.

In traditional developmental psychology, for example, the emphasis has typically been on *development* in childhood and *deterioration* in adulthood. So for instance, Piaget's work focused on the cognitive development of the child (the development of thinking and reasoning) up until he reaches the full intellectual potential we see in adults.

Interest in adulthood and older age, however, was frequently described as the psychology of *aging* rather than development (Burke and Mackay, 1997; Gross et al., 1997). This meant that research into issues connected with HGD typically focused upon the development of skills and abilities in infancy and childhood while exploring the loss of faculties in adulthood.

More recently though, there has been much greater interest, both within and outside the scope of the discipline of developmental psychology in proposing a pattern of *common stages* of development. This provides a much greater focus upon the role of strengths and resilience in HGD and contrasts with the traditional study

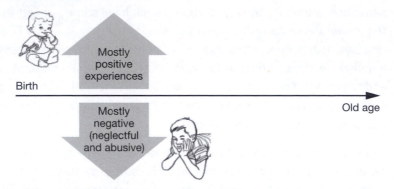

***Figure 4.1*** *Psychosocial balance of emotion and experience across the lifespan*
Images © Vetta/Getty Images.

of aging that emphasizes deficit and weaknesses accompanying the loss of faculties (Hawley and DeHaan, 1996; Levinson, 1986).

This 'strengths' approach has also included what became known as '*Lifespan developmental psychology*', which provides an overarching framework for the study of individual development from conception through to old age. This perspective emphasizes successful (effective) development, within which there are individual and cultural variations (Baltes et al., 2007) (see Figure 4.1).

### The life-cycle and life course approaches

The related concept of the life-*cycle* was originally seen as a radical move away from the idea of development/decay towards ideas of 'normality'. It was taken from an ethological approach to HGD – the scientific study of animal behaviour under natural conditions. This idea will be explained further in Chapter 5 when we look at 'bonding' and 'attachment'. However the term 'life-cycle' is now mostly used to examine animal and plant life-cycles (Bateson, 1966; Hall et al., 2005) although it has also been used by economists to look at cycles of behaviours (Ben-Porath, 1967; Gourinchas and Parker, 2002).

Another term, the 'life course' (Levinson, 1986) was also originally intended to replace the traditional psychological child-based, growth-oriented accounts of the person. This model emphasizes the importance of timing, social context, and organization of human lives from birth to death (Elder and Shanahan, 2007). It is a version of the age/stage model that various researchers from different theoretical traditions have employed (see the discussions of Freud's and Piaget's models in Chapters 3 and 2, respectively). The concept of the life course has gained new energy in recent years among social work and related academics (Floyd and Bakeman, 2006; Green, 2010; Lutfey and Mortimer, 2006; Shanahan, 2000). The life course, however, is more commonly focused on health and well-being, generally directed at biology, experience and adjustment (Elder and Shanahan, 2007).

However, it is often difficult to distinguish between the way that life course and lifespan are used by psychologists and sociologists, with some authors arguing that they have the same focus, use and meaning (Baltes et al., 1999). You will have to decide for yourself. What is most important to think about, though, is how the findings from studies inform social work practice.

## Lifespan development

I think that the term 'lifespan', as developed by Erikson and others, e.g. Leonie Sugarman (2001), works better for social work students and practitioners studying HGD, not only because of its implications for resilience but also because of the implied idea that being older does not separate an individual from their own early life and childhood. The concept of the lifespan manages to integrate individuals' experiences of their lives while at the same time linking generational issues such as parenthood or grandparenthood. The student/practitioner consequently is made aware, for instance, that in their work with young adults they might also have to hold their aging parents in mind. Similarly, the lifespan concept helps us to remember that older people have interests in younger generations because they are connected or disconnected with children and grandchildren. So even where those older people are without children and grandchildren, or where their relationships with them are disrupted or dysfunctional, the inter-generation involvement remains a live issue.

As proposed above, Erik Erikson's model of psychosocial development provides a dynamic and thoughtful model of HGD and, although essentially psychoanalytic, the anthropological dimension ensures that it successfully attends to culture and identity in an interdisciplinary way (Erikson, 1950/1963, 1959/1980). See Table 4.1 overleaf.

### ERIKSON'S MODEL

The first year of life, characterized by Erikson as a stage of *basic trust versus mistrust* involves the infant in interacting with her parent or care-taker, and it is the quality of that care that will give or deny the infant a sense of predictability or trust in the world. If the child's major experience leads to a sense of *trust* then the child is likely to go on to have a degree of trust that they will make successful relationships and have a positive sense of self. Of course, during the first year of life we do not have a grasp of language and, therefore, conceptualizing this sense of trust will be instinctive rather than intellectual. You might want to take a look now at Melanie Klein's work, which is outlined in Chapter 6 and is particularly valuable for the development of the 'intra-psychic' element of the MDI approach.

The second stage, of *autonomy versus shame and doubt*, takes place when the child has developed basic skills of communication, physical dexterity and mobility.

*Table 4.1* Adaptation of Erikson's eight ages of man and psychosocial development

| Age | Stage | |
|-----|-------|---|
| 0–1 | **Basic trust** Trust is a fundamental concept in the experience of becoming human – being able to trust yourself to cope (at this stage with managing to eat, grasp, develop accurate vision and so on and to develop strategies to interact with the social and physical environment). | **Basic mistrust** An infant who is let down by his care-taker(s), whose needs are neglected or who is abused, does not manage to trust himself in the world or to trust others. |
| 1–3 | **Autonomy** If enough sense of trust in self and others has been gained, the infant/young child tries out his relationship with the social and physical world around him. He begins to experience parts of the environment that are 'not' him (other people, toys etc.) and starts to get a sense of what gives them a feeling of pleasure and achievement. For example, he is able to manipulate certain objects and use a potty. | **Shame and doubt** An infant who has been let down and treated inconsistently, particularly by his primary care-taker(s), such as a parent who has not managed clear boundaries between the infant and themselves (e.g. regularly hit the child because they are in a bad mood or under the influence of an intoxicating substance), will experience difficulty in making sense of what 'belongs' to him and what relates to another. He will begin to feel shame and doubt in his capacities because he lacks a sense of personal management. |
| 3–5 | **Initiative** As the child enters school he is rewarded for using his cognitive and social skills by praise and the discovery of friendships. He increases his potential support networks and his sense of autonomy and trust in his abilities. | **Guilt** This continued failure to achieve precipitates a sense of guilt – sometimes guilt about even being in the world. |
| 5–12 | **Industry** The achievements in the early school years become enhanced and the child's experiences and sense of he is are become broader. | **Inferiority** The child recognizes that others have skills, praise and experiences that are denied to him because of his inabilities in intellectual, practical and social domains. Also there is a recognition that other children's experiences and families might be very different from his own. |
| 12–18 | **Identity** A strong sense of being in the world – where a child has come from, where he is heading. An adolescent who is becoming aware of who he is is further able to test things out and cope when things go wrong. | **Role confusion** The young person continues to be confused about who he is, how he relates to his peers, families, school and his own future. |
| 18–25 | **Intimacy** The young person continues to form close and important relationships including, but not only, sexual ones. He also begins a different quality of relationship with his family of origin. The future as an independent adult is becoming tangible. | **Isolation** A young person might apparently have many friends and sexual partners but not manage intimate relationships and 'fall out' with people. His serial relationships might be portrayed as demonstrating popularity, but are frequently desperate attempts to discover the 'secret' of companionship which he may never have had. |

**Table 4.1** *continued*

| Age | Stage | |
|---|---|---|
| 25–50 | **Generativity**<br>This is about procreation and rearing the next generation but it is also about other achievements at home and work. | **Stagnation**<br>The individual does not have the experience of development in any domain of his life and becomes 'stuck'. This could lead to clinical conditions such as depression and/or alcohol and substance abuse. |
| 50+ | **Ego integrity**<br>The older person knows who they are, is able to love and feel love and can look back over his life so far and recognize who he is. | **Despair**<br>The individual has a sense that his life has not led to anything of value and he is adrift. |

At this stage she has gained some control over her bladder and bowels. If she makes too many mistakes in the learning process then she will increasingly develop a sense of shame rather than a sense of accomplishment. Once again, the quality of the care she receives will make a difference for better or ill.

*Initiative versus guilt* refers to the crisis around the child's ability to plan and take the initiative for some of her actions. She may also be interacting with other children during this stage. This means there is scope for a great many 'mistakes', and if the child is not supported by her care-takers she may experience too much of a sense of guilt about her failures.

Around the time of starting school, the emotional crisis is about *industry versus inferiority*. For the first time the child is put into competition with several other formerly unknown children. She is faced with the need for approval from strangers, and that is achieved via the quality of her work at school rather than her other personal qualities. If she doesn't do well, she risks feeling inferior to her peers.

The crisis for the adolescent is to resolve the battle between developing a sense of *identity versus role confusion*. There are so many opportunities and obligations that a teenager might be faced with, including those that surround sexual identity and the development of relationships. Successful resolution of this crisis is the development of an integrated sense of identity and entry to successful adulthood.

In young adulthood, during the crisis period of *intimacy versus isolation*, the task for the young woman or young man is to manage to develop close relationships without losing their own identity. The middle period of life, *generativity versus stagnation*, involves creativity and development of self and one's talents including parenthood. (Erikson's view that midlife ends at 40 has been seriously disputed, and this is particularly uncharacteristic of women's experience because many don't return to their career tracks until they are around their early 40s because of child care responsibilities.) *Ego integrity versus despair*, the final stage, comprises the sum of life's parts. Did she manage to make sense of her life, achieve what she sought in the way that she wanted to? If there are too many regrets, too many unresolved issues from earlier in life, then a sense of hopelessness may set in for the last stage of life.

## IDENTITY

In this lifespan model the development of *identity* is a 'cumulative' experience. It is rather like a snowball which is never composed only of pure frozen water. It contains stones, bits of twig and other less pleasant substances, but it is nevertheless held together by frozen water. It also grows in size and substance as it rolls along. Identity is a useful idea for thinking about HGD because as it develops, accumulating the good and bad elements of biological, social and psychological life, there is still a kernel of the individual that remains in essence who they always were and retains their fantasy about who they will become. In other words, their sense of identity spans their life – the life lived, being lived and the life to come.

Identity, ego or self are complex concepts that are important to understand across all elements of HGD. Identity has been the nucleus of HGD theory and research included in the work of sociologists (Giddens, 1991; Jenkins, 2002), psychoanalysts and psychotherapists (Knight and Poon, 2008), biologists (Martin, 2007) and psychologists (Sugarman, 2001), all of whom have developed slightly different perspectives. However, for all of them, identity is about the development and relationships of the individual person.

According to George Herbert Mead (1934), whose work I discussed in the section on symbolic interactionism in Chapter 3, the development and *meaning* of identity arises from the reflexive interplay between the 'I' and the 'me' (that is, the immediate consciousness and the self we think about in retrospect) in the context of a changing society. In other words, identity is not a static concept, and what it means for each of us is connected to the context in which we live and work. Thus Mead has made us realize that we interpret and reinterpret *who* we are and *how* we are in the social context of our lives and the lives of others to whom we relate. Sometimes we hear in popular media about people who have 'reinvented' themselves after, say, career failure, a spell in prison or similar life disruption. However, Mead's work has shown how we all reinvent ourselves at various times of our life and probably at different times of our day (with our children and then with service users) or week (out with friends and then back to office relationships).

For Erikson, too, identity was central to lifespan development.

## RELATIONSHIPS

Human *relationships* are fundamental to becoming a person with an identity. Identity helps us to make sense of how each of us is recognized and responded to by others. All major theories about all or part of HGD identify the role of others in any one individual's lifespan. Throughout this book, from consideration of bonding and attachment in Chapter 5 to successful and failed relationships described in subsequent chapters, we see that relationships and identity are inseparable.

From the beginning of life, then, there is a family configuration that the baby enters. Each one is different, but each of us also shares common attributes and, as I show throughout the book, it is the quality of these relationships that most impacts on HGD and lived experience.

## A material-discursive-intra-psychic perspective

Taking a material-discursive-intra-psychic (MDI) perspective to make sense of HGD gathers the best information from all the theoretical perspectives and developmental themes identified in the previous chapters and in Chapter 5.

MDI takes account of HGD in all its features, from the biological to the societal, while paying close attention to the ways in which socio-political-historical constructions of subjective knowledge interconnect with emotional experience. This means that our sense of ourselves (subjective knowledge) connects with ways in which we understand the role, experiences and expectations of a person in a particular political and historical time (socio-political-historical). So if you were a Russian peasant in the time of the Tsars when there was no social mobility but a sense of knowing your place, 'subjective knowledge' would involve a sense of the limitations of your life-chances. This would contrast sharply to your view of yourself living in twenty-first century Britain where the world might be your oyster provided you gain an education and embark upon a profession.

Within this framework, then, individuals are able to make sense of, and therefore negotiate and manage, their biographical 'selves' as they move through the lifespan.

To begin to explore this model in greater depth and detail, I outline each element as set out in the 'material', 'discursive' and 'intra-psychic' positions. In subsequent chapters each lifespan stage is described broadly and, where most appropriate, in terms of the MDI model.

### *The material context*

The material context comprises a complex interconnected set of factors that include:

- the physical environment in which we operate through the lifespan (socio-economic circumstances, housing, work-life, family size, the community in which we live);
- our biological and biographical (the meaning we give to our background) make-up;

- strong intra-personal cognitive, sociological and social psychological components as well as strong genetic/EP elements, which include our strengths and weaknesses such as ability to reason and think effectively or our tendency to anxiety or violent behaviours when stressed.

Naturally these vary across the lifespan for each of us, as well as between individuals. As we grow, mature and age our biological *materiality* changes and we become variously able for that reason. We develop new physical competencies and in-competencies at almost every stage of our lives. One example is how I now (in my 60s) find it very difficult to tie my shoelaces because of reduced flexibility, while at the same time my young grandson also finds it difficult to tie his shoelaces, but in this case because his manual dexterity and hand/eye co-ordination are still developing.

For instance, Uri Bronfenbrenner, whose aim was to think beyond what he perceived as a 'negative' developmental psychology, saw HGD as being about 'progressive [mutual] accommodation, throughout the lifespan, between the growing human organism and the changing [immediate] environments in which it [sic] actually lives' (1977). By this he meant that the bio-psychological person (the organism) adapts to the social and physical conditions in which he or she lives and that this is an ongoing process. The process is affected by relationships in the immediate settings and the larger social contexts in which the settings are

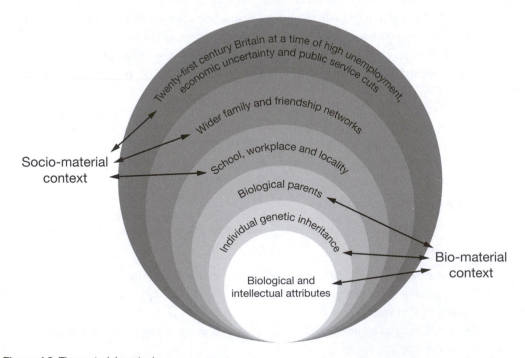

*Figure 4.2* The material context

embedded. Furthermore, the organism/person has an impact on the various systems it/he inhabits – changing the physical and social structures in which it/he
lives (Bronfenbrenner, 1977).

The material, therefore, extends beyond those factors that are observable and
(potentially) measurable. Our biographical *stories* that we tell ourselves and others and which, as we have seen, are part of the glue of our identities change as we
pass through the lifespan. This happens both in terms of the sheer length of the
biographical tale (or tail if we think about our life in a slightly different way) but also
how we recall and fail to recall what has happened to us and give these real and
imagined events meaning. The meanings we ourselves place on our experiences
and the contexts in which we live/have lived them are part of the materiality of the
lifespan.

For example, one elderly woman recently recalled how for many years she had
had no idea how much her husband had earned until she saw his pay advice by
accident. They had been together for most of their adulthood and brought up a
family together. She considered it to be typical of her generation of women and
housewives to be given housekeeping money, so she had never considered herself
in any way disadvantaged by not knowing how much money came into the household. She had believed that they, as a family, were quite poor and as a consequence
she had managed sparingly, denying herself many luxuries that had tempted her.
Neither had she been able to provide her children with all she believed they de-
served. When she discovered the truth that they had in fact been comfortably off for
some considerable time, the sense of who she was and the meaning of her life with
her husband changed her biographical context dramatically. She felt that she and
her children had been betrayed and for some time she was effectively traumatized
by this knowledge. It took her a while and work with a social worker interested
in individual counselling to come to terms with her life and her relationship with
her husband. It was not only the relationship itself that had been shaken, but her
sense of her own judgment about the *socio-material context* in which she had lived
her life.

A case reported widely in the media of a baby aged eleven months who died of
malnutrition and vitamin deficiency is another and different type of example of the
material context impacting on life. The mother was a vegan but had taken on board
in good faith the message that 'breast is best' for babies so she had breast-fed
the baby from birth. However, she was unaware that her own limited diet and the
limited diet of breast-milk fed to the baby was, in fact, depriving the baby of life-
giving nourishment. This is an example of the *bio-material context* impacting on life
chances.

In both cases, the material context was complex. The mother in the second
scenario felt she was doing the best she could for her baby. Her choice of eating

regime coupled with her misunderstanding of what impact her own diet would have on her baby through the breast milk was part of the baby's material world, demonstrating the complicated, inter-generational relationships between people across the lifespan.

Focusing solely on a material context to understand HGD, however, fails to reveal what is below the surface of someone's life, although the impact of materiality as described above, should not be neglected.

### The discursive context

The discursive context refers to the ways in which both individual and social experiences are *constructed*, or formed, through the institutions in which they are described and discussed. 'Discourse', the basis of a discursive context, includes conversation, written texts such as newspapers or books, images including fine art and film, and what are called *social practices*. Social practices refer to culturally accepted and desirable ways of behaving and ways of portraying social action within discourses.

This might happen through the development of a technical phrase or label such as 'mental illness'. The phrase 'mental illness', as you will know, is widely used, and comes from an authoritative source (psychiatry) to describe the experience of someone who has problems in their life about what is reality – whether they are schizophrenic and 'hear voices' or whether their sense of hopelessness and helplessness, their depression, does not reflect their real access to resources and opportunities. The dominant discourse surrounding mental illness during the late twentieth and early twenty-first centuries constructs a person suffering mental ill health as someone with a *medical* problem which is 'treated' by doctors in hospital in-patient or outpatient facilities or general practice surgeries. By contrast, however, remember that I discussed debates around this topic in Chapter 1. There we thought about the 'anti-psychiatrist' R.D. Laing's question 'who is mad here?' – the system/family or the patient? This discourse from the 1960s constructed 'madness' as a rational response to insane institutions.

Psychotherapy, particularly longer-term approaches such as psychoanalytic psychotherapy, is rarely provided by the NHS now because of the power of genetically-based theories of mental illness. However, genetic theories of depression and even schizophrenia are just as speculative as the social science theories, but some forms of science currently have more power than others. (See the discussion of this and references to some key studies in Chapter 1.)

Discursive contexts also refer to the way society is understood through the discourses around its historical structures. So, coming back to the example of the Russian peasants under the Tsarist regimes, the use of the term 'peasant' then was a description of a lifestyle embedded in a culture where there was little opportunity for social mobility and where the land was owned by the gentry who in turn 'owned' those who lived and worked the land. 'Peasant' was a description constructing a group who took a pride in their ancestry and practices. Using the term 'peasant' now, in Russia and in the West, is mostly used to insult someone by implying they are uneducated and/or not very bright. The meaning and the construction underlying the word are formed according to social and historical culture.

It is also important to see that discursive construction suggests fluidity. In other words, contemporary constructions of peasants and people suffering mental illness are not fixed – meanings and experiences associated with these constructions shift over time and context. This is part of what sociologists and social psychologists have called the post-modern project. *Post-modernism* is an approach to society, human relationships and behaviour that challenges the traditional (or modern) grand theory method, thus suggesting that some concepts are *social constructions* and therefore not fixed. Freud's model of psychosocial development and evolutionary psychology are both examples of grand theories in that they attempt to explain processes through looking at a set of relationships (such as human development or human reproductive choices) overall rather than in small bites. Consequently, thinking about ideas in a post-modern way means that some ideas are fluid and subject to change over time. For example, notions of good parenting vary according to culture and time period and are *socially constructed*, contingent upon how a society chooses to give meaning to evidence about how parents might behave (Woodcock, 2003). A strict parent who physically chastised their children was seen as a good parent who had control of their family in Victorian times. In contemporary society this behaviour by parents may well provide grounds for care proceedings.

Another example might be the way the word 'riot' is used. Riots can be constructed as an indication of justified social unrest and even a form of 'people's democracy'. The Poll Tax riots of the late 1980s and early 1990s in Britain were described thus, and even though cars were burned, window smashed and, in parallel to these events, many refused to pay their tax bill, the dominant discourse then and now was to locate them in history as a mass disturbance against political oppression. This is in direct contrast to the riots that took place during the summer of 2011, which were discursively constructed as mass action by people with criminal (rather than liberationist) intent. The concept of *moral panic* is a useful way of understanding differences in the meanings given to some social phenomena which sometimes leads to national soul-searching, as with the 2011 riots. Another example is that of obesity. Is there in fact a public health epidemic of child and adult obesity or is it a moral panic – a discursive construction (Campos et al., 2006)?

Discursive (or social constructionist) psychology and post-modern thinking in sociology form the basis for understanding and explaining the discursive context *which has external and social origins rather than bio-material or intra-psychic ones.*

Foucault, a highly influential French philosopher whose work I introduced at the beginning of Chapter 3, developed ideas of the relationship between power and knowledge, proposing that power is fluid rather than fixed and that the influence of what we 'know' as factual varies over time and is dependent upon the dominant beliefs during a particular era.

*Symbolic interactionist* ideas (see Chapter 3) also inform the discursive context and the ways in which we give meaning to our selves, relationships and society – symbolically – with language being the core symbolic characteristic.

There are debates within discursive social science about how far analysis of discourse 'liberates' or 'regulates' – the 'light' side or the 'dark' side of discourse (Danziger, 1997).

### THE 'LIGHT' SIDE OF DISCOURSE

In some contexts, through *deconstructing* (i.e. tracing the ways in which a discourse has been constructed) the meaning and language used to convey aspects of that meaning, it is possible to appreciate important insights and to make sense of some relationships. A powerful example is that of domestic violence. As Featherstone and Trinder (1997) proposed, the existence of domestic violence is not a 'given' but discursively *constructed*. In other words, there is no objective, universally and historically stable concept of 'domestic violence'. Their argument goes as follows:

- Firstly, in Western twenty-first-century societies domestic violence is illegal but also perceived generally as aberrant and the perpetrator culpable. This is not the case even today in all societies. The same behaviours are not perceived in the same way in Afghanistan as they are in the USA, but neither has domestic violence always been identified as problematic in Western culture. Thus history and culture have constructed different meanings for the same behaviours.
- Secondly, many women themselves fail to recognize that their relationship could be described as living with *domestic violence*. They might understand that their partner behaves violently but, until they have discourses to draw upon which name domestic violence and abuse, some women might see what is happening as a characteristic of their lives rather than as an observable fact and social discourse.

The way that our lives are constructed through discourse has consequences for the actions we take and the meanings we give them. It could follow that being able to name a set of behaviours sets someone on the road to being able to change their situation and perhaps reconsider the meaning that, in the case of domestic abuse, a violent relationship has had on their life. Therefore these concepts can act as a *resource* for someone to re-evaluate their life and relationships. This is the light side of discourse in that it supports critical thinking.

## THE 'DARK' SIDE OF DISCOURSE

The 'dark' side of discourse (Foucault, 2002a, b) is not necessarily about negative experiences and processes. This phrase refers to the regulation of conduct
through discursive practices. This means that those in power (and who have power
over knowledge) construct social practices that survey and regulate behaviours.
Thus, for example, 'evidence' about what makes us human is regulated by the
knowledge-claims of the most powerful scientists. We can see this routinely in
contemporary science reporting by the media, as shown in Chapter 1, and the
'maternal deprivation' thesis discussed in Chapter 5 (Riley, 1979).

An example of the outcome of discursive regulation is the discourse that 'biol-
ogizes' health and attributes 'discovery' to genetics, with other approaches being
portrayed as outdated. This biologizing of health, for instance, has given rise to
some women choosing to have 'preventive' mastectomies, even though they do
not have any signs of breast cancer, because there is a history in their immediate
female family members (Canter, 2012).

Forty years ago the idea that gay couples might be able to form legally recognized civil partnerships, let alone be married, would have been unimaginable. The
life story of Quentin Crisp bears witness to this. Crisp, whose ninety years of life
spanned the twentieth century, was persecuted and physically attacked for being
'queer' and those attacks on him were socially acceptable at the time – Crisp was
positioned (or constructed) as the one at fault and to be blamed for being deviant.
Neither Crisp's lifestyle nor his behaviour would be regulated formally in contemporary Western societies, although nothing fundamentally 'biological' or 'psychological' has changed.

Foucault, with these kinds of historical and cultural practices in mind, argued
that power and knowledge are linked and that discourses are created to regulate
behaviour through operating as constraints and norms. Foucault himself particularly highlighted discourses on mental illness, criminality and sexuality as regulating social behaviour (Burkitt, 1999; Foucault, 2002a, b).

Expert power and knowledge, such as that of medical researchers, is also used
to regulate behaviours, although this kind of regulation is constructed as 'beneficial'. For example, it is now inconceivable to recall that some of my colleagues and
students used to smoke in their offices and lecture-rooms. The consequences of
science and the construction of the dangers of both smoking and passive smoking
have led to changes in the law characterized by seating areas outside pubs and
restaurants and notices, such as those in my institution, forbidding smoking within
three metres of a building. Following Foucault, the smoker comes under the 'gaze'
of health workers and politicians who have identified what behaviour is healthy and
what is damaging. The high profile reports of the deleterious effects of cigarette
smoking to the smokers themselves and those around them effectively focused a

disciplinary *gaze* upon them which therefore regulated smokers' behaviours, defying them to transgress these *newly constructed n*orms (Haggerty and Ericson, 2000).

## Being 'agentic'

The lifespan is not simply about the growth of experience and identity, but also concerns actively interpreting one's *biography* and making sense of one's own and others' lives. Unlike the traditional versions of developmental psychology (such as behaviourism and some (mis)understandings of cognitive developmental and psychoanalytic theories discussed in Chapters 1, 2 and 3), it has become accepted among academic researchers that individuals are not only 'acted upon' but have their own 'agency'. They have a sense of being the cause of behaviour and thought rather than a passive recipient of what life throws at them (Giddens, 1991; Reavey and Brown, 2007; Sylva and Lunt, 1983).

Discursive approaches demonstrate that individuals are not passive in relation to ideas, other people or themselves, but they are thus *agentic.* Human agency, or being agentic, describes how each of us actively presents ourselves to others and to ourselves, engages with the environment (human and material) and generally acts in the world. It involves the management and negotiation of events such as starting school, losing a parent, having a baby, becoming a grandparent, bereavement and the death of loved ones and of oneself. It even refers to the baby's initial primitive engagement with its carer (see Chapter 7) where there is evidence that interaction, and the infant's role in that interaction, have meaning and purpose.

To recap:

- Each of us interacts with the world, making an impression and taking autonomously conceived and planned action to manage the relationships around us at different levels.
- The baby/child has an impact on the family who cares for her – which is not simply the fact of having this baby as a family member, but because the baby has her own demands. Her distinct personality and behaviour also have a particular impact.
- A recently widowed elderly person will have an individual impact on the environment he moves to (the care home, the family) because he has his own demands that attempt to shape the context he moves to.
- Groups and communities can take action to change their lives by resisting policy or action by governments and local authorities.

The different theories described in Chapters 1 to 3 vary in the extent to which that agency is seen to be important, depending on the degree of *determinism* – the belief that biology is destiny – at the centre of the theoretical framework (Kondrat, 2002).

### Lived experience: 'agency' and 'performativity'

We can draw upon discourses of criminality, victimhood, madness and betrayal at various times and stages of our lives, and these ideas interact with and bisect our sense of identity/selfhood.

We draw on these discourses in an immediate sense when we become, say, a victim of burglary attributing our experience of shock and loss to increased criminality in the community. When our partner tells us they love someone else and plan to leave us, we see this as a betrayal. Using language and symbolism in this way, we can make sense of our individual experiences and find a way to see them as 'shared' and in some way integral to the culture. Burglary happens. Betrayal happens. And neither of these things has happened just to us, but the label provides a symbol through which the experience can be communicated to others.

This is how we construct a sense of who we are which is both *material* and *discursive* in character. We draw on expert discourses to explain experiences, particularly those that have traumatic causes or consequences such as divorce, family bereavement or serious ill health. We also understand that our experiences are influenced by the material context of our lives – previous histories of illness, lack of education, a car accident or a neglectful parent.

This may be discussed in *phenomenological* terms as 'lived experience' (Ellis and Flaherty, 1992; Lindseth and Norberg, 2004). Phenomenology refers to the philosophical idea that we structure our own experience and make our own sense of our own 'being in the world'. We feel, behave and give meaning to the 'story' of our lived experience and as such we 'perform' our biography and re-tell it to ourselves and to others to make sense of it (Daly, 2001; Goodley and Tregaskis, 2006; Goodson, 1995).

Judith Butler's work on gender constitution and *performance*, similarly, follows such a phenomenological view. For Butler, identity per se may be seen as a performance with the lived experience of, say, 'alcohol addiction' as the *'object of belief'* (1988: 520) that sustains the *performance of the self*. That is, the *material fact* of our addiction gets reconceived as a process that gains a cultural meaning. In other words, we come increasingly to see ourselves as being addicted to alcohol and behaving accordingly, separating our sense of our 'self' from things that other people 'do' or 'are'. This is also relevant to Goffman's perspectives on the 'asylum' discussed in Chapter 3.

To illustrate these ideas about human agency and performativity, I draw upon the story of a well-known, but anonymised, business family. Their lives are constantly lived in the public gaze and as such create a 'performance' to manage their image and to manage the performance of who they are taken to be and feel they are. After the brief case study, I show how their performances of self might be analyzed using a discursive framework. This management of performance occurs particularly in show business, forming the basis for magazine stories and chat-show material. You might like to think discursively about the next celebrity interview in your newspaper or chat show.

## The Kingmans: A family in distress

The family of the veteran entrepreneur and businessman, Malcolm Kingman, were interviewed in the press about twenty-five years ago with their confessions about drinking, alcoholism and violence. They also gave (perhaps) unintended information about sibling rivalry and anxiety. What is particularly interesting in this context – and partly why I have chosen this family's story – is how stories from and about the family are told and retold. I have also chosen the story because, although it was in the public domain, it is easy to make anonymous as it appeared more than two decades ago.

It had become apparent that the director of a subgroup of Malcolm's parent company, William his son aged 45, suffered from alcoholism and drug addiction that caused him to be physically violent and have apparently psychotic episodes in public.

Malcolm, then aged 70, declared publicly that he too had had problems with alcohol and drugs when he was younger, although he had been sober for the past twenty years (roughly since the age that William was when the articles appeared in the press).

When stories of William's drunken outbursts hit the headlines Malcolm talked about his son being 'emotionally crippled'. Malcolm's theory was that any period of abusing alcohol and drugs in someone's life can be written off as a non-*developmental* stage of life so that an addict and substance abuser effectively misses out on maturation and remains at the life stage prior to their dependency and addiction. By this, Malcolm appears to have meant that a person will lose any sense or experience of maturing or emotional development during the years of abusing drugs and alcohol.

What he did not identify were triggers to the behaviour itself. Malcolm suggested that his son had been courageous in coming off drugs and drink rather than continuing to be the violent, aggressive wastrel that the media portrayed him to be.

In the meantime, one of William's brothers, Trevor, perhaps a rival for power in the wider company, had wondered publicly in numerous press interviews, why his brother's emotional development had turned out to be so different from the way he himself had managed adulthood when neither of their parents drank any more and their other brother (Terry) had stopped drinking ten years previously.

In this family it is possible to see the intricacies in a family pathology and dysfunction.

- The addicted and drunken father who has reformed his life.
- The middle-aged man who is addicted, drunken and acting out his violence(s).
- The brother who has chosen to position himself apart from *this* brother, commenting that, having witnessed his father's volatile behaviour at home when they were young, he cannot understand why William followed the same path.
- This brother and his father also separate themselves from William.
- Terry was an invisible force, used by Trevor to punish William a little more by comparing him favourably.
- The family drew upon different discourses to explain and story their own lives and to interpret what they have been seen to act out.

The Kingmans had talked about their lives publicly in various media outlets, and you will be able to conduct a similar analysis of other people in the public domain, particularly sports and entertainment celebrities. It might be interesting to find such a story, which doesn't have to be about misfortune, it might be about someone gaining celebrity status, having a baby or being reunited with a family member from the past. If there are enough reports about them then you may be able to see patterns of how performance is negotiated through language. You may get some hints on what to look for in the next section.

### ANALYSIS

As Reavey and Brown (2006) have shown when discussing adults' memories of abuse in childhood, there is pressure (from self and others) to recall detailed events as evidence of their memories. This is both to bear witness to the reality (that is, confirming its truth) and to the cause of ongoing trauma (that is, identifying that an event or period in one's life had an impact on the behaviour and experience being discussed in the present).

In other words, when something traumatic or degenerative has taken place in someone's life they, and those closest to them (which might include their social worker), have to *tell* of what happened and more so to provide a theory.

Survivors have to publicly rehearse that they *are* survivors, linking their lived experience with the performance of survivor. So, when a service user tells a social worker about their lives, they are in fact attesting to the trauma of, say, a bereavement, providing a theory about why it caused them to behave in the way they are currently doing – abusing alcohol or experiencing severe depression, for example.

In the case of the Kingmans:

- Malcolm, as a survivor of drug and alcohol abuse is telling his own story, distancing himself from what he himself might have done during his drunken and abusive years by talking of his *son* as being emotionally crippled.
- Trevor, similarly, is explaining himself as the son of parents who don't drink (any more), perhaps revising memories of childhood in which he may have chosen to be different from his father.

Memories have to be managed and, in the case of traumatic lived experience following abuse, condensation or simplification takes place so that 'there is the conflation of multiple episodes of abuse in a singular image' set alongside 'the reduction of an ambiguous set of conflicting forces and an indeterminate set of motivations into a manageable, dramatic structure' (Reavey and Brown, 2006: 193). This means that the person combines the events around the trauma or extended distressing episodes, such as an accident which caused her to be confined to a wheelchair despite successive surgical and physiotherapy interventions, in order to ensure that the importance of what happened is flagged up. But, in the telling, the event needs to be disentangled from what might be significant but mundane events to the listener/observer, such as weeks of exercises to gain power in the muscles.

### *NARRATIVE*

As well as being *performative* and *agentic* we also have a personal history constructed through memories which is managed by being story tellers with 'narrative intelligence' (Mateas and Sengers, 2002). We 'furnish our worlds not just with data but with meaning ... by telling stories we make sense of the world. We order its events and find meaning in them by assimilating them to more-or-less familial narratives' (Mateas and Sengers, 2002: 1). The shift among many social psychologists towards a discursive approach and, more recently for some, a material-discursive approach (Ussher, 1997; Yardley, 1996) lends impetus to the use of *narrative* to understand lived experience. This means the telling of a story, such as the recounting of an identity or life story, and emphasizes that language and the construction of concepts, such as HGD and identity, are based on *talking about them* rather than, for example, observable aspects of biology.

To explain further, when we tell the story of something we did, or even the story of our life, we put various actions and events into a context. You might link the story of meeting your partner in the context of your university social life or a practice placement. Similarly, when you left school you might describe your first job in the context of leaving your family home or moving to another part of the country or making new friends. When we talk to others and to ourselves about who we are, we tell a story – or produce a narrative to explain who we are and the context in which we lived through certain key moments.

### NARRATIVE AS A RESEARCH METHOD

A narrative approach to psychological and sociological research and analysis is particularly important for making sense of questions of self and identity (Andrews et al., 2007; Fraser, 2004). It is from research conducted explicitly to make sense of how people talk about themselves and their lives that we have learned how people manage their lives and the performance of their stories. Understanding the experience of service users is clearly relevant here because when you meet them they will want to ensure that you have the full context to explain their life that led to their meeting you.

Michelle Crossley (2003), who has continued to focus on what she calls 'the methodology of self', takes the 'storied' nature of human life as a means of attributing a central role to language 'but more specifically to "stories", in the process of self-construction' (p. 290). Since the late 1990s the concept of narrative has also entered social work research and practice (Fraser, 2004; Riessman and Quinney, 2005).

This is suggestive of what Crossley proposes – that narrative psychology (and, of course, related social sciences) goes beyond the idea that stories are simply used to make sense of unexpected events and that human psychology has 'an essentially narrative structure' (p. 291). That is, we each need to make sense of our lives and the relationships we have in a way that could be structured as a coherent story.

Thus, the Kingman family *needed* to see and talk about William in a context of his and their own lives even though, or perhaps because, Trevor and Malcolm told the story differently. Thinking about this family might lead you to think about the families described by Laing and Esterson (in Chapter 1), for example, in which, although a particular member was constructed as the 'mad' or bad one and presented to the doctors as such, the observer did not necessarily perceive the interactions they saw in the same way.

---

**PAUSE AND REFLECT**

The idea of narrative will have resonance too with the families we work with and it would be a useful exercise to choose one such family and consider the way that each might tell the story of the other members.

What might you understand through this process that was missing from your previous analysis of their troubles?

---

One study of domestic violence narratives (Wood, 2001) offers 'insight into the cultural authorisation of violence and women's toleration of it in romantic relationships' (p. 241). In other words, once a discourse has become recognized as having some culturally accepted meaning then a woman can use it to decide for herself how acceptable some behaviours (in this case domestic violence) might be. The three premises on which Wood's paper operates are similar to Michelle Crossley's ideas that:

- We all rely on narratives to make sense of our lives.
- Narratives are social in nature in that we look at the story of our life in relation and in comparison to others.
- Narratives are most urgently sought when experience does not make sense as, for example, with the Kingman family, where violence had been publicly displayed, or in cases of childhood sexual abuse.

For women living with domestic violence, for example, it may be hard to make sense of and story what is happening. However the research experts, as we have seen, suggest that we are all almost compelled to provide a narrative in order to remain in touch with our sense of self. For women experiencing domestic abuse then the stories might be answering the questions: 'How did the abuse begin?' 'Whose fault is it?' 'What should I do to survive (physically and emotionally)', and (perhaps) 'Why couldn't I leave?'

A group of midlife women living alone also told stories of who they were, how they achieved well-being and managed their future concerns including disability and finance (Segraves, 2004). For these women, the story and identity of living alone was central to who they considered they were and their well-being, and their negotiation of relationships was based upon this narrative.

This lens of the storying of self can be applied to most other situations that service users might find themselves in to explain how they arrived at the point of needing social work support.

### A METHOD FOR SOCIAL WORK?

There is more to consider than just the social nature of the story-telling and construction of the narrative. There is clearly a relationship between performing a narrative and experiencing a sense of sharing (and perhaps justifying) one's self. This could happen in the context of a research project when the topic of the study is mutually recognized, talking to the media, as with the Kingmans or other high profile families (Enosh and Buchbinder, 2005), or during therapy when a patient/client might either want to reveal or conceal material or during a social work assessment.

These interventions might explore the narrative with a particular purpose beyond simply constructing the story for the story-teller themselves (Ferro, 2009; Iliffe and Steed, 2000; McLeod and Balamoutsou, 1996). The narrative will help the social worker to understand in greater depth the meaning that particular events had for a service user. It will also allow social workers to reflect on their own personal values in relation to the story being told. A service user who had been convicted in the past of a violent crime might be able to contextualize this experience

## PAUSE AND REFLECT

**Story-telling and 'battles with truth'**

Gitta Sereny's (1995) detailed account of the life of Albert Speer, Hitler's architect and Minister for Armaments, which she subtitles 'his battle with truth' provides a fascinating story of how he constructed (and it would seem reconstructed) his life as a member of the Nazi administration and the aftermath during his twenty-year sentence in Spandau prison. Apart from being a senior member of an administration that was associated with genocide, his position as Minister for Armaments meant that his Ministry used thousands of people as slave labour to support the Nazi war machine. He presented himself as unaware of this, or at least unaware that they were treated in an inhumane fashion.

What is particularly relevant here is that, despite her interest in Speer as part of her work on the nature of evil, Sereny also came to like him. Her feeling was based on the way he accounted for himself, although the subtitle of her book still identifies him as having a problem with integrity.

Sereny's account of Speer may relate to experiences that a social worker might have while hearing a complex history from a service user in which it is essential that prior ideas and other people's views need to be disentangled as part of listening and evaluating the narrative. This may be the case if the service user's account of their experiences touches us in some way.

as part of a process when explaining things both to themselves and to the social worker.

Continuing with the theme of domestic violence, Enosh and Buchbinder in their research interviews with male perpetrators and female survivors identified four different styles of interaction when accounting for themselves. These were narrative as a *struggle*, as *deflection*, as *negotiation*, and as a *self-observation* process. This is reflected in Sereny's analysis of Speer's story, and countless others in which the story-teller is in some way culpable. The story of the Kingmans, similarly, can be seen in this context.

## PAUSE AND REFLECT

It may be useful to think about stories you have been told by particular service users and how far (if at all) you might be able to identify similar categories.

This framework illuminates and structures how a narrative can represent a struggle with anxieties and guilt about the role that other members of the family might have played. It thus deflects from the pain they are feeling, and it is noteworthy that the Kingmans, for instance, negotiated to express William's behaviour as that of the *emotional cripple*, and thus they performed their self-observations by the very act of telling the story.

These processes are reflected in all assessment interviews and interventions with vulnerable children, families and adults and will be considered in more detail in the following chapters.

### The intra-psychic dimension

The concept of intra-psychic owes much to psychoanalytic explanations of the *unconscious*, described in Chapter 3, and in aspects of attachment experiences, described in Chapter 5. The intra-psychic dimension to HGD that is part of the MDI model comprises contributions from Freudian, Kleinian, post-Kleinian and Eriksonian theories of development. The unconscious comprises innate instinctual material as well as repressed material, and it is generally accepted (albeit with variation) that the ego develops and acts as a control mechanism and gateway between the conscious and unconscious elements of the psyche (Smith et al., 2012). This, of course, is a complicated set of processes which operate around unfamiliar structures. I shall describe them again briefly but it is worth re-reading 'Psycho-dynamic theories of HGD' in Chapter 3 which deals with the detail.

Psychoanalysts following Freud identify three elements to the mind – the id, the ego and the superego. The id operates *unconsciously* as an innate storehouse of instinctual drives (towards pleasure or towards despair) and material *repressed* by the conscious part of the mind. Repressed material refers to things that we feel or know about ourselves and those nearest to us that we find too painful or too scary to think about – and therefore we don't. But they don't go away – they are lodged in the id and this may impact on many things we feel, think and do without being aware of their influence.

The ego is the part of the structure of the mind that we are most familiar with. Ego is the Latin word for 'I' and it is no surprise then that the ego is the *conscious* part of the mind which 'manages' how we act and perform.

The superego, or the conscience, makes us feel guilty sometimes, as well as giving us advance warning about whether our proposed behaviours might be right or wrong.

The work of Jan Fook and her colleagues on *critical reflection* in social work practice may also be seen in this context as an intra-psychic dimension, even though in a practical way (Fook, 2002; Fook and Gardner, 2010). They envision critical reflection as a complex way of linking 'awareness' and 'action' and, although they do not concern themselves with the unconscious per se, the content and context of their work begs to make sense of what is *out of our immediate awareness*. Similarly the work of Gillian Ruch writing on relationship-based and reflective practice in social work focuses upon the role of anxiety in making sense of the self as a professional engaged in the practice of life-long learning (Ruch, 2002, 2005).

While classical psychoanalysis remains distasteful to some in social work, perhaps because it is frequently not taught and people may think there is an awful lot to learn, there are, however, key evident truths that might be observed in the everyday life of children and adults.

Consider why a threesome, the feeling of being left out, is often unbearable – someone who is your 'best friend' is spending time with others or your wife is having a sexual relationship with another man or one of your peers has been promoted and now spends time with the team leader rather than with you. It is apparent that these patterns, which of course vary somewhat for each of us, shape our family, friendship and working relationships for the rest of our life. Some gain insight into this, perhaps through therapy or being involved in some other form of consultation at work, others never do. And while we become competent adults over time, the infantile images remain and they retain the power they had when they formed our whole world (Schwartz, 2010).

Classical psychoanalysis is built around the *Oedipus complex* (Britton, 1994; Freud, 1914; Schwartz, 2010). This refers to the primal scene in which the infant is fully cared for and loved by the mother, and in a primitive way perceives that relationship as unboundaried: the infant and mother are ideally fused and the infant is the centre of a loving world. This is the ego ideal and the place to which we all want to return in every subsequent relationship. We want to be loved just for being ourselves with no questions asked: unconditional love – the ultimate place of safety.

In the infant's developing life though, a rudimentary sense is gradually gained that they are not the only person in the mother's life. The father/mother's lover seeks and attains intimacy with the mother – appearing to supplant the infant herself as the centre of the mother's universe. As shown in the earlier chapters, the infant/child's sense of who they are and their place in the world expands as they grow. In psychoanalytic theories this means that the pain of being displaced, along with the realization of the existence and power of others, gets partially resolved when the father becomes acceptable and the rage and impotence felt towards the father for supplanting the infant becomes manageable and managed by the development of the superego and defence mechanisms (Sylva and Lunt, 1983).

It is finding a comfortable place in the world and managing to accept that not everything or everyone is perfect that enables life to go on, and this characterizes the resolution of the Oedipal situation – the centrepiece of the intra-psychic experience.

To contextualize the role of the unconscious we also need to draw on the work of the sociologist Anthony Giddens (1986/2003, 1991) and symbolic interactionist ideas (Mead, 1934/1967) about reflexivity (see the discussions of their work in Chapter 3).

Anthony Giddens' theory of structuration makes an important contribution to understanding lived experience across time and ways of being and thinking that, in turn, play a key part in understanding a MDI approach to the development of relationships and selfhood. Giddens (2003) proposed that it is important to be able to

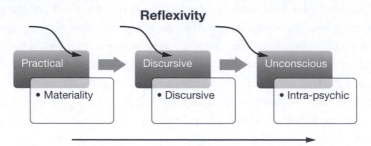

**Durée** – the passing of time and the routines of daily life

*Figure 4.3* *Levels of consciousness*

test a theory empirically – that is, through scientific methods rather than as just a personal story. Therefore, from his social theory it is possible to draw out foundations of a MDI perspective that supports analysis of the stories of lived experience.

Simply put, Giddens' theory explores both a process and a structure of lived experience, suggesting that human mental life is organized in time and space that is a 'banal and evident feature of human day-to-day life' (2003: 35). This is reminiscent of the ways in which narratives are constructed (see the section on narrative in this chapter): we organize our experience, in this case with specific attention to time and space (or place).

The *durée*, or daily duration and flow of life that he describes, indicates that time is *repetitive* (as in day-to-day) but also for the human individual it is *finite* and *irreversible*. All social institutions (the material) are expressed in the routines of daily life, enabling the physical and sensory properties of the human body to function, the latter being the locus of the active self. Our body then is the means by which we interpret time – looking older over the years or getting tired during the course of the day.

Giddens' theory also resonates with Bronfenbrenner's model of *ecosystems* discussed in Chapter 3. Students have to attend their university classes and practice placements and, although some events and days are more memorable than others, over a period of three months, say, time and the experience of the course or placement become routinized (or banal) through repetition. However, during that period the student will have gained knowledge, experience and perhaps self-confidence which may be difficult to describe.

The day-to-day passing of time, however, could be overshadowed by time passed in the past (i.e. our memory of daily routines is less significant to us than previous life events), but it is that ability to experience time passing that supports the ability to experience and know self and others. So a person who has experienced past trauma might express themselves mostly as that victim of their past and not the person they experience in their daily work and home routines.

Our daily existence and its repetitious routines enable us to tell our story to our 'self' and to others, and this repetition makes the stories 'ours'. This returns us to Mead's ideas about the conversations held between the 'I' and the 'me' (Chapter 3) which form the basis of our human ability to reflect upon ourself and our actions and give them a meaning, and which in turn becomes part of who we are and how we see the world.

Giddens' stratification model of consciousness involves not only *durée* (passing time) but three levels of consciousness: the *discursive*, the *practical* and the *unconscious*. As he describes it:

> The reflexive monitoring of activity is a chronic feature of everyday action and involves the conduct not just of the individual but also of others. That is to say, actors not only monitor continuously the flow of their activities and expect others to do the same for their own; they routinely monitor aspects, social and physical, of the contexts in which they move. (2003: 5)

Therefore an individual has a motivation (or drive), takes action, rationalizes the action and reflexively monitors the consequences and conditions of that action. Giddens' sociological/philosophical understanding of human motivation and experience (as described thus) also turns us towards the psychoanalysis of Freud and Erikson to examine how 'the psychological foundations of the interweaving of the conscious and unconscious can be represented' (Giddens, 2003: 41). While, what Giddens calls, 'competent actors' discursively report their intentions and reasons for acting as they do they cannot necessarily do the same about their motives, which may be unconscious.

The discursive consciousness he describes refers to the level at which we reflect upon and account for our self to our self and others. This is similar to Mead's (1934) I as subject and me as object. The I reflexively and continuously makes sense of the me (see Chapter 3). A student came to see me, worried that at the end-of-placement party held in his honour, he had given a brief speech which he later felt was embarrassing because he had said some things about colleagues that he thought had been misunderstood. He had felt anxious about this throughout the Christmas vacation period and was concerned that his former supervisor and colleagues would think that he was not the person he really was – dedicated and serious.

The practical consciousness, although different from discursive consciousness because it lacks the same degree of reflexivity, is the awareness of what is simply and practically done. For example, practical consciousness is the awareness that 'I am divorced' or 'I have left him' or 'I am dying' or 'I made a fool of myself at the party'. However, to become divorced or to *recognize* that one has been abused or is terminally ill requires the discursive level of consciousness. Giddens says that he does not intend 'the distinction between the discursive and practical consciousness to be a rigid and impermeable one ... Between discursive and practical consciousness there is no bar' (2003: 7). This makes sense in the context of all the accounts and approaches such as those of Ussher (1997) and Yardley (1996) as well as Crossley's exploration of narrative psychology (2003).

However, barriers *do* exist between the unconscious (which contains material repressed and thus 'inaccessible' to consciousness) and the other two levels of consciousness.

Giddens' consideration of the unconscious is based largely on Freud's model and his concepts of the discursive, practical and unconscious structure of the individual are parallel to or in place of the ego, superego and the id (Freud, 1925; see also Chapter 3 for reference to the superego in particular).

For Giddens, following Freud, the unconscious includes repressed material and material denied to consciousness, particularly *motivation*. Why did the student give a silly speech at his farewell party? He thought that he had been overcome with exhaustion and relief that the placement had gone well. He had also had some champagne which would have distorted his sense of the occasion. However, was there an unconscious edge to his speech that made fun of himself and his colleagues because at some deep level he meant it? Neither he nor I know the truth here, and there were no obvious consequences. It is likely that everyone in his team had all had a glass of champagne and was equally exhausted.

Giddens also draws on Erik Erikson's work, building upon Freud's structure of the psyche and his psychosexual developmental stages (Erikson, 1950/1963), he places its emphasis on *psychosoc*ial development. Through this process individuals come into contact with the potential for a range of outcomes in their development and sense of a secure, autonomous selfhood. In Chapter 6 I discuss attachment issues and provide more detailed evidence of how this secure and autonomous selfhood is developed.

## CHAPTER SUMMARY

This chapter has examined the reasons why Erikson's model of the lifespan is helpful in understanding how we develop through our lives, and also how at different ages and stages we can make decisions that have an impact on what happens to us and how we feel about it. You will remember that this model is dependent, relational, social, reflective and imperfect, and employs unconscious and conscious processes.

The lifespan clearly is a diverse and complicated concept but you will now recognize that understanding it critically may be supported by the use of an MDI perspective. The details of the material, discursive and intra-psychic contexts have been described in this chapter, enabling us to look more closely at the elements that impact upon our individual experience of the lifespan. You will see now how the lifespan is negotiated and managed, although within material and psychological contexts that constrain us.

From birth we are engaged with others – adult care-givers, siblings and, as we develop, more and more people at different stages of their own lifespan come into our lives. Having parents, grandparents, friends, children and grandchildren all brings us back to thinking and experiencing other parts of the lifespan than the one representing the age/stage we occupy. We are also active in our management of and socially constructing the meaning and narrative of our lives, working around the constraints of the material context, dominant discourses of the period and place in which we live and our intra-psychic experiences.

Furthermore, we have to find ways of reconciling our past and the baggage we bring with the everyday routines to which we cling in order to make sense of ourselves. Because we have the capacity to reflect and be reflexive we also have the need and ability to compose the story or narrative of our life.

Underpinning the lifespan are the unconscious processes – defences against anxiety and the rerunning of the primitive object relationships of our early lives.

Reading this chapter therefore should help you become aware that:

- No one theory or academic discipline rovides a definitive understanding of HGD or the human motivation to act in any particular way.
- We all live in a complex set of interconnected social, emotional and interpersonal environments.
- We all 'story' our lives within these complex environments in order to develop, grow and maintain a sense of who we were, are and will become (identity).
- In order to become an effective practitioner, which involves managing self as well as supporting others, social workers need to have (at least) an overview of HGD theories and their complexities.
- All theory can (and perhaps should) be 'deconstructed' in order to identify whose interests it serves.

## FURTHER READING

Some early ideas about material-discursive understandings of health and gender will be of interest to you now:

Ussher, J. (1997) *Body Talk: The material and discursive regulation of sexuality, madness and reproduction.* London: Routledge.
Yardley, L. (1996) Reconciling Discursive and Materialist Perspectives on Health and Illness. *Theory & Psychology,* 6(3), 485–508.

Then read about the addition of the intra-psychic and narrative research to the material and discursive perspectives:

Ussher, J.M., Hunter, M. and Cariss, M. (2002). A Woman-centred Psychological Intervention for Premenstrual Symptoms, Drawing on Cognitive-behavioural and Narrative Therapy. *Clinical Psychology & Psychotherapy,* 9(5), 319–331.

Thinking further about the intra-psychic dimensions, this paper on the Oedipal complex is easy to read:

Nicolson, P. (2012) Oedipus at Work: A family affair? *Psychodynamic Practice.* 18(4), 427–440.

Further detail about the intra-psychic dimensions can be found in both:

Howe, D. (2008). *The Emotionally Intelligent Social Worker.* Basingstoke: Palgrave Macmillan.
Smith, V., Collard, P., Nicolson, P. and Bayne, R. (2012). *Key Concepts in Counselling and Psychotherapy: A critical A–Z guide to theory.* Milton Keynes: McGraw-Hill/Open University Press.

**FURTHER READING** *continued*

For a helpful account of the discursive dimensions:

Reavey, P. and Brown, S.D. (2007). Rethinking Agency in Memory: Space and embodiment in memories of childhood sexual abuse. *Journal of Social Work Practice: Psychotherapeutic Approaches in Health, Welfare and the Community*, 21(1), 5–21.

To explore further ideas about narrative research and practice the following chapters and articles are useful places to start, although they will require some prior thinking and reading:

Andrews, M., Day Sclater, S., Squire, C. and Tamboukou, M. (2007) Narrative Research. In C. Seale, G. Gobo, J. Gubrium and D. Silverman (eds), *Qualitative Research Practice* (pp. 97–112). London: Sage.

Crossley, M.L. (2003) Formulating Narrative Psychology: The limitations of contemporary social constructionism. *Narrative Inquiry*, 13(2), 287–300.

Fraser, H. (2004) Doing Narrative Research. *Qualitative Social Work*, 3(2), 179–201.

Erik Erikson himself wrote clearly and sympathetically about his theories and the ideas they were based on:

Erikson, E. (1950/1963) *Childhood and Society*. New York: Norton.

Anthony Giddens' work on the individual and society is enduringly valuable:

Giddens, A. (1986/2003) *The Constitution of Society: Outline of the theory of structuration*. Berkeley and Los Angeles: University of Calfornia Press.

# 5

# ATTACHMENT, SEPARATION AND LOSS: THEMES IN HGD

**LEARNING OBJECTIVES**

- To develop awareness of the role that attachment, separation and loss play in HGD across the lifespan.
- To recognize some of the historical and controversial aspects of attachment research and theory.
- To explore how the theories of attachment style link with our knowledge of attachment experiences in infancy.

## Introduction

In the previous chapters where the nature/nurture debates and controversies were reviewed, it became clear that the processes around HGD result from a mixture of biological (including genetic), psychological (cognitive, behavioural and psychodynamic), environmental and social structures, which in turn represent all developmental phases across the lifespan. The lifespan approach, described in Chapter 4, also captures a range of interdisciplinary perspectives from the core fields of biology, sociology and psychology, particularly when taken together with the MDI perspective. By now you will have realized that no single theoretical or disciplinary approach in itself will explain how we grow and develop into human beings embracing common and individual strengths and weaknesses.

In this chapter I build on these ideas to show how early attachment relationships become inscribed in our genes, brains and nervous systems, as well as in the way we behave socially and emotionally. This means, once again, taking account of evidence offered by these different academic disciplines and attempting to make links between them – which may not necessarily be very easy. So be patient with yourself if you have to read this chapter (or, indeed, any of the others) more than once, or if you have to read articles from the *Further Reading* sections before you are ready to progress to subsequent chapters. None of this is uncomplicated work.

Taking account of all of the diverse scientific approaches, even if difficult, is ultimately worthwhile as it helps us to understand fully the impact of attachment, separation and loss on HGD across the lifespan. It also illuminates the diversity of influences that make up humanity in general and our own experiences of being human.

The focus in this chapter is specifically upon understanding the *origins in infancy* of *attachment, separation* and *loss*. However, the same concepts will also be used in subsequent chapters to show how experiences which influence our abilities to withstand the pain of, say, *loss through bereavement* can be traced through the lifespan. What happens to us in infancy sets out the template for how we deal with subsequent events and emotions. Some of this is explained in our discussion of work on attachment *styles.*

The key concepts in this chapter are fundamental to social workers' theory-practice tool kit, especially moving forward to the *reflective-relational approach* I introduce in Chapter 6.

### Attachment theory and practice

Attachment is both a *theory* and a *practice*. The idea of the emotional bond was the focus of research that developed into theory. Attachment is also a practice because it describes a relationship, initially between an adult and infant, that continues throughout life when we make close friends, form intimate relationships, have our own children and grandchildren. The practice of attachment refers firstly to the *fact* that we attach ourselves emotionally to others. As you shall read in this chapter, there is scientific evidence from a range of disciplinary perspectives that clearly demonstrates that attachment is essential to human (and animal and bird) life.

Secondly, we all practise attachment in ways that potentially vary enormously in style and application. So, for example, some of us need and thrive on strong and close attachments. This can be a very positive experience if you and the other person have similar needs. It could, however, be a negative experience if you need a very close attachment and the other person prefers a lighter touch. We call these differences in the practice of attachment *styles,* and we explore attachment style later in this chapter.

## Definitions and background to attachment theory

Attachment refers to an important emotional link between two (or more) people beginning in infancy (Klaus and Kennell, 1976) but repeating throughout the lifespan in various ways, including falling in love, friendships and attachments to your wider family. Attachment, as we shall see, is a basic condition for life. Some theories of attachment propose that it is instinctual or innate, while others suggest it is learned shortly after birth. This debate fits within the nature/nurture controversies with which you are now familiar.

Attachment theory combines knowledge derived from psychoanalytic, experimental developmental psychology, naturalistic ethology, evolutionary psychology and, most recently, cognitive neuroscience (Schore, 2005; Swain et al., 2007). Thus it both complements and enhances understanding of the lifespan and MDI lenses on HGD described in Chapter 4.

As John Bowlby, one of the key researchers in the field of attachment theory, describes it (1977), attachment is an *affectional bond* between two people, initially between the mother-figure and the baby although of course the experience of this attachment relationship is transferable to other relationships – with siblings, father, other relatives and friends.

It is the basis of early attachment relationships through which we form sexual relationships and fall in love. It is when these bonds become broken irreparably that we grieve. These attachment bonds vary in their quality and strength and Bowlby was one of the first to argue that the initial attachment – its strength, its offer of safety and other qualities – sets out a template for all future relationships. Psychological and emotional damage as a result of disruptive early attachment might, he argues, be softened via psychotherapy (1977, 1988).

The extent of researchers' interest in attachment behaviours and feelings is clear when you consider the breadth of different perspectives in attachment studies. Knowledge of attachment has been informed by research conducted on infant and toddler development (Ainsworth et al., 1978; Klaus and Kennell, 1976); primate development (Seay and Harlow, 1965); with young people who have been adopted and fostered (Howe and Fearnley, 2003) or who live with poor mental health or are otherwise socially excluded (Bowlby, 1977) as well as with adults to examine attachment styles and their consequences for well-being and interpersonal relationships (Bifulco et al., 2003; Shemmings, 2006). You can see from that list that we know a great deal about attachment and, unsurprisingly, attachment is widely agreed to be of crucial significance for understanding the lifespan and HGD.

Understanding attachment draws upon a wide range of evidence. This spans studies of the quality of the infant/mother(care-giver) relationship to interactions and patterns of attachment in later life (Shemmings and Shemmings, 2011).

It is important to note that attachment behaviours and individuals' *styles* of attachment (formed during the early life phase) potentially endure throughout the lifespan and influence our relationships with others and our identity and self-development (Holmes, 2010; Zeanah et al., 2011) and well as our sense of security and mental well-being (Bowlby, 1988).

I am now going to look initially at attachment styles because they help you to understand the ways in which early attachment practices influence how we behave to others, and give clues to aspects of our emotional lives. After that, I shall review the research and theoretical background that led us to understand attachment style and its importance in the lifespan. Understanding the origins and implications of attachment styles underpins adolescent and adult phases of the lifespan, although much of the core research was on infant children or newborn birds and non-human primates.

## Attachment styles and emotional security

Research on attachment has identified the existence of different *styles of attachment* (Ainsworth et al., 1978). This begins in infancy as a response to very early interactions, and the pattern persists as the child develops. Some attachment experiences become styles that are more positive, providing greater resilience, for instance, than others that might lead to relationship anxieties.

John Bowlby, whose ideas were instrumental in early thinking about attachment styles, talks about how an effective attachment relationship provides a *secure base* to explore the social and physical environment and specifically how the degree of security and trust established during early attachment relationships impact on subsequent emotional and social development (Bowlby, 1988). Following Mary Salter-Ainsworth, who talked about *secure* and *insecure* attachments, Bowlby described the following styles and their characteristics. These are:

- *Secure attachment* in which the individual is confident that the parent figure will be available, responsive and helpful in adverse and frightening situations. This individual feels emboldened to explore the world and develop relationships with others.
- An *anxious, resistant attachment* pattern that reflects the experience of the individual who is uncertain whether his parent will be responsive or available. This individual tends to be prone to separation anxiety, clingy and cautious about exploring the world and anxious about relationships.
- An *anxious avoidant attachment* when the individual has no confidence that he will receive a helpful response and, instead, expects to be rebuffed. Such individuals are likely to be suspicious and also might seek to betray trust because they think others will do that to them (see Bowlby, 1988: 124).

Subsequently, work on defining, describing and applying attachment styles to social work and clinical practice has expanded and may be used effectively to predict the outcome of interventions with vulnerable people of all ages (Shemmings and Shemmings, 2011).

Patterns of infant attachment seem to endure throughout life, and attachment styles present in adults may be assessed in different, but overlapping, ways to provide attachment profiles. These may be used as part of an assessment process in social work for planning work and assessing risk in families and with vulnerable adults.

## Assessing attachment styles in adults

During the 1980s and 1990s there was increased awareness and interest in the USA of the significance of attachment for understanding adult responses to loss and trauma (Hesse and Main, 2000; Main, 1995). This work led to the development of the Adult Attachment Interview at Berkeley (in California) (Main, 1995) which taps into the *narrative style* of the respondent, demonstrating how the relationship is talked about and is 'represented' in their own mind (see the discussion of narrative and storytelling in Chapter 4). This procedure enabled Main and her colleagues to identify the insecure disorganized style described above, as well as to understand how individuals are able to make sense of their lives despite poorly supported early lives.

Antonia Bifulco and her team at the Lifespan Research Group at Royal Holloway, University of London (and later Kingston University and most recently Middlesex University) developed a series of attachment style *interviews* that assess characteristics of current adult attachment style in relation to a person's ability to access and utilize social support, an approach of particular value to social workers.

The Attachment Style Interview (ASI) provides a categorization of attachment style for individuals, as well as assessing their specific support context and quality of close relationships. The attachment profile that results from the data collected not only determines which style best characterizes the respondent – *Secure, Enmeshed, Fearful, Angry-dismissive* or *Withdrawn* – but also the extent to which the insecure styles are dysfunctional in terms of whether the person is Markedly, Moderately or Mildly Insecure. This is important, given evidence that 'Mildly Insecure' styles carry less risk of mental health problems than do the 'Markedly'.

To date two versions of the ASI have been developed. The ASI for Research, Clinical and Practice use (ASI-RCP) is tailored towards psychologists and psychiatrists working in research and clinical and forensic practice fields, and the ASI for Children's Services is tailored towards the practice requirements of Adoption & Fostering and Child Care services.

### PAUSE AND REFLECT

You can read much more about this on the Lifespan Research Group's website where they identify a number of applications of the interview, but this one is a useful example for those of you working in children's services: www.attachmentstyleinterview.com/ ASI_for_children.html

The styles identified by Bifulco and colleagues (Bifulco, 2004; Bifulco et al., 2008) are:

- **Clearly secure**: this is the most stable and flexible style with comfort, closeness and appropriate levels of autonomy. This style enables the ongoing ability to make and maintain relationships with at least two others. This would also suggest that an infant/mother combination who manage this stage will also produce a sense of basic trust over mistrust.
- **Enmeshed**: This style is dependent, and the individual infant and later the adult will have a high desire for company and low self-reliance. Bifulco et al. predict this style is represented by superficiality across many relationships. It is positively characterized by sociability and warmth, but there is also the tendency to anger and 'push-pull' relationships.
- **Fearful**: This style is characterized by anxiety about rejection or being let down. Early life experiences of rejection may be generalized to all others. There is frequently a desire for closeness coupled with fear of becoming close to someone. The positive characteristics might be sensitivity to others.
- **Angry-dismissive**: this is the angry avoidance of others, with high levels of mistrust and self-reliance as well as a low desire for company. The key characteristic is anger. Individuals with this style are self-reliant but in conflict with those around them, and frequently need a high level of control over their lives.
- **Withdrawn**: This is characterized by high self-reliance and high constraints on closeness, perhaps expressed as a desire for privacy with clear boundaries and with a closed style of relating.

In my work with families, and couples in particular, these styles become apparent fairly quickly, as they will with you when you think about them in the context of your practice. So, for example, the man with the *withdrawn style* might be the businessman or lawyer who focuses on work, his colleagues and cases, and providing the family income through gaining more business for his company and, thus, promotion. This couple is likely to have difficulties because of the isolation the wife/ mother experiences and his inability, due to his style of attachment, to make her feel part of his life. The relationship between the partners consequently becomes fraught, and most particularly if she herself has a *fearful style* of attachment. In such a case, *she* is likely to feel rejected when *he* feels he is doing what he ought by providing for his family. She is likely to accuse her partner of having an affair or simply not loving her. He most probably will withdraw even further into his work. I have experienced this relationship pattern in many such couples. Bifulco and her colleagues have developed a version of the ASI which focuses on couples (www. attachmentstyleinterview.com/pdf%20files/ASI_Relationship_flyer.pdf).

By the age of four children will have established attachment relational styles that should be easy to identify using the ASI. Bifulco and colleagues (2008) suggest that this measure is of great use to social workers in a number of ways, but it is particularly valuable for predicting parenting abilities in prospective adopters or foster parents (Howe and Fearnley, 2003; Howe et al., 2001).

The same team have also developed the Vulnerable Attachment Style Question-naire (VASQ) which detects two factors – 'insecurity' and 'proximity seeking' – and identifies individuals whose attachment styles make them vulnerable for depressive disorders (Bifulco et al., 2003).

## PAUSE AND REFLECT

### Attachment styles

Attachment styles become very apparent in team management and relationships. The team leader or supervisor with a withdrawn style, for instance, will find it difficult to engage in an emotionally intelligent way with staff, particularly those whose work needs close supervision.

As you will recall from above, a withdrawn style means that the manager will be highly self-reliant and, therefore, not used to discussing or sharing ideas and feelings with other people. As you also know from your own work, supervision does require a degree of sharing personal experience and emotion about cases. Even if you are only talking about your own responses, your withdrawn style manager with her high constraints on closeness, clear boundaries and with a closed style of relating might find it very difficult to help you with your feelings about a particular case or conflicts in the office.

Perhaps even more difficult for a team leader or senior practitioner, regardless of their own attachment style, could be a team member with an angry-dismissive style who would resist supervision and being managed.

Thinking about your team and your own experience of being a member of that team is a useful way to understand what is going on in a number of professional situations you are likely to find yourself in. Understanding what is going on in groups and organizations you work in and with is an important way for you to handle your own anxieties and the stresses that are normal for your type of work. So, do try to use your understanding of attachment styles to make sense of your own day-to-day circumstances.

- Can you find your own attachment style in the descriptive categories above?
- Has this impacted upon your work with colleagues/supervisors/managers?
- Do you think you can loosely assess the attachment styles of your colleagues?

## The work of John Bowlby and the research tradition that followed

I want now to return to the core research and thinking that led to these developments through understanding the role of attachment in lifespan development. John Bowlby, a psychiatrist and one-time head of the Tavistock Clinic, was one of the principal early attachment theorist-practitioners. His clinical work in the 1940s focused on neglected, affectionless and disturbed children. This led him to identify the need for attachment between children and parents which he saw as stemming from the human propensity to make strong *affectional bonds* to particular others. Bowlby (1951) was commissioned by the World Health Organisation (WHO) to investigate the psychological state of homeless and refugee children after the Second World War.

From that work, the controversial *maternal deprivation thesis* developed. This thesis suggested that infants needed consistent care, attention and love from their mother (or one mother-substitute figure). It had to be the same person, and the mental health of infants whose mother was not present or attentive during these early weeks and months of life would be negatively affected in years to come. Bowlby had proposed that this view of the centrality of mother/infant attachment relates to a universal human *dependency* need (1951: 127).

## PAUSE AND REFLECT

### Maternal deprivation

The maternal deprivation thesis became controversial because Bowlby's work, including the WHO report, was used by governments as evidence for closing day nurseries and thus forcing women, who had successfully engaged in war-time work outside the home, back to full-time child care. It was claimed that this initiative was implemented to prevent maternal deprivation and its mental health consequences, although it became clear that it was actually intended to provide employment for returning servicemen. The women had been too effective in managing their work at home and outside, and many wanted to remain employed.

In the USA, the famous 1942 song and later documentary *Rosie the Riveter* demonstrated clearly that women could do 'men's work'. You can see memorabilia including photos and posters at www.rosietheriveter.org which also has a link to a video, *Rosie's Girls*, intended to build young women's self-esteem as workers including mechanics. This present-day initiative is sponsored by (among others) Wells Fargo, famous for stage coaches in the Wild West and more contemporary forms of public transport now. However, its message is not just for American women and girls; it is used widely in education in the UK and other countries.

Attachment theory, although in part discredited by feminist thinking and reactions against the idea of maternal deprivation caused by mothers with aspirations outside the home (Riley, 1979), has nonetheless experienced a revival among contemporary practitioners and researchers. This is not so much as a criticism of working mothers now, nor is it used to gain political currency, but because of the accumulating evidence in the intervening years that provided powerful insights as to how early attachment patterns affect HGD. It is particularly influential in clinical psychology, psychotherapy (Holmes, 2010) and social work (Howe et al., 2001) research, as well as in practice where attachment style is used to make decisions about the well-being of, and practice with, service users, such as looked-after children and vulnerable families (Bifulco, 2004; Shemmings and Shemmings, 2011).

Attachment capacities develop most strongly over the first year of life, although there are individual differences in the ways that it is experienced and enacted. The impact of *separation* from attachment figures for infants also varies depending upon the quality of that initial attachment relationship (Bifulco, 2004).

I shall now look at the way attachment theory has developed and been used to understand separation, loss and grief. This represents the other side of the attachment coin – what happens when attachments are broken.

## Separation

Between the 1950s and 1970s, increasing attention was paid to research on the separation of mother and infant (maternal deprivation). The ways in which attachment quality influences the emotional and psychological security of children was particularly emphasized. Mary Salter Ainsworth, a developmental psychologist, was commissioned by the World Health Organisation, following on from Bowlby's work, to look further into maternal deprivation (Ainsworth, 1962). Her work explored the ways infants set about discovering the world beyond the immediate proximity of their mother. She ran experiments and conducted naturalistic observations of children when apart from their mother/care-givers.

Ainsworth examined how babies managed the *'strange situation'*. In this experiment, an infant aged between 18 months and 2 years was in a room playing with its mother. The mother then left the room and a stranger entered the room. The stranger then left the room and, later, the mother returned. This stage, which was crucial for the theory Ainsworth was developing, is called the *reunion.* It is the reunion that is used by researchers to develop their ideas about attachment styles.

Different variations of the situation included the mother being in the room while the stranger entered, or returning while the stranger was still there. Observations of all of these situations with a large number of infants were recorded and the differences that were noticed in the infants' behaviours at each stage were used to identify attachment styles.

**PAUSE AND REFLECT**

You can watch an excellent example of separation studies on YouTube via the website www.simplypsychology.org/mary-ainsworth.html.

It has been written and produced by Saul McLeod, a lecturer at Wigan and Leigh College. Have a look at this video and also take advantage of some of the reading and ideas listed and linked to the same web page.

The strange situation procedure and subsequent classifications are now seen as the gold standard for clinical assessment of attachment patterns (Zeanah et al., 2011).

The style of most concern to clinicians and social workers has been the *disorganized attachment style* (Hesse and Main, 2000). During brief separations in the strange situation, the infant exhibiting a *disorganized attachment style* would be frightened, disoriented and disorganized. It also appears that as children who have experienced disorganized attachment in infancy grow up, they feel contradictory biological arousal and show fear on occasions when they are stressed and distressed. This style is frequently found in prison and adult psychiatric populations (Hesse and Main, 2000; Lyons-Ruth and Jacobvitz, 1999).

In the strange situation, researchers observed infants' and toddlers' reactions to brief separations to classify them into securely or insecurely attached. This work led to ideas about providing infants and young children with a secure base, which Bowlby himself had proposed as the central feature of parenting. He and Ainsworth claimed, from their clinical and research-based evidence, that parents (carers) need to ensure the child can make sorties into the outside world and return to the parents knowing that 'he will be welcomed when he gets there, nourished physically and emotionally, comforted if distressed, reassured if frightened' (Bowlby, 1988: 11).

Other observations of children who had been separated from parents, under usually traumatic circumstances, supported the thesis that the relationship between an infant and the mother/carer is a fundamental requirement for mental health, and also that disruption of the relationship produces a great deal of anxiety and distress, both at the time and in later life (Bowlby, 1982).

Michael Rutter (1979), reassessing the concept of maternal deprivation, supported the conclusions of Bowlby and Ainsworth but emphasized human *resilience*, proposing that even as infants we have the opportunity to form attachments and bond with people other than the mother herself. He also stressed that there are clear individual differences across the lifespan in children's responses to early emotional deprivation. However, Rutter did indicate that for some children, who were deprived of parental/consistent attachments through prolonged separation, mental health and conduct disorders might result if they were unable to form other satisfactory attachments. This was early thinking about what came to be known as 'disorganized attachment' (Shemmings, 2011).

## *Loss*

Talking about attachment and how we handle it, based on our early experiences, has implications for experiences of separation and loss. This is particularly pertinent when thinking about separation and loss for those who have suffered poor quality or disrupted attachments earlier in the lifespan.

Loss occurs throughout the lifespan to various extents (Bowlby, 1988; Parkes et al., 1991) so going to nursery school is an early loss of the comfort of being at home, getting married is a loss of personal independence and being promoted is a loss of a former professional identity and the relationships that surround it. It is a major experience for everyone when core bonds are broken (Bowlby, 1977) but it is not necessarily only a negative experience. It is associated with events such as a bereavement, being placed in foster care, or even the loss of a community and way of life (Marris, 1986), but it is also associated with change which can have both good and bad elements. Research into bereavement and life events including moving house, divorce, retirement, marriage (Holmes and Rahe, 1967) and having a baby (Nicolson, 1998) has frequently emphasized the processes of *mourning* the loss. Furthermore, it appears that attachment quality and style originating in infancy impact upon the ways in which we later deal with mourning (Parkes, 1998). So we can have and enjoy a much-wanted baby or move to the dream house in the country and experience happiness and fulfilment at the same time as we have a sense of grief for what we have left behind or what we have lost through making the gain. Mostly, though, we usually talk about loss as being the loss of something good such as a partner we love. It is also most likely that social workers support service users whose experiences revolve around the kind of loss that lacks redeeming features.

One of the first to identify how we cope with the loss of a loved person was Freud (1917), who distinguished between the normal process of *mourning* in which time and remembering act to heal the pain and *melancholia*, whereby a dysfunctional attachment to the lost person triggers a seemingly permanent state of depression. Subsequent research suggests that loss of this kind when a person's background includes early disrupted attachment is probably at the heart of most forms of persistent clinical depression (Leader, 2009).

## Human attachment: material, discursive and intra-psychic perspectives

Attachment between people occurs on several levels: material (environment and context), discursive (the way that attachment is socially constructed – thought about and given meaning) and intra-psychic (the emotional and unconscious experiences).

### THE MATERIAL CONTEXT

The *material context*, as we discussed in Chapter 4, includes both bio-material and social/cultural perspectives. So, for instance, the *bio-material* refers to a biological response that attracts two or more people – sometimes referred to as interpersonal chemistry. This occurs as part of the infant/mother/care-taker 'dependency' and is a mutual attraction that may be seen in the way that some mothers/fathers and others meet the gaze of the infant. It also occurs later in life when people fall in love and, conversely, following bereavement or leave-taking of loved ones when, apart from psychological distress, there is a physical pain. It may be, for instance, that a social worker and service user become attached and moving on can bring about powerful physical feelings of pain or disturbance.

The *social and cultural* contexts in which attachment relationships take place also have an impact upon the interaction. For the early life attachment experience this will be about the size of the family, its economic status and the home atmosphere, such as happy, depressing or aggressive. The social and cultural context of the early attachment will influence later relationships and experiences of separation and loss.

Piaget's (1990) stages of cognitive development (Chapter 2) demonstrate that, even though our brain and nervous system grow regardless of environment, the child *interacts* with what he finds around him, and that might inhibit or stimulate reasoning and relational abilities.

The ecological context of development (Bronfenbrenner and Morris, 2007) is also a critical factor through which a child develops a sense of his own place within the various systems in which he grows and develops (see Chapter 3 for further detail). Cultural patterns of child rearing are also important in making sense of what is conducive to well-being, and this changes across the socio-historical system. The work of John and Elizabeth Newson (E. Newson and Newson, 1965; J. Newson and Newson, 2007) has added substance to Bronfenbrenner's theory, through their detailed observations and interviews with parents in England about their beliefs and practices on child rearing.

### THE DISCURSIVE CONTEXT

The *discursive* context is one in which the meaning of attachment is socially constructed. It is interesting, for example, to think about why and how attachment and separation in the relationship between infants and mothers became so important after the Second World War. The idea was actively employed to encourage women to return to the home and full-time child care and, in order to achieve this, the concept of maternal deprivation was constructed around the research evidence. Other concepts might have emerged from the early studies – for instance, resilience which Michael Rutter emphasized in his work reassessing maternal deprivation. This, as you will have seen from the earlier discussion and from the theory in Chapter 4, shows how the maternal deprivation thesis was a *regulatory discourse* which constructed the working mother of pre-school children as a woman who put her children's emotional development at risk (Foucault, 2002a, b; Riley, 1979).

The discursive context here also involves discourses around attachment styles. As you will have read above, different researchers and practitioners describe similar styles in different ways. In other words, each style is a social construction rather than an objective phenomenon. However, attachment styles are measurable, although of course the device for its measurement relates to the way the style is constructed. The very concept of attachment itself is a discursive device used to describe and give meaning to a relationship practice and process.

### THE INTRA-PSYCHIC CONTEXT

The *intra-psychic context* is particularly salient when considering infant/carer relationships. Infant/mother attachments are related to a sense of emotional well-being (or the opposite). Seeking proximity to the infant and nourishing her and the infant's feeling of security are observable, but they have an important emotional and intra-psychic dimension too. Intimate couple relationships in adolescence and adulthood often replay (unconsciously and emotionally) some of the early emotions of the first attachments. It has also been suggested that couples come together *unconsciously* to re-enact those early relationships. Attachment style descriptions pick up some of the behaviours and emotions connected to the first attachments with both their psychological costs and benefits.

## Classical research studies on attachment, separation and loss

In the next section I describe some of the classic studies that have brought the concepts of attachment, separation and loss to the fore. While some were conducted more than sixty years ago, their significance for HGD has only slowly been recognized. The first reason for this resurgence of interest has been (as you will know now) the removal of the political motive. The maternal deprivation thesis was misunderstood and misused in the immediate post-war years to encourage mothers to become full-time carers by depicting women who went out to work as poor mothers. The concept of maternal deprivation is now more clearly understood to occur when the relationship between infant and mother is dysfunctional (i.e. neglectful and/or abusive) and substitute care is inconsistent and/or equally neglectful and abusive.

Secondly, technological developments in brain imagery and genetic understandings have meant that links between early studies of attachment may now be understood more effectively from an interdisciplinary perspective. We can see that neglected infants (humans, non-human primates and birds) suffer emotionally and in other psychological ways, and that the outcome of this neglect becomes biologically established in the brain and nervous system. Some believe it may also be transmitted inter-generationally through genetic means.

Thirdly, attachment styles and their importance for understanding how people manage their relationships in the family, with their partners and at work are relatively recent developments. But their application to practice has taken off with social workers and clinicians because understanding attachment style helps diagnosis and treatment in relation to comprehending separation, loss and change in vulnerable people.

Remember that the conclusions drawn from the studies and the relevance of the findings for practice are dependent on the societal context. The studies

described below are organized according to whether they are predominantly material, discursive or intra-psychic, although there is clearly overlap between each of
these perspectives. (This arrangement is designed to help you begin to use this
taxonomy, or way of organizing your ideas.) The material contexts also divide into
bio-material and socio-material ones as you will see in the following sections.

### Bio-material perspectives

The bio-material context of early attachments has a strong history, demonstrating
that birds, non-human primates and human beings have a biological predisposition to attach to a care-giver because of early dependency needs for food, warmth
and shelter. It has also been demonstrated that there is a biological need for *affection* among animals as well as humans.

Evolutionary psychologists (Geary and Bjorklund, 2000) and ethologists studying naturalistic animal and bird behaviour (Hazan and Shaver, 1994) concur that
the importance of early attachment relationships is paramount to well-being,
safety and security. These researchers argue that there are genetic imperatives
in individual humans, non-human primates and other creatures (such as ducks)
to attach to others (Lorenz, 1966). Cognitive neuroscientists (who study brain patterns, structure and development as they relate to thinking) further suggest that
early attachment quality becomes embedded in the developing structures of the
brain and nervous system (Schore, 2005).

#### IMPRINTING AND BONDING

Ethological studies of bird and animal behaviour have established, through controlled observations, what can now be re-examined in brain science. One of the
most important early discoveries to influence our thinking about attachment was
made by Konrad Lorenz (1952/2002) who identified the *imprinting instinct*. Imprinting is a phenomenon exhibited by several species. Upon coming out of their eggs,
ducklings and chicks will follow and become attached (socially bonded) to the first
moving object they encounter (which usually, but not necessarily, is the mother
duck or hen). Lorenz observed that his Greylag geese, reared by him from hatch-
ing, treated him like a parent. The goslings followed Lorenz about and even when
they were adults they courted *him* in preference to other Greylag geese. Lorenz
proposed that the sensory object met by the newborn bird is somehow stamped
immediately and irreversibly onto its nervous system. It is this process he called
*imprinting*. This too has been captured in a useful YouTube video www.youtube.
com/watch?v=2UIU9XH-mUI

Klaus, Kennell and colleagues (Klaus et al., 1972) subsequently examined *human* imprinting or, more accurately, the bonding process between the newborn infant and mother. They suggested that there was a *critical period* immediately after
birth for the formation of a human *mother's* attachment to her infant (and thus,

probably, the infant's attachment to the mother). They consequently argued successfully that maternity units should support new mothers to hold and feed their babies immediately from birth rather than have the baby taken to a nursery, which was typically the practice up until the late 1970s.

Successive research confirmed that there are short-term negative effects of mother/infant separation at this critical period, so that some mothers temporarily reject their babies. However there is no clear evidence to suggest that long-term damage ensues from short-term separation at that initial stage provided a secure attachment is established subsequently (Klaus and Kennell, 1976).

One essential element of the bonding experience is the concept of 'reciprocity', a termed coined by Schaffer and Emerson. Their work focused on the mother's response to the baby, which in turn is influenced by the baby's response to her (Schaffer and Emerson, 1964a, b).

It is now generally believed that, while the human baby has the capacity and desire to bond with the mother-figure, it also has the capacity to make attachment relationships to more than one adult such as the father, grandparent or foster/adoptive parent if they are introduced at a key developmental stage and if the practitioners involved are sensitive to the impact of separation, loss and forming new attachments.

This research all points to the importance for practice of handling the early stages of the relationship empathically when placing children with foster and adoptive parents or returning a looked-after child to her birth-parents. Although attachments in the child's life might have been disrupted, attention to the context will minimize future damage to the development of the relationship in the new situation and the individual's future well-being.

### SEEKING AFFECTION, MATERNAL DEPRIVATION: THE CASE OF HARLOW'S MONKEYS

One set of experimental studies indicating the bio-material importance of the attachment of the infant to a mother-figure has been Harry Harlow and colleagues' studies of infant monkeys (Seay et al., 1962; Seay and Harlow, 1965). The inspiration for these studies was Bowlby's demonstration of the importance of attachment, the distress of separation and its long-term consequences (Bowlby, 1982).

In Harlow's initial experiments, infant monkeys were separated from their mothers from between six and twelve hours after birth and were presented instead with substitute or surrogate mothers made either out of heavy wire mesh or of wood covered with cloth. Both mothers were the same size, but the wire mother had no soft surfaces while the other mother was covered with foam rubber and soft terry cloth to make her cuddly. Both were warmed by an electric light placed inside them.

In one experiment both types of surrogates were present in the cage, but only one was equipped with a nipple from which the infant could nurse. Some infants received nourishment from the wire mother, and others were fed from the cloth mother. However, even when the wire mother was the source of nourishment (and a source of warmth provided by the electric light) the infant monkey spent a greater amount of time clinging to the cloth surrogate.

These results led researchers to believe the need for closeness and affection goes deeper than a need for warmth and even food. Subsequently the monkeys raised by the dummy mothers engaged in strange behavioural patterns in their adult life. Some sat clutching themselves, rocking constantly back and forth; a stereotypical behaviour pattern for excessive and misdirected aggression. Normal sexual behaviours were replaced by misdirected and atypical patterns: isolate (or attachment deprived) females ignored approaching normally attached males, while isolate males made inappropriate attempts to copulate with normally attached females.

As parents in adulthood, the isolate female monkeys (the 'motherless mothers', as Harlow called them) were either negligent or abusive. Negligent mothers did not nurse, comfort or protect their young, nor did they harm them. The abusive mothers violently bit or otherwise injured their babies, to the point that many of them died.

As with the other classic studies, useful YouTube posts can bring the experiments to life. The following video link shows the work with Rhesus monkeys: www.youtube.com/watch?v=hsA5Sec6dAI.

Harlow's research points clearly to the importance of mother (adult)/child bonding and the potentially dire effects of deprivation in humans. Not only does the child look to his mother for basic needs such as food, safety, and warmth, he also needs to feel love, acceptance, and affection from the care-giver. Harlow's findings show some long-term psychological physical effects of delinquent or inadequate attentiveness to child needs. However, once again, these results point to the potential for new adult/child relationships to flourish if human warmth in the dyad can be supported by the social work practitioner.

Harlow demonstrated firstly that relationships between mothers and infants were *emotional* rather than just physical. This indicates, for instance, that a secure and long-term relationship between adoptive or  foster parents and an infant is likely to be better for the infant/child in the long term than a dysfunctional and disruptive relationship with a biological parent.

Harlow's work also supported the view, following Konrad Lorenz (1952/2002) that there is a *critical period* for the development of the capacity for attachment in an infant. If a good attachment does not occur then, it is possible that the child will have mental health problems in later life.

Further, it is clear that the need for attachment is a *biological necessity* although it need not necessarily be with the birth-mother.

Much later, Cozolino (2006) suggested that secure attachments have a beneficial and observable effect on the developing *brain* in that evolution has selected human relationships involving attachment and bonding to shape and build complex social brains. He stresses that human (unlike animal) brains are capable of *mending* because they are capable of adapting and, thus, a damaged brain (i.e. starved of affection or experiencing distorted relationships in infancy) is capable of adapting following more secure and affectional relationships.

## Socio-material perspectives

The term 'maternal deprivation', as you will recall, has been used to explain nearly every negative interaction between a woman and her baby/young child including rejection, hostility, cruelty, over-indulgence, repressive control, lack of affection (Ainsworth, 1962) as well as neglect and abuse (Bernazzani and Bifulco, 2003). As almost every developmental psychology textbook demonstrates, it was exposure to some of the terrible cases identified in orphanages and other situations where many babies were warehoused, following the trauma and devastation in Europe during the Second World War, that made maternal deprivation and its consequences a fundamental matter for all work on HGD from ethology to cognitive neuroscience (Schore, 2005). Below I describe the findings from these classic studies, particularly the well-known studies of post-war orphanages and Anna Freud's study of child refugees.

### THE RESIDENTIAL NURSERY

The claim made by Spitz and Wolf (1946) as well as Bowlby (Bowlby, 1952; van der Horst and van der Veer, 2008) that early deprivation of maternal care may have led to long-term developmental and psychiatric consequences has continued to be controversial (Ainsworth, 1962; van der Horst and van der Veer, 2008) but has also informed judgments about child care over the intervening years (Howe, 2001).

Immediately after the war Spitz and Wolf carried out a long-term study of a residential nursery for infants during which they observed 123 unselected infants each for a period of twelve to eighteen months. The infants were physically cared for but by a number of different nursery staff, who were so busy that there was no time for them to play or stimulate the babies or form a relationship bond. The researchers found that, by the second half of the first year, a few infants had developed weepy behaviour in marked contrast to their previously happy and outgoing behaviour when they were first admitted. After a time this weepiness gave way to *withdrawal*. The children in question would lie in their cots with averted faces, refusing to take part in the life of their surroundings. When the researchers approached, they were ignored.

Spitz and Wolf believed that these children, deprived of adult attention and affection, would probably suffer long-term psychiatric consequences.

However there is some later evidence, as we see in the next section, that attachment relationships can be formed between peers, even among young children, and if this happens there is hope that psychological damage from deprivation might be mitigated. This is illustrated in the case of the war orphans discussed below.

### WAR ORPHANS

There continues to be a steady increase in the number of war orphans, particularly since the 1990s with conflicts in the Balkans, Middle East and Africa. What does the future hold for war orphans? How do children overcome traumatic experiences in which they are victims and/or witnesses to brutality, violence and murder? We do know some answers from observational studies, particularly the classic study by Anna Freud and Sophie Dann of war orphans brought to the UK after the Second World War.

They (Freud and Dann, 1951) studied six children (around the age of three years) rescued from the Tereszin Nazi concentration camp by the Russians and sent to England with other rescued children. They did not have an easy or straightforward journey to London. Immediately after their rescue they were taken to a Czech castle and fed and treated with great care and skill by the authorities, who were eager to ensure they returned to health as soon as possible. The children stayed there for a month and then went to a reception camp in the British Lake District before moving to London. They were, in fact, destined to be fostered in the USA, and funding had been provided from the American Government for a year's rehabilitation in the UK. The project was provided with accommodation in England, and the staff were drawn from the Hampstead Nursery run by Anna Freud and colleagues. The careful observations and recording of the children's behaviour provide us with a unique account of development in the absence of adult attachment and recovery from severe deprivation.

Initially on arrival in London, the children reacted badly in that they were wild, restless, noisy and uncontrollable, showing no pleasure in their new surroundings. In the first few days they destroyed all the toys they were given and much of the furniture. They were either coldly indifferent to the staff or hostile, making no exception, even for Maureen who had travelled with them from the Lake District, and was thus their only link with their recent past. At times they would not even look up when one of the adults came near them. Interestingly, though, when they did have a need they would turn to one of the adults, but then ignore the same person after the need had been met.

If they became angry (which was often) they would hit, bite and spit at the adults and shout and scream using 'bad' language – mostly in German but with some Czech words. The English words gradually increased as well.

The positive feelings among the children were centred exclusively among themselves as a group of children, and it was clear they were very attached to, and cared for, each other but not anyone else. They wanted to stay together all the time and became very upset when separated, even briefly, for any reason. *This made it impossible to treat any one of them as an individual.*

They gradually managed to build relationships with the adult staff, however, but unfortunately there is no information about what happened when they finally left the nursery, although it has to be assumed that at least some of them were separated from each other in order to be fostered or adopted.

The issues arising from this study suggest that the socio-material context has the potential to restore or repair some of the psychological damage:

- Children who have had an early secure attachment that becomes disrupted through trauma (such as war) will be able to develop attachments later in life if the context is supportive of *repair*.
- Children who have not made secure attachments to stranger adults *can* make strong attachments to peers.
- Children deprived of adult relationships will respond to adults in very immature and aggressive ways, at least initially.
- Children who have severe behavioural difficulties are not necessarily deficient, delinquent or psychotic but may have had a traumatic past experience.

This is particularly pertinent information in the context of fostering and adoption with children who have had traumatic backgrounds. It suggests the potential for healing, if the new family (and hopefully the relevant agency) has strengths that provide support and are well supported themselves.

### Discursive perspectives

Studies on attachment which use narrative methods (i.e. the respondents are asked to tell their own story rather than complete a questionnaire, as described in Chapter 4) (Crossley, 2003; Riessman and Quinney, 2005) have shown that both attachment experiences and emotion are socially constructed (Harris, 1999). One Swedish study demonstrated that grief itself may also be socially constructed, so that when disasters occur, accounts broadcast on the mass media serve to shape a normative (and apparently internal) model of grief and loss (Reimers, 2003). In other words, we all (including the victims) have expectations of a particular set of emotional reactions that are considered to be normal.

Harris' work, for example, indicated that children develop an understanding of emotion through *talking* about it. Even so, different children attribute different meanings and feelings to particular events and their responses. Harris' work raises the question of whether the *sensitivity* of the early care-giver is responsible for the differences between the meaning children give to their emotions or whether *family discourse* (e.g. 'stiff upper lip', or being expressive) shapes the meaning of emotional reactions and emotional relationships. Perhaps here it might be worth re-reading the description of the family dynamics in Chapter 1 discussing Laing and Esterson's ideas about 'who is mad here?'.

Maternal discourses on emotions, however, do appear to be more influential in children who have securely attached relationships, with the mother suggesting that sensitive and secure attachments support the experience of the next generation in reflecting and feeling secure in emotional responses (Ontai and Thompson, 2002).

### Emotional and intra-psychic perspectives

While it is important to note that the ways in which each of us is able to deal with loss relates in some way to the early years' attachment and separation experiences, this may not necessarily predict how such events might be managed in adulthood.

Over the years since Freud identified the psychological conscious and unconscious impact of mourning loss (Freud, 1917) and the strength of grief, followed up by Bowlby's work, large numbers of studies and observations have focused on the processes of attachment and loss as fundamental to the human condition (Howe et al., 2001; Shemmings, 2006).

Work on attachment styles, for example, has shed light in a number of ways onto the internal representation of other people in an individual's life, because it seems that close relationships and the ability to manage them bears some relation to *feelings* about other people (Holmes, 2010; Shemmings, 2006; Shemmings and Shemmings, 2011).

Another related approach to the same process has been the development of theories of *mentalization*. This is the capacity to put oneself in the emotional shoes of another. It has proven to be an effective predictor of good or poor mental health and particularly relevant in cases of borderline personality disorder – typically people unable to empathize with others (Fonagy, 2000, 2001). The care-giver's ability to consider the child and to understand that others might have different needs and ideas from one's own, and the ability to reflect upon that, is likely to lead to a healthy outcome in a parent/child relationship. Parents' ability to take account of their child's mental states was strongly linked to security of attachment in their own backgrounds as well as their relationship with their own children. Thus, security and insecurity are transmitted across generations of parents and children.

Social workers and others in similar professions clearly need to develop their capacity for mentalizing in order to both support service users and monitor the risks related to them.

## CHAPTER SUMMARY

Attachment theory, including the multidisciplinary perspectives, its history from classic studies to contemporary technological innovations and identification of attachment styles and their contribution to understanding relationships, separation and loss, all combine to make this a crucial and yet complicated chapter. Attachment in all its facets is central to HGD as a theory and to social work as a practice, which means that it is important to have a working knowledge of this work before you move on to read the following chapters.

As you will have noted, attachment theory has now progressed beyond its discursive construction as a political ploy to make women feel guilty, driving mothers of young children from the workplace. We are now confident that it is not the absence of mothers that causes emotional problems leading to poor mental health in adulthood, but sustained neglect and abuse which may be transmitted across generations by parents who are unable to care for their infants due to social and biological factors.

Consideration of the work of psychoanalytic psychologists such as John Bowlby (1982) and social work academics such as David Howe (2001) and David Shemmings (2006), psychoanalysts Melanie Klein (1975) and Erik Erikson (1950/1963) is crucial to understanding the importance of attachment in theory and practice. There is also sustained, persuasive and increasing evidence from social and biological scientists in different epistemological traditions that early *attachment relations* (i.e. the experience of being cared for by one or two consistent adults) have the power to influence how far someone has an enduring sense of security and ability to form relationships with other people and the degree to which each person is able to trust both themselves and others (Fonagy, 2001). We also know from both social and neuroscientists that, while attachment styles (secure and insecure) persist over time, it may be possible to repair emotional damage if a secure context can be provided and

the individual is supported to develop within it (Cozolino, 2006).

Research has brought together ideas that demonstrate human resilience and our ability to repair emotional damage alongside a broader and deeper understanding of what actually constitutes maternal deprivation leading to disorganized attachment behaviours. Social workers need to use their understanding of attachment, separation and loss to make decisions about child development and protection, as well as working with adolescents and vulnerable adults, particularly those with mental health difficulties (Holmes, 2010; Howe and Fearnley, 2003; Shemmings and Shemmings, 2011).

To recap, attachment theory has provided practitioners with:

- A means of understanding how human beings of all ages interact and relate to others.
- The means to develop a capacity for understanding how individuals come to have a sense of self-awareness, emotional intelligence, and an empathetic awareness of the *experiences of others* . This process has been called *mentalization* – that is, the capacity to put oneself into the mind of others (Holmes, 2010). We look at this in more detail in Chapter 6.
- The ability to work reflectively (Fook and Gardner, 2010) and relationally (Ruch, 2005) (and therefore effectively) (see Chapter 6).
- A sense of their own identity across the lifespan.

Reading this chapter therefore should help you to understand:

- The long-standing, broad foundation of the evidence base showing the importance of attachment relationships for HGD.
- That appreciating the role of attachment also leads to understanding how separation, loss and disrupted and dysfunctional attachment relationships impact across the lifespan.

**CHAPTER SUMMARY** *continued*

- That both the psychosocial approach to lifespan development and the MDI lens for understanding life events provide valuable means of making sense of HGD theories and key relationships in your personal life and practice.

- That human beings are resilient and, although poor early attachment relationships frequently lead to mental ill health and conduct disorders of various types, there is enough evidence to support the value of well-considered social work intervention (probably within a multidisciplinary context) to assuage some of the impact of this early distress.

**FURTHER READING**

There is a wealth of reading on attachment but perhaps the most relevant here are:

Bifulco, A., Jacobs, C., Bunn, A., Thomas, G. and Irving, K. (2008) The Attachment Interview (ASI) as an Assessment of Support Capacity: Exploring its Use for Adoption-Fostering Assessment. *Adoption and Fostering*, 32, 33–45.

Howe, D. and Fearnley, S. (2003) Disorders of Attachment in Adopted and Fostered Children: Recognition and Treatment. *Clinical Child Psychology and Psychiatry*, 8(3), 369–387.

Shemmings, D. and Shemmings, Y. (2011) *Understanding Disorganized Attachment: Theory and Practice for Working with Children and Adult*. London: Jessica Kingsley.

chapter

# 6

# FROM THEORY TO REFLECTIVE-RELATIONAL PRACTICE

**LEARNING OBJECTIVES**

- To introduce the reflective-relational approach to social work thinking and practice.
- To consider how theory from earlier chapters might inform the reflective-relational approach.
- To consider theory in the context of real-life examples.

## Introduction

The previous chapters explored the theoretical bases of HGD, especially nature versus nurture, psychosocial development across the lifespan and attachment theory, and introduced the MDI approach. In this chapter, I highlight all these different perspectives and how they both help us by informing our critical thinking and also support a *reflective* and *relational* social work practice. As you will see, this is an approach to practice that draws upon evidence from research and evaluated practice. It therefore tries to ensure effective work with service users as well as reducing anxiety among practitioners by reinforcing the importance of thinking and reflecting.

In order to illustrate this approach, in this section I focus on cases involving (a) child protection, (b) long-term mental health problems arising from neglect and abuse and (c) family relationships disrupted through substance abuse.

However, the main objective in using these illustrations is to demonstrate theory as a *tool kit* that practitioners can refer to and take from when assessing best practice with all service users in different situations.

### Defining reflective-relational practice

As identified in previous chapters, the psychosocial approach to the lifespan, including attachment theory, and the MDI perspective take account of the *complexities* in HGD. These complementary models offer practitioners immediate access to the characteristics of a particular stage of lifespan development, which assists their assessment. For example, using Erikson's characterization, if you are working with a woman in her late fifties whose marriage has broken down and whose children have flown the nest, you might recognize her sense of stagnation which she experiences and expresses through a sense of hopelessness and depression. You will then be able to consider the support that might best suit her by evaluating her material (financial and environmental), discursive (the everyday construction of the lives of late middle-aged women) and intra-psychic (the meaning and emotional reactions she herself experiences) context.

So, for instance, it is also possible to assess the vulnerability of a person in older age who is recently widowed by focusing on how they are thinking about their future life and reviewing how their narrative fits within the framework of integrity versus despair.

The intervention may then be planned giving consideration to

- Material context (biological, social and physical);
- Discursive context (the meaning the woman attributes);
- Intra-psychic (emotional) status.

In other words, the knowledge needed to reflect upon the lifespan *stage* benefits from being informed by the MDI status of the service user. Using the same example of the widowed older person, the bio-material (perhaps the person's physical capacities and age), the socio-material (such as support networks and quality of housing), the discursive (such as the person's account of their own life and identity) and the intra-psychic (their emotional state and their capacity for separation) add to the practitioner's repertoire. It is important to remember, also, that this form of analysis is evidence-based.

In order to make the most effective use of what the practitioner has learned in *theory* it is also necessary to develop *skills* and the *capacity to link* these through a reflective-relational method. This means engaging with:

- **Reflective practice** (Fook and Gardner, 2010). This is essentially a method of learning to implement best practice using a critical incident. Using this technique, the social worker identifies a particular service user episode, such as a visit to someone with psychotic symptoms. He then reflects on how he felt about the visit and how he took decisions and implemented interventions and actions (including personal ones such as talking to colleagues) and then reconsiders what this meant overall for him and the service user's life.
- **Mentalizing techniques** (Fonagy, 2000). These involve the practitioner in reflection, but particularly from a *relational* perspective as discussed in Chapter 5 which talked about attachment behaviours and experiences. Being relational is an approach whereby the practitioner needs to think about *what the other person is feeling* at any one time. This technique has been developed from a therapeutic perspective based on attachment theory, but it also resonates with the

symbolic interactionist ideas I described in Chapter 3. That is, we learn about ourselves in relation to others, others' responses to us and ours to them. This might be described as *empathy*. This leads us to ideas about emotional and social intelligence.

- Using **emotional and social intelligence** (Goleman, 2006; Ingram, 2012) bears a relation to empathy while holding in mind your own emotional reactions to a personal, interpersonal and more broadly social situation. Team managers need to access emotional intelligence in order to be effective leaders and to support their team, and for their own emotional survival. This involves some use of intuition when hard evidence isn't available (Nicolson et al., 2011). Emotional intelligence has been demonstrated to reduce vulnerability to negative life events and to increase resilience (Armstrong et al., 2011) as well as enhancing the social worker/service user relationship (Ingram, 2012).

In Figure 6.1 you will see ways in which a social worker might apply a reflective-relational approach to decision-making about practice. The lifespan stages in Erikson's psychosocial model provide a positive to negative *sliding scale* for each stage, as we discussed in Chapter 4. This establishes the core of the intra-psychic level of theory – although as you will be aware from the previous chapters, it also gives insights on how other theories contribute to this dimension too.

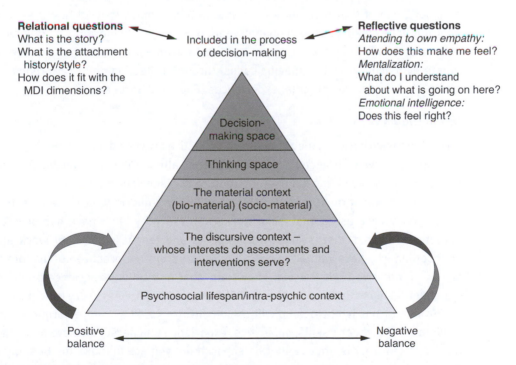

*Figure 6.1* From theory to reflective-relational practice

Similarly, the discursive and material contexts each have positive and negative elements, and may also be assessed on a sliding scale. So, for instance, the *thinking space* might use information on the extent to which a procedure (such as a multidisciplinary case conference) serves the vested interests of an organization (discursive) as well as the family and socio-economic circumstances (material) of a service user.

This tool-kit approach should not be used as a means of *calculating* an outcome for the service user however. The social worker has to respond in a reflective-relational way (particularly using emotional intelligence) in considering the relevant information – this model provides *a guide for thinking rather than a recipe for practice.*

Therefore, from the information in the thinking space, the story and how it fits with theoretical knowledge needs to be reflected upon so that a combination of experience, empathy, mentalization skills and emotional intelligence come into play for decision-making.

These techniques take account of the ways in which an individual practitioner might place herself *in the position of another person,* considering empathically about how the other might be thinking and consequently behave.

Thus, the practitioner can make an effective judgment and appropriate intervention, if and when necessary, informed by their reflective-relational practice.

Thus in reflective-relational practice, a social worker is best informed to make their judgment if they themselves are able to think *empathically* of how a service user might be making sense of an intervention (Howe, 2008; Ingram, 2012). Also, if the social worker links awareness and action, he is able to consider how to develop practice (in general and in specific cases) through reflecting on his *awareness* of his own role and developmental experiences (Fook and Gardner, 2010).

### Using theory

The relationship between theory, skills and effective practice does not display itself as a straightforward trajectory. It is complicated, although once you have grasped the technique you will find it a useful structure to guide your thinking.

Theory is sometimes seen as irrelevant to the important practicalities that impact on service users and social workers in everyday life. I have had several, sometimes heated, discussions with students and teachers of social work and counselling who have wanted to get rid of theory from the practice curriculum in favour of intensive *skills training*. They claim that it is skills, experience and personality that make up the effective practitioner, and theory plays very little part.

But I know this isn't true and will try to convince you! My counter-argument to students is that theory, skills, capacities, experience and personality are all intrinsically linked. That is, they cannot be separated if you are to make the best decisions and let clear thinking guide intervention. It may be true that someone might have a good grasp of theory but cannot develop effective skills to assess what is happening with people. It is unlikely, however, that a practitioner can operate skilfully without some knowledge of theory – even though in some cases it might have been instilled a long time previously and seem to be common sense.

The practice of *critical reflection* (Fook and Gardner, 2010), which involves social workers in thinking deeply about a particular incident, making notes, thinking back over the encounter and bringing it to a discussion with a group of colleagues, emphasizes this very point. Although some of you might think you are employing experience (as indeed you probably are), your knowledge of theory also comes to the fore as the means by which you identify the critical incident itself.

This holds true for whatever theoretical tradition you might have trained in, whether it be psychoanalytic, person-centred counselling or radical social work action and practice.

In what follows I demonstrate how the theory discussed in previous chapters might be applied to practice using a reflective-relational approach which I will illustrate through examples of child abuse and neglect, mental illness and substance abuse.

### Working to prevent child abuse and neglect

Much of what we know about working to prevent child abuse has sadly come from cases where a child in the care of social services has died, or been seriously injured and neglected, at the hands of his or her carers. The *Munro Review of Child Protection* (Munro, 2011) was commissioned to examine why previous reforms to child care and protection practices still demonstrate such serious failures. The wider content of the report is outside the scope of this book but Munro's overarching brief – to provide effective help to children at risk of neglect and abuse – is central to concerns about HGD. She emphasized that social workers need to be well informed about the latest research and relevant theory.

---

**PAUSE AND REFLECT**

In order to think about theory in a reflective-relational way you might consider

- What should social workers hold in mind about HGD theories in order to inform their judgments on how to support particular children and their families?
- Think about a family you have worked with and recall a critical incident. This might be when someone broke down in tears, which might have surprised you at the time. Equally it might be when someone thanked you for

asking a particular question or making a specific suggestion.

- How might each of material, discursive and intra-psychic dimensions inform your thinking about a possible intervention around that incident?
- How could poor decisions you might have made about that incident be put right and improve well-being?
- What were your *feelings* about involvement in that work?

It is not simply the prevention of a child's death that is at the heart of child pro-tection, though. Abused and neglected children's life chances and quality of life may be damaged significantly if there is no effective intervention by social workers. Remember the discussion of maternal deprivation and disorganized attachment from Chapter 5.

Munro makes it clear that there is irrefutable evidence of the long-term im-pacts of abuse and neglect and indicates the potential consequences to develop-ment across the lifespan following abuse and neglect. Although she has not put it that way, she too is thinking about how the lifespan and the material-discursive-intra-psychic dimensions of life have an effect on the abused and neglected child (Table 6.1). Despite the plethora of reports into cases of child abuse, neglect and death and the comprehensive work of Munro, there remain questions that social workers need to ask themselves on a daily basis.

Thinking now about these questions and how to make them come alive, I have selected the tragic case of Maria Colwell who died at the hands of her step-father in 1973. The description of what happened to her is used here to illustrate, and

*Table 6.1* The lifespan trajectory

| Type of abuse and neglect | Infant | Young child | Older child | Adolescent | Young adult | Midlife | Older age |
|---|---|---|---|---|---|---|---|
| Physical (material) | Injury | Injury | Obesity, skin disorders, bruising | Hair loss, eating disorders, self-harm | These problems will be exacerbated without support | | Severe weight loss |
| Emotional (intra-psychic/ discursive) | Hyper-attentive | Crying | Hyper-alert/ cries easily | Unable to make effective relationships | | | Atypical grief reactions |
| Behaviour (material/ discursive) | Flinching/ watchful | Aggressive and fearful | Hitting, pinching others | Behavioural disorder/ bullying | Aggressive and possibly violent or bullying | Domestic abuse (victim and perpetrator)/ abuse of own children | Self harm, failure to eat |
| Underlying psychological/ mental health status (intra-psychic) | Unfocused anxiety | Anxiety | Anxiety/ depression | Sense of failure/victim | Borderline personality | | Isolation |
| | These symptoms and behaviours will accumulate over time if there is no treatment or support | | | | | | |
| | Without support consequences persist over time | | | | | | |

**Birth to old age**

**PAUSE AND REFLECT**

Table 6.1 describes a pathological or dysfunctional model of development. If a child suffers abuse and neglect and the outcome of injury from infancy, then affect regulation (or mood self-control), attachment and growth (getting older and bigger) are all disrupted. Table 6.1 also makes it clear that, without effective intervention, material, discursive and intra-psychic problems recur across the lifespan to adulthood. The MDI and Erikson's lifespan models provide a more nuanced or subtle model than that used by Munro, which is the basis for Table 6.1.

It might be useful to see whether you would like to add information to that already in Table 6.1.

question again, the social work decisions that failed to protect her and other children who have suffered similarly and, perhaps more importantly, to think about what might have been better practice.

## The death of Maria Colwell in 1973

Maria Colwell was beaten to death by her step-father in 1973 when she was eight years old. Maria was the fifth child of her mother Pauline's first marriage, to Mr Colwell. Maria also had an older half-sister who had been cared for by her maternal grandmother since her birth. Maria's father had left home soon after Maria's birth and died shortly after that.

Maria's mother had a mental breakdown soon after Maria was born (and after Maria's father left) and was unable to cope with all the children. The local social services, therefore, decided to take Maria (the youngest) into care when she was four months old, placing her with her mother's sister-in-law's family (the Coopers) for fostering (see Figure 6.2).

Maria was assessed by her social worker to be living happily with her foster parents and thus continued working to support the Coopers and Maria. Her mother, however, decided she wanted Maria back home when she was six years old and social services decided to return her. By then, Pauline was living with William Kepple and their three new children (all, of course, younger than Maria).

Maria's mother had maintained some degree of contact with her over the intervening years but *Maria did not want to leave her foster parents*. She had lived with the Coopers for most of her life and, of course, they were the family she remembered growing up with.

At some point in the previous six years she had gone back to stay with her mother for a week, but it is unclear whether this was an attempt by social workers to resettle her which had broken down, or simply that she had gone there for a short holiday.

For the fourteen months before she died, when she was living with her own mother and the new family, Maria was assessed as steadily deteriorating in her

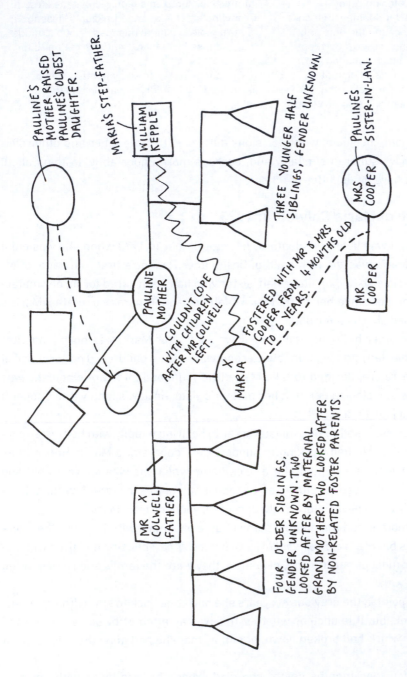

*Figure 6.2* Genogram of Maria's family

PAULINE'S MOTHER RAISED PAULINE'S OLDEST DAUGHTER.

MARIA'S STEP-FATHER.

WILLIAM KEPPLE

THREE YOUNGER HALF SIBLINGS, GENDER UNKNOWN.

PAULINE'S SISTER-IN-LAW.

MRS COOPER

PAULINE MOTHER

COULDN'T COPE WITH CHILDREN AFTER MR COLWELL LEFT.

FOSTERED WITH MR & MRS COOPER FROM 4 MONTHS OLD TO 6 YEARS.

MR COOPER

X MARIA

MR X COLWELL FATHER

FOUR OLDER SIBLINGS. GENDER UNKNOWN. TWO LOOKED AFTER BY MATERNAL GRANDMOTHER. TWO LOOKED AFTER BY NON-RELATED FOSTER PARENTS.

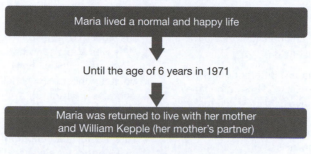

- Maria was born in March 1965

- She was taken into care and placed with foster parents from the age of 4 months

Maria lived a normal and happy life

Until the age of 6 years in 1971

Maria was returned to live with her mother and William Kepple (her mother's partner)

- For 14 months after that Maria lived with her mother, younger half-siblings and step-father
- Despite evidence of cruelty and neglect reported to the authorities, Maria remained living with her mother and step-father

In January 1973 when Maria was 8 years old she was beaten to death by William Kepple

*Figure 6.3* The time line of Maria Colwell's short life

health and behaviour. She appeared depressed and unhappy. It was subsequently found that she had experienced neglect and cruelty at the hands of her mother and step-father, causing her great distress. During the last months of her life, neighbours had apparently made more than thirty representations to various authorities about Maria's state of health.

Maria's death occurred one night when Kepple returned home at 11.30 pm to find her up and watching television. He beat and kicked her to death.

Before you read any further, look at the *Pause and Reflect* box overleaf. In the Colwell case it becomes immediately apparent that HGD theories have something to offer in trying to make sense of what happened – not only within the family but surrounding the decision-making contexts. No one theory in itself can provide the answers but, using the lifespan and MDI approaches together, it should be possible to focus on what would have been best for Maria. In the end, the social worker needs to make a judgment – weighing up what she has observed and the sense she makes of the observations *in the context of theory*. The material context of the 1970s favoured the birth parents over foster parents, but this has changed since in favour of considering the child's needs to be paramount.

### Using theory in the case of Maria Colwell

Now I want to explore some further issues for reflection to make you think about how you might use theory if you were faced specifically with Maria Colwell's family

**PAUSE AND REFLECT**

**Maria Colwell**

It might be useful to read the case details for yourself (DoH, 1974) and consider the answers to some of these questions.

- Might you have made a different decision from that of the social workers at the time? What would you have considered in making that decision? Think particularly about the material-discursive and intra-psychic dimensions of Maria's life.
- How effectively could a six year old communicate her needs to the social workers, teachers, doctors and other professionals involved in making the decision to let her return home?
- Is it possible to assess depression in a six, seven or eight year old child? How was knowledge of attachment used in this case?
- Was attachment to the Coopers ignored in favour of the discourse on *maternal*

deprivation? (Remember that this was in the early 1970s.)
- How important are blood ties, i.e. living with your biological mother (or father), in ensuring the welfare of a child?
- Why was Maria's mother so insistent on having her back when she already had three younger children (only half-siblings to Maria) and a new partner?
- Why do many of us turn a blind eye to evidence in cases such as this one?
- How useful is a genogram as a decision-making tool for assessing risk in family relationships?

Try to assess how far the psychosocial lifespan development model, attachment theory and MDI perspectives might have helped you to work with this family and identify the risk to Maria. I have made some suggestions but it is more important for you to think the issues through for yourself.

situation in the months before her death. You might want to consider more than one approach to address these questions or you might think of different questions that should have been asked.

### 1.  HOW MIGHT MARIA'S VOICE HAVE BEEN 'HEARD'?

To communicate effectively with adults, a child needs to have a complex vocabulary and be able to make sense of what is happening to her. She will be using words to think about what is happening to her and how it makes her feel. She will also use words to tell others what she wants them to know. This will, of course, be a *performative* narrative, as you saw in Chapter 4 – the child would choose how and what to present in the story.

From Piaget's work, described in Chapter 2, you will have seen that children should, by the age of six, have developed some key skills (the level of thinking would be at the 'concrete operation' stage) (Piaget, 1990).

Piaget also proposed that as children grow they develop theories about how to negotiate themselves in their world. Thus Maria, at the age she was returned to her mother, would have been developing complex thoughts and possess a sense of how to order people and objects in her internal and social world. This means she could understand that some things remain constant, despite external changes.

Perhaps she knew that she would remain happy if she lived with the Coopers and was aware that she did not want to go back to her mother.

Furthermore, the work of Lawrence Kohlberg on the development of moral reasoning (Kohlberg, 1969), which will be discussed in Chapter 8, would indicate that, following her positive experience with the Coopers, Maria would probably have been able to judge that her step-father's behaviour was 'wrong' and that her mother was also lacking morally by neglecting and failing to protect her *This might be described as the material context.*

However, of course, Maria would not have made an objective, neutral judgment and may, herself, have been facing a moral dilemma of divided loyalties. *These may be the intra-psychic and perhaps socio-material contexts.*

If you take the development of cognitive and verbal skills into account, she should *theoretically* have been able to communicate effectively with the social worker. Furthermore, given that she had had several years of experiencing stability and well-being, she would have known that her family life at the time leading up to her death was not as it should be. She knew it could and should be different (*the bio-material and intra-psychic contexts*). So what prevented her from making this clear to the social workers and other professionals?

### 2. WHAT MIGHT HAVE PREVENTED HER FROM BEING HEARD?

Bronfenbrenner (Bronfenbrenner and Morris, 2007) suggests that growth and development in a child reflects the influence of the *systems* within which she lives (see Chapter 3). Maria's life was influenced by all the adults who were her carers. The foster parents and social workers within her initial microsystem created a context in which she could grow and develop normally and, by all accounts, happily. Sadly, this was then disrupted by the *trauma of transition* to the microsystem represented by a family of hostile strangers (even though one was her biological mother).

Maria had moved from a microsystem where she could freely communicate with those close to her (the Coopers). They, in turn, were willing, on advice from social workers, for her to communicate across the mesosystem, or boundary, to another microsystem, her biological mother's family, where she was kept isolated. What is interesting (and tragic) is how the social workers as part of that damaging microsystem failed to heed warnings from others and from their own observations and engagement with Pauline and Kepple (*bio- and socio-material contexts and intra-psychic dimensions*).

The work of Bowlby and others on maternal deprivation (Bowlby, 1952, 1982) and the experimental studies on attachment and loss (e.g. Harlow's work with primates), discussed in depth in Chapter 5, all reinforced the centrality of the mother/infant relationship to long-term mental health, and separation from the mother as detrimental in the long term. This thinking possibly influenced professionals' practice for several decades after the studies were first reported.

Clinical and academic thinking about the *detail* of what this meant eventually developed a more nuanced and critical stance, ensuring that the child's interests were seen to be complex (i.e. not simply a case of 'blood being thicker than water') and put before socio-political thinking. Very sadly this thinking came too late for Maria. (Here perhaps is a case of discursive influences – dominant discourses regulating behaviour based on the knowledge-claims of experts and the vested interests of government.)

There is new evidence, though, that might have introduced a powerful note of caution into this particular case. Evolutionary psychologists have, to some degree, reinstated the blood-tie debate. Through analyzing anecdotal as well as experimental evidence, some suggest that it is frequently the step-parent, rather than the biologically-related parent, who harms the child. This was certainly the case with Maria (and other child abuse cases, as we shall see in later chapters).

From an evolutionary psychology (EP) perspective the theory proposes that the adult *invests* time, effort and attention in their genetic offspring, thus ensuring the survival of their own genes (Workman and Reader, 2008). This concurs with the general EP perspective discussed in Chapter 2 that human beings channel their resources (emotional and material) to their own kin. Strong feelings of pleasure derive from nurturing your own young and feelings of pain come from the thought or reality of them experiencing harm. Therefore, it is most likely that a parent would *privilege* the well-being of their own biological child over that of a step-child. So when there is a biological and a step-child in the family it would be 'natural' for the adult's love to flow towards the biological child first, however fond they might be of the step-child. The EP theory is not in any sense suggesting that a step-, foster or adoptive parent would cause a child deliberate harm. However, if that adult has had an abusive and neglectful upbringing, then the risk of them directing abuse towards a step-child becomes increased (*bio- and socio-material context*).

### 3. IS IT POSSIBLE TO ASSESS WHETHER A CHILD UNDER TEN IS EXPERIENCING DEPRESSION AND THEREFORE LIMITED IN THE ROLE THEY MIGHT PLAY IN DECISION-MAKING?

Psychoanalytic theories such as those of Freud, Klein and Erikson (Erikson, 1950/1963) outlined in Chapters 3, 4 and 5 would suggest that Maria's experiences of sudden, negative and traumatic changes would have produced problems for her development. Being removed from the care of her mother in infancy might have impacted on her sense of trust in herself and others, and this would clearly have become exacerbated when she was returned to her mother full-time. These negative experiences, translated into psychosocial development (as described in Erikson's lifespan stages), would most likely lead to a sense of hopelessness and depression. She would be at the stage of 'latency' which, unlike the label, is a time of profound emotional development and of new learning for children beginning to be increasingly independent and finding their 'feet' with peers and wider social relationships (Waddell, 2005). Look at Table 4.1 (p. 62) where Erikson's model of the lifespan is described.

The ability to understand the emotional differences between her life circum-stances while with her foster parents and then with her 'real' mother and Kepple *may* have contributed to Maria's depression. This would link with her thinking and the construction of her own narrative about her life discussed above. Maria might well have appreciated that her life with her foster mother had come to an end and that she would have to adapt to living with her mother's new family, which would have been likely to cause a severe sense of disruption and grief. The importance of attachment relationships and the trauma of disruption would also have accounted for depression and the inability to make herself heard, and probably she would not have had the chance to have peer support from Kepple's biological children (in fact they might have intensified her isolation) as did the war orphans discussed in Chapter 5 (*intra-psychic and material contexts*).

## PAUSE AND REFLECT

### Emotion and reflection in social work

Social work has had a special love/hate relationship with psychoanalytic ideas and, despite the 'hate' predominating since the late 1970s, versions of psychoanalysis are now returning to the social worker's core repertoire. During the 1960s and into the mid-1970s psychoanalytic psychology was influential as part of social work training and practice, literature, sociology and art studies although, apart from (aspects of) clinical psychology, it was never central within the discipline of psychology.

Traditional human development books for social work students and practitioners relied on psychoanalytic approaches (e.g. Rayner, 1986). Other more recent texts of HGD, for example Beckett and Taylor (2010), have several psychoanalytic ideas underpinning their approach and, more directly, Marion Bower (2005) has proposed the value of psychoanalytic theory for social work practice.

Psychoanalytic theories of development, particularly those of Freud and Erikson, still remain a key basis for understanding the stages of development across the lifespan. Further, the work of psychoanalysts such as Melanie Klein (Klein, 1959/1993; Waddell, 2005) and Wilfred Bion (1994) has come more into focus in recent years to explain infant emotional and social development. Their work is particularly valuable for social work practitioners because of their interest in 'states of mind' and how these change according to situation rather than life stage.

The interest in emotional intelligence in professional practice of various types, including social work, hints at the need for a deeper, intra-psychic understanding of what goes on between people (Howe, 2008; Ingram, 2012; Morrison, 2007).

Furthermore, the work of the sociologist Anthony Giddens (described in Chapter 4) includes the unconscious as an important factor in his approach to understanding human experience (1986/2003).

- Consider how much reflective-relational social work owes to psychoanalytic practice?
- How important is understanding unconscious motivation to social work practitioners when reflecting on yourself?
- How important is it when reflecting on service users?

## Further intra-psychic issues in decision-making: turning a blind eye to evidence

Reflective-relational practice acts as an antidote to the 'blind eye': taking a reflective-relational stance facilitates our ability to *turn towards* unbearable behaviours that you might witness in practice. Sometimes what is 'in front of our eyes' is so unpalatable that we fail to see it. This is not to say that social workers (or others) deliberately *ignore* evidence of abuse, but sometimes the possibility of some abusive relationships is so agonizing to consider that they are plainly *not seen. This is particularly relevant because social workers and their managers are frequently held to account for not noticing evidence of physical abuse and neglect.*

Turning a blind eye means literally 'not seeing' evidence of behaviour, processes or events taking place in front of our eyes. While it is often the case that social workers are pilloried for failing to spot the signs of abuse and violence towards a child, the phenomenon of turning a blind eye seems to be both common and universal. No doctor or nurse, it seems, spotted the serious facial and bodily injuries of baby Peter Connelly (a seventeen-month-old boy who had had more than fifty injuries over an eight-month period, eventually dying at the hands of his mother's boyfriend in 2007). Why did the locum paediatrician, Dr Sabah Al-Zayyat, who saw the baby two days before he died not 'see' that his injuries were horrific and deliberately inflicted? A post-mortem examination subsequently revealed a broken back and ribs, among a number of other injuries that are believed to have predated the medical examination.

One week before his death, the baby had stayed the night with his biological father and his maternal grandmother. The grandmother had tried to stop him from crying in the night. She reported that there were bruises and cuts on his head and his hands were bandaged but, until the persistent night-time crying, she did not seem to 'see' these for what they were. She later reported that she had said to his father that there was something wrong with the baby and that they should take him to hospital *but they did not do so.*

The social workers who have been sacked following the inquiry after that baby's death had been acknowledged as extremely competent and well respected in their field, and this included Maria Ward, the social worker assigned to the Connelly case. Although the authorities admitted things were missed, they also argued that resources were depleted because of the high number of child protection referrals.

But was it really the lack of time and other resources that prevented an effective judgment being made by such an experienced social worker? What might have happened to prevent highly experienced and competent practitioners (medical as well as social workers) from identifying the risks to this baby?

Psychoanalysts and others have addressed this phenomenon of knowing/not knowing and seeing/not seeing which has become part of reflective practice. The 'blind eye' can happen at both a conscious and an unconscious level.

Remember Gitta Sereny's (1995) reflections (outlined in Chapter 4) on how much Albert Speer knew/didn't know about the treatment and fate of slave labourers, Gypsies and European Jewry? What did he know? He talked to her about sensing things but not knowing. Stan Cohen, the sociologist, also talked of how, during his South African childhood in the period of apartheid, he had some knowledge of how Black people were treated but knew he didn't want to face it, particularly when it was about people he knew. He later wrote about the lies we sometimes tell ourselves to defend against unpalatable truths (2001, 2004).

The underlying message is that it may be emotionally *intolerable* to face full knowledge of what is going on between the actors/participants in some scenarios, such as serious child protection cases. As a result, key information may be 'missed' because social workers might experience disbelief at taking in knowledge of the behaviour of the protagonists and then *refuse to think* as a defence mechanism (see Chapter 3) (Cohen, 2001, 2004; Smith et al., 2012).

Over the years, policy-makers and academics have attempted to develop rules for practice and the management of practice to prevent such tragedies. The divergence between what are clear and mostly sensible rules and human nature is what will continue to bedevil social workers and other practitioners whose work leads them into painful and distasteful situations.

## Reflective-relational practice in a therapeutic community: the case of Orla

Not all infants and young children who are neglected and abused experience the same developmental lifespan pathway. The long-term and extensive studies of neglect and abuse by Antonia Bifulco and her colleagues at Royal Holloway, University of London led them to make this telling statement:

> the world of the child and adolescent is complex, encompassing a variety of potentially influential experiences in the first sixteen years of life. Harmful experiences do not necessarily come singly, neither do they exist in a vacuum devoid of any happier ones. Intuitive understanding cannot hope to grasp the complex mechanisms by which various interrelated childhood experiences influence different adult outcomes. (Bifulco and Moran, 1998)

This is important because it speaks to all of us. Even Maria Colwell, for example, may have had some happy memories and feelings about her biological mother which led her to construct a narrative convincing herself and others that things were not as bad as they might have looked to others in hindsight after her death. We shall never know of course.

With all this in mind, I want to explore the case of a young woman named Orla, whose early life had been one of extreme abuse and deprivation. As she grew into adolescence, Orla was unable to function in everyday social settings (school or work despite being intellectually able). She persistently self-harmed by cutting her arms and sometimes taking overdoses of drugs. I met Orla several years ago when I was a group worker in a therapeutic community for sociopathic adults (most of whom were young) but she was one of the people who stayed in my mind.

### Background to the therapeutic community movement

The therapeutic community was part of a post-war mental health strategy, called social psychiatry. It was based on the work of the psychiatrist Maxwell Jones, who believed that traumatized ex-service personnel needed to be resocialized in order to regain confidence (Jones, 1956). The idea was that patients should be in a group and community setting all the time so that they experienced what other people thought of them and could express their views about other people. Wilfred Bion's (1961) classic studies of group behaviour were based on people who had difficulties being with others, often for reasons of traumatic experiences in their past, and who were also hard to treat. This approach was later seen as particularly effective for alcohol and drug abusers and addicts (Aron and Daily, 1976; Wexler and Williams, 1986) and people who self-harmed (Schwartz et al., 1989). It also proved a successful method of rehabilitating some types of personality-disordered offenders (Hobson et al., 2000). Recent studies, particularly in the USA, demonstrate the effectiveness of medium-term psychoanalytically oriented therapeutic communities for treating this population (Chiesa et al., 2004). Unfortunately this method, although effective for hard-to-treat and hard-to-manage mental health service users, has fallen by the wayside in the UK because it is more expensive than traditional drug-based psychiatry. Lessons may still be learned, though, about working with disturbed and borderline service users in mental health settings of different kinds.

Social psychiatry and therapeutic communities in particular are examples *par excellence* of reflective-relational practice. Not only did the 'residents' of therapeutic communities (as the patients were called) meet in groups at which they received feedback on all their behaviour which they had to reflect upon, but the staff also had group meetings – at least one a day – to consider the residents, often specific residents, the community as a whole and the staff group themselves. The work in therapeutic communities thus worked to a reflective-relational model, although it was not named as such.

### Orla's background

Orla was a typical resident in that she was young (early twenties), had suffered from a set of early traumatic experiences, was intelligent and articulate but unable to sustain herself in everyday social settings. She might take offence at something someone had said or, more likely, feel guilty for offending someone else and want to punish herself for it. She had a sense overall that she didn't deserve help and was often depressed or, as she put it, 'unable to feel anything'.

Orla came from a strict Catholic family in rural Eire (growing up during the 1960s) and became a patient in the institution as a consequence of persistent self-harming. She showed no signs of psychosis (i.e. losing touch with reality). Mostly she would use a knife or glass to cut up her arms, but she sometimes took over-doses of various analgesics that she collected via tortuous routes (frequently described by her doctors as 'devious'). She had been in several psychiatric hospitals but had eventually been referred and admitted to the therapeutic community because she was considered to have the degree of insight and emotional strength to cope and benefit.

Her early history was not on record. However, we can make a guess that rural Ireland in the 1960s was not conducive to women's freedom to have intellectual or sexual experiences without guilt and punishment.

### Orla's experience of abuse

When Orla was about nine her father had seen her with a boy (a friend) and both had been wearing only underpants. Orla and the boy had been 'touching' each other. Her father hit her with a leather belt (*and perhaps we might assume that this was how he typically disciplined his children, although we cannot know for certain – we do know that violent punishment of this kind was not condemned at that time*) and locked her in her attic bedroom for a year.

Orla's brothers and sisters were not allowed to go up and the only person she had contact with was her mother, who brought her food twice a day and emptied her potty. However, her mother had also spoken at length to the priest about what had happened and, although he apparently supported the father's actions in order to prevent her eventual downfall to Hell, he did suggest to Orla's mother that it would do no harm to make sure Orla had some good books to read.

Thus Orla, whose family were generally uneducated, managed to use her obvious intelligence during her isolation to read, learn, think and also gain a (rather strange) closeness with her mother that she had never had before. When her father 'released' her, everyone behaved as if nothing strange had happened. Orla, though, was never the same again – both for worse and a little for better.

It may be worth at this stage thinking back to Chapter 1, where *Sanity, Madness and the Family* (Laing and Esterson, 1970) was discussed, to reconsider hidden communication among family members and its impact, particularly upon children.

## *Reflective-relational intervention*

Orla's life, when I first knew her, was very troubled but there was clearly a sense that something positive had happened to her as well. She took part in a work group I was attached to, which meant that we all interacted as 'equals' (although it was known that I would discuss everything significant that happened during that group in the staff-only group). We spent the sessions mostly cooking cakes and biscuits and cleaning the kitchen area but when interactions took place between residents we would discuss them during that group, as well as bring them to the small and large group therapy sessions.

One reason I was moved to write about Orla years later is that, on reflection, I had felt a strong connection with her. My background and early life bore no similarities to Orla's so there was no easy reference to identify the connection. I also wonder whether having a connection with someone in a therapeutic community/ group therapy context was positive, but she did come to trust that she could work collaboratively with me – producing tea and lunches for the residents – without 'acting out' or getting distressed by the demands of people waiting for their food.

It is important here to emphasize three things from theory related to Orla's childhood experiences.

- Firstly, the context of abuse and neglect is complex and not always easy to identify. It depends, among other things, upon the ecological environments of a family, including the quality of relationships within and between generations (Bifulco and Moran, 1998; Blaxter, 1981; Rutter and Madge, 1977). Thus the material context and the dominant discourse of religious conservatism all served to make her environment one in which any free spirits were potentially crushed.
- Secondly, harmful experiences frequently do not occur as single events or types of experience. So a child might be neglected, sexually abused and bullied or they might be neglected but enjoy some very happy times with members of their family and all the experiences will be given meaning by the individual and woven into their life narrative (Bifulco and Moran, 1998).
- Thirdly, however resilient a child might be, there will be an adulthood outcome. The work of psychoanalytic writers has been particularly important in demonstrating and theorizing this (Bowlby, 1982; Erikson, 1959/1980; Klein, 1953) and their ideas have been reinforced by cognitive neuroscientific studies (Schore, 2001).

Think again about the theories from these perspectives discussed in Chapters 2, 3 and 5.

Orla had worked at thinking about herself and relating to others and that had worked well enough eventually for her to live outside a total institution. After discharge, Orla lived in a group hostel (comprised of ex-inmates of the community) after which she went to live with a young man she had met while a resident at the therapeutic community. I heard she did have occasional episodes of depression and self-hate/cutting up. However she was also able to draw on her own resources to a great extent, the resources which had been built up during her stay at the community.

---

**PAUSE AND REFLECT**

**Complex influences and mental health**

Whether Orla's tendencies for self-harm were innate and supported Orla through her ordeal as a child or whether they were developed and/or strengthened in the therapeutic community is unclear. What was notable was how her life included positives and negatives. Perhaps as a baby she had achieved a greater sense of *trust* in her relationships and herself (Chapter 4) and *secure attachments* (Chapter 5) which prevented her from having a psychotic breakdown when incarcerated, with subsequent repeat episodes (see Chapter 7). Perhaps the socio-material religious context was experienced as supportive as well as punitive by both Orla and her parents. It may be, too, that the very fact of her friendship with the boy when she was very young offers evidence that she had felt free to explore relationships and be curious about others' bodies, and was thus secure in trying to find out more about herself and the world.

It is important to remember that all biographical information is valuable and that gaining the service user's biographical narrative and assessing how they themselves construct and deconstruct the events and emotions in their lives is vital information for practitioners.

It might be a useful exercise here to imagine Orla's complete story.

- What was it like living in her family before her incarceration?
- How did her brothers and sisters experience what happened to Orla?
- How did each of her parents feel about the actions they took?
- What might the priest have done differently?
- How and when would a social worker intervene?
- Might it have been useful to support her parents in trying to mentalize about Orla (see Chapter 4)?
- How might Orla's future have looked after the therapeutic community?

---

## Substance abuse and child neglect

There seems little doubt that there is a vicious cycle of abuse and self-abuse connected with growing up in an abusive family, although it has to be noted that such a cycle is not inevitable (Dore et al., 1995; Dube et al., 2001; Knitzer, 2000). Many shield themselves from their pain using alcohol or other substances, and this frequently precipitates damaging neglect and abuse in the next generation. The websites of charities working to combat child neglect highlight the intrinsic link between alcohol and drug abuse and consequent child neglect. Action for Children's, for example, states:

People choose to take drugs or drink alcohol for many different reasons. This can include prescription medicines as well as illegal drugs and very often starts as something to 'take the edge off' a problem or situation. (www.actionforchildren.org.uk/our-services/family-support/child-neglect/Alcohol-drugs-and-their-role-in-child-neglect, accessed 14 December 2013)

The reasons often become more complex as time goes on and can include:

- to avoid feeling bored;
- to fit in with peers;
- to have more self-confidence (often leading to aggression);
- to belong to a special group;
- to forget about problems;
- to relax and feel good.

Unfortunately, once choice gives way to dependency, people will often pay for drugs and/or alcohol before everyday necessities such as food or even steal to do so. This will, of course, have an impact on any dependents they may have.

The stories of neglect and violence in families where the adults abuse drugs and alcohol are far too common and highly complex.

## Reflective-relational work with Carla

### Carla's background

Carla, who is twenty-four, has four children (Mark aged seven, Jaydon aged six, Mandy aged four and Darren who is three). Mark and Jaydon's father was violent towards her, breaking her jaw during her first pregnancy. He left her after Jaydon was born for another young woman and has since been in prison for armed robbery and sexual assault. He has no contact with Carla or his two sons.

Mandy and Darren each have different fathers. Darren's father lives with the family in social housing just outside London, although he frequently disappears for days on end and then reappears, and no-one seems to know where he was or why he went.

For six years Carla has been abusing drugs and alcohol. Mark and Jaydon frequently have to put her to bed, wake her in the morning and, particularly when there is no food in the house, call their grandmother (who lives nearby but is actually the mother of their estranged father). Carla's mother spent much of Carla's early years in psychiatric hospital following suicide attempts.

Carla's mother had recently had another breakdown and accused Carla of abusing Jaydon. The police called round late at night with an unfamiliar social worker to remove Jaydon. Carla became understandably very upset about this and started drinking before leaving the house, apparently to find her local dealer. She then

129

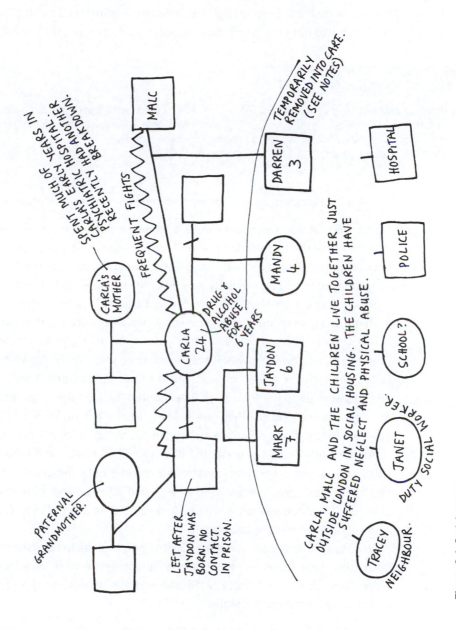

**Figure 6.4** Carla's ecomap

became aggressive to passers-by on the local high street, screaming abuse until she was arrested. Her other children were then temporarily taken into care. All this happened over a period of about twenty-four hours.

The duty social worker, Janet, had to write a report to help make a decision about the next steps. Even though her aims were primarily to safeguard the children, Janet also felt concerned about separating them from their mother.

**PAUSE AND REFLECT**

- What information does Janet need to make her decision?
- What decisions would you make for the short and longer term and why?

- What elements from this case study reflect material, discursive and intra-psychic perspectives?

A disturbing incident took place while Janet was writing her report:

Mandy and Darren (four and three) attended a half-day nursery in a building attached to Mark and Jaydon's school. Tracey, Carla's neighbour, would call in to collect the children one week and Carla would reciprocate the following one.

Monday morning was usually very difficult because Carla had frequently had a physical fight with Malc, her partner and Darren's father, after a weekend of drinking and taking dope (which was easily available because they lived in a large estate of social housing in a suburban area where drug use was common). However, one Monday when it was Tracey's turn to collect the children for school, she called out from the street as usual but the door didn't open. There was silence and she went up to the front door. She shouted through the letter-box and heard one child crying and another one sobbing loudly but nothing else. She called several times with no response and called out to the older children by name.

A police officer had to break the door to gain access. Inside the living room Mark and Jaydon were semi-conscious with an empty vodka bottle on the floor and two empty cans of cider. Darren was tied to a radiator pipe crying quietly, and must have been exhausted as he looked helpless, but Mandy, Carla and her boyfriend were nowhere to be seen.

In hospital it was discovered that Darren had bruises to his back and cigarette burns that were of different vintages, although some were very fresh. The two older boys were clearly intoxicated and verbally abusive to the social worker, police officer and hospital staff.

Apart from the very short-term action of finding Carla and deciding on placements for the children, the child protection team had some important medium- and longer-term decisions to make.

**PAUSE AND REFLECT**

**Complexity in child care**

This is a real case example although I have disguised some details for the sake of confidentiality.

What theoretical perspectives might the social workers draw upon to help risk assessment and decision-making?

Social workers need to reflect on the theoretical tools they might usefully employ to make sense of complex (and at times confusing) situations, such as that in Carla's family life. For those working with this family there were both emotional and intellectual responses to deal with – in the actors (i.e. the family and Tracey, the friend) as well as in themselves. Carla had the potential to be a good mother and loved her children but, when she was abusing substances that influenced her thinking, she was not coping with parenthood.

In this case, the practitioners need to reflect on their own role, the emotional connections or disconnections between the service user and themselves and the members of the family (conscious and unconscious links) and how these might support and/or hinder practice.

- What information does this case description provide about working to support Carla (and Malc her boyfriend) in their roles as mother/step-father of Mandy and the three boys? Remember that Malc is Darren's biological father but step-father to the others.

It was clear to Janet, the duty social worker who became involved, that:

- The members of the family had all experienced neglect and abuse at various times in their lives.
- Carla's early life has not been easy. Nor was her current one.
- Little was known about Malc except perhaps that he was sometimes prepared to leave his own son Darren 'to his fate'. Darren himself had been physically assaulted by someone over a period of time. Whether or not it had been Malc who had caused the injuries, he is implicated either as perpetrator or for neglecting to care for the three-year-old.
- Carla and Malc took drugs and drank heavily and would fight each other when they became intoxicated, particularly at weekends (at least that is what Tracey told Janet).
- Mark had been behaving in an aggressive manner for some time and the other two boys were following him.

In order to assess how useful the theories might be in practice, it is helpful to look at what Janet would know from considering the facts of the case and HGD theories

Janet noted the following in relation to Carla:

- There is an inter-generational pattern of neglect that is being played out in Carla's relationships (Buchanan, 1996; Rutter and Madge, 1977).
- Her attachment to her mother was disrupted by her mother's absence due to psychiatric in-patient treatment. It would be important to discuss this with Carla and possibly provide ongoing support which pays attention to her attachment problems (Shemmings and Shemmings, 2011). The pattern of early attachment as we know (see Chapter 5) is fundamental to understanding relationships and mental health through the lifespan (Bifulco and Moran, 1998; Bowlby, 1982).
- One result from Carla's own experience of neglect has been her difficulty in sustaining relationships with her children (particularly her sons) (Fonagy, 2000).

- She frequently feels helpless when faced by her children's 'resistance' to her authority. Using Erikson's (1950/1963) psychosocial stages of development (Chapter 4), this indicates once again that Carla's developmental experiences veered towards the negative.

- She has not maintained boundaries between herself (as adult and mother) and her children, in that she 'changes places' sometimes and Mark and Jaydon had to wake her up and suggest she shops for food. She also seems to consider that their resistance and bad behaviour empowers them in some way and indicates that they can look after themselves as well as a three-year-old.

- Carla either perpetrated physical abuse on Darren or colluded/ignored others abusing him.

- Carla has somehow managed to avoid the 'radar' of the children's services up until this crisis. This suggests she has some basic effective social and parenting skills. This would also indicate exploring where she had lived and contacting agencies to see if she was known. If not, then perhaps that supports the view that Carla with appropriate provision might be able to care adequately for her children. Was the recent debacle a cry for help?

## PAUSE AND REFLECT

- What further information would Janet need in order to decide on the package of support measures for Carla's children?
- What might Janet recommend to support Carla?

- What would you include in your report to assess the risk to Carla's children if they remained in her care?
- What might reflective-relational practice look like with Carla and her children?

Ferguson (2001) has proposed a narrative model of work with families where different types of abuse and child-care problems exist. As with the people in Ferguson's selected case study, Malc and Carla initially resisted any extended work with social workers. They felt confused and unable to predict how any involvement might progress, and what the point of it might be. In fact, they were resigned to fighting for the children not to be taken from them, but were not really equipped to do so effectively because of the other things going wrong in their lives.

The social worker involved in Ferguson's case study, whose aim was to develop a greater sense of self-esteem and develop parenting skills, faced the same problem as that confronting any social worker taking on extended work with Carla and Malc. Following Ferguson's model, the social worker in Carla's case arranged to call in twice a week for a month and just had coffee and talked to Carla (mostly).

The aim initially was to think about the social work role on these rapport-building visits. They are not the same as providing counselling/therapy/emotional support but they are vital to building trust, so it is also important for the social worker not to pretend he is coming to see the family, as would 'a friend'. *The danger for social workers is failure to continue to be both 'reflective' and 'relational' (and aware of boundaries) and for this an equivalent style of supervision is needed*. The role requires resilience and persistence as well as other qualities.

After time, in Ferguson's case, it was reported that the work and relationships became 'co-constructed' – the social worker had made it clear who she was and 'where she was coming from' and the parents had made clear their strengths, weaknesses and fears. A relationship was built in which both social worker and parents could describe what was going on in each other's 'mind' in that they could make predictions and helpful comments to each other about what was happening in each meeting.

In Carla's case, the social work team decided to employ mentalization-based therapy (MBT) to provide extra support to Carla and Malc. This was based on the evidence that they had demonstrated some effective social and parenting skills in the past and that it would be possible to develop these over time. A social worker from the mental health team collaborated with the child safeguarding services to this end.

MBT supports a service user in reflecting on past traumas that hindered their development of capacities for sensitivity to others. Sometimes, too, their feelings about themselves become almost meaningless – in other words they become both numb to themselves and others. Many people who have had trauma in childhood will develop disorganized attachment styles which make them vulnerable to social and emotional dysfunction – both unable to care for themselves or for anyone else (Fonagy, 2000; Shemmings and Shemmings, 2011). Evidence from research has indicated that people who have been traumatized in early life may cope well much of the time but in the face of negative events, such as with Carla's recent life experiences, may temporarily be unable to make commitments, experience disturbance of body image and sense of their 'self' and also fail to see anyone else as having a normal range of emotional experience or even physical pain (Bateman and Fonagy, 2000; Fonagy et al., 2003).

## CHAPTER SUMMARY

In social work (like medicine and other similar professions) there is as much art as there is science in the face-to-face work. Each theory of HGD has something to offer to practice and a reflective-relational approach to putting theory into practice which takes account of:

- social work knowledge;
- information available;

- the individual practitioner's ability to think through available theory in context(s);
- professional and personal life experience.

Most people who come to the attention of social workers have highly complex lives and face multiple challenges as with the family of Maria Colwell, Orla, Carla and her family.

**CHAPTER SUMMARY** *continued*

Reading this chapter should help you to:

- Recognize that theory and practice are intrinsically related;
- See that it is helpful to think systematically about practice and theory;
- Employ a reflective-relational perspective to exploit the MDI approach to the lifespan;
- See how the lifespan complements MDI perspectives to provide a 'tool kit' to practice decision-making;

- Recognize also that no tool kit can ever replace *thinking* that is reflective and relational and which also draws upon existing theory.

In Part II of the book I expand the theoretical links between approaches to HGD, while continuing to bear in mind the gap between real life and theoretical explanations.

**FURTHER READING**

For understanding the origins and aims of mentalization-based therapy (MBT) more clearly, see the work of Peter Fonagy, Jeremy Holmes and various colleagues. For instance:

Fonagy, P., Target, M., Gergely, G., Allen, J.G. and Bateman, A.W. (2003) *The Developmental Roots of Borderline Personality Disorder in Early Attachment Relationships: A theory and some evidence.* Psychoanalytic Inquiry, 23(3), 412–459.

Holmes, J. (2010) *Exploring in Security: Towards an attachment-informed psychoanalytic psychotherapy.* London: Routledge.

Jan Fook and her colleagues have written clearly and comprehensively about critical reflection:

Fook, J. (2002) *Social Work: Critical theory and practice.* London: Sage.

Fook, J. and Gardner, F. (2010) *Practising Critical Reflection: A resource handbook.* Maidenhead: McGraw Hill/ Open University Press.

# II

# THE LIFESPAN: A MATERIAL-DISCURSIVE-INTRA-PSYCHIC APPROACH

In Part II I focus on theories from the MDI perspective which are appropriate to understanding the lifespan from infancy to old age. Each chapter begins with a description of the developmental psychosocial 'tasks', based on the psychosocial developmental stages identified by Erikson, and continues with the MDI contexts within which these tasks are conducted. At the end of the chapter, there is an *analysis* of at least one case example using a reflective-relational approach drawing upon these theories and providing a backdrop to practice.

All the cases will be taken from real-life examples. Some of these relate to people I have worked with or cases I have supervised. These have all been anonymized and are sometimes presented as composites. Other examples will be drawn from documents of inquiries where a case has been subjected to public scrutiny.

For each chapter, as before, three learning objectives are identified and reviewed to suggest key points that the reader might have taken up from the text.

# 7

# INFANCY AND EARLY CHILDHOOD: THE IMPORTANCE OF SECURITY AND TRUST

**LEARNING OBJECTIVES**

- To become familiar with the psychosocial lifespan tasks of infancy and early childhood.
- To explore the ways in which the development of attachment relationships is connected to HGD at this stage.
- To consider how the MDI theories presented might be applied to a reflective-relational consideration of real-life case material.

## Introduction

In Part I we considered the theoretical background and showed how Erik Erikson's approach to understanding the lifespan and material, discursive and intra-psychic (MDI) perspectives help us think critically about evidence from research and practice (Chapter 4). Particular emphasis was also placed on theories surrounding attachment relationships and how they interact with the sliding-scale model of lifespan development (Chapters 4 and 5).

Infancy and early childhood, from birth to (roughly) the age of four, represent a critical period of the lifespan throughout all theories of HGD. Even though development and growth take place well beyond infancy and early childhood, across the lifespan until the end of life, patterns established at the start of life continue to exert a powerful impact (Sugarman, 2001). These patterns not only shape our personality, but are the source of our anxieties and influence the types of relationships we have with friends, family, partners and our own children (Bandura, 1973; Klein, 1984; Meltzoff and Decety, 2003; Shechory and Sommerfeld, 2007; Shemmings, 2006). Further, following Chapter 5, attachment relationships at this stage influence brain structures (Schore, 2005). Cognitive neuroscientists also propose that early life experiences shape the configuration of our brains in other ways, for example, in our understanding of moral actions and accountability (Santosuosso and Bottalico, 2009). In this chapter we are going to examine early life with the understanding that the MDI processes impact on everything that follows through the lifespan.

During infancy and early childhood, defined here as birth until about the age of four (preschool), there are opportunities for the individual to gain a feeling of trust or mistrust in themselves and others. This is the beginning of having a sense of your place in the world. This development occurs through the varied everyday experiences that face the developing infant. There are both personal successes and triumphs to be had or shame and doubts which come from experiences of failure.

Examples of 'successes' might be the achievement of crawling across the floor so that the infant is 'rewarded' for having attained his goal. Failure might be the outcome of not being able to reach or grasp something or dropping a bottle and not being able to pick it up. If you watch a baby you will witness moods of both pleasure and rage, which are likely to be the result of having succeeded or having failed (Bick, 1964; Erikson, 1950/1963).

### Psychosocial tasks

Psychosocial tasks at all stages of the lifespan take place in MDI contexts, as I have proposed in Part I. The infant is born into a bio- and socio-material world, he learns to engage his discursive level of consciousness as he develops complex thought abilities, while, from birth, he has the capacity for primitive, and later, complex unconscious activity and emotion.

It is useful now to draw on all of these contexts and ways of thinking and feeling when considering HGD. As you shall see, issues of emotional security (Bowlby, 1988; Holmes, 2010) and the potential for disorganized attachment styles (Shemmings and Shemmings, 2011) correspond to the central struggles in infancy and early childhood. Too great a sense of mistrust and shame and doubt are clearly linked to an insecure and confusing start in life, and you looked at this in more detail in Chapter 4.

In the first stages of life, Erikson proposed that we engage in unconscious and conscious tasks in accord with the physical, social and emotional context. This is the core of what he called psychosocial development, as you saw in Chapter 2.

The first task (in infancy) is about establishing a degree of trust in self, environment and others who inhabit that environment. Failure to achieve this sense of trust results in a greater proportion of mistrust that becomes embedded in that person's identity. This process occurs during the first year or so of life (Table 4.1, p. 62).

The second task, which as with all the others builds upon what has been achieved earlier, involves gaining a sense of autonomy – a rudimentary foundation for identity – over shame and doubt. This state gains hold over a greater part of the developing self in young children who have been treated cruelly, neglectfully and inconsistently. This dynamic conflict takes place between the ages of (about) one year until three or four years of age.

I now consider these two early phases of the lifespan from an MDI perspective in the context of attachment theory, which complements psychosocial developmental matters at this stage.

## PAUSE AND REFLECT

**Trust and survival**

It is, of course, important to note that we all have some degree of mistrust in ourselves and others, and this is not overall a negative outcome. It enables us to think about and make judgments of others. A capacity for mentalization develops through our growing sense that others may not necessarily put our needs first, but we can survive that experience and negotiate our place in the world. Without such an understanding of failings in ourselves and others we would be unable to communicate effectively, our expectations would be unrealistic and we would set the bar too high.

A child who trusts themselves completely, and without question, will be unable to develop insight into his capacities, strengths and weaknesses, because he will assume he can do everything well. Similarly, a child who trusts everyone around to be on her side, with her interests at the forefront of their minds, will be unable to cope with the ambivalence present in all relationships (Finzi et al., 2001; Shemmings, 2006).

We all need to grasp – consciously and unconsciously – the imperfection in us all. If we aspired to perfection and expected the same of others we would find ourselves unable to live, love and work with others.

A child who has no sense of shame or self-doubt may have a poorly developed sense of empathy and be unable to mentalize, possibly displaying borderline personality characteristics (Fonagy et al., 2003).

A social worker would be similarly unequipped to make judgments in their cases, particularly complex ones. They might consider themselves to be omnipotent and their judgment to be infallible. That, of course, would spell disaster on a number of levels. To be able to operate *reflectively* and *relationally* is a consequence of our capacity to cope with uncertainty and the lack of perfection (Mollon, 2006) in self and others (Ruch, 2002).

We need to take these thoughts forward to think about every stage of the lifespan.

## The significance of the early months and years

None of us reaches school age without some sense of mistrust, shame and doubt, as you will recall from the discussion of Erikson's ideas. That is mostly a positive outcome because no-one has the perfect experience of early life. If we did have such a fabled ideal upbringing we would have no resilience to cope with our entry into the imperfect world or to be able to reflect on our own lack of perfection.

As part of the process of striving towards the person we will become, we also develop an understanding, in a primitive way, of what and who cannot be trusted. (See Table 4.1 to recall the stages and tasks in Erikson's model.)

A small baby who has good enough care from her primary carer (Winnicott, 1971/2001) is still likely to experience degrees of mistrust, shame and doubt but will *easily recover* their sense of competency and good feelings about who they are and about the people around them. As you will recall from Chapter 1, 'good enough care' means that parents attend enough for their babies to ensure they thrive, even though they themselves might consider they have not reached perfection, and that the child has experienced reasonably consistent secure attachment to his main care-taker (Ainsworth et al., 1978; Bowlby, 1988) As Michael Rutter emphasized, human beings, given enough basic consistency, are resilient.

On the other hand, the baby who does not receive positive acknowledgement for who he is, or a sense that the carer values him, and experiences inconsistent or even negligent and abusive interactions with important adults, will probably have difficulties in relationships throughout his life, suffer low self-esteem and mental health problems (Mollon, 2006; Shemmings and Shemmings, 2011). There is a danger, although it is not inevitable, that children who experience extreme neglect and inconsistent care or are witnesses or victims of domestic violence in early childhood are more likely than others to replicate these experiences with their own children (Dryden et al., 2010; Nicolson, 2010; Shemmings and Shemmings, 2011).

I want to look now at how the details of an MDI approach might help to make sense of this phase of the lifespan, starting with the material, which I break down into the bio-material and socio-material contexts.

### The bio-material context: conception and early growth

Biological development begins from conception when the egg/ovum is fertilized by a sperm to form the zygote (the fertilized egg). While the majority of conceptions occur *in utero,* through heterosexual intercourse, there are exceptions to this in which conception is assisted, frequently because of infertility and problems with conception (Dancet et al., 2011). However, there are reasons other than infertility for having assisted fertilization, such as lesbian couples where one or both partners wishes to become pregnant (Franklin, 1997).

At conception, the genetic inheritance of the future human being is laid down. This includes their sex, ethnicity, colour of eyes, hair and future height, as well as health, cognitive, intellectual and personality factors. Even so, the basic biology of conception is still not a total blueprint for the child's future. The social environment plays a vital and equally sustainable part in forming the person so that diet and the quality of the physical environment (e.g. housing, air quality) can all affect the outcome of the genetic inheritance.

Basic physical skills are similarly influenced by genes and environment, and within norms (e.g. size, weight, ability to sit up, crawl, walk and talk) there are individual differences based on the material context.

### The socio-material context

The socio-material context in infancy is closely related to the bio-material one in that rapid physical development links with the ability to experience the socio-material world. Think here about the work of Piaget described in Chapter 2 (Burman, 1997; Piaget, 1990). All knowledge of the infant's world begins with information coming through her senses (Sylva and Lunt, 1983). These are sight, hearing, taste, smell and touch. Using these senses the infant becomes aware of the environment and what is around her.

The infant interacts with the material context in order to develop processes that support this communication – *perception* and *cognition*. Perception is about awareness of the sensations that are experienced, thus gradually informing the infant that there is a world outside *and inside* her skin. Perception occurs through the eyes, ears and neurological sensors scattered throughout the skin and the internal organs. The infant can experience light and dark and very quickly can identify shapes. The infant hears and begins to identify specific sounds. The infant feels pain and discomfort and of course pleasurable sensations.

Through these sensations a sense of the world develops, as described in Chapter 2, particularly with reference to Piaget's work. The infant therefore begins to engage in a *relationship with the material context* via and with her own body and with the physical and inter-personal environment (Kellman and Arterberry, 2000). This includes language recognition leading to the ability to form differentiated sounds and speech (Dehaene-Lambertz et al., 2002). In recent years, the information about the bio-material context of infant development has focused on evidence from cognitive neuroscience where the technologies for investigation have become increasingly sophisticated (Schore, 2005; Werker and Tees, 2005).

*Memory* also begins in infancy through the perception of repeated events, demonstrated by the ability to repeat actions and recognize faces, voices and toys (Rovee-Collier and Hayne, 2000). In Chapter 3, particularly in the section on *learning*, you saw how, for example, crawling across the floor could be a reward in itself (a form of operant conditioning) and it might also be accompanied by positive responses from the carer. As a result, a primitive, preverbal sense of satisfaction would be paired with a warm sensation from outside (i.e. praise from the carer) (Kim, 2001; Staddon and Cerutti, 2003).

Look back at the story of Little Albert (also in Chapter 3) in which the baby was conditioned (or had learned) to become terrified of mice (Watson, 2009). Learning and memory are related to each other, primarily in that we mostly memorize what we learn in order to make use of the knowledge. The significance of understanding learning and memory and how we manage them are considered below.

Bronfenbrenner's (Bronfenbrenner and Morris, 2007) bio-ecological model of human development (Chapter 3) highlights the multiple layers of systems which surround us and with which we interact throughout the lifespan. There is a large and growing body of evidence to show how poverty impacts across the lifespan of the individual and is transmitted across generations, and poverty and social inequalities are intrinsically linked (Bird, 2007).

One such study, conducted for Save the Children (Harper et al., 2003), examined the conditions of childhood that might lead to poverty throughout life and transfer poverty to the next generation as well. Using UNICEF's basic framework for survival, protection, development and participation, the authors concluded that social relationships impacted on the immediate environment, so that children benefitted if they were able to engage in enabling relationships, and that the 'assets' transferred across generations – such as property or debt, nutritional care, education, freedom from disease, value systems and gender biases – impact as enabling or inhibiting mechanisms, depending on their quality.

---

**PAUSE AND REFLECT**

**Poverty and early childhood**

Consider this news headline that was stimulated by the recession in the UK.

A rising number of children are going to school tired, hungry and poorly dressed because they are living in poverty, a survey of teachers suggests.*

It was reported in this article based on a study by the Association of Teachers and Lecturers that nearly 80% of teachers say they have pupils living in a family below the poverty line.

One in four teachers reported that poverty among their pupils has increased since the start of the recession.

One teacher told the researchers about a boy who had been laughed at by classmates when changing for PE because he had not been wearing underpants.

In another case, a teacher said one sixth-form student had not eaten for three days because the child's mother had no money to give the child for food.

With these examples of child poverty come shame and humiliation and a lasting sense of inferiority.

*uk.news.yahoo.com/5/20110415/tuk-children-going-to-school-hungry-and-45dbed5.html, 15 April 2011

---

## The discursive context

In some ways infants and very young children have but a rudimentary ability to draw on language to make sense of their lives, implying that a discursive consciousness and the ability to reflect will be relatively primitive at this age. However, following Piaget on cognitive development (Chapter 2), Giddens on levels of consciousness (Chapter 5) and Mead on symbolic interactionist perspectives on development (Chapter 3), each of us has a degree of *reflexivity* through which we make sense of the symbols and repetitions in the material context. This is a form of elementary discursive consciousness. Thus Piaget (cited in Burman, 1997) talked of the child as telling stories in order to organize a version of himself (a narrative) and organize his active memory (Piaget, 1946/1969). Mead and subsequent symbolic interactionists also outline how mind and society are intimately linked and how reflexivity enables the sense of who we are and how we fit into the outer world and our own world.

As Mead describes it, the *I* is the stream of our consciousness and sense of subjectivity that then automatically focuses on the *me* (object) to understand and explain our *self* to ourselves and to others. So, for example, you might have an angry exchange (I) on seeing a colleague using the last drop of (your) milk in their

coffee and then wonder what on earth possessed you to make such a fuss, potentially endangering a relationship (me).

David Ingleby (1977) argued that the study of child psychology generally is based
on ideology because what becomes scientific knowledge is based upon the political
context. Think also here about fashions in research. Erica Burman (1997) further
suggests that psychologists (and other scientists) also draw on discourses around
infants/infancy and all children/childhood to *construct* a developmental psychology. She argues that infancy and childhood are, therefore, constructed around such
concepts as vulnerability, innocence, dependency and hope for the future, and it is
these discourses that reflect cultural and ideological practices.

These ideologies and discursive constructions have a profound impact on what
are believed to be norms of behaviour and they potentially undermine social work
assessments of risk and plans for support to children and families. Remember it
was not that long ago, perhaps in the late 1960s when some of your own lecturers
and managers might have been at school, that school students might be caned
– sometimes in front of the school, and that parents might even be urged to beat
their children. In some quarters this is still advocated as either an effective deter-
rent or a means of encouraging children who might otherwise behave badly or be
lazy (Grogan-Kaylor, 2004; Larzelere, 2000).

## The intra-psychic context

Freud's ideas about infantile sexuality, and thus infantile *agency*, described in detail
in Chapter 3, have mobilized thinking around HGD in a way that contrasts with the
experimental developmental psychology perspective, which focuses mostly on the
non-emotional, objective and measurable features of infancy such as vision and
perception. However, even the mainstream developmental psychology textbooks
refer to Freud, mostly because of the need to examine the relationship between
the infant and the mother (and later the father) as integral to intellectual, biological
and emotional development (Freud, 1923/2007; Gay, 1995). Freud's ideas also now
coincide with some contemporary neuroscientific studies of the brain. While Freud
did not have access to contemporary technologies, his concern, along with brain
scientists, was with mental structures and their development.

Following from the outline in Chapter 3 of Freud's stages of psychosexual development (onto which Erikson has built), it is important to see how others also
developed ideas from this work which have fed into psychoanalytic therapy and counselling. These are ideas that need to be (re)visited by social workers involved in child
protection, family support and mental health work (Bower, 2005; Waddell, 2005).

Many of the influential ideas about child care and children's mental health,
originating in the twentieth century, came from experts taking a psychoanalytic

perspective. We have already considered the work of John Bowlby at some length (Chapter 5), but the other important contributor was Donald Winnicott. Both Bowlby and Winnicott based their original ideas on work by Freud, Erikson and Klein (1959/1975). Their work focused on the significance of very early life for emotional, social and intellectual development. Winnicott (Smith et al., 2012) made important contributions to our understanding of both the socio-material context in infancy – his thinking about the 'good enough' mother who manages to provide a mostly positive context for her infant to develop – and the importance of play. He was also instrumental in thinking about the intra-psychic contexts of development, particularly about the *false self*. He believed this was a consequence for a child who was influenced to believe that he was perfect by a parent and, unconsciously realizing that he was not, feeling he had to be responsive to the needs of others who thought of him this way, thereby not expressing his own needs. This false self-position, as Winnicott calls it, makes the child feel safer (Gomez, 1997).

### Who was Donald Winnicott?

Donald Winnicott (1896-1971) was a paediatrician and psychoanalyst, one of the founders of the Object Relations school of psychoanalysis and a leading contributor to the British Independent Group of psychoanalysis. He studied medicine, with a break in studies during the First World War, when he was a probationer surgeon in the British Navy. He eventually worked at Paddington Green Hospital in London for around forty years and gave over 20,000 consultations with the mother-and-child couple (Symington, 1986).

Winnicott's career was unusual in that he was a child psychoanalyst who also worked with the *mothers*. One of his influential concepts was that of the good enough mother, in recognition that many mothers constantly worried and felt guilt because they were not perfect. Winnicott saw that, provided enough love and good experiences were provided for the infant/child, their environment would be one that would lead to health (Winnicott, 1965).

The good enough mother was able to provide what Winnicott named a *holding environment* for her child, as did the therapist working with a patient or client. The emphasis in the mother/baby relationship was on physically holding the baby so that the baby would be secure and feel the mother's body. The baby developed a sense of being held, fed, bathed and looked after, and he would consequently feel some comfort from that, psychically. That experience would then develop to an understanding of the family and the outside world. Therefore, the baby would have taken in a sense of how he was mothered and the feelings in response to that and would face his future life with those objects internalized to make sense of his relationships. Winnicott was also interested in children's play, and here he was concerned with the development of the self (Winnicott, 1971/2001). He considered that it was important for children to have opportunities to play early in life and that maturing too early (having a sense of self that is based upon responsibility and others' expectations rather than maturing through play and thus self-discovery) leads to the development of a 'false' self. Therefore, in common with some other analysts, particularly Freud and Erikson, Winnicott argued for a model of maturational stages of development (Winnicott, 1965).

## *Attachment and trust*

Erikson and Freud were both concerned with the impact of loss and change on development, and it was Freud's work that initially sparked clinicians and researchers such as Harlow, Bowlby, Ainsworth, Main and so on (Chapter 5) to consider the damage that early loss from lack of secure attachment might confer on infants and young children and on adults who had had poor relationships in early life (Ainsworth et al., 1978; Bifulco, 2004; Bowlby, 1988; Fonagy, 2000; Main, 1995; Parkes et al., 1991).

Despite the focus on specific stages or events during the lifespan, it is impossible, by definition, to take any process or stage of life as a mutually exclusive, discrete entity. Erikson himself is very clear that we carry with us all that went before, through each developmental stage, and that at each stage our lives are enmeshed in the lifespan of others. This position has been echoed consistently by subsequent writers (Baltes et al., 2007; Bee and Mitchell, 1984; Sugarman, 1986, 2001).

At the early stages of infancy, Erikson suggested that the key task for the infant is to develop a sense of trust over mistrust (in both the self and others). This concurs with Shemmings' view (2006) that the concept of attachment itself implies that the self is constructed as socially embedded. In other words, the individual/self/ identity is not an objective observable entity but is dynamic or fluid and develops biologically, socially and psychologically with all these characteristics constantly intertwined and interacting.

Erikson also identified the central role of attachment in the process of gaining trust or mistrust. He emphasized the highly complex nature of these processes, showing how behaviour and styles of attachment might seem the same but have very different meanings to the people involved:

> to hold on can become a destructive and cruel retaining or restraining, and it can become a pattern of care: to have and to hold. To let go, too, can turn into an inimical letting loose of destructive forces, or it can become a relaxed 'to let pass' and 'to let be'. (Erikson, 1950/1963: 226)

This notion that holding on can be destructive is interesting because it is somewhat contrary to the current emphasis on strong early attachment relationships being secure and thus, overall, positive. Erikson's concepts of holding and letting go, however, have important implications across the lifespan, and particularly for the consideration of attachment styles.

As we saw in Chapter 5, attachment styles vary. Bowlby's initial categorization only focused on the positive experience of secure attachment and the ambivalence of the anxious/resistant and anxious/avoidant styles which are both about rejection. Main (1995) and Bifulco (Bifulco et al., 2003) also stress that strong attachment is, on the whole, likely to lead to positive emotional health. It might be, though, that, for some parents/parent substitutes, the strong attachment is focused on *their* needs and might thus lead to a sense of disorganized attachment (Hesse and Main, 2000; Shemmings and Shemmings, 2011).

To think about this further, Bion's idea of *maternal reverie*, which I shall explain shortly, is suggestive of a communication between the infant and mother/mother substitute that either relieves or heightens unconscious anxiety. In other words, Bion indicates the potential for toxicity (or a negative force) in some close relationships.

As Erikson indicates, therefore, it is the infant's capacity to understand, albeit in a primitive way, that the mother/primary care-taker will return time and again, and when she does it will be for *the sake of the infant's care*, that enables the infant to trust other people to 'keep their word'. The infant needs to experience positive security and trust. This sense of security also enables the infant to trust herself to be lovable enough not to be deserted.

It may also be worth thinking about how we can either hold on to or let go of particular experiences in our lives, including those that are deeply disturbing and influence how we see the world in adulthood. This will be explored further in later chapters that are concerned particularly with trauma and bereavement (see Chapter 12).

The overall emphasis of this work on holding was initially to explain how the infant experienced the bio-social context. It was developed to show how the relationship with the mother/mother substitute and the father (or father substitute or absent father) is fundamental to psychological (conscious and unconscious) development throughout the lifespan. This is particularly important for thinking further about the origins and development of attachment styles (Bifulco, 2004; Bifulco et al., 2003; Holmes, 2010).

### Object relations and intra-psychic development

Particularly relevant to this early stage of development is object relations theory, based on the work of Fairburn (Gomez, 1997; Waddell, 2005) and including that of Winnicott, Bion and Klein among others. Object relations, considered a British development, although developed from Freudian psychoanalytic theory was distinct from it. Object relations focuses upon the person having a dual relationship with their 'inner' world of phantasies (conscious and unconscious) and the external world of others. Gomez suggests that, while there are clear overlapping ideas and interests among those whose work is considered to be part of the Object Relations school, they are actually a diverse group of theorists.

Fairburn was concerned to show that life was more about relationships than in-stinctual drives, in contrast to Freudian ideas (Gomez, 1997). Bowlby, whose work was arguably among the most significant from this group, adhered to object rela-tions ideas, but his work on attachment became appreciated in its own right.

### The roots of anxiety

Klein (whose work preceded and supported the development of the Object Rela-tions school) was concerned with the nature and origin of unconscious phantasies in early infancy of anxiety, their impact on adult life, and of how preverbal, primitive *defences against anxiety* characterize an individual's inner world and their experi-ence of social and emotional relationships (Klein, 1959; Segal, 1964). In contrast to Freud, Klein (e.g. 1959) considered that the ego and id develop from the start of life. She suggested that the ego – the *manager* of the conscious – defends against unconscious impulses in a number of ways, some helpful to mental well-being and others not. Through meticulous observations of infants she hypothesized that from birth we experience anxiety of a 'persecutory nature' and, without being able to grasp it intellectually, the infant, unconsciously, feels every discomfort 'as if' it were being inflicted by hostile forces.

Frustration, discomfort and pain are experienced as persecution and their con-comitants (frustration and hate) become destructive impulses that *are still opera-tive in later life* (1959: 248–249). We unconsciously take in the world around us (our experience of others, i.e. objects and how we relate to them) and expel impulses we cannot tolerate (e.g. extremes of anxiety and hatred) onto others as a means of defending the ego. This process is called 'splitting'. The ego splits off the bad, in-tolerable feelings of frustration and badness that produce feelings of persecutory anxieties and we *project* them into others.

Early infancy and the primitive unarticulated feelings that arise are brought to the surface again in adulthood, particularly when individuals go through stressful situations such as living with or leaving an abusive partner. If the woman's mother/ carer during infancy had been good enough at containing the persecutory anxie-ties during what Klein terms the *paranoid-schizoid position*, the person will grow up with a sense of autonomy (or basic trust) and the ability to care for themselves. In this position the infant, and at times the adult (who will return psychically to that infantile state when she is under extreme pressure), fears retaliation for their ag-gressive and phantasized envious attacks on the mother figure. When the baby is about three months old she becomes able to tolerate frustrations and integrate her experiences rather than split them off. This is what Klein called the *depressive position*. If the baby has experienced enough good care and containment for their persecutory anxieties in the paranoid-schizoid position, then it is likely that the individual will be able to hold within herself some representation of good objects (Smith et al., 2012).

Most of us believe that our inner world is manageable and that either we our-selves or another (friend, relative, therapist) can take care of us and support some of our overwhelming feelings. However, we cannot overcome unconscious impuls-es if we continue to expel rather than acknowledge and work through them.

### Containing anxiety

During infancy and childhood the responsible adults/parents have the opportunity to modify the feelings of persecutory anxiety by holding the boundaries between phantasy and reality, while acknowledging the feelings that persecutory phanta-sies of anxiety may represent. This includes not only containment of the child's fears but also of their aggression, cruelty and sadism, all of which are part of nor-mal primitive behaviours seen in infancy (Segal, 1993). In other words, the carer of the infant will tolerate the infant's frustrations, rages, upsets and fears, try to understand them and give back to the infant a sense of security from those fears. Some carers, who have not had their own anxieties and frustrations so contained, still experience primitive fears and will exacerbate the infant's feelings rather than containing and comforting. This is not making a case to 'blame' the mother/parent/ carer but an indication of how support might be offered to them in order to soothe their own primitive fears and enable them to do the same for their own children.

The counsellor or psychotherapist performs a very similar role vis-à-vis the cli-ent or patient seeking help, that is to 'hold' (or contain) the client's unacceptable and distressing feelings that have been brought about by a trauma or pain that resonates with early anxieties from infancy (Klein, 1959).

Cognitive neuroscientists have suggested that uncontained anxiety in infancy shapes neural pathways in the brain (Swain et al., 2007).

### Wilfred Bion and the concepts of container/contained and 'maternal reverie'

Bion, an important British psychoanalyst, developed the concept of the container/ contained which has important implications not only for infant development but also for the role and experience of professional social workers, counsellors and psychotherapists (Bion, 1962; Smith et al., 2012). Bion theorized these concepts as a fundamental inter-subjective experience of emotional communication between an infant and her mother, and thus between the analysand and analyst (Grotstein, 2007). At the beginning of his life, the baby does not have access to a thought/

thinking because his mental apparatus is not mature enough to *metabolize* and integrate these very first mental or proto-mental materials. Bion has described this as having thoughts without a thinker (Grotstein, 2007). These primitive experiences correspond to extremely archaic bodily feelings, to emotional states linked to the infant's very earliest sensory and relational experiences, which he cannot utilize as such. The baby, therefore, has to divert these feelings through an Other, which in this case is the maternal object (Bion, 1962, 1963, 1967).

The infant thus projects undigested/indigestible feelings into the psyche of her mother (or maternal object) who lends the infant her own 'thought-thinking apparatus' to reshape, detoxify and transform these primitive fearful feelings into manageable ones. This material can then be assimilated by the infant and integrated into her own mental functioning. This transformation is due to the mother's capacity for maternal reverie, which thus takes away the overwhelming toxicity of primitive fearful feelings produced and felt by the infant (or by the patient).

### MAIN IDEAS OF THE OBJECT RELATIONS SCHOOL OF PSYCHOANALYSIS

The Object Relations School of psychoanalysis (mostly based in Britain) focused on very early infancy, and thus has been influential in developing theory and practice related to this period of the lifespan. It is, of course, almost impossible to test these theories empirically (i.e. experimentally). However, researchers at the clinic based at the Tavistock and Portman NHS Trust in London have conducted hundreds of hours of observational studies and evaluated therapy outcomes (including child psychotherapy) which have ensured that their contributions are taken seriously. Recent use of MRI scanning and brain imaging have contributed further to the validity of much of the psychoanalytic ideas about infancy while challenging others. Also, it is important to remember that there are critical debates between and within the psychoanalytic schools themselves (Gomez, 1997; Smith et al., 2012).

## PAUSE AND REFLECT

### Relationships and infancy

What happens when parents seem to have little ability to bond with their children or to keep them safe?

How might you identify good enough parenting and a holding environment?

What knowledge supports social workers in:

- Identifying potential cases of child neglect and abuse?
- Developing an effective formulation of the problems?

- Formulating a strategy for intervention?
- Deciding on support procedures?

As you have seen, experiences in infancy and early childhood revolve around the meaning of relationships. Whether we mature to become secure, moderately trusting, resilient and able to manage our own and others' anxiety depends on those early attachments and the quality of relationships (see also Chapter 5).

An ability to understand self in a relationship and reflect accordingly is the overriding prerequisite for social work theory and practice.

The case of the murder of four-year old Jasmine Beckford is a story of generations of abuse, neglect and dysfunctional family life. While Jasmine's mother and
step-father were unequivocally culpable in her torture and death, in the proposed
reflective-relational formulation, I want the reader to consider the impact of their
early years' experiences on all of the protagonists.

I particularly want you to think about whether an analysis of cases such as this
can help provide insight into:

• Social work practice and supervision;
• The organizations involved;
• The role of blame in trying to repair systems after such tragedies (Blom-Cooper,
  1985; Cooper, 2005; Dingwall, 1986; Model, 1986; Rustin, 2005; Sheldon, 1987).

## The murder of Jasmine Beckford and the transmission of inter-generational abuse

Jasmine Beckford weighed just 23lbs when she died in 1984 at the age of four
from a blow, inflicted by her step-father Morris Beckford, that dislodged her brain.
The case of the Beckford family was highly complicated. For the final months of
Jasmine's life, Morris had kept her chained to a bed in a tiny attic. Her death was
finally attributed to brain damage, although the pathologist found she had 40 other
injuries covering her face and body, including 20 broken bones. Some of the injuries happened in the days before she died. Other injuries, including leg fractures,
broken ribs, burns and cuts were months old.

In what follows I look at some of the circumstances of Jasmine Beckford's life
and death from the perspectives of (a) the family and (b) the social workers who
were involved at various stages. I then review some of the literature that has refo-
cused on this and other cases to consider practice.

There had been generations of abuse and neglect in the families of both Jasmine's mother, Beverley Lorrington, and her step-father, Morris Beckford. From
the information available about Jasmine Beckford's step-father and mother it is
apparent that there were *attachment problems* between both of them and their
parents and grandparents, which probably damaged their abilities to look after
Jasmine and her sister. It is also worth noting (although with caution about making too great a generalization) what evolutionary psychology has to say about the
way that step-parents might have less investment in the welfare of non-biological
children than the biological parent.

### The people involved

**Morris Beckford** was born in Jamaica in June 1959. He arrived in Britain as a nine-
year-old with two of his sisters to be reunited with his parents who had left him in

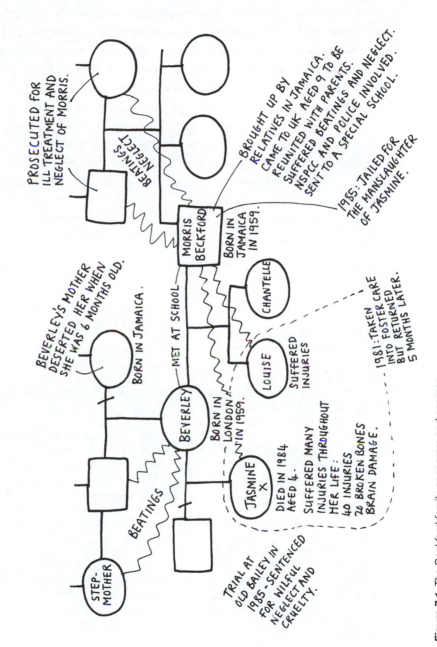

**Figure 7.1** *The Beckford family genogram and ecomap*

PROSECUTED FOR ILL TREATMENT AND NEGLECT OF MORRIS.

BEATINGS NEGLECT

BROUGHT UP BY RELATIVES IN JAMAICA. CAME TO UK AGED 9 TO BE REUNITED WITH PARENTS. SUFFERED BEATINGS AND NEGLECT. NSPCC AND POLICE INVOLVED. SENT TO A SPECIAL SCHOOL.

1985: JAILED FOR THE MANSLAUGHTER OF JASMINE.

MORRIS BECKFORD

BORN IN JAMAICA IN 1959.

MET AT SCHOOL

BEVERLEY'S MOTHER DESERTED HER WHEN SHE WAS 6 MONTHS OLD.

BORN IN JAMAICA.

CHANTELLE

LOUISE SUFFERED INJURIES

1981: TAKEN CARE INTO FOSTER CARE BUT RETURNED 5 MONTHS LATER.

BEVERLEY

BORN IN LONDON IN 1959.

JASMINE ✗

DIED IN 1984 AGED 4.

SUFFERED MANY INJURIES THROUGHOUT HER LIFE: 40 INJURIES 26 BROKEN BONES BRAIN DAMAGE.

STEP-MOTHER

BEATINGS

TRIAL AT OLD BAILEY IN 1985 - SENTENCED FOR WILFUL NEGLECT AND CRUELTY.

Jamaica with relatives. By the time he was thirteen he had been accused of stealing from his own home and was being beaten by both his parents. The teenage Beckford had been forced to sleep in an outhouse without a bed. After attention from the Police and NSPCC (National Society for the Prevention of Cruelty to Children) both of his parents were prosecuted for his ill-treatment and neglect. He was eventually sent to a special school where he met fellow pupil, Beverley Lorrington.

**Beverley Lorrington** was born in November 1959 in London. Her Jamaican-born mother had deserted the family when Beverley was only six months old. Beverley later claimed that her childhood was a miserable succession of beatings by both her step-mother and her father. She began living with Morris Beckford when she was 19 years old and several months pregnant with Jasmine, who was not Beckford's child. Jasmine was born on 2 December 1979 in London and given the name Jasmine Lorrington. Shortly afterwards, her birth records were changed at the insistence of Morris Beckford.

*Morris and Beverley therefore both had histories of separation, loss, disruption, physical abuse and neglect that should have been identified as major risk factors*

## PAUSE AND REFLECT

**Case details in summary**

- Two-and-a-half years after Jasmine's birth, Beverley gave birth to Jasmine's sister, Louise Beckford.
- When Louise was only five months old, she was admitted to hospital with a broken arm and eye hemorrhages.
- Doctors warned that Louise's injuries were non-accidental.
- Three days later, 18-month-old Jasmine was taken to the same hospital with a broken femur. Jasmine was discharged from hospital after six weeks.
- Both children were then made subject of a *Place of Safety Order* – so the local authority had full parental rights over the children.
- The children were placed on the *At Risk* register and taken into foster care.
- Two months later, Morris Beckford was found guilty of assaulting Louise, causing actual bodily harm, and given a suspended six-month jail term and a £250 fine.
- Five months later, in April 1982, a case conference of professionals in Brent decided

that both Jasmine and Louise, who had been with foster parents, should be returned home on a trial basis.
- Between April and November 1982, Beverley spasmodically took Jasmine to a day nursery. Between January and June 1983, Jasmine attended nursery school – but on increasingly irregular occasions. Her last recorded attendance was on 9 September 1983.
- The family had a family aide (who gave support in the home to Beverley) but, when she left the employment of Brent, she was not replaced.
- The couple's third child, Chantelle, was born shortly before Christmas 1983 – seven months before Jasmine was to die.
- At 5.30pm on 5 July 1984 Jasmine was dead on arrival at hospital.
- Following their trial at the Old Bailey in spring 1985, Beckford was jailed for ten years for Jasmine's manslaughter while her mother, Beverley Lorrington, was sentenced to 18 months for wilful neglect and cruelty.

I shall now offer an analysis for you to think about using a MDI framework.

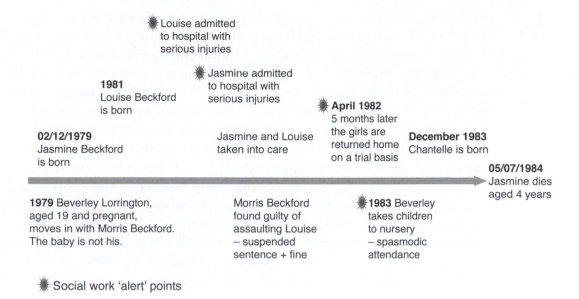

*Figure 7.2* *Events leading up to Jasmine's death*

## The material context

I am keeping the bio- and socio-material context discussions together for this section. The bio-material context mostly involves the physical injuries and neglect, including lack of nourishment.

It is important to consider, first, how relationships, constituting the socio-material context, were experienced in the lives of Jasmine's mother and step-father. Beckford could never be excused for what he did, but it is important to note his journey to becoming such a monster. He had been separated from his parents early in life and, although he may have managed to form an attachment relationship with his sisters and relatives who looked after him as a young child, he was separated again and sent to live with two strangers – his parents. These parent/strangers appeared to have little care for what he had been through and made his life more shameful by their accusations, their violent physical abuse, cruelty, humiliation and rejection.

Morris was raised in anger and violence and possibly projected his shame and humiliation onto his children and step-daughter. In meeting Beverley he found someone who needed him, but perhaps she herself was unaware of how to meet and manage Beckford's unmet needs, and may also have been unable to do so.

At six months of age, Beverley herself suffered a sudden painful and cruel separation from her mother who had not managed to bond effectively with her. What would this have meant to the infant? It would have been confusing and it is likely that Beverley would have grown up to feel that she was unlovable. Also, as we saw in Chapter 5, infants who have had no comfort in their lives also become emotionally stilted. This would suggest that Beverley found difficulty with putting herself in the place of another (thus she would have a low capacity for mentalization).

Beverley was subsequently humiliated and shamed by her father and stepmother who did not seem to want her around them. This would not merely have reinforced her feelings of being unlovable, but provoked the need to find an attachment figure who needed and valued her. She became pregnant at an early age, possibly while trying to find love, and (presumably) was deserted by Jasmine's biological father. She is unlikely to have understood how to read others' signs about relationships, although attuned to being used, shamed and humiliated, so (perhaps unconsciously) was drawn to Jasmine's biological father, who then deserted her.

It is noteworthy, therefore, that Morris wanted to stay with her and to act as a father to Jasmine, which must have made Beverley feel that she was loved – perhaps for the first time in her life. What the couple did to their children needs to be thought through carefully to understand both the emotional (intra-psychic) and socio-behavioural (bio- and socio-material) contexts. Why didn't the assessment of risk to the Beckford children not take account of the psychic and social histories of Morris and Beverley?

The Inquiry into Jasmine's death was chaired by Louis Blom-Cooper QC (Blom-Cooper, 1985). Olive Stevenson, a distinguished and well known social work professor in the 1980s, wrote an editorial (1986) in which she drew similarities and distinctions between this case and that of Maria Colwell. The concern in these and all the subsequent reports about child deaths following abuse and neglect had been with finding out what had gone wrong and apportioning blame – with the aim that this kind of thing would never happen again (Braye and Preston-Shoot, 2006; Cooper, 2005; Ferguson, 2001; Munro, 2005). But of course it continues to do so.

It is not within the scope of this book to look in detail at the Inquiry findings or the recommendations. It would be useful, though, for you to read the report and Stevenson's editorial, and also other texts that are recommended at the end of this chapter. However, to summarize, the inquiry identified the following points of blame:

- Jasmine's death was predictable and preventable.
- There was poor communication between health visitors and social workers; similarly communication was poor between the nursery staff and the key workers. Therefore, the significance of Jasmine's injuries and absence from nursery went unheeded.
- The foster parents had believed the placement with them was to be long term and when they found the children were to be returned they became 'obstructive'

– again poor communication between the service users and departments in the social work agency.

- When Jasmine was home on trial the social worker did not see her alone. She visited while Jasmine was watching the TV along with her mother and Chantelle the new-born half-sister.
- The failure to consider a care order for Chantelle was also noted in the Inquiry report.
- There was, overall, a lack of appropriate monitoring of the Beckford children.

The report recommended higher competency training for social workers in both specialist areas and for duty work.

It is the matter of blame – both blame levelled at the organization (mainly child protection services) and the social worker and her manager that warrant further scrutiny and thought here. The paper written shortly after the Inquiry by Elizabeth Model reinforces this (1986). She draws attention to the report's reference to the quality of social work practice. Talking of the social worker, Model suggests:

> Her gaze was focused on Beverley Lorrington and Morris Beckford; she averted her eyes to the children to be aware of them only as and when they were with their parents, hardly ever to observe their development, and never to communicate with Jasmine on her own. The two children were regarded as mere appendages to their parents who were treated as the clients, although [the social worker] did tell the Magistrates in 1981 that her 'primary role is the welfare of the children'. (p. 293)

The supervisor was also criticized for not advising and supporting the social worker to ensure that Jasmine (along with Louise) was seen and talked to away from their parents. There are very strong echoes in the things that Eileen Munro has said in the *Munro Review of Child Protection* (2011) about the role and experiences of social workers.

## PAUSE AND REFLECT

### Some lessons to be learned from inquiries into child-care failures

Social services and individual social workers were ascribed much of the blame for this tragedy. Other cases preceded it and others have followed, so it is important to reflect on how, as a practitioner, you might make decisions based on available evidence.

Issues raised by inquiries such as Blom-Cooper on Beckford consistently appear to focus on two problematic areas:

- the dysfunctions in the system, and
- the poor practice of individual social workers and their managers.

In the Beckford case, the system within the London Borough of Brent and other agencies revolved around communication failures – both

## PAUSE AND REFLECT

➡  internal and external. Subsequent reports about child protection failures have also identified this as a point of serious weakness in the systems, and the solution has always been to reinforce the protocols and bureaucracy. Thus, the professionalism of the workers and their agencies has been attacked (Cooper, 2005; Rustin, 2005). Both Rustin and Cooper have drawn attention to the 'profoundly disturbing impact of what they are trying to manage' (Rustin, 2004: 11). That is not to say that the social work practitioners in all these cases are blameless – it is to raise a fundamental question about practice and the ways in which the system both supports and undermines it (Howe, 1996).

Therefore, it is important to explore the relationship between bureaucracy and 'tick box' protocols and to examine what happened to the social work practitioners and their practice below the surface.

Some further questions related to HGD theory are:

- What were the risk factors that might have alerted the social work and other professionals to the dangers to Jasmine and her sisters?
- What were the relevant attachment issues in this family?
- Would explanations from evolutionary psychology about blood ties help to throw light on the behaviour of the adults in this case?
- Could you distinguish Morris' behaviour towards his biological children from his behaviour to Jasmine?
- What would you try to observe when visiting a family that might be at risk of violence?
- At what points and in what ways might more effective social work intervention have prevented Jasmine's death and injuries to others (Ingram, 2012; Munro, 2005)?

## CHAPTER SUMMARY

This chapter explored the MDI approach in infancy and early childhood. Early childhood and infancy are critical times in the life of humans, and there is much evidence that mental health and social relationships throughout life will be undermined by early deprivation of secure attachment, being unable to invest one's self and others with sufficient trust, and being overwhelmed by shame and self-doubt. These problems in infancy and early childhood will have further consequences, in all likelihood resulting in social exclusion, poor physical health, poverty and failure to support the next generation.

Evidence for these consequences comes from the clinical studies of Freud and Bowlby, experimental studies about imprinting and bonding, cognitive neuroscience evidence about the impact of neglect in infancy on the brain and the work of Howe, Bifulco and Shemmings

on the importance of understanding the role of attachment styles for adult relationships. This also needs to be seen in the context of Erikson's early stages of the lifespan in which, consciously and unconsciously, the infant and young child begins to gain a primitive sense of self-esteem.

It would appear from the evidence that beliefs about the impact of the early attachment relationships have become taken-for-granted and the consequences of this may be grave.

Reading this chapter should therefore:

- Help you to understand both how potentially vulnerable, but also how resilient, human beings can be.
- Draw attention to some of the ways in which social work as a social institution has failed, and perhaps crucially *been* failed by the socio-political system.

**FURTHER READING**

Blom-Cooper, L. (1985) *A Child in Trust: Report of the Panel of Inquiry into the circumstances surrounding the death of Jasmine Beckford.* London: London Borough of Brent.

Howe, D. (1996) Surface and Depth in Social Work Practice. In N. Parton (ed.), *Social Theory, Social Change and Social Work.* London: Routledge.

Rustin, M. (2005) Conceptual Analysis of Critical Moments in Victoria Climbié's Life. *Child & Family Social Work*, 10(1), 11–19.

Stevenson, O. (1986) Guest editorial on the Jasmine Beckford Inquiry. *British Journal of Social Work*, 16, 501–510.

Waddell, M. (2005) *Inside Lives: Psychoanalysis and the Growth of Personality.* London: Karnac.

# chapter

# 8

# OLDER CHILDHOOD: FINDING A PLACE IN THE WORLD OF THE FAMILY AND SCHOOL

**LEARNING OBJECTIVES**

- To understand the challenges for development on entering school and the social world.
- To recognize the risks to children at this stage of the lifespan, including a sense of failure in the development of their skills, bodies and ability to interact with others.
- To consider the ways in which the MDI contexts influence the development of moral reasoning and behaviours.

## Introduction

In Chapter 7 we considered the early years of childhood from infancy until starting school. All childhood represents periods of massive changes physically, intellectually, socially and emotionally, but starting school marks an important turning point in a child's life. It is a turning point mostly because, regardless of how social a child's early years have been and how populated by friends and extended family, going to school means turning outwards. Your back is towards home and you begin to face your life in social institutions. You may have been to nursery or play-group, but school is the first organization that you *have* to attend.

Following early childhood and before reaching adolescence, children make major developmental advances towards abstract thought, including the ability to reflect upon their sense of selfhood, recognizing also that there is a world of others whose lives go on even when the child himself is not there. You will have read and thought about this while reading all the earlier chapters (Erikson, 1950/1963; Giddens, 1991; Piaget, 1990; Sylva and Lunt, 1983). The ability to be reflexive is important because it enables the child to understand concepts of time passing and mortality, thus gaining a sense of a future and a past in their own lives and the lives of others. It also marks the beginning of a sense of morality – an understanding that their actions might harm others (Arsenio and Lemerise, 2004; Kohlberg, 1981; Waddell, 2005).

## Psychosocial tasks

In Erikson's lifespan model the child will be dealing with *initiative*. This includes, of course, entering school and operating independently from the family by coping with schoolwork, developing competitive sporting skills and making new relationships with peers and teachers. If this all leads to too much failure the child will have a sense of *guilt* about his place in the world. We probably all know adults who seem to feel unworthy and guilty about almost everything they do. These are the people who constantly apologize for themselves. It is likely that they found the early school weeks and months very difficult, maybe because they were not supported in taking the initiative at home (smothered or spoiled) or perhaps because they were neglected and abused at home and their sense of unworthiness predated their feelings from school.

Later, at the pre-adolescent stage, the psychosocial task becomes more about achievement through putting effort into work and friendships. Erikson has called this 'industry versus inferiority', the latter representing a more long-lasting sense of personal failure because by now children are able to compare themselves and their lives with those of others. Do remember that these tasks represent a sliding scale, so that no-one is likely to be totally at one or the other end of this scale. We all have bits of the positive and negative and, without the latter, we may not manage to develop resilience to situations where things go wrong.

According to Freud's model of development, this age is the time when the development of the superego or conscience occurs. Thus the ability to mentalize (or to be empathic) is a vital achievement at this life stage.

So, by the age of around five to eight years, children are facing life outside the home and developing social and intellectual capacities. They also have to be with others, compete and co-operate with them and, therefore, develop a personal moral or ethical code, which they can reflect upon and which helps to define who they are to themselves as well as to others. They learn to have a sense, too, that they have a future and that there is a part for them in shaping that future. Underlying all of this is the complex array of emotional reactions that arose from living their life up to this point.

To illustrate the contexts of these active and complicated years, using initiative and guilt as an organizing framework, I highlight:

(a) obesity and other eating disorders;
(b) bullying and violence.

Then, as case examples, I explore morality and guilt in a more dramatic sense, employing the material, discursive and intra-psychic elements in the lives of children who have killed. Albeit exceptional, these histories reveal clear risk factors associated with the disorganized attachment patterns that arise from severe neglect and/or abuse (see Chapters 5 and 7). They also provide evidence about moral reasoning, emotion and guilt.

These children's experiences are then contrasted with those who are carers in order to emphasize the ways in which contexts across the lifespan may exacerbate differences.

## The contexts of older childhood

From Piaget's work (Beckett and Taylor, 2010; Piaget, 1990), it is clear that children's cognitive development leads, at least, to the ability to think about complex issues in concrete terms. Although they may not have the skills to consider abstract ideas in any depth, they are able to learn and apply what they have learned to understanding their own lives and the lives of others (see Chapters 2 and 3).

Between the ages of (around) four to twelve there is rapid physical growth towards the transition to puberty. The body and mind change over this period and there is a clear sense of a growing personality. Freud described this period as latency, suggesting that nothing much happens. However, as Margot Waddell (2005) proposed, latency is in fact a time of 'a new kind of flourishing' (p. 82). The flourishing at this stage, though, is social rather than psychosexual.

Challenges occur in the transition from being mostly at home with a parent-figure to mostly at school with adult strangers (teaching assistants and teachers) and a large peer group. Further, perhaps for the first time, a child experiences direct competition in relation to their physical and mental prowess which influences their growing awareness of who they are and their place in the world. Early attachment relationships (Chapter 5) will have had a major part to play in preparing the child for the way he will experience and cope with these new challenges (Hamre and Pianta, 2001; Rothbart et al., 2001). Waddell (2005) again, taking a psychoanalytic view, suggests that this might result in a child becoming unconsciously troubled about possible unmanageable situations, perhaps with their peer group or with a teacher.

This all implies that the time between entering school and adolescence is beset by rapid change in bio-material (such as growing taller and stronger), socio-material (making new relationships) and intra-psychic contexts (emotional turmoil and new attachments). The overwhelming significance of early attachment relationships comes to the fore, particularly about how children deal with their bodies and minds and relate morally towards others (Shemmings and Shemmings, 2011).

## Bio-material context

Physical, emotional and psychological development all enhance and constrain what is possible for the developing person. Older childhood brings many changes in capacity and with those, of course, come risks of injury, illness and emotional damage, as well as demonstrations of prowess.

Some of the easily observable changes in the bio-material context include the increased co-ordination in small muscles that facilitate activities such as drawing, writing, making things and managing electronic games, mobile phones and other devices. Large-muscle skills also develop to allow more skill in sports, bicycle riding, skateboarding, swimming and running. The environment of the nursery school and primary school will enable further development of these physical capacities.

Height, weight, colouring and some other factors such as eyesight capacity are influenced in part by environment and in part through heredity (Bee and Mitchell, 1984; Sudbery, 2010; Sugarman, 1986). These are implicit in the development of personal and social identity, particularly via gender, ethnicity and attractiveness.

The development of identity awareness includes a growing feeling of sex and gender identity as children become overtly alert to the differences between themselves physically, socially and mentally and the other sex. With new relationships come new challenges and risks for children, and at this age children risk a sense of 'inferiority' that will trigger the shame that may have been consigned to the unconscious (Malson, 1998; Mollon, 2006; Sylva and Lunt, 1983).

### Diet and nutrition

Eating *behaviours* during older childhood become particularly visible because the child spends more time outside the home and also because, as the child reaches puberty (or at least anticipates puberty in the context of her peer group), body size and shape become a source of identity (Reiter and Lee, 2001). Gender and sexual identity are also linked, and there is evidence that for both girls and boys eating *disorders* might be connected to anxieties about gender identity and sexual development, particularly, but not exclusively, to worries about sexuality (Boroughs and Thompson, 2002; Carlat et al., 1997; Ryan et al., 2006).

Also important is the impact of *nutrition* upon growth (Wolock and Horowitz, 1984). The child neglect and abuse cases outlined already in this book (for instance, Maria Colwell and Jasmine Beckford) identify how these children's low weight should have been a marker of risk. This is also evidenced in cases of neglect, separation anxiety and trauma in which young children either lost weight or failed to increase their body weight (Block and Krebs, 2005; Slack et al., 2004).

In Chapter 9, eating disorders in adolescence, which have different origins and behaviour patterns, will be considered in detail.

### Childhood obesity

Body size and shape are among the challenges a child has to meet on entering this phase of their lives. The full force of the almost global epidemic of childhood obesity has come into the spotlight (Lobstein et al., 2004). Being overweight not only places children at risk of illness but also has serious psychological and emotional

consequences. Obesity and hatred of one's own body often co-exist with being bullied (Murtagh et al., 2006). Coming into contact with other children exacerbates
the ways in which a child may gain a sense of achievement or inferiority, and pre-
adolescent overweight boys and girls are more likely than others to be victims of
bullying because they deviate from appearance ideals. However, some older obese
*boys* are likely to actually be the bullies, possibly because of physical dominance
(Griffiths et al., 2006). Overweight children, overall, are at risk of general unpopu-
larity (for instance, not chosen during team games), all of which can lead to withdrawal and depression, the latter possibly exacerbated by a poor diet (Janssen et
al., 2004).

As research and anecdotal evidence below shows, obesity may be an indicator
of family dysfunction and the need for support (Gustafson and Sarwer, 2004). More
obviously, there are severe mental health consequences for overweight children at
the age when they begin school. Many experience teasing and bullying, and there
is some evidence of suicide brought about through this spiral of consequences.

Childhood obesity is widespread. The 2013 Health Survey for England (HSE)
data shows that nearly 1 in 4 adults, and more than 1 in 10 children aged 2–10,
are obese (www.hscic.gov.uk/catalogue/PUB10364/obes-phys-acti-diet-eng-
2013-rep.pdf). In 2007, a British Government-commissioned report predicted that,
if no action was taken, 60% of men, 50% of women and 25% of children would be
obese by 2050. Obesity can have a severe impact on people's health, increasing the
risk of type 2 diabetes, some cancers, and heart and liver disease. The Department
of Health (DH) has therefore developed strategies for dealing with the relatively recent increase in the body mass index (BMI) of children in the UK (dh.gov.uk/health/
category/policy-areas/public-health/obesity-healthy-living/). BMI is a measure of
body fat based on height and weight. Children are classified as overweight if their
BMI is between 25 and 30 and obese if their BMI exceeds 30. A National Childhood
Obesity Database (NCOD) was set up in 2006 in England and Wales with the aim
of tracking and analyzing trends in childhood weight and nutrition (dh.gov.uk/en/
Publicationsandstatistics/Publications/PublicationsStatistics/DH_063565).

Altogether, the database contains measurements of 538,400 children in school
Reception Year and Year 6. Nationally, 12.3% of girls and 13.4% of boys in the Reception Year were overweight, and 9.2% of girls and 10.7% of boys in that year
group were obese. In Year 6, 13.8% of boys and girls were overweight, and 15.4% of
girls and 18.9% of boys were obese. Children seem to become more obese during
their primary school years. There is debate about whether obesity in children occurs because parents are killing with kindness or whether they are neglecting the
health of their children.

## Discursive practices and childhood obesity

Beliefs and discourses around feeding the family are influential in adults' under-standing of how best to provide nutrition for their children. There are competing beliefs and social pressures that impact upon both families and professionals working with them. Rebekah Fox and Graham Smith (2011) investigated the case of the South Yorkshire 'Rawmarsh Sinner ladies' who were accused by the media, and pilloried by the public at large, for feeding their children chips through the school fence. This happened during a campaign fronted by Jamie Oliver, the ce-lebrity chef and food campaigner, in which healthy lunches (balanced meals with meat, vegetables and less toxic fats) were provided by the school. But the chil-dren were apparently not content with this. They claimed they were still hungry after eating these meals and did not enjoy the healthy options as much as they had their previous diet. So some of their mothers went to the school in the lunch break and passed their children chips through the fence. The mothers believed they were helping their children and the children were happy their mothers had done this for them.

In analyzing the public outcry and the mothers' behaviours, Fox and Smith fo-cus on the discursive construction of the obesity crisis and what is positioned as healthy eating for children. They suggest that discourses of blame were employed to denounce working class families as bad parents (particularly bad mothers) and, as such, being unable to care appropriately for their children. Thus while on one level the nutritional status and BMI of a child is part of the bio-material context and the practical level of consciousness, what is healthy, desirable and normal, both in terms of appearance and understanding of diet and eating behaviours, is culturally and historically constructed. Jamie Oliver's ideas and recipes were 'good', higher calorie, fried foods were 'bad'.

*Table 8.1 Identifying psychosocial problems in children*

| The emotional damage of being bullied | Risk factors |
|---|---|
| Poor sleep: sleep apnoea and anxiety about abuse at school | Parent figure should notice – discussion with child and possibly seek medical support |
| Absence from school: bullied children either feign illness or skip school | Teachers and social workers need to be aware and investigate the psychosocial context – problems such as poor school performance and bad company |
| Avoiding physical activity: worry about being seen in a negative light | Risk of spiralling mental health problems and increased obesity |
| Eating disorder: binge eating, bulimia and poor sense of body image | Indicator of mental health problem and low self-esteem |
| Suicide and attempted suicide | High risk if previous symptoms ignored |

### Intra-psychic dimensions of eating behaviours

Eating is also associated with *states of mind*. This varies from person to person – many people eat more when they are depressed while others hardly manage to eat at all. Being overweight in itself might make a young child feel depressed for physiological reasons (it is difficult to do ballet, play football, ride a bike, wear nice clothes and so on) and/or because jokes are made about them by other children who are imbued with cruel stereotypical ideas about fatness. The cruelty and re-jection is in part a response to the fear of being fat in those who taunt and bully overweight children, and there is increasing evidence that overweight school-age children are being bullied (Janssen et al., 2004; Tischner, 2012).

Psychoanalytically, moving from latency to an awakening of sexual awareness and the onset of puberty, the unconscious experience of the body is central. Fol-lowing Giddens (1986/2003, 1991) from a MDI perspective, the knowledge of being overweight and a discursive consciousness of what that means socially are medi-ated powerfully by early patterns of relationships which linger in the unconscious about food and comfort (Dale, 1993; Klein, 1959/1993). Klein's concept of the un-conscious 'splitting off' of the primitive experience of oneself as hateful may impact upon behaviour in childhood and result in a child engaging in bullying and violence towards others. There is some evidence that a child who is bullied at school or in their home-locality (whether or not it is because of obesity) will probably put on (more) weight.

The American website EzineArticles.com carries a review of the process (ezine-articles.com/?Overweight-Children-and-School-Bullying&id=3200591). It appears that there are significant associations between a student's BMI and negative peer victimization. Friendship can be withdrawn and rumours spread about overweight children. Once a child has been rejected in this way, finding themselves friendless, they are likely to look for comfort in food, put on more weight and encounter dif-ficulty in reintegrating with peers. There is thus a vicious circle. Unhappy children are vulnerable to being made more so by being isolated, bullied and then may eat for comfort, which exacerbates the bullying and unhappiness. Unhappy children also feel hated and hate (Klein, 1959/1993). There is ample anecdotal and empiri-cal evidence in a variety of articles in magazines and the worldwide web that obese children are continuing to go through this spiral of physical, social and emotional distress (O'Dea, 2005; Tischner, 2012).

Thus it is not simply being overweight that is the epidemic, but the con-sequences to the child's long-term development and mental health (www.fightingdepression.co.uk/obese-children-likely-to-be-bullied-and-suffer-depression-anxiety). It appears that, regardless of any other factors such as race, gender, social status or educational level, obese children are more likely to be bullied (Nishina et al., 2005). Also, children who are victims of bullying suffer more from depression, anxiety and isolation (Kumpulainen et al., 2001). Bullying is a complex problem and does not happen in psychological or social isolation, but it must be remembered that most children do not bully.

### Bullying among children

There is now increased public awareness of bullying among children. This alone may be helpful in drawing attention to the difficulties some children face (Gladstone et al., 2006; Glew et al., 2000). In an Australian study (Rigby and Slee, 1991) it was reported that approximately 1 child in 10 had been subjected to peer group bullying. Boys reported being bullied more often than girls, who tended to be more supportive of victims so that it was less common to find one girl bullying another. With increasing age, there was a slight but significant decline in reported bullying; notably, however, attitudes toward victims became less supportive as children grow older. The researchers in this study also found a tendency to *despise* the victims of bullies while there was general *admiration* for school bullies. This contrasted with avowed support for intervention to assist the victim. They suggest that deeper understanding of these complex, and in some respects apparently contradictory, attitudes need explanation in order to develop effective interventions.

There are different types of bullying, which may make it difficult to identify and label initially. It is only since the 1990s that it has been possible to draw upon the child-bullying discourse to explain some of the relationships that take place in schools. It is now no longer possible for either parents or teachers to turn a blind eye to bullying behaviours.

They have been recognized as consisting of:

- Verbal bullying (calling a child names);
- Social exclusion and isolation (the child is not befriended and efforts to make friends with others are rebuffed);
- Physical bullying (pushing, pinching, kicking or, even worse, being attacked by one or more of the children doing the bullying);
- Bullying through lies and false rumours;
- Having money and possessions taken and/or damaged;
- Being threatened, humiliated and forced to do things that are distasteful or anti-social;
- Racial bullying (name calling and other things listed above);
- Sexual bullying (this can include sexual assault or even rape);
- Cyber bullying (unpleasant texts and e-mails or possibly pictures circulated among other children that the individual victim is made aware of).

What we do know is that being bullied attacks a child's sense of self-esteem, and this might be connected to the child who already has low self-esteem or a sense of inferiority and shame being placed in the potential victim position.

## Anti-social personalities and moral dilemmas: when do children know right from wrong?

Morality remains a key concern among developmental psychologists who see moral development and the ability to distinguish right from wrong as fundamental to being human and living in a society with others. It is also of interest to policy makers and those involved in child protection. Cognitive neuroscientists have identified a relationship between the evolution of the brain and the ability to make moral judgments (Cushman et al., 2006; Loye, 2002). Judgments of this kind are not, of course, the same as moral *behaviour*. You may be able to distinguish right from wrong but, for many reasons, this awareness might not govern your behaviour. As with the discussion of Milgram's studies of obedience to authority and those about bystander apathy discussed in Chapter 1, what you believe and what you might say or do in certain conditions are not always predictable. Nor might you always feel comfortable about what you have done or were going to do, but that may not stop you.

Behavioural and social learning psychologists have all tried to explain children's understanding of what constitutes moral behaviour, particularly aggression and violence, through learning and modelling as well as taking account of how actions are symbolized by children and given a meaning (Bandura, 1978) (see Chapter 3). In other words, what goes on in a child's mind when they make judgments, and when they make decisions about how to handle a situation where moral judgments have to be made?

Freud made it clear that human beings had to exercise some mechanism of self-control at an early stage if they were to be able to live together. In Chapter 3, the structure of the psyche with the id, ego and superego were described. It is the function of the superego, which develops around the ages of five or six, that acts as the conscience so that the child has to defend herself against the pressures of the superego to hold back the feelings of shame and anxiety. It is important to remember that the superego does not necessarily govern behaviour, although it does induce guilt if the person engages in behaviour that she may be ashamed about.

### *The material context: behaving and reasoning about morality*

Cognitive developmental theorists such as Piaget (1965) and Kohlberg (1981) have explored moral reasoning and the development of a sense of justice in children, looking behind behaviour to the meaning each of us attributes to our actions.

   Piaget believed that children made moral judgments based on their own observations of the world, which is particularly important to remember when considering some extremes of behaviour. Piaget focused on how children reasoned about
good and bad behaviour in themselves and other children and, in particular, how
they developed and applied their own sense of fair rules. He eventually identified
two stages of reasoning about moral development. The first he called 'heteronomous morality' (other-directed). This meant that children responded to outside
rules developed and applied by other people, usually parents or teachers. The second stage he called 'autonomous morality' (self-directed). At this stage the child
has developed her own sense of what is right and wrong and knows whether or not
she is transgressing. These different moralities represent stages of development
in reasoning ability.

   These are typically illustrated as follows. Children of different ages were told
stories of other children's behaviours and asked to say which child was the naughtier, and why? One comparison might be:

> A little boy called John was asked by his mother to get a plate out of a high cup-
> board to help her set the table. He stood on a chair and reached up. He got the
> plate but lost his balance and managed to knock six other plates off the shelf and
> onto the floor, breaking them all.

> One day, a little boy called Henry tried to get some jam out of a cupboard when
> his mother was out. She had told him never to eat jam without her permission.
> He climbed onto a chair and stretched out his arm. The jam was too high up, and
> he couldn't reach it. But while he was trying to get it, he knocked over a cup. The
> cup fell down and broke.

   Piaget found that even though 5- to 10–year-old children were able to distinguish between deliberate and unintentional acts, they still tended to base their
judgments on the outcome of the act: the more severe the outcome, the naughtier
the act. This was an example of *heteronomous morality*.

   Older children were able to make judgments based on the person's motives:
Henry was doing something he shouldn't have been doing, so he is naughtier. This
is *autonomous morality*.

   Piaget saw these two phases as overlapping rather than as clear developmental
phases so that a child might reason in a different way according to the context and
their personality. In the heteronomous phase there was a belief that bad behaviour
can be seen by authorities such as parents, teachers or God and that rules should
never be broken. The autonomous phase was understood by children as being
judged on the basis of intent and that it is possible under certain circumstances to
break the rules or tell a white lie if it prevents someone getting upset.

*Table 8.2* Kohlberg's stages of moral reasoning

| Stage 1 | **Obedience**<br>If you don't obey the rules you are a bad person |
|---------|---------------------------------------------------------------------|
| Stage 2 | **Self-interest**<br>It is better to keep yourself happy and safe, regardless of what else is going on |
| Stage 3 | **Conformity**<br>Misbehaving is a bad thing to do and you should obey rules even if you cannot agree with them |
| Stage 4 | **Law and order**<br>You should not break the rules (and steal, for example) because the law prohibits it |
| Stage 5 | **Human rights**<br>Everyone has a right to make a considered and ethical decision regardless of the rules |
| Stage 6 | **Universal human ethics**<br>Decisions about what is right and wrong should be made according to philosophical principles having weighed up the situation before you take action |

Kohlberg's theory of moral development, which built on Piaget's work, suggests a developmental sequential process of reasoning, or 'stages', in the application of a moral principle to a dilemma to derive a solution (Carpendale, 2000). It has been criticized because it predicts a greater consistency in moral reasoning than has been observed experimentally and in life. Kohlberg's theory of the development of moral reasoning (see Table 8.2) like Piaget's, was based upon telling stories such as the Heinz dilemma to children, adolescents and young adults.

The Heinz dilemma, one of the famous vignettes which you will find in most textbooks, is as follows:

A woman was near death from a special kind of cancer. There was one drug that the doctors thought might save her. A pharmacist in the same town had recently discovered this treatment but the drug was expensive to make and he was charging ten times what the drug cost him to produce. He paid £200 for the basic ingredient and charged £2,000 for a small dose of the drug. The sick woman's husband, Heinz, went to everyone he knew to borrow the money, but he could only get together about £1,000 which is half of what it cost. He told the pharmacist that his wife was dying and asked him to sell it cheaper or let him pay later. Heinz was told 'No, I discovered the drug and I'm going to make money from it.' So Heinz got desperate and broke into the man's store to steal the drug for his wife.

Should Heinz have broken into the store to steal the drug for his wife? Why or why not?

The stages in Table 8.2 are not necessarily *sequential*. Someone might reason about their decisions differently according to the situation in which they find themselves. For instance, you may have been in a similar position to the Heinz dilemma and use that experience (whatever your decision and the outcome) to assess the vignette about what Heinz should have done. Thus the context, individual background and the details of the dilemma itself, in real life, would impact upon your reasoning.

---

**PAUSE AND REFLECT**

**Women's voices and moral reasoning**

Carol Gilligan, a feminist psychologist working during the 1970s, asked why women were not included in the voices that were identified in research about moral behaviour and emotion. She was particularly interested in moral pronouncements by the State, with her interest initially being sparked by a US Supreme Court judgment that made abortion legal on the justification of women's right to choose. To her mind, this meant that women had been charged with a moral responsibility for life and death in relationships which also involved men as the father of the unborn and future children.

This inspired her research on young women's and girls' moral reasoning, and not only about abortion. *In a Different Voice* became a classic feminist text (Gilligan, 1983) and inspired subsequent generations of feminist scholars to follow up this project, taking a *relational* stance (Brown and Gilligan, 1993).

**What is relational morality?**

Gilligan's work on moral reasoning employed studies of moral conflicts and life choices, including the Heinz dilemma. She found that girls' answers differed fundamentally from those offered by boys. For instance, a typical answer from a boy might be based on a sense of *mathematical logic* – there is a problem, it needs to be solved, so we solve it.

However the (typical) answer from a girl proposed a more complex *relational* solution to the problem. They might ask what would happen to these same 'actors' in different scenarios? The most telling result was frequent suggestions that the dilemma was best discussed among the protagonists.

- But are girls and women less likely to break moral codes than boys and men?
- What evidence can be drawn on to make a case either way?

Think about this in the following example about Mary Bell a young girl who committed murder.

You might also like to think about how your colleagues and classmates might make moral judgments – are there gender differences?

---

## Getting away with murder? The material and intra-psychic contexts and the case of Mary Bell

Gilligan's critique of moral reasoning has implications for making sense of the social and psychological influences on child murderers. An extreme and terrifying case is that of eleven-year-old Mary Bell. While Mary's behaviour is by no means typical of a child whose life had been one of abuse and deprivation, her relational behaviour and its consequences are far from unique.

Mary Bell, was convicted of the manslaughter of four-year-old Martin Brown (murdered just before her eleventh birthday) and the murder of three-year-old Brian Howe two months later (Sereny, 1998).

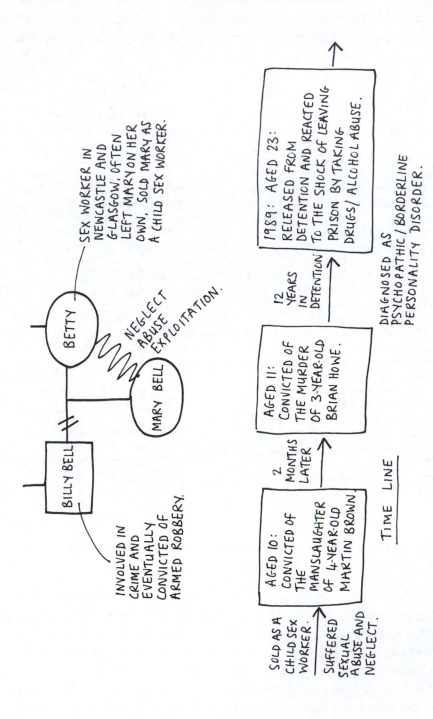

**Figure 8.1** Genogram and ecomap for Mary Bell

Mary strangled both of her victims. Between the two killings, she and her friend Norma broke into and vandalized a nursery in their neighbourhood, leaving a note confessing to Martin's killing, which at the time was dismissed by the police as a prank. Mary also apparently returned to the scene of the crime against Brian and carved the letter 'M' into his stomach, using scissors to cut off some of his hair, scratch his legs and mutilate his penis.

After Mary's conviction (manslaughter on the grounds of diminished responsibility) her mother sold articles about her to various newspapers. Psychiatric reports identified Mary as psychopathic (see APA, 2010).

Mary served twelve years in custody and was released from detention (anonymously) when she was twenty-three in 1989. She was released on parole, but with minimal support or supervision, and reacted to the shock of release from prison by taking drugs and drinking heavily, claiming that she longed for the security of a prison cell. At one stage she turned to shoplifting, and apparently said it was an unconscious desire to be returned to prison (Dub, 1947; Goodstein, 1979; Zeitlyn, 1967).

But did Mary understand what she was doing at the time of the killings? Since the Bell case there have been other instances where abused and neglected children have bullied, abused and sometimes murdered others, as we shall see in the next chapter. The debate about blame, though, has not yet been resolved to everyone's satisfaction. How far are such children *criminals*? Are they mad or bad?

Mary Bell was certainly demonized by the press and the public, who painted her behaviour as if she were inhuman. Commenting on subsequent related and similar cases, some sociologists have argued that these events – a girl murdering other children – contravened the public perceptions of the innocence of childhood. This applied particularly to girls who were seen as the gentler of the two sexes, and this made the vilification of Mary even more intense (Hall and Montgomery, 2000; Jones, 1999).

The case of Myra Hindley reflects this too, indicating that women are not expected to commit the kinds of criminal acts that men might. Hindley was one of the 'Moors Murderers', who, with her boyfriend Ian Brady, tortured, murdered and buried the bodies of children on moorland near Manchester in the 1960s. It is reported that she herself claimed that she was worse than Ian Brady because *she* had a sense of what was right and wrong and knew what she was doing. Childhood, and female childhood in particular, has been imagined by sociological theorists to be a period or process of social integration, while any fracture of this image is perceived as a threat to social traditions and therefore socially disruptive and morally alarming (James and Jenks, 1996).

**PAUSE AND REFLECT**

### The psychology of the child who murders

What do we know about the development of moral reasoning that might be relevant to the experiences of Mary Bell (Cushman et al., 2006; Greene and Haidt, 2002)?

Research into social learning and morality suggests that the ability to empathize or understand reciprocity in interpersonal relations is important (although not totally necessary) to make appropriate judgments about what is right and wrong during middle-childhood (Bandura and McDonald, 1963; Selman, 1971) (see Chapter 3).

Subsequent research suggests, however, that emotion and affect (mood or state of mind) are as important as reasoning in morality (Greene and Haidt, 2002). This evidence is based both on experimental observations of children and on the use of functional MRI scanners to explore the brain during different types of moral behaviour (McGuire et al., 2009). It has been suggested that early life experiences, particularly those of separation and abuse, might impact upon brain development which in turn might influence moral decision-making (Schore, 2005).

Is there a public perception that somehow children (and possibly women too) are 'innocent' so the shock of a child murderer stimulates greater public outrage and concern? (James and Jenks, 1996)

The mental image of a girl and her friend apparently taunting the murdered child's sister – an act that had been widely reported by the press – and risking both the discovery of the body, and thus Mary's guilt, is unthinkable and unbearable for most of us.

But Mary's behaviour needs to be considered in the context of developmental psychology:

- How sophisticated would Mary's moral reasoning have been?
- What would she understand about right and wrong at the age of eleven?
- What had she learned in her short life about morality and moral behaviour and from whom?

As you will see below, Mary had very poor attachment experiences and no role models to guide her towards moral reasoning and social behaviour. However, the discursive context of the innocence of childhood pervaded the Bell case: she was a child who had transgressed, she had corrupted her friend Norma and she had murdered two children.

## From the material to the intra-psychic context: consequences of disorganized attachment?

Mary's mother, Betty, was seventeen when Mary was born. Betty was a sex worker in Newcastle-upon-Tyne but she also worked frequently in Glasgow, leaving Mary to her own devices. Mary's father was unknown, although it was suggested that he was Billy Bell, an habitual criminal who had been briefly married to Betty. Billy Bell was later convicted of armed robbery. It was suggested that Betty had made several attempts to kill Mary and make her death appear accidental. Mary was also repeatedly sexually abused from the age of four by men procured by her mother.

Reading about Mary's life and background, it is apparent that there was little there to provide her with comfort or any sense of a secure base (Bowlby, 1988; Holmes, 2010). Role models were abusive and uncaring at best and at worst, like her mother, were trying to kill her (Bandura, 1978). The social mechanisms that were transmitted to her were all about brutality (Buchanan, 1996) and also, perhaps, that no-one cared or would do anything to help, even if they knew of the abuse Mary was suffering. It seems that a series of men took advantage of her mother offering Mary to them for abuse, and no-one stopped what was happening. Even so, Mary has survived.

Disorganized attachment was discussed in Chapter 5, which presented Shemmings and Shemmings' (2011) review of the evidence on the causes and consequences of disorganized attachment and work by Bowlby and Ainsworth. It was initially labelled 'unclassified' by Bowlby (1970) and Ainsworth (Ainsworth et al., 1978) who recorded fearful and avoidant children's behaviour, but lacked the evidence to positively associate it with abuse and neglect. What the unclassified infants in the Ainsworth study had in common was contradictory intentions – approaching their parent with their head averted, being apprehensive and fearful of the parent and being disoriented as if dazed and in a trance. Sometimes they froze all their movements when the parent approached.

The kinds of behaviour (Hesse and Main, 2000; Main and Soloman, 1990) now labelled as having origins in *disorganized attachment* include shutting down emotionally and being fearful 'without solution'. This fear is characterized by a lack of preparedness, an absence of foreboding without respite from an avalanche of fear that cloaks the infant/child. It seems that after a time this initial form of infant attachment becomes hostile towards the parent – controlling, using verbal aggression and even physical aggression. Alternatively it might result in a more apparently caring approach – with behaviour appearing cheery and helpful towards the parent although very much directed by unpredictability and malevolence geared to controlling the parent.

Even by the standards of those who have had abusive and neglectful parents, where parenting typically leads to disorganized attachment, Mary Bell's behaviour was extreme. However, so was the context in which she spent her very early years. Her desire and ability to control her friend Norma and her two victims resonates with extreme consequences of disorganized attachment. Her early fears were turned into an emotional shut-down, unpredictability and malevolence.

### *Memories, identity and guilt*

This emotional shut-down was also true in the cases of Robert Thompson and Jon Venables, the children who killed two-year-old James Bulger in Liverpool in 1993 (Rowbotham et al., 2003). However the case of Venables, in particular, indicated that, despite capacities for emotional dissociation, for some it is difficult to overcome guilt (Sereny, 1998). Mary Bell showed similar indications. Jon Venables, imprisoned when he was eleven for the gratuitous torture and murder of the toddler, was released with a new identity along with his friend and fellow murderer Robert Thompson.

While Thompson, seemingly the leader when they killed James Bulger, assumed his new identity with apparent success, Venables resumed notoriety. He was imprisoned again for breaking various sections of his parole, and for having child pornography. When his identity was exposed, various new-found friends came forward to quote him as saying things similar to 'If you really knew who I am...' or 'You would not be so happy if you knew what I might be capable of'. He spent a great deal of his leisure abusing drugs and alcohol, which precipitated his arrest and re-imprisonment, and, with his identify made public, he would clearly be in some danger in the future.

It is likely that Venables, like Bell, needed the paradoxical comfort of being able to forget who he was while at the same time confessing who he was. He was trying to drown his memory with alcohol and other substances, but while under the influence his sense of who he was became more acute. We cannot know for sure, but it would appear that the shame of what he did and who he was (i.e. a murderer of a child) cannot be wiped from his memory (Raine, 2002).

## Child carers

In direct contrast to the betrayal of the image of innocence, represented by Bell, Venables and Thompson, are the pre-adolescent children who act as carers to disabled adults (usually a parent) or other children (siblings) (Aldridge and Becker, 1993; Barnett and Parker, 1998). Young carers, of whom there are at least 51,000 in the UK, have long been the subject of concern among social care services. Life for young carers is under-researched although, clearly, their opportunities are limited and they are likely to miss out on all but the basic educational facilities. Their friendships with other children are also likely to be restricted. There is also evidence that such children are secretive about their lives (Thomas et al., 2003).

It has been suggested that these children suffer from a degradation in mental and physical health, have damaged educational careers, restricted social networks, and will suffer long-term consequences in adult life as a result of their childhood caring roles (Newman, 2002). Newman argues that limited empirical evidence exists for these claims and that, where legitimate concerns arise, they are frequently related to poverty, social exclusion and unsupported or inadequate parenting. While dedicated services to young carers have made a valuable contribution in highlighting an important social issue, a radical review of their place in the overall structure of support services for families affected by illness or disability is surely long overdue.

These young people make a choice to sacrifice much of their normal childhood to care, providing physical, practical and often emotional support to the parent they look after. This suggests that in many cases the young carer may be securely or anxiously attached (rather than disorganized as in the case of Bell). It may be part of the reflective-relational stance to identify the attachment style in order to make decisions on how to support such children (see Chapter 6).

The characteristics of the young carer are described on the Barnardo's website (www.barnardos.org.uk/what_we_do/our_projects/young_carers.htm) as:

- The average age of a young carer is twelve.
- The 2001 Census showed that there were 175,000 young carers in the UK, 13,000 of whom cared for more than 50 hours a week.
- More than half of young carers live in one-parent families and almost a third care for someone with mental health problems.

Sometimes young carers are subject to being taken into care, potentially increasing the stresses they experience.

## CHAPTER SUMMARY

As children get older they develop a growing sense of who they are and who they will become. Children are able to make moral judgments and, through understanding what is right and what is wrong, they are able to evaluate their own behaviour and motives and decide whether they are basically good people. Most children develop some degree of positive self-regard that enables resilience. But for many children whose lives are blighted by cycles of disadvantage, whether exhibited through neglect or abuse or even illness brought about by poor diet or the stigma of poverty, a sense of shame lingers into adolescence and adulthood. This might lead to a paucity of moral reasoning, which is unlikely to lead to the extremes of behaviour described above but certainly could lead to bullying, criminal actions and consequent incarceration.

You should be able to identify and understand the range of challenges children face at this age. Also you should begin to recognize the material, discursive and intra-psychic contexts of the challenges that young girls and boys face in the years around entering and engaging with school.

## FURTHER READING

The reading recommended at the end of Chapter 7 will also be relevant here, but you might also be interested in reading further about Mary Bell and children like her:

Sereny, G. (1998) *Cries Unheard – Why Children Kill: The story of Mary Bell*. New York: Henry Holt & Co Inc.

Other relevant readings focusing on young carers are:

Newman, T. (2002) 'Young Carers' and Disabled Parents: Time for a change of direction? *Disability & Society*, 17(6), 613–625.
Thomas, N., Stainton, T., Jackson, S., Cheung, W.Y., Doubtfire, S. and Webb, A. (2003) 'Your Friends Don't Understand': Invisibility and unmet need in the lives of 'young carers'. *Child & Family Social Work*, 8(1), 35–46.

# 9

# ADOLESCENCE: IDENTITY, ROLE AND SEXUALITY

**LEARNING OBJECTIVES**

- To explore identity development as a consequence of puberty and the teenage years.
- To review the material, discursive and intra-psychic *challenges* at adolescence.
- To understand the pivotal role of adolescence in HGD.

## Introduction

Chapters 7 and 8 examined the immense challenges for young and older children faced with developing bodies, minds and relationships. Adolescence though, as we shall see, is a time of life when these changes and developments are consolidated, and this provides a platform for looking forward to adulthood. Your body and mind are no longer those of a child. Intellectually and emotionally you are able to think, reason and reflect upon your life, although the myriad influences you will have encountered up to this point in life will impact upon how these processes work. Erikson's idea that adolescence is a pivotal time provides a helpful framework for us to make sense of how it is positioned within the lifespan.

Erikson (1959/1980) remains one of the key authorities on adolescence across several academic and clinical disciplines because, as with the other stages he describes, he includes biological, social and emotional (unconscious) elements. He identified the stage of adolescence as an important element of the lifespan beyond a simple transition from childhood to adulthood, as some had suggested (Sugarman, 2001). Adolescence, according to Erikson, is a time of self-consciousness and attention to how we think others see us. It is also a time for reflecting on what we have achieved and what we might become. It is, additionally, a time when social behavioural patterns become laid down in the brain (Nelson et al., 2005). Biologically, adolescence is also when young people reach puberty and face the hormonal and physical changes that accompany it. It is therefore potentially a terrifying and tumultuous phase in the lifespan. If we think we have not lived up to our desires or others' desires and expectations of us, then there is a sense of failure emotionally and physically.

## Psychosocial tasks

Adolescence is, for many, either a turning point or the stage of life at which future possibilities are fixed or become limited. In adolescence, battles are fought and fought again with parents, friends, siblings, teachers and social workers. 'Who do you think you are to tell me (whoever I am)?' is a common taunt to parents and carers (Dasen, 2000; Resnick et al., 1993)?

At this stage the psychosocial task is to cope with the possibility of developing your identity versus role confusion (Erikson, 1959/1980). The future begins to hit the individual with spurts in growth akin to those in early childhood, puberty and the physical and emotional uncertainties, the fear of what lies ahead in adulthood and the struggle to discover who you are and where you belong. It is also a time when you might make enemies and face serious competition and rivalry for the first time (Erikson, 1950/1963)

Erikson has been particularly influential within HGD theory for his identification of the importance of adolescence and the crisis surrounding identity (1959/1980). He related the bio-material context (the onset of puberty) to the psychosocial ones in which the place of the young person in the family and wider society was subject to specific historically and socially-constructed discourses (Foucault, 2001; Tolman et al., 2003). The negotiation of this stage of the lifespan is critical for mental health and well-being and future prospects in relationships and work.

I now explore the importance of physical change, gender and sexuality in the development of relationships and identities.

## The bio-material contexts of adolescence: sex and gender

Adolescence mostly coincides with puberty, giving rise to both sex and gender as sensitive areas in the development of identity. Both are key lenses through which we see the world and the world sees us (Bem, 1994). Sex, sex roles and gender are related concepts (Lachance-Grzela and Bouchard, 2010; Manstead and McCulloch, 1981), but each requires definition and explanation for the part they play in the construction of gender identity and health.

Social, biological and psychological influences on our lives come together in a complex way in relation to sex, which is basically about whether the adolescent is

*Figure 9.1* Adolescence – the pivotal stage

male or female (Ickes, 1993). While biologically-designated sex has a significant part to play in the way human experience is defined, it is subject to layers of psychological experience mediated by personality, socialization, sexuality and gender divisions which are themselves socially constructed (Archer, 1984).

Gender is different from sex in that it refers to the social characteristics whereby women and men exist in a dynamic structural relation to each other. In other words, the social system positions women and men into particular patterns of relationships towards each other – some might describe stereotypes of this as the 'war between the sexes'.

But why does designated sex appear to make so much difference within the lifespan of individuals? Most of us are born female (with a vagina and emergent ovaries) or male (with a penis and future testicles) and that designation is called our sex. This is initially dependent upon genetic endowment, and subsequent characteristics related to the development of our bodies to resemble the adult of each sex depend upon hormone distribution prior to birth and at various stages of the lifespan (Martin and Ruble, 2010).

However, some people are born without the features that distinguish them as either female or male, with possibly the features of both (Wiesemann et al., 2010). Clearly this (mostly congenital) condition, *intersex*, will be of key consideration at the time of birth, but also as the child grows towards puberty when sex and gender are highly significant with developmental concerns about dress, grooming, acceptable behaviour and so on. While biological and anatomical differences between women and men are strikingly visible, female and male bodies also have *much in common* that makes them human (Tolman et al., 2003).

From birth we are compelled to seek confirmation of our gendered identity because it tells us and others so much about our future life chances. This raises problems for children with the characteristics of intersex. From the time we recognize whether we are female or male, before we are sure we know how those in each category are meant to behave, it has been argued that all human individuals actively pursue the project of becoming gendered. At the same time, we are aware of the contradictions that separate experience and desire from social constraints on girls (who are influenced to be feminine and who may want to play football and climb trees but are persuaded against doing so) and boys (influenced to be masculine and not cry) (Coward, 1993).

The physical characteristics of females and males as they grow represent further clear anatomical distinctions: body fat and hair distribution, reproductive functions and genitals.

However, the anatomical distinctions are not simplistic. They represent social and ideological constraints as well as biological ones (Baron-Cohen, 2004; Ussher, 2003). Debates proposing that male and female brains are constructed differentially have become highly charged. On the one hand, Baron-Cohen argues that his work shows unequivocally that the female brain is organized to be *empathetic* (i.e. to identify the emotions and thoughts of another and respond with appropriate emotion) while the male brain is structured around *systematizing* (i.e. to analyze, explore and construct a system to identify underlying rules).

The other side, led by Cordelia Fine (2010), challenges him and his like-minded colleagues with being *neurosexist*. While the jury may still be out about the science, and although most of us hold our own views, the discourse of brain science appears to have held its own as the dominant voice in the early twenty-first century.

Successful sexual and gender identity development are fundamental to a sense of well-being and a positive belief in being alive (Busseri et al., 2006; Savin-Williams and Diamond, 2000) while failure to feel secure in one's sexual body indicates a risk of mental illness (Gonsiorek, 1988; Zucker, 2005).

Erikson proposed that we arrive at each stage of the lifespan with an accumulation of baggage, or emotional debris, as well as some degree of strength and resilience. We are all a product of what went before in our lifetimes (biologically, socially and emotionally). Evolutionary psychologists, as we saw in Chapter 2, point out we are also products of our bio-cultural heritages (Geary and Bjorklund, 2000).

The physical changes during adolescence are dramatic and for many they temporarily eclipse the ideology of sex and gender (Lerner et al., 2010).

- The proportions of the body change significantly and the head changes shape.
- Boys begin to grow facial hair and their jaws and foreheads become more prominent.
- During puberty the width of the shoulders and hips change dramatically. For both boys and girls the pelvis becomes substantially bigger but girls don't have such an increase in the size of their shoulders.
- Muscles, fat and hormones also change in character. Boys' muscle growth differs from girls in that the muscles are more pronounced while girls have more body fat.

However, it is the sexual characteristics that develop during adolescence that are particularly salient and potentially disturbing to the developing person, although the rate of these changes is relatively slow and subtle (Lee, 2009; Tolman et al., 2003).

### Challenges for girls

Girls develop breasts and begin to ovulate during adolescence. For girls, when menstruation begins, it comes with the associated psychological implications related to fertility (Brooks-Gunn and Ruble, 1982; Koff and Rierdan, 1995). While there are, indeed, hormone changes during puberty, and possibly genetic factors, it would be unwise to neglect the ways in which gender discourses are played out and give meaning to the experience of becoming a woman in a sexist world (Lee, 1994). There are cross-cultural differences and socio-historical shifts in how menstruation is received by the community, the family and the girl herself.

One study of girls in the USA showed that adolescent girls receive mixed messages about menarche (the onset of menstruation): it is traumatic and upsetting but they should act normally, or it is both an overt symbol of sexual maturity while also a mysterious, secret (covert) event. Girls in the study reported a clear distinction between scientific knowledge about the anatomy and physiological functioning, and what they termed 'realistic', pragmatic knowledge about managing the lived experience of menstruation. Using methods of critical, feminist analysis, Kissling (1996) examined social texts of menstrual socialization – including girls' conversation about their menstrual education, their mothers' discussions of the preparation for menstruation and instructional materials presented in their health education classes – to discuss the communication and the silences of contemporary menstrual socialization. For many young women though, menarche remains a source of shame although there has been a shift in women's experiences. Contemporary adolescents starting to menstruate have a more positive attitude to the reproductive body than generations of their predecessors (Lee, 2009).

For some young women, menarche is a time of high emotion and it has been argued that the hormone changes and the meaning (i.e. becoming fertile and no longer a child) might have a role in adolescent depression. Prior to adolescence boys and girls are equally prone to depression but Born and colleagues (Born et al., 2002) asked why the onset of puberty in girls so dramatically shifts the proportion of gender depression. They found that two girls to every boy are depressed at this stage of life. These authors argue that vulnerability to depression may be rooted in an intricate meld of genetic traits, normal female hormonal maturational processes and gender socialization.

Adolescence may also coincide with the onset of eating disorders, and many are girls who have memories of abuse or are in two minds about gender identity. One study suggested that strong familial relationships may decrease the risk for disordered eating, while both sexual and physical abuse are strong independent risk factors for disordered eating among both adolescent girls and boys (Neumark-Sztainer et al., 2000).

The rise in heterosexual intercourse among adolescents in the late 1970s and early 1980s gave rise to numerous studies about the different ways that girls respond to sex. One such study, drawing on 400 in-depth interviews with teenage girls, examined the quality of sexual initiations, comparing the family and sexual histories of girls who described sexual initiation as painful, boring or disappointing with those of girls who emphasized sexual curiosity, desire and pleasure, and concluded there was a need for more sex education (Thompson, 1990).

Becoming pregnant during adolescence is identified as a problem in Western industrial societies, although in some other cultures it may be seen as desirable. Being pregnant and having a baby as a teenager have a number of negative effects on education (Harding, 2003), developing friendships, developing an intimate sexual relationship (with the baby's father or another man), employment and career prospects. Thus there is a high risk of poverty. Research has mostly focused on the reasons for becoming pregnant, including investigations into whether sexual abuse is a causal factor (Roosa et al., 1997).

A review of studies in the UK and USA (Bunting and McAuley, 2004) suggested that family support is particularly important to teenage mothers and has a positive influence on parenting behaviours and practices. However, the mother/daughter relationship is not always a straightforward one, and conflict between the two can diminish some of the positive impact.

Research on partner support highlights how support from fathers and/or other male partners has been linked with improved financial and psychological outcomes for teenage mothers, as well as having a positive influence on parenting behaviours. There is also evidence to suggest that support from partners may become increasingly important to teenage mothers over time. While the research available on peer support is much more limited, it does suggest that the emotional support of peers is also perceived as being important by teenage mothers. Current research findings indicate that families, partners and peers tend to provide different, but complementary, forms of support for teenage mothers which, on the whole, appear to contribute to more positive outcomes for this group (Bunting and McAuley, 2004; Koniak-Griffin et al., 2003).

### Challenges for boys

For boys the changes in their reproductive organs start around the ages of eleven or twelve with the enlargement of the testes and scrotum, followed by the enlargement of the penis around the age of fourteen. During this period the boy's height dramatically increases and his penis gradually gets longer and wider. Nocturnal emissions take place and may at first be seen as secret and shameful (as with the onset of menstruation in girls) but the discourses of gender dynamics might reshape this as something to be proud of.

The association of the first ejaculation with sexuality makes it an emotionally-charged event. North American researchers considering the importance of the first ejaculation, which is biologically significant in sexual and reproductive functioning, showed how it is also psychologically meaningful while at the same time socially invisible. The mean age at semenarche (first ejaculation) is 12.9 years.

All of the boys in the group had had sex education in school, yet many felt unprepared for their first ejaculation, which occurred earlier than they expected and before formal education. Those who felt prepared expressed more positive feelings and coped better. Common responses to semenarche included surprise, curiosity, pleasure and confusion. Most boys did not tell anyone that this event had occurred and many had initially confused ejaculation and urination (Stein and Reiser, 1994). 'Risk-taking' behaviours (pregnancy for their partner, sexually transmitted diseases including HIV infection) are common when adolescents start being sexually intimate and are often linked with other health-risk behaviours, such as substance misuse (Tripp and Viner, 2005).

In a Swedish study with forty 17-year-old boys, adolescent fatherhood was considered to be a catastrophe while abortion was seen as a moral dilemma (see Chapter 8). Most participants agreed that the unrestricted right to decide on abortion rests upon the girl, but some were frustrated by not having any legal right to influence the decision. Contraceptive failure was viewed as common and mainly due to the influence of alcohol or in relation to unplanned sex. Boys perceived girls as having a greater responsibility in avoiding pregnancy, and they often put a blind trust in the girls' use of hormonal contraceptives or initiation of emergency contraception.

Several groups had insufficient knowledge about foetal development and other aspects of reproduction. Many were unsatisfied with the sex education they had received at school, but still considered it to be an important counterweight to other sources of information concerning sex, such as pornography (Ekstrand et al., 2007).

Evolutionary psychologists see sexual relationships slightly differently from many other commentators on adolescent behaviour, as you will recall from Chapter 2. Schmitt and his colleagues (2001), for instance, proposed, based on an experimental study, that men and women have evolved short-term and long-term mating strategies that are pursued differently by each sex depending on theoretically derived dimensions of context. According to their sexual strategies theory (SST), the sexes tend to differ in the nature and prominence of the short-term component of human mating – particularly in their short-term desire for sexual variety. They considered that short-term mating (a fling or brief affair) was unrelated generally to psychological dysfunction and may in fact be related to mentally healthy personality characteristics in men, while the opposite is the case for women.

One study emphasized the difficulties adolescents face if they think they might be gay (Chambers et al., 2004), describing how homophobic and misogynistic abuse were used as key instruments in teenage peer regulation.

### Eating disorders

There is no simple definition of what constitutes an eating disorder or who is most at risk (Cooper and Fairburn, 2003) and there are several different explanations of causes from genetic (Bulik et al., 2005) to psychosocial and emotional, based on body image and low self-esteem (Malson, 1998). It is strongly argued by clinicians that there are more eating problems requiring attention than the ones categorized in the popular understanding (such as bulimia and anorexia), and these are now frequently given the label 'NOS' or 'not otherwise specified' (Fairburn and Bohn, 2005).

Studies of the antecedents and risk factors in relation to eating disorders vary but there is evidence of links between personal histories of abuse and neglect, depression, domestic violence and eating disorders in general, including obesity (Wonderlich et al., 1996). While the findings indicate that sexual abuse is a risk factor for the development of bulimia nervosa, it does not appear to be specific to bulimia nervosa nor is it relevant to most cases (Murray and Waller, 2002; Smolak and Murnen, 2002). Sexual abuse appears to be a risk factor for psychiatric disorder in general (including bulimia nervosa) among young adult women. There was no evidence that secondary referrals of bulimia nervosa are necessarily indicative of sexual abuse (Waller, 1991; Welch and Fairburn, 1994). The incidence of bulimia was 4.9 times higher among the study participants who reported having multiple episodes of childhood sexual abuse, however, than those who reported having no such history, even after statistical adjustment for factors such as parental divorce and educational level (www.medscape.org/viewarticle/571082).

## The socio-material context of adolescence

Identity at this stage of the lifespan reflects social norms and prominent discourses about what counts as important in contemporary life, such as gender, sexuality, social class and ethnicity.

In the late twentieth and early twenty-first centuries post-pubescent young people would most probably be in full-time education and looked after at home or by social services. In the nineteenth century they would most likely have been working. In some societies, even in the twenty-first century, young teenage women (and sometimes young men) may be married and even become parents shortly after puberty. In the USA and Europe teenage pregnancies are seen as a social problem, however.

Much has been written in the later twentieth and early twenty-first centuries about ethnicity and identity. This has focused particularly on the process of searching and feeling comfort/discomfort about ethnic identity and on how tensions between identity and culture, in every sense, provide major risk factors for mental ill health (Martinez and Dukes, 1997; Roberts et al., 1999). On the whole though, it appears that adolescents who have a clear sense of their ethnicity also have higher self-esteem (Umaña-Taylor et al., 2002).

### Drugs and alcohol

Sexual abuse in childhood and adolescence is widespread, pervasive and corrosive. It is also an important exacerbating factor in adolescents' subsequent lifestyle and the choice of protective behaviours, including abusing drugs and alcohol to ease the pain (Medrano et al., 2002; Tyler et al., 2000).

In a study of runaway adolescents, relationships between sexual abuse and sexual risk, substance use, emotional distress and conduct problems were examined. Those who had been abused were significantly more likely than non-abused peers to engage in unprotected sex, have more sexual partners and use alcohol and drugs, but did not differ in their levels of emotional distress. Those abused after the age of 13 were more often engaged in sex work than non-abused peers. Boys abused before age 13 had more sexual partners than those not abused, and runaway boys were significantly more likely to have been sexually abused than has been reported in prior research (Rotheram-Borus et al., 1996).

Many young people end up in custody because of substance abuse, and that is problematic in its own right. But it might also lead young women into the hands of gangs of men who exploit vulnerable adolescent girls for sex work.

### Adolescents in custody

Teenagers in custody are particularly vulnerable. In a review of teenage deaths in custody in the UK, Coles and Shaw (2012) reported that, between 1990 and 2011, 30 young people had died in custody and 28 of those deaths were self-inflicted. Of the other two, one was homicide and another restraint-related. Coles and Shaw argue, with evidence, that judiciary and prison staff frequently fail young people through being unable to assess the risk when a child/young person is highly vulnerable. Many staff working with young people in trouble have not been trained to work with their specific and special needs. These authors also identify what they call a discourse of 'adult-centrism'. Some staff working with fully developed, tall adolescents in custody tend to see them as menacing rather than being young people just out of childhood with all the related confusion and challenges.

Coles and Shaw cite the case of Gareth Myatt (a mixed race 15-year-old) to demonstrate how vital qualities, such as containment and support, are lacking in the judicial and custody system for adolescents. Gareth's death was caused by restraint following what was initially a minor incident. The problem escalated for Gareth when he was taken back to his room, isolated and, one by one, his few personal possessions were removed from his room as punishment. Gareth did not react until a small scrap of paper with his mother's phone number was taken – then he swore and begged them to leave it. Interpreted as a threatening situation by the staff, he was physically restrained and that led to his asphyxiation and death.

Such an example as this exposes the gap between the staff and teenagers, and how this misunderstanding can lead to the ultimate tragedy. For Gareth, his personal possessions were all that he had to give him a link with his own past, his sense of family and who he really was. For him, the very last straw was the removal of the last link with his mother – her phone number.

It may be surprising that the staff in such specialist units had no sense of the importance of this link, but it is also apparent that adolescents are frequently unpredictable and adults feel physically threatened by them.

---

**PAUSE AND REFLECT**

- What do you imagine happened between the young person and the staff members in the example of Gareth Myatt?
- If you were supervising the staff how would you have advised them to manage this young man?

- What would be your feelings about Gareth's death if you were his social worker?
- What do you think would be the staff members' feelings?
- What, apart from the death itself, is important in the scenario described?

---

### Chances of survival

While there have been many other unthinkable stories about children who have lived in residential homes and places of adolescent and child detention, there have also been stories of survival (Canham, 1998/2012). Celebrity accounts of being in care, such as the television programme about the actor, Neil Morrissey and his brother Steve, have provided some engaging evidence of what it feels like to be a looked-after child – what led to the experience and what happened afterwards. *Neil Morrissey: Care Home Kid* (BBC, 2011) described his extraordinary childhood. Neil and Steve had grown up in Stafford in the 1970s and, after being caught stealing from shops and the changing room of the sports club, they were taken into local authority care. At the ages of ten and twelve, the brothers were placed in different children's homes and the outcomes of their experiences also differed. While Neil was there until he was seventeen and became a successful actor, his brother Steve had a far tougher time and, aged 37, was found dead in his flat on his own. For some adults brought up in difficult circumstances, including inadequate or damaging foster or children's homes, their personality and previous life experiences enable the degree to which they are resilient in their adult lives. It is clear, though, that life in a children's home is not on the whole positive, although for some, like Neil, it could be bearable.

Canham (1998/2012), a child psychotherapist who had also worked in residential care homes for children, talked of the number of children who come and go, often to their birth parents or to a foster home. Sometimes children's homes were like waiting rooms. However, some other children remain in the home for many years and that has the effect of making them feel left behind. The staff group in care homes also has a high turnover, which is not conducive to the children's health, particularly in maintaining the ability to mentalize in the context of (reasonably) secure attachment relationships.

Many of the children who end up in care, particularly those who stay in residential homes until they are eighteen or for significantly long periods of time, will probably not have managed a secure and loving attachment or the establishment of trust with either staff or peers.

A report on a survey of the mental health of young people in care makes their widespread distress very clear (Meltzer et al., 2002). The researchers provided the following disturbing results from their study, for those both within and outside the adolescent age group. Among young people aged 5–17 years looked after by local authorities, 45% were assessed as having a mental disorder. Of these, 37% had clinically significant conduct disorders (anti-social behaviour which indicates a disturbed state of mind). Furthermore, 12% of the young people with a mental disorder were assessed as having emotional disorders – anxiety and depression – and 7% were rated as hyperkinetic (hyperactive). This suggests that among the population of looked-after children, nearly half experience severe emotional disturbance, of whom more than one-third were highly disturbed with conduct disorders and nearly one-fifth were anxious, depressed and hyperactive. None of this is conducive to a positive sense of identity but leads to role confusion and social exclusion. Around the ages of 11 to 15 these problems are particularly acute, reflecting the difficulties inherent in adolescent challenges.

## PAUSE AND REFLECT

**Supporting mental well-being throughout adolescence**

During adolescence, mental well-being is fragile for many who lead apparently normal lives and go on to develop as relatively untroubled members of society. For young people at risk, with histories of family dysfunction, abuse and neglect their present lives and futures may be intolerable and mental breakdown, turning to drugs and alcohol for support or criminal behaviour is a possible outcome.

A website was launched in 2013 so that disturbed adolescents could find help for their mental health worries. Many young people find it hard to let anyone among friends, families or health professionals into their personal worlds if they are feeling pressure such as anxiety and depression, which might lead to suicidal feelings and behaviours.

A look at the website www.mindfull.org would give you helpful insights, by following the links to counselling, mentoring and self-help to gain a picture of what vulnerable adolescents are going through but might neither choose nor be able to share with you. The link to professionals, for instance, includes mental health professionals, some of whom will be reading this book.

## The discursive context: the social construction of adolescence and gender

Adolescence, is a relatively new construct, defined as teenage dependence with the individual being positioned in the family as *not grown up*. It was invented in the face of increased affluence and stability arising from technological development, urbanization and structural changes in employment which led to more stable families and thus increasing teenage dependence on their parents in Western societies (Fasick, 1994). These demographic patterns have had their benefits and challenges but it has been suggested, with good evidence, that the adolescent condition has led to disaffection and problems for young people themselves, their families and their communities (Bakan, 1971; Gergen et al., 2004). Teenagers living at home as *children* are likely to find their energies frustrated and suffer from a confused sense of identity. In the twenty-first century the typical adolescence is perceived as a time of *problems* rather than the launch-pad for maturity and a productive and peaceful adulthood (Dasen, 2000).

### *Constructing gender*

Gender, as we have seen, is a *process* through which social life is organized at the level of the individual, family and society. Puberty and its biological changes has become the objective centre for the construction of contemporary adolescence. Biological development per se has been positioned as a significant social process and, in particular, one that brings gender issues to the fore because the biological changes at this time of the lifespan highlight diversity. Gender, however, is more than simply a description of biological difference and diversity because it prescribes and defines the parameters of individual human experience in that women's lives are different from men's lives.

Sex and gender are about biology, culture, power and discourse. Almost all societies are patriarchal – they obey the rule of the father and are run by men or masculinist value systems.

Marie Maguire (1995) takes on the Foucauldian notion (see Chapter 3) that sex and gender are discursively constructed, suggesting that, although there are objective biological differences between men and women, the practice of gender and sexuality depends on the dominant discourses and knowledge–power relations of the historical period.

What are 'masculinity' and 'femininity'? Every society has ways of distinguishing the sexes – socially, culturally, psychologically. Historically, however, the way this division has been drawn has varied enormously. What counts as maleness or femaleness in one period or cultural setting can look radically unlike its equivalents in other times or places. And similarly, how an individual comes to identify him or herself as belonging to a gender also varies greatly (Maguire, 1995: 1).

This is a good description of how gender has become a socially constructive discursive practice: the concepts are built through language and that language defines and limits the behaviours of each one. Furthermore, discursive practices inform both social and self-surveillance in that we reflect on the way we see and perform the narratives of our identity.

It is not only accepted now, but *expected*, that mothers of children over the age of five work outside the home, at least on a part-time basis. This would have been unthinkable in 1950s post-war Britain (see Chapter 5) because it was widely proposed that children would suffer from maternal deprivation. As we now know, relationships between mothers and children are far more complicated.

Women and men use their bodies to express everyday femininity and masculinity and experience sexual sensation. For example, we emphasize our physical shape and attributes, which have been socially defined as attracting sexual partners, through dress, hair-style, posture, make-up and physical movement. As a result, women's (stereotypical) passive/responsive qualities are emphasized, as are men's (stereotypical) aggressive/active ones.

Gender differences between the way women and men experience these competing and complementary forces are emphasized in both scientific literature and in everyday life, where they are taken-for-granted and frequently characterized as the 'battle between the sexes' (Baron-Cohen, 2004).

- hides emotions
- dominant
- assertive
- reckless
- intelligent
- logical
- sloppy
- aggressive
- competitive
- active

- considerate
- gentle
- cries more easily
- understanding of others
- aware of others' feelings
- interested in appearance
- feelings easily hurt
- passive
- able to devote self to others

*Figure 9.2* Gender stereotypes

## PAUSE AND REFLECT

### Gender and stereotyping

It has become a cliché, but even so a useful illustration, that the British Prime Minister Margaret Thatcher was more masculine in her values than many men and that she paid little heed to 'women's issues'. However those who knew her also said she was a very feminine woman who used female wiles to get her way.

But what does this mean? There is clearly a suggestion here that what counts as masculine, feminine and female wiles are not clearly observable ideas that we can all agree upon. It would seem that each of us (presumably within some limits) has a different image of what is involved. Sex and gender represent a conundrum so it is perhaps not a surprise that young people have difficulties getting used to their changing bodies and the discursive consciousness that accompanies each sex.

'Who am I going to be?' varies across generational cohorts and the decades as social norms, values and the social construction of gender vary.

What discursive practices position women as being powerful and getting their way within a patriarchal system?

Think for a minute about a situation that is common to your everyday life, for example, going to work, going to a party, involvement in a family occasion, asking for help with an assignment, taking part in a sporting activity. You can choose others.

Imagine in detail how things would be both different and similar for you if you were to take part in that activity as a member of the other sex/a different ethnicity/an adolescent.

- How would you feel?
- What would be different about the way you would behave, speak, move and so on?
- Would you approach people differently?
- Would you talk about different kinds of things or in different ways?
- How would you imagine others would react to you?
- Would you be thinking differently about aspects of the chosen situation?
- Make a list of the things that are the same and the things that are different.
- Would you feel comfortable and why would that be?

It is difficult to separate anatomy and biology from their *meaning* – either their meaning to individuals or to a society. The crucial aspects of anatomy/biology in relation to gender are the ways in which men and women are physically different, and the fact that those differences are endowed with values that consistently disadvantage women. Women's bodies, with the capacity for child-bearing and breast-feeding, are clearly different anatomically and biologically from men's. These anatomical and biological differences are the source of different behaviours associated with reproductive function (see Chapter 10). This is not in dispute (Choi and Nicolson, 1994; Ussher, 1997). What is problematic however, are the various ways in which the female body has been positioned as subordinate to that of the male (Lee, 2009; Nicolson, 1998). This is often achieved in relation to women's reproductive capacities by patriarchal science describing female possibilities, such as the ability to have babies, as if they were deficiencies (Ussher, 2003).

Masculinity, on the other hand, is positioned as positive and competent in youth, middle and old age. This is not to say that all men are destined to be successful in their professional and personal lives, far from it. Masculinity is about competition, often to the death of the rival. It is not uncommon for newly-appointed senior managers, for instance, to express open hostility to rivals, particularly towards those in slightly junior positions who might be ready to take over from them if they show weakness. The male body is built to fight and, whereas the older woman is seen mainly in terms of her faded femininity, the older man who is no longer in the running for power is frequently seen as wise and experienced.

Feminist social science, psychoanalysis and post-structuralist critiques have all made significant contributions to understanding the meaning of the gendered body, and feminists in particular to the power connotations of these meanings (Paechter, 2006). The meaning of the gendered body is best described as a *process* rather than a set of facts, and this process takes place throughout an individual's psychological development, responding to social development and change. Consequently, it is difficult for an individual to experience one without the other. Thus we give our own body meaning which develops through our reflexive work in relation to different levels of consciousness, and this becomes embedded, albeit in a dynamic way, as part of our biography. However, the meaning we give our own body is linked in with the social construction of the female and male body. We evaluate and regulate ourselves accordingly.

## The intra-psychic context of adolescence

The intra-psychic nature of adolescence revolves around the complex negotiation of the material and discursive contexts and how they fit into the emotional level at which you have come to operate. For most of us, adolescence is a time for catching up – bringing our emotional (often unconscious) experiences and reactions towards some kind of equivalence with our biological bodies. For example, how do you, as an adolescent, *handle* the physiological changes and the changes in others' reactions to you? Once you become a sexual being, how do you cope with and process the feelings that connect you to others? What happens when you are rejected by someone you have sexual feelings towards (Orbach, 2010)?

Take the case of the adolescent boy who has fantasies (and even sometimes the experience) of a sexual relationship with a school-teacher. The young person involved may be the size and shape of an adult, he may even appear to have the emotional maturity of one but his experience of managing his sexual body and *mind* exposes him to stress. Young people who have been securely attached and developed supportive relationships (see Chapter 5) will be able to cope and develop their skills and abilities to distinguish sexual from emotional feelings of attachment. But for other, more vulnerable people, this represents damaging abuse. In the 2006 film, *Notes on a Scandal*, Cate Blanchett's character, who was in love with an adolescent school-boy, debated these issues with the teacher played by Judi Dench (who had her own fantasies about her colleague). In a situation such as this, there is rarely a positive outcome.

The real-life case of 30-year-old married teacher, Jeremy Forrest, and a 15-year-old school girl is interesting for conflicting reasons. Forrest and the pupil had been in a relationship for some months before travelling to France and staying there together for a week. He was convicted and imprisoned for abducting the pupil in June 2013, There are several website accounts from national newspapers with different angles and opinions on the story: some of the more emotive ones call him a 'pervert teacher' but several also include the young woman's version that *she* 'groomed' the teacher. You will have to come to your own conclusions, of course, about what motives underlie the story, but it highlights the conflicting conscious and unconscious experiences and expectations around adolescence – their own and our perceptions of them.

Even so, what takes place in such real or fantasy relationships needs to be explored and understood to increase understanding of HGD. Erikson's phase of identity versus role confusion remains helpful as a template for understanding the emotions surrounding these and other experiences (Erikson, 1950/1963). This phase also acts as a signpost to the unconscious levels of managing this pivotal experience.

Much of what happens *psychically* (or emotionally and unconsciously) during adolescence represents a response to the individual's personal *past*. By contrast, much of the discursive construction of adolescence is about *who you will become* as a future individual (or at least the tensions that constrain who you will become).

During adolescence memories and stories of the self play a critical role in negotiating identity. These memories may or may not represent fact but the narrative, as it develops, does represent a personal reality for the individual and one on which their future life is built. The story of the famous actress Marilyn Monroe is a poignant account of adolescent confusion that remained unresolved through her relatively short life (see Box 9.1 overleaf). I draw links as far as possible between the material, discursive and intra-psychic contexts.

Like any other life, the background to our own story is constructed through memory and telling and retelling some events to ourselves and/or others (Le Carre, 1997; Reavey and Brown, 2007). Everyday life is very difficult for looked-after children, particularly during adolescence when they are struggling with the developmental task of making sense of who they are. It is also critical, as Neil Morrissey said, to bring identity development to the fore although survival means shutting out much of the past and that in itself brings problems of making sense of one's story.

## BOX 9.1

### The story of Marilyn Monroe

Marilyn Monroe was born Norma Jeane Mortenson in 1926 to a single woman who was unsure of the identity of the baby's father (Banner, 2012). He was believed to be a man called Stanley Gifford who worked in the film industry. When she was a teenager, Marilyn tried to contact Gifford but he always refused to see her. It has been suggested that she felt a profound loss at never knowing a father, a scar that never healed, and much of her adolescence and young adulthood was spent dealing with fantasies about her parents, and her father in particular.

Marilyn, like many other children who grow up in care, came from a maternal background of mental health and financial problems. Marilyn was boarded out with foster parents when she was only 12 days old. The religious couple with whom she lived repeatedly told her she would end up in Hell because she liked to sing and dance. When her foster mother died suddenly, Marilyn was returned to her mother, but her mother had a mental breakdown shortly afterwards and attacked a friend with a carving knife. She was institutionalized for the rest of her life. Marilyn entered (what was then called) an orphanage, which she found unbearable. She was there for two years before going to live with a family friend but, after that arrangement broke down, she lived in a series of foster homes. During her adolescence she was apparently sexually abused by at least one of the foster fathers whose wife then attacked Marilyn, accusing her of seducing her husband and refusing to recognize the adult man's responsibilities and role.

Just before her death in 1962, Marilyn filled out an official form in front of her secretary, who witnessed the melancholy star bitterly scribble 'Unknown' on the line marked 'Father'.

In later life Marilyn often exaggerated, embellished, and fantasized about the dismal events of her childhood, but there is little doubt that her early life contained disorganized attachment relationships and sexual abuse.

### False memories?

It is frequently stated that Marilyn Monroe embellished stories of her childhood (Banner, 2012). In many other cases where accusations of physical and sexual abuse were made it has also been said that the adolescent was lying or mistaken. Questions have been raised for several years about whether 'recovered' memories are 'false', and taking this view sometimes represents an attempt to discredit social workers, counsellors and psychotherapists, as well as those whose memories of physical and sexual abuse are recovered. There are suggestions that some memories can be implanted by the professional (Pope, 1996). While this idea is used to discredit the 'talking professions', research has shown that it may be possible to implant memories in ways that might benefit people, through changing the memory of trauma for instance (Laney and Loftus, 2010). Even so, this is an exciting area of fast-developing research and many questions have yet to be answered, which has serious implications for memory experts and those who have to make judgments about risk to mental health in criminal-legal and safeguarding settings (Read, 1999).

One study examined whether false memories of emotional events could be implanted and, if so, whether real, implanted and fabricated memories had distinctive features. Results indicated that 26% of participants recovered a complete memory for the false experience and another 30% recalled aspects of the false experience. Real, implanted and fabricated memories differed on several dimensions (e.g., confidence, vividness, details, repeated details, coherence, stress).

These findings have important implications for the debate over recovered and false memories, suggesting that it is highly possible to recall clearly and in some detail events that did not happen (Porter et al., 1999).

Another study to examine the same phenomenon did not concur fully with these findings, although the methodology was different. Susan Clancy and her colleagues (Clancy et al., 1999) tested whether asking participants to imagine unusual childhood events inflated their confidence that these events happened to them, and then investigated whether this effect was greater in women who reported recovered memories of childhood sexual abuse than in women who did not. Participants were pretested on their confidence that certain childhood events had happened to them before being asked to imagine some of these events in the laboratory. These results suggested that individuals can counteract memory distortions potentially associated with guided imagery, at least under some conditions. Both of these studies, however, were conducted under laboratory conditions and involved manipulation of the memory process by the experimenter.

Chris Brewin (2007) reviewed empirical research since 2000 on trauma and autobiographical memory in adults. He identified four enduring controversies. These are whether (a) traumatic memories are inherently different from other types of autobiographical memory; (b) memory for trauma is better or worse than memory for non-traumatic events; (c) traumas can be forgotten and then recalled later in life and (d) special mechanisms such as repression (when memories are buried deep in the unconscious to save the ego from the pain, see Chapter 3) or dissociation (whereby a person is able to literally disassociate herself from the acts which comprise the memory) are required to account for any such forgetting.

Brewin concluded that traumatic and non-traumatic memories differ substantially, but only in clinical, not in healthy, populations. In other words, people who have suffered from mental health problems have a different sense of their own pasts than those with robust mental health. So, whereas involuntary memory is enhanced in clinical populations (that is, comes into consciousness in a very sharp and vivid way), voluntary memory is likely to be fragmented, disorganized, and incomplete. Brewin anticipates more information from neuropsychology advances and brain imaging which will help us to understand more.

How do people who have been abused (whether or not they have had a history of mental illness) make sense of their traumatic memories (Reavey and Brown, 2007)? Memories are highly complex and central to identity construction. Making sense of your memories of your own life means finding a way of reconciling the trauma and coping with the past pain, as well as making sense of what that means for your life. In Neil Morrissey's case, he was able to recall his experiences in care as including the experience of some 'love', although that had not been the case for his brother. Marilyn Monroe was described as being scarred by her past – things she knew and things she didn't (the identity of her father and any relationship with him) as well as being accused of 'making things up' about her life-story.

## Case study: Andy, the self-abusing bully

Andy had spent time in a young offender's unit by the age of fourteen. He had spent much of his pre-teen years in care, mostly in a children's home, but he moved to live with foster-parents when he reached the age of eleven. While in the children's home (aged nine) he had been accused of sexually assaulting a girl of his own age. No-one was ever sure what had really happened but Andy's behaviour became increasingly aggressive and beyond the control of the professionals in charge. The foster-parents were distant relatives and for around a year it seemed as if Andy might have settled down. Then the foster-father became ill with pancreatic cancer and died very soon after diagnosis, Mary the mother could no longer manage to care for Andy, even though she always maintained contact. He was moved to another family but by then he was involved with crime – breaking and entering, buying, using and selling hard drugs.

### *Family background*

Andy had been a physically unappealing child, but some of that was seen to be self-inflicted because he ate prolifically and did not wash properly. He didn't seem to care about himself at all. Andy was unable to make or sustain a relationship and even the adults around him did not like him.

Andy was born into a single-parent family. He was Millie's fourth child – her first three were girls and each of them had a different father. Andy was a more difficult baby than the girls, but Millie was in no state to care adequately for any of them. She was at breaking point when Andy came along. All her daughters had spent some time in care and plans had been made for Andy to be placed on the at risk register when he was born. For that reason he was very soon placed with temporary foster parents and then in a children's home. Then, Millie's mother, Bex, agreed to move in with Millie to care for her and the new baby. However, Bex herself had a history of psychiatric difficulties – she had been sexually abused by an older brother.

Bex tried her best to look after Millie and Andy, and mostly dealt with Andy by feeding him high-calorie, sweet and highly unsuitable foods and drinks. When he

195

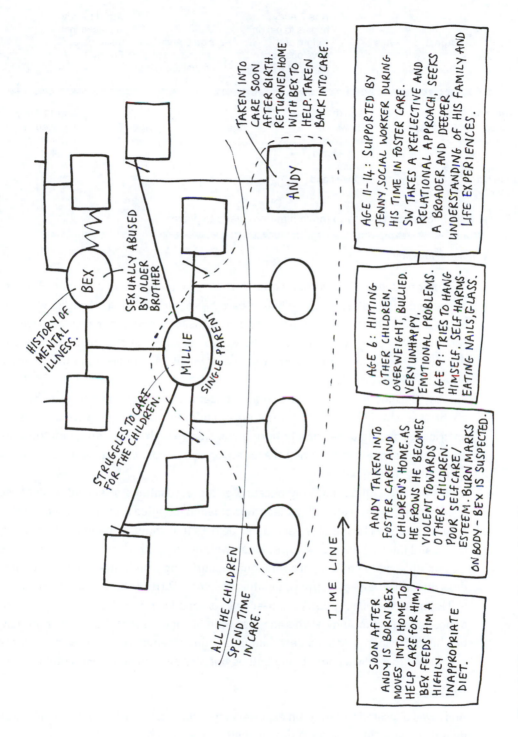

**Figure 9.3** Genogram and ecomap for Andy

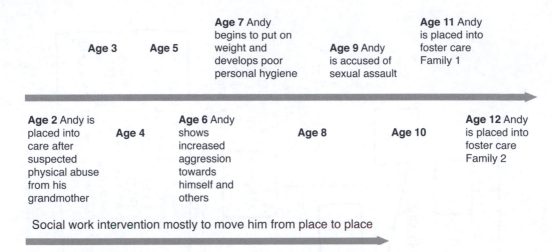

**Figure 9.4** *Timeline for Andy*

was placed under a care order, some burns were found on his body and Bex was suspected rather than Millie. While in care he rarely smiled or engaged with any of the staff. As he grew older, he increasingly lacked a sense of personal hygiene. His favourite activity was eating and he would spend as much time as he could in the kitchen doing just that. He grew very overweight, soon becoming the victim of other children's cruelty.

Andy became depressed, but he also became violent and by the time he was six he was strong enough to hit the other children, mostly using weapons such as cricket bats. He once tried to burn a child's arm with a hot pan taken from the stove. Andy seemed to have no care for anyone and, most distressingly, apparently cared little for himself.

When he was nine, possibly because of the accusations of sexual assault, he tried to hang himself and after that attempt failed (bungled and discovered in time) he tried to eat nails and glass and other objects that could damage his alimentary canal and internal organs. Andy seemed well on the path to becoming diagnosed 'sociopathic' or, in contemporary language, suffering from anti-social personality disorder or now anti-social/psychopathic type (APA, 2010) or borderline personality.

Not all of the description of anti-social personality in the *Pause and Reflect* box opposite applied to Andy at the age (between six and eleven) that I focus on now, but his behaviour was considered unusual and extreme. The care workers were concerned that he was both being bullied but also seen to be bullying others.

### Practice

Andy was allocated to Jenny, an experienced social work practitioner, when he was about 11 years old, during his time in foster care, until he was 14.

**Anti-social personality**

The formal description of anti-social personality is that these individuals seek power over others and will manipulate, exploit, deceive, con, or otherwise take advantage, in order to inflict harm or to achieve their goals. An arrogant, self-centred, and entitled attitude is pervasive, along with callousness and little empathy for others' needs or feelings (Fonagy et al., 2003). Rights, property, or safety of others are disregarded, with little or no remorse or guilt if others are harmed. Emotional expression is mostly limited to irritability, anger and hostility; acknowledgement and articulation of other emotions, such as love or anxiety, are rare. There is little insight into motivations and an impaired ability to consider alternative interpretations of experience.

Temperamental aggression and a high threshold for pleasurable excitement are typically associated with this personality, linked to reckless sensation-seeking behaviours, impulsivity without regard for consequences, and a sense of invulnerability. Unlawful or unethical behaviour is often pursued, including substance abuse and physical violence. Aggressive or sadistic acts are common in pursuit of personal agendas, and sometimes pleasure or satisfaction is derived from humiliating, demeaning, dominating or hurting others. Superficial charm and ingratiation may be employed to achieve certain ends, and there is disregard for conventional moral principles (Finzi et al., 2001). General irresponsibility about work obligations or financial commitments is commonly present, as well as problems with authority figures.

• Think about how much of this might apply in your assessment of Andy.

Like everyone else, Jenny found it almost impossible to establish any rapport with Andy, and was initially very worried about the consequences for his future if she could not find a suitable placement. She began looking at the files on his life to date and focused particularly on the significance of his earlier highly negative attachment experiences. He had been moved almost immediately from his mother (who would have been unlikely to offer him much of a bonding experience) to foster and residential care and then to his mother's home with his grandmother Bex, whom it is believed systematically chastised him physically. Millie, his mother, expected her children to be separated from her and placed in medium- to long-term care at some point in their early childhood (as with Andy's sisters). There was no obvious father figure in the household, nor was there any attempt to make links with Andy's father who was technically 'unknown'.

Jenny could have simply mounted a holding operation for Andy, except that he became increasingly violent as well as personally at risk with his substance abuse. His appearance and general demeanor, despite efforts of care staff and foster parents, remained unkempt.

Jenny could not bear to think how much Andy repulsed her, but this also meant she was unable to reflect on their relationship and what she might learn about working with Andy if she could think beneath the surface in a more reflective-relational way (Cooper, 2005; Howe, 1996).

Notwithstanding that Jenny had a sound grasp of theory, particularly in relation to the difficulties Andy had in making relationships based on his early experiences, she could not help wondering why anyone would like this young man.

In supervision she worked at developing a reflective-relational approach towards Andy which involved:

- Taking a general MDI perspective on adolescence as a stage of development, recognizing the importance of physiology and psychology concerning the body.
- Refocusing on the importance of identity development as central to adolescence, thus reinforcing for her the relationship between Andy's physical appearance and his sense of who he was.
- Focusing on herself and her reactions to an angry, unattractive young man with a history of violence and a suspicion of sexual assault.

  - She reconsidered what she thought about Andy – recalling her understanding of disorganized attachment.
  - She had tried to monitor her feelings about Andy recognizing that, for the most part, she tried to avoid either seeing or thinking about him, which is not best practice.
  - She, therefore, tried to reconcile her academic knowledge with her feelings and consequently, rather than simply taking a reactive role, and working with Andy as a holding operation, she attempted to probe into his feelings and discuss his relationships, identity and sexual feelings.
  - As a consequence she also began working with his family (sisters, mother, grandmother) and care staff, focusing on feelings and what might be different in the future.

Andy, as described here, is an amalgamation of two similar teenage boys, and the social worker in both cases attempted something different from the box-ticking, reactive approach. They had previously managed to avoid engaging with him but could cover themselves by listing their visits and other activities to support him. They discovered in both cases a vulnerability with these young men that could actually be worked with, intra-psychically and socially. The boys began to gain a sense of their place in the world and, particularly in one case, an embryonic empathy towards others emerged to enable them to develop relationships.

## CHAPTER SUMMARY

Adolescence is a period of profound change at all levels, material-discursive and intra-psychic. Western industrial societies, particularly in times of recession, have shown that they are not ready to offer young people much in the way of a guaranteed future. This has meant that adolescence for many is a time of dependency on parents or the State or of facing the marginality of social exclusion, which might mean turning to gang culture, violence, drugs and alcohol abuse with the likely consequences of illness, death or time spent incarcerated. The result is further exclusion, poor health, especially mental health, poverty and poor prospects for a satisfying life and relationships. This is not to say that, despite the tragedy and sadness, there are not many stories of adolescents successfully negotiating the extremes of the changes their bodies and emotions are facing.

In many ways adolescents are more challenging for social workers to support than individuals at other stages of the lifespan because they are at such a crossroads. Despite appearances, there is a gulf between teenage perceptions of the world and those of social workers and other adults.

Reading this chapter should therefore:

• Help you to understand the pivotal role of adolescence in the lifespan, which suggests that it provides some degree of opportunity for intervention to support healthy development in some damaged young people.
• Emphasize how, despite the fact we have all passed through this tumultuous stage of the lifespan, it is easy not to see the vulnerabilities that lurk behind frequent bravado.

## FURTHER READING

Briggs, A. (ed.) (2012) *Waiting to be Found: Papers on children in care* (pp. 61–70). London: Karnac.

Erikson, E. (1959/1980) *Identity, Youth and Crisis*. New York: Norton.

Waddell, M. (2005) *Inside Lives: Psychoanalysis and the growth of personality*. London: Karnac.

chapter

# 10

# YOUNG ADULTHOOD: INTIMACY VERSUS ISOLATION

**LEARNING OBJECTIVES**

- To review the psychosocial tasks of young adulthood particularly those connected to forming intimate relationships.
- To explore key events in young adulthood and consider what might lead a young adult to happiness.
- To think about how you might use national statistics to identify what is going on for adults at this stage of their lives (and for other stages too).

## Introduction

Young adulthood, following the teenage and adolescent years, represents the time in life when some degree of identity and continuity has been established. Erikson, for example, indicated that young adulthood is typified by a further quest for identity and a move towards coping with intimacy with another person. This can be very hard for those who mostly failed to cope with adolescence very well.

It is at this time, following adolescence, puberty, growing identity and the awakening of a sense of sexuality, that the young adult might seek a partner to help repair some earlier emotional damage by forming a close attachment bond. This may work well or may exacerbate deep relationship difficulties. The fear at this stage of development is rejection and as Erikson says: 'ego-loss may lead to a deep sense of isolation and consequent self-absorption' (Erikson, 1950/1963: 237). In other words, rejection now might prevent someone from feeling that they belong in any way to the world in which they live – they might feel unwanted, unlovable and an outcast. You will recall that there are mental health challenges in adolescence which frequently lie undetected and unresolved. If this happens then the demands of adulthood may well be overwhelming and prevent the individual from looking out into the world to see what it might offer him.

### Psychosocial tasks

Probably the most important task in young adulthood is to discover more about your own identity, motivations and potential happiness by forming intimate

relationships – as friendships and with sexual partners. Frequently, success depends on what you do with your life and opportunities for making relationships
(Bunnell et al., 2012). Also, whether you make friendships easily or keep friendships over time depends, at least partly, on attachment style (see Chapter 4) (Davis
et al., 2004). Of course, intimacy is not the only concern at this stage of the lifespan.
Young adults will also be grappling with starting work, learning a trade or engaging in higher education – choosing their future life at some level. For young adults
graduating from an elite university, who are likely to have their skills sought after,
there may be a sense of achievement that feeds positively into identity. However,
academic or professional achievements might have been gained at the price of losing opportunities for intimate friendships and sexual partnerships.

Many young people coming out of care, or those who have had tragic and stressful backgrounds, may have a firm sense of identity as losers or bad people. Those
who have been in care for longest (over two years) are more likely to be at risk
of anxiety and depression in adulthood (Shechory and Sommerfeld, 2007). Many
young adults from problematic backgrounds may, consequently, have mental
health problems, break the law or abuse drugs following failure to cope with the
role confusion of adolescence (Smith et al., 2005).

Failure to engage effectively with another person of choice can be extremely
wounding and turn an individual back in on themselves. Those with a reasonably
secure experience of early attachment who survived adolescence without too much
of a sense of role confusion will manage to come to terms with being rejected by
some people on some occasions, realizing that 'it is not the end of the world' and
'life goes on'. Those with a poorly functioning sense of identity who found adolescent struggles difficult may find their difficulties intensify, with their stress levels
leading to a low sense of well-being in young adulthood.

While it is often considered that adolescence is a particularly difficult time of
life, expectations held by individuals and those around them as they reach adulthood – that they should be grown up, independent, have successful relationships
and be heading for some successes – can be doubly daunting.

## The bio-material context of young adulthood

Evolutionary psychology has much to say about mating behaviour or seeking sexual relationships (see Chapter 2 in particular, but also Chapter 9). Evolutionary
psychologists propose that women and men have different strategies for maximiz-
ing their genetic potential. Women are more choosy because their investment in
each offspring is nine months, and longer in terms of breast-feeding and care. For
men, their interest is in making sure they impregnate as many women as possible in order to ensure their genetic inheritance (Schmitt et al., 2001). This means,

therefore, that women and men are going to have difficulties agreeing on their relationship behaviours because the implication is that, while men have to ensure female sexual fidelity in order to be certain they have passed on *their* genes to the next generation (i.e. that woman's babies), men themselves are better off not being sexually faithful so that they ensure maximum opportunities for reproduction.

One typical study (Buss et al., 1992), conducted as an experiment, indicated that women were more jealous than men about infidelities, particularly emotional and sexual relationships outside the primary one. It has also been suggested, therefore, that one goal of male-perpetrated domestic violence is control over female sexuality, including the deterrence of infidelity. According to this hypothesis, domestic violence varies with women's reproductive value or expected future reproduction, declining steeply as women age (Peters et al., 2002).

The perspective that gender roles and behaviours are governed by evolutionary fitness continues to be challenged by feminist scholars (Bayer and Malone, 1996; Nicolson and Burr, 2003; Sayers, 1982) taking a more social/societal perspective on gender and power relations. There is a discussion of evolutionary psychology and rape in Chapter 2 that you might like to think about once again as a background to reading this part of the chapter.

For both women and men, questions of fertility and decisions about parenthood are part of the bio- and socio-material context of young adulthood (Aisenberg Romano et al., 2012). These decisions and experiences related to fertility can be fraught with anxiety – both unplanned pregnancies (Bouchard, 2005) and the failure of fertility treatments (Schmidt, 2010; Verhaak et al., 2005).

### The socio-material context

There are many other pitfalls and risks to expectations of young adulthood in the context of twenty-first-century life, with some evidence that three or more generations may remain living in the same household for mostly economic reasons, including the lack of affordable housing. Thus, there is an increased dependency at both ends of the lifespan, by which I mean that families living together may include older relatives, possibly grandparents, the householder, middle-aged parents, and not infrequently their children as young adults who have children of their own (see Chapters 11 and 12). All this impacts particularly on the choices and opportunities for those entering adulthood and, while there may be many positives to be drawn from families living together and sharing resources, it also militates against the development of independence and securing a strong identity (Shanahan, 2000).

The statistics that are available to demonstrate the material context in which relationships are developed tends to be about marriage and civil partnerships because these events are recorded officially. Have a look at the variety of information about marriage, civil partnerships, divorce and family size on the UK Government website:

## PAUSE AND REFLECT

### Independence and risk

The normal expectation in young adulthood – to become increasingly independent of their family of origin, more able to withstand the everyday and exceptional stresses of life, have their own friends and move towards a serious intimate relationship and parenthood – represent major pressures for all young adults.

The consequent risks include:

- Economic hardship due to poor educational and employment prospects.
- Health-related vulnerabilities.
- Relationships may be difficult to form.
- Relationships may break down.
- Parenthood doesn't happen or doesn't work.

All of these risks potentially lead to isolation because wealth and health in particular provide the opportunities and skills for developing intimacies on several levels to enhance the sense of who we are and our place in the world. However, it is important to note that not everything is to be judged on the surface. Just because someone is married with children does not mean that they are not isolated/experience intimacy – the stress of becoming a parent in itself might cause a relationship breakdown with mental ill health consequences (Flora and Segrin, 2000; Nicolson, 1998). Isolation in marriage is common, frequently in the medium to longer term, with some violent relationships beginning early on (Bacchus et al., 2004; Featherstone and Trinder, 1997; Nicolson, 2010; Wood, 2001).

You might like to listen again to the BBC Radio 4 programme *Generations Apart* (www.bbc.co.uk/programmes/b01pztjf), which identifies some of these issues, with interesting examples comparing the generation born soon after the Second World War with people who were born in the 1990s.

www.statistics.gov.uk/hub/population/families/marriages--cohabitations--civil-partnerships-and-divorces/index.html

Once you are used to looking at information from the Government Office of National Statistics you will see there are statistics about all aspects of British society They can become addictive! However, smaller academic surveys may also give information about people living together to provide depth and more detailed insights (Cherlin, 2004; Cheung, 2000; Schoen and Standish, 2001).

The following information about trends in intimate relationships for the first decade of the twenty-first century is based on reported statistics from the UK Government (news.bbc.co.uk/1/shared/bsp/hi/pdfs/11_04_07_social_trends.pdf). (This document comprises more than 150 pages and includes all recorded social trends – only download it if you have caught the statistics bug.)

Forming and sustaining intimate relationships are difficult tasks and the statistics for England and Wales mirror those of the USA in supporting this contention. While sustaining or breaking up from a long-term partnership may be within the province of mid- and late-adulthood, the energy that goes into meeting people and choosing a partner takes place early in adulthood.

It appears that young people have been delaying marriage, with the average age for first marriage in England and Wales in the first decade of the twenty-first century being 32 for men and 29 for women – an increase since 1971, when it was 25 and 23, respectively.

At the start of the second decade of the twenty-first century, almost 60% of men and 40% of women aged between 20 and 24 in England still live with their parents, and more than seven million people in Britain live alone, compared to three million in 1971.

Data issued by the Office for National Statistics gives a clear and invaluable picture of trends. In England and Wales the rate for marriage, for instance, has dropped dramatically over the last 100 years. In 1901 there were 259,400 marriages with 53.3 men per 1,000 of unmarried men getting married and 44.6 women per 1,000 of unmarried women. By 2001, fewer marriages took place (249,227), despite the increase in population, with 27.4 men and 23.7 women per 1,000 of the unmarried population of each sex getting married (www.guardian.co.uk/uk/office-for-national-statistics).

However, divorce rates also went down, suggesting that more heterosexual couples are choosing to live together rather than marry. (In 2005 there were 155,000 divorces in England and Wales compared to 180,000 in 1993, which was the peak year.)

However the Office for National Statistics data showed that children in the UK in the 1990s were three times more likely to live in one-parent households than they were in 1972 (news.bbc.co.uk/1/shared/bsp/hi/pdfs/11_04_07_social_trends.pdf).

These figures suggest that young (and older) heterosexual adults still opt for one significant intimate relationship, although they are perhaps more cautious than previous generations about the age at which they make a long-term legal commitment.

### Same-sex relationship patterns

Gay marriage, which has been possible in Canada since 2005, is now on the agenda in the UK and USA. Same-sex marriage became legal in England, Wales and Scotland (but not Northern Ireland) in March 2014. In the USA, same-sex marriage was recognized by the federal government and by some jurisdictions at the time of writing (2014). While religious rhetoric has been applied to prevent this from happening, it is clear that gay couples are keen to commit.

Same-sex couples formed 6,281 civil partnerships (3,227 male and 3,054 female) in the UK in 2009. This figure represents a fall of 12% compared with 2008 but, presumably, in the earlier year there were many couples who had been waiting to legalize their existing relationships.

Although more men than women formed same-sex civil partnerships in the UK in 2009, the proportion of all partnerships that were male decreased to 51%, compared with 53% in 2008. More men than women formed partnerships in England (52% male) while the situation was reversed in Scotland (44% male), Wales (46% male) and Northern Ireland (48% male).

In 2009, male civil partners in the UK were, on average, older than female civil partners (41.8 compared to 40.0), although the average age at formation had fallen since 2008 for both sexes. In the same year, 11% of men and 21% of women forming a civil partnership in the UK had been in a previous marriage or civil partnership.

## Becoming a parent

Patterns of fertility and the decision to become a parent have a complicated connection with women's and men's lives overall (Bouchard, 2005; Schmidt, 2010). Better-educated, middle-class women appear to have ensured greater control over when, if and how many children they have than women from less privileged backgrounds. Further, control over fertility means more scope for education and employment for women, which in turn provides opportunities for independence and autonomy. As a consequence, this impacts upon the lives and expectations of men.

The statistics quoted above make it clear that more couples in the 1990s were divorcing, separating, marrying later and not marrying, more frequently than was the case in the 1970s and 1980s. This data is almost certainly connected to the fact that women's lives are no longer solely prescribed by their role as mother in the traditional family.

It is not only the quality or length of a relationship that determines whether a couple become parents. Approximately one in six couples in the USA, as in most other developed economies, experience difficulty conceiving. The global figure is estimated to be 60–80 million people. Likewise, approximately 15% of couples of childbearing age seek medical help for infertility, usually after about two years of failing to conceive. Among these couples, infertility is exclusively a problem with the female in 30–40% of cases and exclusively a problem with the male in 10–30% of cases. In 15–30% of cases, both partners have detectable abnormalities. After thorough medical examinations, the causes of infertility remain unexplained in 5–10% of couples.

There are US government websites (e.g. www.census.gov/hhes/fertility/data/cps/2010.html) that have further data of this kind. While it is definitely worth a look if you are interested in how the data are broken down between different social and ethnic groups, the above information sets the scene adequately.

The couples who do seek medical help for infertility have to make difficult choices because treatments are scarce, expensive and not always successful. Furthermore, there are cultural and personal values that influence people's decisions (Verhaak et al., 2005)

## Mental health and abortion

Some social workers may be faced with ethical dilemmas in relation to women who want or who have had abortions for social reasons (Furman et al., 2004; Gilbert,

2000). Women who have terminated a pregnancy are a vulnerable group (usually of young adults) who are frequently confused and distressed and may feel that they have been betrayed by their partner, family and others (Boyle, 1997; Faria et al., 1985). There may be not as much stigma associated with abortion in the early twenty-first century as there was in the 1970s and 1980s when the possibility of a legal termination in the UK was relatively new. There is also more general support for adolescent women who have babies and choose to bring them up than in previous generations (see Chapter 9).

## PAUSE AND REFLECT

### The experience of abortion

Women seek and obtain abortions for different reasons; at different times of gestation; via differing medical procedures; and within different personal, social, economic, and cultural contexts. All of these may lead to variability in women's psychological reactions following abortion. Consequently, global statements about the psychological impact of abortion on women can be misleading.

The American Psychological Association (APA) appointed a task force to consider the impact of abortion on the mental health of women (Major et al., 2008). Their brief included psychological responses following abortion. The task force reviewed and evaluated the relevant literature to address four primary questions:

- Does abortion cause harm to women's mental health?
- How prevalent are mental health problems among women in the United States who have had an abortion?
- What is the relative risk of mental health problems associated with abortion compared to its alternatives (other courses of action that might be taken by a pregnant woman in similar circumstances)?
- What predicts individual variation in women's psychological experiences following abortion?

According to the report, scientific evidence indicated that, among adult women who have an unplanned pregnancy, the relative risk of mental health problems is no greater if they have a single elective first-trimester abortion than if they deliver that pregnancy. That supports the idea of a woman's right to choose.

The evidence regarding the relative mental health risks associated with multiple abortions is more ambiguous, however. Statistical connections observed between the experience of having multiple abortions and poorer mental health outcomes may be linked to co-occurring risks (i.e. other life events, histories of vulnerabilities or other problems) that predispose a woman to have more than one unwanted pregnancy and the factors and pressures in her life that might lead to mental health problems.

The few published studies that examined women's responses following an induced abortion due to foetal abnormality suggest that terminating a wanted pregnancy late in pregnancy for this reason appears to be associated with negative psychological reactions equivalent to those experienced by women who miscarry a wanted pregnancy or who experience a stillbirth or death of a newborn. However, the strength of the negative mental health reaction is less than for those who deliver a child with life-threatening abnormalities.

The differing patterns of psychological experiences observed among women who terminate an unplanned pregnancy versus those who terminate a planned and wanted pregnancy highlight the importance of taking pregnancy intendedness and wantedness into account when seeking to understand psychological reactions to abortion.

None of the literature reviewed by these researchers adequately addressed the prevalence of mental health problems among women in the United States who have had an abortion. In general, however, the prevalence of mental health problems they observed among women who had a single, legal, first-trimester

**PAUSE AND REFLECT**

abortion for non-therapeutic reasons was consistent with normative rates of comparable mental health problems in the general population of women in the United States. Nonetheless, the authors concluded, it is clear that some women do experience sadness, grief and feelings of loss following termination of a pregnancy, and some experience clinically significant disorders, including depression and anxiety.

This review identified several factors that are predictive of more negative psychological responses following first-trimester abortion among women in the United States. Those factors included:

- Perceptions of stigma, need for secrecy, and low (or anticipated low) social support for the abortion decision.
- A prior history of mental health problems.
- Personality factors such as low self-esteem and use of avoidance and denial coping strategies.

- Characteristics of the particular pregnancy, including the extent to which the woman wanted and felt committed to it.

Across studies, prior mental health status emerged as the strongest predictor of post-abortion mental health. Many of these same factors also predict negative psychological reactions to other types of stressful life events, including childbirth and, hence, are not uniquely predictive of psychological responses following abortion.

Well-designed, rigorously conducted scientific research would help to disentangle confounding factors and establish relative risks of abortion compared to its alternatives, as well as factors associated with variation among women in their responses following abortion. Even so, there is unlikely to be a single definitive research study that will determine the mental health implications of abortion 'once and for all', given the diversity and complexity of women and their circumstances.

## Stress and motherhood

Becoming a mother is something that most women do, that only women can do and that on the whole they think about during young adulthood. While, increasingly, women recognize that they have the choice to opt out of motherhood, it is still the case that nine out of ten have at least one child. So, most women take the fact of motherhood or future motherhood for granted.

*Being* a mother, though, is increasingly a *life-style choice* for women. Do I stay at home and engage in full-time child care? Do I have children in my early 20s or late 30s? Do I have them with or without a partner? Do I combine motherhood and a career? What kind of life-style are we talking about when we include motherhood in the equation?

Academic study after academic study has shown the following patterns of motherhood to be true:

- Most women opt to become mothers if they can (Maxwell and McDougall, 2004).
- Increasing numbers of mothers work outside the home (Maxwell and McDougall, 2004).
- Most women combine work/career and motherhood. For some it is purely for economic reasons but, for a significant and increasing minority of working mothers, it is so that they can continue a successful career (Lewis et al., 2007).

- Women who are the most successful in their careers tend to have fewer children. In academia in the UK, for example, where promotion to full professor is only likely to happen to 1 in 30 women, those who are promoted are more likely to have no children or only one child. Women in all professional jobs mostly put off motherhood until their late 30s (Nicolson, 1996, 2003).
- Despite the rhetoric about the 'new man' and men wanting to take a fully active part in parenting, the basic *management* of the home child-care tasks still falls *mainly* to women (Smithson and Stokoe, 2005). If the man opts for the primary parent role, the family is likely to be less well-off financially, because women are almost always paid around 25% less than their male counterpart in any job (Burnett et al., 2011). This poses problems in many families.
- A woman who would normally want to have a stimulating job or an active career, is unlikely to be happy for very long if she opts for a long career-break or leaves work altogether for full-time motherhood (Bernazzani and Bifulco, 2003).
- Children who are cared for by a reluctant or depressed person are less likely to be well-adjusted socially or develop intellectually (Weinberg et al., 2006) as well as children who have more than one regular carer. Thus, two parents, or sharing child care with a good, regular nanny, is the best approach to infant/young child care, but may well prove out of most people's reach for financial and/or social reasons.
- Mothers are made to feel guilty for almost every possible problem their child might have at present or in their future lives, and most mothers accept this guilt as their own! It is almost impossible to consider yourself a good mother. All mothers feel guilty – whatever kind of lifestyle they have – at least some of the time. Donald Winnicott's notion of the 'good enough mother' discussed in Chapters 1 and 7 has been an excellent antidote to the misuse of John Bowlby's original studies of attachment and the discourses surrounding maternal deprivation.

### Stress and fatherhood

Contemporary men want to be fathers and involve themselves in parenting (Henwood and Procter, 2003), although this may present challenges for both the man and his partner. Fatherhood is not without its stresses. Balancing work and family life can leave many men feeling as if they're drowning in a sea of work, bills and the general responsibilities of being a father (Duckworth and Buzzanell, 2009; Maxwell amd McDougall, 2004). According to a poll from the APA, men said work, family and money, as well as worries about the economy, are significant causes of their stress. APA's 2007 *Stress in America Survey* found that 50% of men were concerned about their stress level. Men, more often than women, said stress negatively affected various aspects of their lives, such as job satisfaction (50% of men vs. 40% of women) and their overall satisfaction with life (45% of men vs. 38% of women). Even though there are many social differences in the culture and welfare structures of the UK and USA, some of these issues remain germane to both societies.

Couple counsellors and psychotherapists in the UK have identified a high level of stress among middle-class, middle- to high-income families in which the man (or one of the male partners), in particular, works long hours, perhaps as a lawyer or a city trader, while his partner (who may well have had his or her own profession) looks after the young children. These couples frequently seek help to work through these almost intractable difficulties and many case examples are available in the literature (Clulow, 2007; Ludlam and Nyberg, 2007).

## The discursive context of young adulthood

Young adulthood is a *subject position* (i.e. there is an available discourse to iden-tify and distinguish the position of young adulthood from that of adolescence or midlife) and a *social construction* that both reflects the material context and im-pacts upon it. As you have seen above, for example, there are various positions that might be taken up in relation to doing motherhood.

The subject position of young adulthood *reflects* the material context because, since the early twentieth century, improvements in diet, health care and hygiene have influenced biological development and enabled people in their late teens and early twenties to physically manage independence and parenthood. Also, economic changes have meant that it has become possible, and sometimes necessary, for young adults to seek and manage financial and domestic independence. The sub-ject position of young adulthood *impacts* upon the material context, drawing on the discourse of adulthood, to claim a stake in adulthood with its associated rights and responsibilities.

Discursive constructions of young adulthood come clearly into focus when think-ing about gender, as is the case with earlier phases of the lifespan, particularly adolescence. Women's and men's lives are variously and differently constrained through the life course, but particularly when entering adulthood. Discursive pres-sure towards (relatively) early parenthood, career development, 'having it all' and so on have been positioned differently as desirable, so that women have experi-enced guilt, and sometimes even depression or other mental health issues (Sayers, 1982; Turner et al., 2004; Ussher, 1997) if they transgress the dominant discourse (Ringrose, 2006). This is the process described by Foucault as *self surveillance* in that individuals are aware of social norms and rebukes *themselves* for transgres-sion (Haggerty and Ericson, 2000). In a study of pregnancy, early motherhood and eating behaviours, for instance, this process was identified in relation to medical advice. Women felt anxious and guilty if they, for example, had taken a glass of wine, too much tea or ate soft cheese if they were pregnant or breastfeeding (Fox et al., 2009).

Images and expectations about young adulthood have changed over the years. Shanahan (2000) identified two emerging themes in the way that young adulthood is constructed. The first theme is the increasing variability in pathways to adult roles through historical time, indicating that adult roles are a consequence of social discourse rather than biological capacity. So, for instance, whether a young adult is charged with becoming a parent, developing a career or taking financial responsibility for caring for elders is the outcome of historical and cultural constructions.

The second theme is that a heightened sensitivity to transition behaviours as developmental processes has meant the active efforts of young adults to shape their biographies in the context of the socially structured opportunities and limitations that define pathways into adulthood (Shanahan, 2000). In other words, at this time of young adulthood, perhaps more than other life stages bar adolescence, individuals take up roles that they see as appropriate to someone in their *position*. Consequently, there is often a rush to enter into an intimate relationship so as not to be left 'on the shelf'. Although this bears some relationship to biology (because of fertility limitations), it is more relevant to a construction of what it means to be a normal young adult. 'Perhaps if I don't have a partner people will think there is something undesirable about me' (Chambers et al., 2004). Further, partner choice and image position a young adult as, for example, heterosexual or gay or able to attract a particular type of partner, perhaps one who is rich and ambitious or interested in children (Kenrick et al., 1990).

It seems that young adulthood means taking your identity forward. You may have come to certain conclusions about who you might become as you struggle with adolescence but now, in adulthood, you need to manage and perform the narrative construction of your life to come.

## The intra-psychic context of intimate relationships

Forming intimate relationships with others is clearly an important task in young adulthood, and this is contingent upon experiences earlier in the lifespan, as we have seen throughout this book. Research has increasingly focused on the role of early attachments and attachment style for forming and sustaining intimate relationships (Chapter 5) (Belsky, 1997; Cozolino, 2006; Field et al., 1999; Fonagy, 2001; Grossmann, 1999; Hazan and Shaver, 1994; Shemmings and Shemmings, 2011).

What is at stake for young adults depends a great deal on how far their attachment experiences in infancy were disorganized and frightening versus how far they were secure and warm (Ludlam and Nyberg, 2007). The former would be likely to lead them to shut down emotionally (see Chapters 5 and 7). The work of Lyons-Ruth (Lyons-Ruth and Jacobvitz, 1999) in the USA and, more recently, Shemmings and Shemmings (2011) in the UK has explored the ways in which we seek to repair, while unconsciously replicating, our early experiences with our primary care-taker.

Intra-psychically all of us attempt to resolve inner and embedded anxieties through a relationship with another. Often, as we know, love is blind and we attribute, in an initially idealized way, properties to our significant other, that are unconscious *projections* and *transferences* (see Chapters 3 and 6 for more detailed discussion on unconscious mechanisms).

*Projection* here refers to the mostly unconscious process of experiencing your denied feelings (those you have blocked but at such a deep level that you are unaware of the denial) or repressed (deeply buried) feelings as belonging to another. These feelings are frequently ones you find unpalatable. However, they also might be ones about unconditional love so you might think that the person you have just met has the qualities you most wanted in a partner and fall in love with them because of this. For example, you might see that they are intelligent, ambitious, kind, humorous and so on. However, if the feelings do not relate to reality, then over time (short or long term) you will experience messages from the other person themselves which you might have been blinded to and become disappointed, or find that they reject you because you don't really understand them (Smith et al., 2012).

Freud first wrote about projection in 1895 and the concept has gone through several iterations since then because it has been an issue that fascinated psychoanalytic scholars and practitioners (Hinshelwood, 1991). However both Freud and Klein (1946) used the concept *to attribute certain states of mind to someone else*. Thus, the hatred that someone might feel is unconsciously attributed to another person in such a way that the feeling of hatefulness in oneself (which may be a shameful experience in itself) is alleviated.

*Transference*, again a mostly unconscious process, occurs when you think that someone has the qualities of another (possibly a parent or early carer) and you redirect feelings from the first person to the one you have just met. There is no basis for this in reality so you might experience your partner as potentially frightening or all-forgiving because you have transferred your experience of your other relationship to the relationship with your partner (Clulow, 2007; Ludlam and Nyberg, 2007).

There are, therefore, things we need to understand about how *unconscious processes* impact upon our own and our service users' lives because they are active in all relationships. Projection and transference are both unconscious defence mechanisms which are helpful in enabling us to function in relation to other people, but we need to be aware of them and not let them take over our sense of reality.

**Instinct and the unconscious**

How often have you met someone – a colleague or service user – to whom you take an instant liking or disliking? This is a dangerous process if you allow it to go unexamined because you are responding to something in your self, from your past, that the other person has triggered. That will bear no relation to the reality of that person's life and personality or the new relationship you are forming. Therefore it is vital that you reflect upon your feelings about others – service users or friends – to check out the evidence from real life.

- Have they shown you by their behaviour that they are angry, dishonest and potentially poor parents?
- Or is it the person from your past who you are experiencing when you interact with them?

## Madeline: the intra-psychic and everyday life

Neither Madeline nor David, her brother, both in their mid-twenties, had left home to go to university. Because they lived in commuting distance from London, they continued their studies there on leaving school. It had 'never occurred' to Madeline to leave. 'My parents don't seem to be pressurizing us. In fact I think we help with the grocery, heating and other bills. I have my own bedroom and my boyfriend used to come to spend the weekends with me.' David similarly feels at home but tends to go out with friends and stays in London most weekends.

However, Madeline became severely and suddenly depressed when her relationship with her boyfriend broke down and she unexpectedly realized that she 'had nothing to show for my adult years'. This was in stark contrast to how she had perceived herself before breaking up with her boyfriend – so much so that she felt she needed to re-examine her life. Through psychotherapy, she gradually came to realize that her loving parents had unconsciously transmitted (projected) their anxieties about separation and loss to her and she had felt a sense of anxiety and guilt about a probable future in which she would leave them to set up home with a boyfriend.

This is an example of projection by the parents – who were unconscious of these feelings – but Madeline had unconsciously experienced a fear of separation and a fear of growing up or at least growing apart from her parents (Baumeister et al., 1998).

Madeleine hadn't had any reason to face this before her relationship ended. Because she had continued to live at home and had never experienced any restrictions on her behaviour, particularly related to who could visit and stay with her, she hadn't questioned what was happening in the family.

During psychotherapy Madeline focused on her awareness that both her parents had had disturbed early lives and both had had treatment for clinical depression. Her mother had spent time as an in-patient in a psychiatric ward and had met her husband, Madeline's father, at a day centre for people with mental health issues. It is likely that Madeline had unconsciously felt obliged to remain at home with her parents, and what appeared to be a *freedom* was actually an *obligation* that obscured her ability to think for and about herself. Her brother had reacted differently, managing to spend time away from what Madeleine now saw as a claustrophobic home life, and he had therefore achieved an important degree of independence

## PAUSE AND REFLECT

### Change in adulthood

While adolescence is identified as the pivotal stage of the lifespan (see Chapter 9), there is little doubt that young adulthood may represent a key stage of life during which we are potentially emotionally vulnerable while trying to take our lives forward. Madeline's case is one example. She found that, while on one level she was feeling and behaving as if she were socially and emotionally secure, in fact there were levels of mostly unconscious turmoil taking place. The event of a relationship breakdown brought that to a head.

Her brother appeared to have remained unscathed, but in some ways he was still living the lifestyle of his student days where the emphasis was on friends and a social life, so it is likely that at some point he too would need to face up to himself in order to grow.

We see in young adulthood how early life experiences – social and psychological (including some preconscious, primitive emotional experiences) – do not disappear as the individual enters adulthood. The pressures of trying to build an independent life for oneself may possibly mask the emotional pressures from an earlier set of experiences. Being unaware of these can sometimes mean that, when something unexpected happens that knocks you off balance, you might find yourself returning unconsciously (and then consciously) to that earlier time and having to deal with those issues as well as the current ones.

Young adults, then, are vulnerable. They have to overcome issues of attachment and separation, the patterns of which are laid down in infancy (see Chapter 5). It is the ability to make secure attachments, which allow another significant person to 'leave the room' with confidence that they will return to you, that is the essence of a secure and confident identity (Bonanno, 2004; Bowlby, 1988).

Some young adults may have buried less-than-happy pasts and often appear to outsiders, as well as to themselves, to have coped well. However, frequently these people have fooled themselves.

Sandy, for example, found it difficult to make a relationship with any man, even though she wanted the heterosexual lifestyle of partnership and children. Her best friend Alan recounted how each man she introduced to him as her potential partner was worse than the one she had just dumped. They treated her badly and she had even experienced violence from her most recent 'ex'. What was going on? Sandy sought counselling and revealed in counselling that her mother had sexually abused her young brother when they were both under ten. She knew something of the facts of life while this had been going on, but could not fathom things between her mother and brother. Whatever was happening to him seemed to distress him a great deal, but he would not talk about it to her or anyone. For some reason, the upset occurred when her father was working nights.

She held on to the story, for herself, that they had all had a happy and successful family. Many of her school friends' parents had divorced and some had never known their own fathers, so Sandy thought her problems minimal. It was only when Sandy and her brother had left home and lived their own lives did he tell her what had happened to him. But Sandy's problems had begun before she knew this – she had turned away from the knowledge (her blind eye) (Smith et al., 2012; Steiner, 1985) when she was a child, but it had festered in her unconscious and grown into a phantasy that had disturbed her subsequent relationships and sense of her own worth.

Whatever individual strengths a young adult has gained from their earlier life, the challenges remain.

### RESILIENCE

It is the positive experiences in early life, either in the family or the wider community, that bring about resilience and the ability to survive (Hawley and DeHaan, 1996; Theron et al., 2011). However, because much of psychology's knowledge about how adults cope with loss or trauma has come from individuals who sought treatment or exhibited great distress, loss and trauma theorists have often viewed this type of resilience as either rare or pathological.

Bonanno (2004) has challenged these assumptions by suggesting that resilience in the face of loss or potential trauma is more common than is often believed, and that there are multiple and sometimes unexpected pathways to resilience. A British study, for example, showed that 10% of individuals who reported repeated or severe physical or sexual abuse in childhood experienced increased rates of adolescent psychiatric disorders, and in this group, rates of adult psychopathology (severe mental health difficulties) were also high. A substantial minority of abused individuals, however, reported no mental health problems in adult life. Resilience of this kind was related to perceived parental care, adolescent peer relationships, the quality of adult love relationships and personality style. The researchers, therefore, concluded that some experience of good-quality relationships across childhood, adolescence and adulthood appear especially important for adult psychological well-being in the context of childhood abuse (Collishaw et al., 2007). Good social work *can* make a difference.

Most of the discussion so far has concerned people with difficult backgrounds of some description. I now consider the relationships of two middle-class couples.

Meg, a colleague, had told me that, although Audrey her daughter and Edward her daughter's husband had what appeared to be a fairy-tale relationship (two

## PAUSE AND REFLECT

### Intimate relationships

Regardless of the figures on singlehood and relationship breakdown, it is clear that we need to relate to others and have attachment/intimate relationships with some other(s). Research and rhetoric on what makes a relationship work shows that people looking for a good marriage need to see whether they can manage key psychological/psychosocial tasks (Wallerstein and Blakeslee, 1995). These are:

- Separate emotionally from the family you grew up in, not to the point of estrangement, but enough so that your identity is separate from that of your parents and siblings.
- Build a sense of being a couple and together based on a shared intimacy and identity, while at the same time setting boundaries to protect each partner's autonomy.
- Establish a rich and pleasurable sexual relationship and protect it from the intrusions of the workplace and family obligations.
- For couples with children, embrace the daunting roles of parenthood and absorb the impact of a baby's entrance into the partnership. Learn to continue the work of protecting the privacy of you and your spouse as a couple.
- Confront and master the inevitable crises of life.
- Maintain the strength of the marital bond in the face of adversity. The partnership should be a safe haven in which partners are able to express their differences, anger and conflict.
- Use humour and laughter to keep things in perspective and to avoid boredom and isolation.
- Nurture and comfort each other, satisfying each partner's needs for dependency and offering continuing encouragement and support.
- Keep alive the early romantic, idealized images of falling in love, while facing the sober realities of the changes wrought by time.

These tasks emerged from, and were reinforced by, Wallerstein's longitudinal studies of marriage and the impact of divorce on partners and their children (Amato, 2003; Boyer-Pennington et al., 2001; Wallerstein, 1986).

lovely children, excellent careers, a great house and prospects of more career and financial success), she dreaded to think what would happen if they faced any stumbling-blocks. Audrey had decided to work part-time in her general medical practice, but six months later Edward was made redundant from his engineering post. If he had not found another job almost immediately, Meg believed they would have split up. There had never been any stress or failure in Audrey's life. Everything seemed to turn out well without her ever having to try very hard. Meg believed this meant Audrey and Edward had little ability to be resilient if they were faced with difficulties.

Kelly, who had worked as a nursery nurse but was now a housewife and mother of three, walked out on Cliff during the global recession when he was sacked as a hedge-fund manager. She sued him for alimony and within two years had found another husband, also in the financial business sector.

Had these apparently fortunate couples really tried or expected to make their relationships last? Why should these privileged people concern social workers?

Although financial security and privilege do protect against many challenges, there are still psychological issues that impact upon the children, in particular, and many young adults, offspring of the rich and famous, have ended up as suicide or drug abuse victims. Harry Ferguson has suggested that social work needs to recognize a role in the methodology of life-planning. His paper aimed to advance 'practice which take the life political domain, emotionality and the depth of social relations as their primary focus'. Radical/political social work had been seen to neglect the distress that the loss of intimacy might cause. Support for making sense of what intimacy might mean would enhance 'the capacities of (vulnerable) clients to practice effective life-planning, find healing and gain mastery over their lives' (Ferguson, 2001).

## CHAPTER SUMMARY

This chapter will enable you to analyze the transition from adolescence to adulthood, to understand how young adulthood as a life stage represents the means to what lies ahead for each of us. This may involve consideration of the risks to future vulnerabilities. You may also have had a chance to review some Government statistics on formal arrangements, such as civil partnerships and marriage, to see the ages at which people begin to commit to long-term relationships. You can also see from divorce figures that these formal arrangements do not always survive emotional, financial and developmental crises.

Crises can be many at this phase of the lifespan. We look for relationships, and may be rejected or make mistakes. We become parents or fail in trying to do so. We become parents unwillingly and perhaps terminate pregnancies or find parenthood and the relationship with the other parent intolerable. Some of us find our perfect fit in a partner and manage a relationship that mirrors our attachment needs and styles.

It will be becoming increasingly apparent by now that the lifespan cannot be understood as discrete stages. Each phase is a complex cluster of transitional experiences that overlap as we develop through them. These developmental experiences take place at the material, discursive and intra-psychic levels, revolving around the psychosocial tasks that are entangled with each of these levels of experience.

Not only is development cumulative, but development through the lifespan involves inter-generational relationships, and we see clearly how people either repeat or (try to) resist patterns from their earlier life which will reflect the lives of those in the previous and the next generation.

Young adulthood faces each of us with the challenge of moving towards autonomy and into relationships that are independent of our families of origin, even though many seem reluctant to take this responsibility for themselves. Successful negotiation of young adulthood and a positive sense of the future returns is the outcome of successful negotiation of adolescence which, of course, means having developed a capacity for dealing with emotional difficulties to secure some sense of who you really are or will turn out to be.

## FURTHER READING

Michael Shanahan's paper provides a useful sociological analysis of pathways to adulthood.

Shanahan, M.J. (2000) Pathways to Adulthood in Changing Societies: Variability and mechanisms in life course perspective. *Annual Review of Sociology*, 26, 667–692.

He has also co-authored a textbook:

Elder, G.H. and Shanahan, M.J. (2007) *The Life Course and Human Development*. John Wiley & Sons, Inc.

Toni Bifulco's work provides important insights into mental health vulnerabilities in adulthood arising from inter-generational neglect and abuse, particularly:

Bifulco, A. and Moran, P. (1998) *Wednesday's Child: Research into women's experiences of neglect and abuse in childhood and adult depression*. London: Routledge.

Bifulco, A. (2004) Maternal Attachment Style and Depression Associated with Childbirth: Preliminary results from European/US cross-cultural study. *British Journal of Psychiatry*, 184(suppl 46), s31–s37.

Other important readings are:

Howe, D., Shemmings, D. and Feast, J. (2001) Age at Placement and Adult Adopted People's Experience of Being Adopted. *Child & Family Social Work*, 6(4), 337–349.

Shemmings, D. and Shemmings, Y. (2011) *Understanding Disorganized Attachment: Theory and Practice for Working with Children and Adult*. London: Jessica Kingsley.

# 11

# MIDLIFE: GENERATIVITY VERSUS STAGNATION

## Introduction

We have explored the turmoil of adolescence and early adulthood and now move on to examine midlife, with its particular costs and benefits. Midlife is a difficult phase of the lifespan to define, as the meaning of midlife (or middle age) has shifted over the years. Does it begin at 30 or 50? Is it, as suggested by Erikson's 'eight ages' model (see Table 4.1), the long period between growing into adulthood and old age? For Erikson, this was represented by the ages between 25 and 50. However, in the twenty-first century, midlife is more likely to end around the age of 65. Is midlife so named, therefore, because it is representative of the middle of lives – in-between generations (parents, children and even grandchildren)?

Among all these possibilities, we can say that it refers to mid- to late-working-age adulthood – some time after thinking of yourself as young but not yet feeling older. It is clear, though, that midlife and middle age provide a (flexible) boundary between youth and older age. This suggests that, far from a period where turmoil and uncertainty have become resolved, there are different kinds of tasks and challenges across this lengthy phase of the lifespan.

In this chapter I define midlife as beginning from around the age of 25, following on from the individual's experiences of their first intimate relationships. By midlife we will have developed a reasonably clear sense of sexual identity, addressed fertility issues and parenthood but not yet faced psychological and actual retirement from public life and the sense of living in an empty nest. These phases, though, may be anticipated by some of us, variously with pleasure, terror or most likely something in between which is marked by ambivalence and possibly curiosity.

People in midlife have the knowledge and experience to offer support and advice to their families and their colleagues. They are also the ones in the way – they interfere (in family life) and they stand in the way (of promotion in working life, for example). Less attention is paid overall, in the media and in psychological/ sociological research, to people in midlife, possibly because they are expected to be grown up and responsible for themselves and have generally passed beyond the early parenting years. However, for some it represents invisibility (Greer, 1993). Social workers generally are involved with people in midlife only if there are safeguarding issues or the adult is vulnerable from mental illness or other disabilities, all of which are likely to have been flagged up at an earlier stage and, consequently, will not be identified as characteristic of this stage of the lifespan (Banister, 1999; Collishaw et al., 2007; Dare, 2011; Turner et al., 2004).

## Psychosocial tasks of midlife

While midlife can be a period during which people reap the benefits of earlier hard work, it is also a time when difficulties may have to be faced or longer-term ones that may have been swept under the carpet resurface (Colarusso, 2006). Life events for those of us in midlife are either taken in our stride because we have learned various coping strategies along the way or have others we can trust to help us through them. People divorce, lose or change their jobs, move house, town or country and grieve the loss of aged parents and children leaving home.

Additionally, life events and non-events (such as a change in the general zeitgeist, i.e. 'spirit of the time', or shift in moral values) can prove to be major stumbling blocks that can send a person into a mental health and/or relationship crisis (Banister, 1999; Dare, 2011; Hayes and Anderson, 1993).

Erikson (1950/1963) proposed that in midlife we are faced with the possibilities of ongoing *generativity* or *stagnation*. In midlife a person feels their life is either settling down, continuing to be eventful and productive, or falling apart because they don't have the possibility, in reality or in the psyche, of a productive future.

We all, it seems, want to feel that something about us will live on into the future, whether as parents and then grandparents, or that investment in work and careers will lead to something exciting and even potentially lucrative. Material and socio-economic inequalities, however, may make some forms of generativity difficult, if not impossible, for those who are marginalized or excluded. Also, some may feel unable to be successful parents or may find it difficult to find employment (Ferguson, 2001; Hayes and Anderson, 1993; Parke and Buriel, 2007; Ritchie and Woodward, 2009).This has implications for mental health, a sense of well-being and the ability to manage relationships, particularly for those who have become embittered when career and family life have not gone to plan or the acclaim they believed to be due to them in midlife has not materialized (Collishaw et al., 2007).

It has been claimed in one famous example that the heavyweight boxer Henry Cooper, who died in 2011, ended his life with some bitterness because his career was lauded for what he didn't quite achieve (beating Mohamed Ali) rather than what he did achieve (becoming Commonwealth and British Champion).

Ronnie (R.D.) Laing the anti-psychiatrist, whose work was discussed in Chapter 1, became vulnerable in midlife. This was apparent in his book of poems called *Do you Love Me?*, which was published in 1976 when he was in his late forties. By then his career and family life (he had had ten children with four women) were disintegrating. After a brilliant start to his career with academic and clinical acclaim leading to work with many famous patients, his career began to slow down. He had many drunken rages and became violent at home and bitter towards his close colleagues. All of this was exacerbated as his career dwindled. This was partly because of fashion in psychiatry (see Chapter 1), but also because he had become distracted by his own celebrity. He had several affairs with glamorous women and his focus was upon this rather than on work. As he drank more and more, his friends disappeared and he fell out with his children, some of whom had developed their own problems with poor mental health and alcohol dependence (Collishaw et al., 2007; Cooney and Uhlenberg, 1990).

## The bio-material context

Midlife is not simply a period of extremes where a person experiences their self at one or the other end of the generativity/stagnation spectrum. Biologically, we are likely to become less physically able, even though many of us in the twenty-first century are fitter in midlife than the previous generation had been (Folkman and Lazarus, 1980; Kawachi and Berkman, 2001; Taylor and Bury, 2007). Despite previous beliefs that intellectual functioning declines with aging, we now know that keeping an active mind and learning from experience enhances brain power for those in midlife (Rabbitt et al., 2007). Consequently, there is a complex midlife mixture of enhanced intellectual functioning interacting with reduced physical abilities. Chronic illness or the effects of life events (such as accident or disease) may also impact upon the physical and psychological context of those in midlife (Goodley and Tregaskis, 2006).

During the twentieth century, demographic (trends in human population characteristics) and epidemiological (patterns of disease across populations) transitions had a radical impact upon health and health service provision. Subsequently, a considerable body of research on the sociological aspects of living with chronic illness has accumulated (Bury, 1982; Taylor and Bury, 2007).

Adults who had experienced a serious illness in earlier life were over twice as likely to be disabled, with certain conditions, such as polio, being associated with a particularly high relative risk. Those who had experienced a socially disadvantaged start to life were more likely to be physically disabled at 43 years than those who had started life with physical health as an advantage. Even so, if someone experienced social disadvantage throughout life, or during adult life, this too increased the risk of disability. Overall, then, it has become increasingly apparent that social disadvantage has a deleterious impact on physical abilities, whatever age the onset of such disadvantage. It will be no surprise to note that the relative impact of disability on income and employment was found to be greatest for those from unskilled and semi-skilled backgrounds (Williams, 2000).

## The socio-material context

At midlife, then, there are risks of losing what had previously been gained. The sense of moving forward (generativity) inevitably slows down because opportunities and energy are both reduced. This sense of growth may be replaced by an appreciation that life experience and successes are being consolidated. However, under the influence of negative events (e.g. divorce, redundancy), a feeling or fear of stagnation emerges. Most of us experience a mixture of growth and stagnation.

For many years psychologists and other social and clinical scientists have examined statistically the ways in which different negative events (bereavement, divorce) and potentially positive events (moving house, marriage, childbirth) can have an impact on mental health and well-being (Holmes and Rahe, 1967). The scale developed by Holmes and Rahe has been used subsequently for different events across the intervening years (Williams et al., 1981).

For example, one study compared personality and life events to see whether some personality types fared better in adversity or when a positive but significant event occurred, and asked which types of individuals are most likely to be affected by negative life events (Emmons, 1991). It appeared that achievement-oriented individuals (who focused on moving forward with careers, for instance) tended to be affected by good achievement events (such as winning a contract or gaining promotion). Similarly, the moods of affiliation- and intimacy-oriented individuals (those people who focused on enjoying the company of others and their social and family lives for example) were affected by interpersonal events (meeting a new lover or potential friend). Thus someone who was striving for career success would be more greatly affected, for better or worse, if they were promoted or made redundant than someone less concerned with achievement in this way. Similarly, people focusing on social and emotional relationships will probably suffer more adverse effects from the loss of a friendship than, say, a person who is focused on achieving power.

While the Holmes and Rahe instrument, as influential as it has been, is used less frequently now, the concept of a *life event* remains live. The impact of life events, for example, is understood as contributing to studies of attachment experiences and attachment style (Bifulco et al., 2000) or other risk factors in earlier life including resilience (Bonanno, 2004). See Chapter 5 for a full discussion of attachment.

A large number of studies have demonstrated a correlation between positive marital (or intimate partner) relationship status and good mental health, in that married people experience greater well-being than single or divorced people. However, the relative importance of the intimate relationship, as compared to the impact of other factors in those people's lives related to mental health, is not known. One study showed that it was the *quality* of a marriage and not marriage per se that links marriage to positive mental health (Gove et al., 1983). It is generally agreed now that social ties do play a beneficial role in the maintenance of psychological well-being although some individuals benefit more than others. Once again, this depends on personality and context (Bifulco et al., 2000; Kawachi and Berkman, 2001).

Antonia Bifulco and the Lifespan Research Group, whose work we talked about in relation to assessing attachment styles in Chapter 5, have also developed a measure of the association between stress and depression in relation to adverse childhood experience. The Adult Life Phase Interview (ALPHI) examined the number of chronic stressors (or 'adversities') experienced over the adult lifespan in relation to chronic or recurrent clinical depression. Adult adversity, both at settled/fixed times and at times of major life change, was shown to be significantly higher among those with prior childhood neglect or abuse, and childhood neglect or abuse were related to chronic or recurrent episodes of clinical depression (Bifulco et al., 2000).

The research emphasis on subjective reporting of well-being and happiness, in addition to the measurement of objectively evaluated life events, has added a different dimension to our understanding (Diener, 2000). For instance, people's cognitive and emotional evaluations of their own lives, including the importance of their subjective view of their goals, were found to be related to feelings of well-being. This suggests that we interpret our life events according to what they mean in the context of our material and intra-psychic consciousness. This is, of course, something of a tautology, or circular argument, because our emotional and mental health status, to an extent, dictate the meaning we put on the events in our lives.

Graham Smith and I realized the truth of subjective perceptions in this way when we re-analyzed some of his interviews with midlife and older chronically homeless men. We expected the men to tell us they were dissatisfied with the things that had happened to them, mostly because their lives were out of the ordinary and they themselves were socially excluded and economically vulnerable. We were very surprised to note how many of them reported that they had enjoyed their unconventional lives and particularly enjoyed positioning themselves as rebellious or free of the bonds of those with more conventional lifestyles (Smith and Nicolson, 2011) (see Chapter 12).

## The discursive context

In midlife we can take up a number of subject positions around the spectrum of generativity/stagnation, particularly in relation to health. So, for example, regardless of the bio-material context (e.g. physical disability), the London Paralympic Games of 2012 demonstrated that the position of *athlete*, or being variously *abled*, sits in a discursive relationship to *being disabled* or *doing disability*. A discursive consciousness in which a person positions themselves as having challenges to meet differs from that of someone taking up the position of being defeated by physical challenges.

One research study showed women making psychological adjustments to their thinking about their bodies with age. As they grew older, they shifted their focus from the external (beauty, shape and so on) that is socially constructed to be positive for younger women, to the internal (intelligence, thoughtfulness, experience). They discursively valued the internal attributes more as they engaged with midlife, which contributed to their acceptance of having an older body (Ogle and Damhorst, 2005). The experience of embodiment in midlife, therefore, may be understood as a *performance* or taking a position (Nelson, 1999).

Similarly with mental health, the *Hearing Voices Network* embodies resistance to the power of psychiatry. This group of people have positioned themselves differently from those who are labelled/label themselves as having a mental health problem. Those positioning themselves as mentally ill are more accepting of the voices as symptoms of schizophrenia, while those in the network regarded their internal voices as simply part of their lives (Blackman, 2007). Further, by taking account of women's narratives of their mental health issues, such as postnatal depression (Nicolson, 1998) and more general depression (Crowe, 2002), those discourses that differ from the mainstream, it appears that the people involved no longer position themselves as being mentally ill.

Radley (1999) argued that the process of becoming chronically ill colours people's lives so that they understand both their illness, their ordinary day-to-day experiences and commonplace interactions as reflected through their understanding of their disease experience. They position themselves as ill, so that the biographically embodied self (that is the sense of being in your own life and body) exists for them in a situation of *chronic reflexivity* in which their bodies/selves are continually seen as failed or pathological in some way.

## The intra-psychic context

Anthony Giddens work on self/identity and structuration were discussed and his model of the practical, discursive and unconscious levels of consciousness were outlined in Chapter 4. To recap, he suggests that we experience ourselves in the world on all of these different levels. Thus, the practical level of consciousness represents the experience of just getting on with it: 'this is what is happening and this is me doing it'.

The discursive level of consciousness is more reflective, with a developing awareness about one's place in the world. The unconscious, or the intra-psychic and emotional levels of being, suggests levels of experience under the surface which we may or may not be able to tap into at different times in our lives. Frequently we need help from an experienced social worker, counsellor or psychotherapist to work at this level.

Various midlife events, which are part of the socio-material context described above, also resonate at the emotional and intra-psychic levels. The ways in which we experience the outcome of these events frequently link to attachment experiences, particularly the disruption of early attachments. You will already understand how positive and secure early attachments enable strong intra-psychic coping mechanisms to manage trauma and disruption (see Chapter 5).

### Events with risk of stagnation

There is a close link between attachment experiences and attachment styles, and consequent outcomes related to adverse life events. Thus, if someone who had experienced disorganized attachment has a marital breakdown or loses their job, it is more likely that, without support, they will suffer mental health and social consequences. Below I review some research evidence suggesting how specific life events might impact upon midlife.

#### THE DEATH OF A PARTNER

One major vulnerability in midlife can be the failure of an intimate relationship or loss of a partner through a fatal illness or accident (Daggett, 1999). For many gay men there has been an epidemic of partner death through HIV/Aids (Cadell and Marshall, 2007). Bereavement will be discussed more fully in Chapter 12, as it is more common in older adulthood. However, midlife bereavement has very specific characteristics that need to be noted, and perhaps they are all the more important because the loss is considered untimely.

Researchers in a study of attachment following midlife bereavement interviewed 70 midlife bereaved people. They showed that when bereaved people use the dead person's possessions to gain comfort for themselves, grief levels fail to reduce over time. The researcher suggests that this indicates a relatively unhealthy grieving process. By contrast, attachment to the deceased through focusing on fond memories led to less distress over time (Field et al., 1999). It may also be that the avoidance of unpleasant emotions following bereavement helps with healing (Bonanno et al., 1994), but this may be difficult to achieve without a great deal of care and skilled support.

At midlife it is not always just the grieving partner who needs to be considered. There are likely to be children involved as well. One child in five who has experienced the death of a parent is likely to develop psychiatric disorder. In the year following bereavement, children commonly display grief, distress and depression. Non-specific emotional and behavioural difficulties among children are often reported by surviving parents and the bereaved children themselves. The highest rates of reported difficulties are found in boys, but other factors such as the extent to which death was expected, the age of the child, the way the surviving parent and others helped the child to mourn and the mental health of the surviving parent all influence the child's mental health (Dowdney, 2000).

## PAUSE AND REFLECT

### Peter's story

Peter's wife died when their son Lenny was just eleven. She had been ill with cancer for some time and in and out of hospital, but one night she didn't return and neither Peter nor Lenny could take in the fact she had died. In order to support his son though, Peter tried to manage his own grief through denial and, without intending to, failed to give Lenny (who was going through puberty and associated adolescent struggles) enough attention. Peter was also unable to help Lenny move forward with his life because he changed the subject whenever Lenny mentioned his mother. To Lenny at the time it appeared that Peter had forgotten his mother.

Lenny became sullen and angry and would throw things around the house – ink and paint at the walls – and he kicked over and smashed the television. After a while, Lenny seemed to regress further. The vicar's wife, who was also a familiar neighbour to the family, reported how Lenny would hide behind the sofa like a young child when she visited (which she did frequently because she was worried about the pair of them). He would then leap out and shout something like 'Enemy approaching' or 'Watch out for aliens', but he would not communicate with her directly.

She also discovered that Peter wanted to sell the house and move away in order to make a fresh start, while Lenny wanted to stay where he best remembered his mother. Over time, Peter managed to re-establish his own life and, as he spent more time with Lenny, he became calmer and could talk directly to him about his mother,

enabling some positive change in Lenny's behaviour and feelings.

Grief therapies with children are becoming increasingly popular, although questions persist about how well these treatments actually help with children's adjustment to the death of a loved one. One important review of research literature demonstrated that child-grief interventions do not appear to generate the positive outcomes of other professional psychotherapeutic interventions. Even so, studies that intervened in a time-sensitive manner and implemented specific selection criteria about who might benefit produced better outcomes than investigations that did not attend to these factors. (Currier et al., 2007).

Jan Fook's approach to reflective practice (Fook and Gardner, 2010) combined with below-the-surface responses (Cooper, 2005; Howe, 1996) might inform a reflective-relational stance to support Peter and Lenny.

- How would you work with Peter and Lenny?
- Why might you be involved?
- What happened?
- What did (or might) you do?
- What stance did you take?
  - What were you thinking might happen?
  - What made you think that?
  - What did you take for granted?
  - What else might you have done or seen differently?
  - What might have been the outcome?

There might also be issues about attachment and attachment styles that will help you analyze the relational context (see Chapter 5 to think about this further).

Therefore, suicide is more prevalent with people who are in crisis and who lack the internal and social resources to cope. There are gendered patterns in that men are at risk of suicide because of a crisis of work, while for women it is more likely to be because of a crisis of family. The researchers drew particular attention to suicide among those in midlife, and to the role of the social bond, especially in the form of attachment, suggesting that for this group relationship breakdown is central to understanding the demography (i.e. the characteristics of the population) of suicide and the significance of social bonds (Shiner et al., 2009).

There are gender differences also in the way life events, such as midlife bereavement or marital/relationship breakdown, are handled. One Australian study suggests that midlife women are particularly vulnerable following a relationship breakdown, proposing that, while most women manage the classic transitions of menopause and the 'empty nest' relatively well, the impact of divorce and the aging and death of parents present more serious long-term challenges to women (Dare, 2011). These include psychological, social and economic adjustments, although it has been shown that most women establish a positive self-identity within five years after divorce. Hayes and Anderson (1993) identified one pitfall for women who fail to manage their finances, which impacts on their economic situation in older age. However, that study is more than twenty years old and women are now more likely to have had experience in the workplace and of their own financial management. In spite of widespread interest in both aging and divorce, relatively little research has linked these topics.

Findings from a study using data from the US Census, *Vital Statistics, and Current Population Survey*, to determine current divorce patterns for women aged 40+ indicated a dramatic increase in the proportion who will be divorced and a marked decline at midlife in the proportion of future elderly women who will be married or widowed. The data also show that the socio-economic well-being of divorcees is significantly below that of widowed or married women (Uhlenberg et al., 1990).

Turner and colleagues (2004) examined the relationship between three midlife transitions and depressive symptoms among 952 women aged from 50 to 59. Using longitudinal data (data captured over time from the same people) about women interviewed for the 1992 and 2000 *Health and Retirement Study*, changes in marital status, change to a parental care-giving role, and changes in perceived health across the eight years could be identified. The findings were consistent with the perspective that individual development occurs in context and across the lifespan, suggesting that psychological and social support enables divorced and bereaved women to develop emotionally and socially.

For men, there are both short- and long-term consequences of divorce on their relationships with their children (Cooney and Uhlenberg, 1990). Cooney and Uhlenberg examined post-divorce parent/child relations, focusing on the extended

effects of divorce on men's relations with their adult offspring. Father/child relations for divorced men aged 50–79 were compared with those of never-divorced
married men on the basis of data from the *National Survey of Families and Households*. Divorce had a pronounced negative effect on the frequency of men's contacts
with their adult offspring, significantly reducing the likelihood that men will have
an adult child in their household, and sharply reducing the probability that fathers
consider their adult children as potential sources of support in times of need.

All of the above studies on divorce refer to the USA. However, there is every reason to expect that men and women in the UK have similar experiences but social
science research in the UK is rarely undertaken in such a robust way and on such
a scale. This is likely to be through lack of financial resources but also might be a
consequence of research 'fashions' in the UK discussed in Chapter 1.

## PAUSE AND REFLECT

### Dai's story

Dai was very depressed and confused about his
life when I first met him in a counselling context
in his middle age. He was forty when I saw
him, but I found that his difficulties appeared to
stem from decisions made in his early twenties.
Dai had met his wife Sissy during his final
year at medical school. She was a nurse and
slightly older than him, and took control of their
relationship from the beginning.

Several years later, Dai reflected that actually
what she had wanted was a doctor, any doctor.
Not him in particular, and that was a hurtful
realization. He just happened to be caught in
her trap.

Using this language made him sound very
bitter but he said that when he met Sissy he
had never had the chance to experience single
life without the stress of student pressures and
had had very few relationships. There had been
nothing remotely serious in any relationship
before Sissy. She had planned their wedding
soon after his graduation and also persuaded
him they should live in Devon where she had
been brought up and her family still lived. Dai
was from north Wales but had wanted to work
for a few years in London as a junior doctor
after graduation. Sissy also wanted him to
work in general practice – which is what he
did, although he had harboured thoughts of
obstetrics during his training.

I found that Dai had been brought up by his
mother, who he described as 'overbearing'.
Listening to his story, a similar adjective might
also have suited Sissy.

When Dai was seven, his father left for work
one morning and did not return until after Dai
himself was married with his first child. It turned
out that he had left Dai and his mother to live
with a younger woman, who was then his
secretary, and had moved to Yorkshire. It was
an interesting coincidence that Dai's father had
been younger than Dai's mother, just as Dai was
younger than Sissy.

The relationship between Dai and Sissy didn't
work. He felt overwhelmed by her family and
one day on his way to work (living in Devon with
two children by then) Dai thought to himself that
he could at least cheer himself up by having
affairs. He pursued this idea enthusiastically and
declared that by middle age he had lost count
of the women he had slept with. Dai modestly
put it down to his profession – 'every woman
wants to have a relationship with a doctor'. He
was concerned that every time he met someone
he was attracted to, he fell 'madly in love' and
declared his passion to the woman. He would
then, when she was 'hooked', freeze and find
her full of faults and cut the contact altogether.
I wondered whether he had this view of *every
woman wanting a doctor* as a counterpart to his
realization that Sissy had wanted *any doctor*. It
was as if he found it difficult to see himself as
an individual, and this then became projected

## PAUSE AND REFLECT

→ onto the women he became involved with. He saw them as all the same.

Most of the women reacted strangely to that (in his opinion) and started phoning him, trying to see him and demanding an explanation, which he found irritating. He was confused. In the meantime, he had little energy left for Sissy and she seemed to lose interest in sex.

As suddenly as he had decided to have affairs he decided that he couldn't bear to lose Sissy, particularly because he didn't want to leave his children.

- How could he get his partnership to work?
- How could he make sure she wouldn't find out about the other women?
- How could he make himself feel happy?

Dai realized when he stopped to reflect that he had been depressed for many years. That realization made him focus on his lack of personal power or autonomy. He had not had control over his father's leaving (which he realized later had torn him apart) and then allowed an overbearing mother to arrange his life, including his career. He had then moved from her hands to that of an equally overbearing wife, who had carried him off to live near her parents and siblings. He felt he had no idea who he really was – even in midlife.

Dai's multiple and sudden declarations of love to numerous women were intended to secure the feelings of the women he was seeing, so that they might return to see him again. But when he found they *did* come back to him they lost their importance because he had such a low opinion of his own self-worth. His most important person, his father, had never come back, at least not while he needed him so badly.

Taking a reflective-relational stance:

- What happened to Dai to make him depressed?
- Were there implications for and from attachment theory to help understand Dai's issues further?
- What did (or might) you do when working with him?
- What stance did you take?
  - What were you thinking might happen?
  - What made you think that?
  - What did you take for granted?
  - What else might you have done or seen differently?
  - What might have been the outcome?

### DEATH OF A PARENT

In midlife, and especially in the later years, it is likely that our parents will die. This could have prolonged effects on social and emotional functioning, particularly if the death was unexpected or the parent/child relationship had been marked by anxious attachment or a history of childhood separation. These factors will contribute significantly to the extent of unresolved filial grief following the parent's death (Scharlach, 1991).

Who can help with this? Another study from the same author examined the resources considered most helpful by 83 adults, aged 35 to 60, in coping with the death of a parent. Friends, family members and peers who themselves had experienced a parent's death were most often cited as being particularly important resources. Daughters were more likely than sons to report receiving help from friends, family and religion, whereas sons were somewhat more likely to see work as helpful. Implications for practice include the need to offer support groups as well as family counselling for adults who have lost a parent (Scharlach and Fuller-Thomson, 1994).

In midlife, parental death often occurs in a context of many other life events, as in the case of Saffi, a lone parent whose mother died while she herself was in England as an asylum seeker and also new to child-rearing attitudes and practices in a different culture.

This suggests the significance of extreme and potentially traumatic changes in midlife and particularly the death of a parent (Dare, 2011). Also it demonstrates the importance of focusing upon support for children and adolescents in high-risk families through working with projects such as Sure Start (Tunstill and Allnock, 2007) (or Starting Early, Starting Smart, the American version).

## PAUSE AND REFLECT

### Saffi's story

Saffi, a religious Christian black woman from Nigeria, arrived in the north of England where she had been resettled after successfully seeking asylum for herself and her five children aged three to nine. It was customary to use corporal punishment in child-rearing in Nigeria, although it is no longer acceptable or legal in the UK.

Shortly after being re-housed in Sheffield, Saffi heard that her mother had died. Saffi's husband had long since abandoned her and she believed he was living somewhere in London. Saffi had hoped to bring her mother to live with her and the children and, in response to the news of her mother's death, she, literally, went mad. She wandered through the streets at night, leaving her children alone. She said she was waiting for her mother who would be looking for her and would not be able to find her way to Saffi's house if Saffi did not look for her. Saffi went to bed in the morning, didn't feed her children (the nine-year-old daughter took the main responsibility for this, which meant that she didn't attend school very often). Saffi would hit the children with a cane when she did come out of her bedroom in the afternoons, because she claimed the devil was in them all and they were allowing the devil to do his work in the house.

Child protection social workers were alerted as well as the mental health services and Saffi's life was turned even further upside down. The children were taken to foster parents although not all five could live in the same household.

Two were with one family and the other three were looked after elsewhere. Saffi was admitted for a few days to a psychiatric hospital and then sent home under the care of a community psychiatric nurse and part-time attendance at a day centre.

However, perhaps she would have benefitted more from a mental health specialist social work input with attention to her cultural context. When Saffi's condition had stabilized the children were returned home on the condition that the preschoolers and Saffi attended the local Sure Start programme every morning and the older ones regularly attended school.

Despite everything they had all gone through, Saffi had managed to get her family to safety away from their home country where they were being persecuted. Her mother, who she clearly loved, had provided a safe infancy and childhood and from that Saffi knew at one level what she needed to do to keep her family secure.

This had become confused with her views on discipline and 'the Devil' and the isolation and lack of support she had received on settling in Sheffield. As the centre staff paid her attention and discovered that she was interested in attending a church that shared her beliefs, they introduced her and she gradually adapted her parenting skills and beliefs.

The emphasis on the multidisciplinary work with Saffi was very much responsive emergency work, necessary at the time to deal with the urgency of her neglecting the children, physically abusing them and also her psychotic episode that seemed to be the root of the family difficulties.

## PAUSE AND REFLECT

➡   It is highly likely that the neglect and abuse of the children, as well as her cultural and ethnic difference, brought out feelings and fears in the professionals involved. This is rarely identified as an important factor in health and social care work even though a non-professional, under-the-surface response is inevitable in human interactions (Cooper, 2005; Rustin, 2005).

Try to respond in a reflective-relational way to Saffi's story.

- What happened?
- What did (or might) you do?
- What stance did you take?
  - What were you thinking might happen?
  - What made you think that?
  - What did you take for granted?

- What else might you have done or seen differently?
- What might have been the outcome?

In Saffi's case there seemed to be at least a temporary happy ending, but there are other questions that might be considered that did not emerge in dealing with the emergency:

- What was the background that the family had left?
- What implications did this (or might this) have had upon Saffi's feelings for her mother, her children and her husband?
- What were the losses?
- How did she manage to develop resilience (it may be easier to see why she 'went mad')?

### STRESS IN THE WORKPLACE

For both men and women the workplace and career are a potential source of generativity (Kawachi and Berkman, 2001), although there are many ways in which work can turn to stagnation and distress. Contemporary work organizations have become highly stressful, and those who work in them feel the pressure, sometimes 24/7 (Duckworth and Buzzanell, 2009; Maxwell and McDougall, 2004; Parke and Buriel, 2007). Since the financial crisis of 2008, economic austerity has exacerbated existing problems, with threats of redundancies and redeployment, and salaries and pensions being attacked.

### BULLYING AT WORK

Bullying at work is a stressful and degrading experience which frequently happens at midlife to people who had believed themselves to be competent and contributing effectively to the work of the organization. Bullying and harassment are situations where a worker or a supervisor is systematically mistreated and victimized by colleagues through repeated negative acts (Salin, 2003b). Social workers have reported frequently that they have been victims of bullying in their organizations, although relatively little research has been done in this area (van Heugten, 2010).

Data from 14 different Norwegian surveys showed that bullying and harassment at work are widespread problems in Norwegian working life, with as many as 8.6% of the respondents bullied at work during the six months prior to the study. Organizations with many employees, male-dominated organizations, and industrial organizations had the highest prevalence of victimization. Older workers had a higher risk of victimization than younger workers. Even if men and women do not differ in prevalence of experiencing bullying, significantly more men were reported as bullies. Victims reported superiors as bullies as often as they reported colleagues as their tormentor(s) (Einarsen and Skogstad, 1996). Another Scandinavian study found that over 73% of people who had been exposed to bullying at work had symptoms of PTSD (post-traumatic stress disorder) as well as increased negative views on self, others, and the world (Mikkelsen and Einarsen, 2002). (See Chapter 12 for a discussion of the symptoms and treatment of PTSD.) Julia Gillard who was Prime Minister of Australia from 2010 until mid-2013 was the victim of bullying and harassment by her colleagues, and her rival for the leadership had allegedly been behind a sexist campaign to discredit her. In a video on the *Sydney Morning Herald* website, Hillary Clinton was seen telling Julia Gillard that you just have to stand up to it! Unfortunately the video is no longer available to view but it demonstrated that female politicians in the public spotlight have to deal with some unpleasant interpersonal experiences and the advice is to be tough.

The social context of a bullying environment and the energy employed to counter it also come with a physiological cost to the victims and witnesses (Hansen et al., 2006). In Hansen and colleagues' study, the relationships, self-reported health symptoms and physiological stress reactivity were analyzed for a sample of 437 employees (294 women and 143 men). Physiological stress reactivity was measured through the amount of cortisol in the saliva. Of the respondents, 5% of the women ($n$ = 15) and 5% of the men ($n$ = 7) reported bullying, whereas 9% of the women ($n$ = 25) and 11% of the men ($n$ = 15) had witnessed bullying at work.

The results indicated that the bullied respondents had lower social support from co-workers and supervisors, and they reported more symptoms of somatization (physical symptoms), depression, anxiety, and negative emotions than did the non-bullied respondents. Witnesses reported more symptoms of anxiety and lower support from supervisors than did the non-bullied employees. Concentrations of cortisol in the saliva were lower at awakening in bullied respondents compared with non-bullied respondents. Previous studies had reported a lower daily concentration of cortisol for people with PTSD and chronic fatigue.

As we saw in Chapter 8 on bullying among children, it is evident that bullying is destructive and attacks self-esteem, mental and physical health in both victims and witnesses, creating a culture of blame and fear. Colleagues and employers have a responsibility to look out for and report bullying. However some bullies are subtle in their approach and even in their choice of victim (Mikkelsen and Einarsen, 2002; Salin, 2003a).

## PAUSE AND REFLECT

### Mariella's story

Mariella remained a social worker for 25 years even though most of her contemporaries had long since departed the profession for what might have seemed to be more rewarding and revered roles. She was now a senior manager in a hands-on family support team in the busy child protection service of a London borough. She had been enticed to London following the break-up of her relationship with her female lover in Sydney (her home city) 20 years previously. She frequently attests to how she had never forgotten the difference between the recruitment sessions in Sydney and her arrival in the outer reaches of north-east London on a grey February day. No-one had provided her with accommodation. OK, they were not her parents or friends, but there was no clear information about how to find any either. In the early 1990s, England appeared to be in the middle of a recession but food and lodgings were expensive and social worker's pay was even worse then, proportionally, than it is now.

Once she was settled though, life seemed like bliss. She could come out as a lesbian and expect support and friendship. She even believed that her service users were not as prejudiced in England as those she had left (and expected to find in London). She felt she had left behind the vitriolic treatment from family, colleagues and erstwhile friends in Australia. It even seemed that some of her colleagues envied her *her* freedom, and she recalls having been asked by one how easy it was to become gay!

As time progressed, she became more senior (and expensive) in her organization, but always with an eye on practice. But then pressure on the service became more intense, she was older than many of her colleagues and her new young male boss began to bully her. Afterwards, she realized that he had believed her an easy target because of her age and sexuality and because she hadn't 'moved with the times' and changed her approach to working.

When Mariella looked around her she suddenly saw that she was one of the oldest members of staff, and the longest-serving one who had chosen to focus on practice and supervision rather than go up the 'greasy pole' of straightforward management. She also recognized that, because her sense of security and stability had been hard won, she had failed to identify the pressures that some others had been going through. She had been thinking of her own role in the organization and working from there rather than taking note of the broader picture. Mariella had believed she was safe because of her excellent reputation but for others she was a 'dinosaur' standing in the way of some ambitious people wanting their own promotions and seeking structural change.

- If you were her manager how would you have worked with Mariella?
- What might be the best use of her expertise?
- Might you have been encouraging her to leave?
- What could you do as a junior colleague or a senior colleague if you either witnessed or intuited office bullying?

### UNEMPLOYMENT IN MIDLIFE

The loss of a job can be devastating, putting unemployed workers at risk of physical illness, marital strain, anxiety, depression, and even suicide (Brandt and Hank, 2011). The loss of a job affects every part of life, from what time you get up in the morning to who you see and what you can afford to do. Until you make the transition to a new position, stress can be chronic. Some people have quite extreme reactions to losing their job in midlife, and feel it is a loss of identity and status (as well as economic potential). There is evidence in some communities that alcohol abuse and domestic violence may accompany job losses for men (Nicolson, 2010; Thomas et al., 1980).

## Events with potential for generativity

Resilience to the medium- or long-term negative impact life events for people with secure attachment experiences may lead towards generative events such as forming new relationships – friendships and re-partnering – or perhaps step-parenting or adopting/fostering other people's children (see Table 4.1, p. 62).

### New relationships

People in midlife who are bereaved or suffer a relationship breakdown are more likely to re-partner than those bereaved in older age (see Chapter 12) (De Jong Gierveld, 2004).

Having dependent children is a major factor in re-partnering, although this relationship is complicated. Using data from the *General Household Survey*, as well as in-depth interview data examining the attitudes of the formerly-married to future relationships, researchers found that parenthood impacted on the likelihood of formerly-married women re-partnering. The more children someone had, though, the less likely they would re-partner. The presence of children worked against re-partnering as they placed demands on their parents and objected to potential new partners. Parents may also see their parental role as more important than, and a barrier to, a new relationship. However, mothers are typically looking for partners for themselves rather than fathers for their children. Among formerly-married people without children, the desire to become a parent encouraged re-partnering. The paper concluded that parenthood status should be a key consideration in analyses of re-partnering (Lampard and Peggs, 1999).

Another study, using data from the Canadian 1995 *General Social Survey* ($N$ = 2,639), examined two competing re-partnering choices made after first intimate partnership disruption: marriage or cohabitation. About 42% of women and 54% of men form a second committed relationship five years after relationship disruption, with cohabitation being the most prevalent choice. The researchers also found that the timing of second relationship formation is more rapid among former cohabiters than among the divorced, and that widowhood is an acute barrier to re-partnering. Gender is the most crucial determinant in the re-partnering process though, with men having a higher rate of second relationship formation than women. The hazard rate of second union formation also varies by age at relationship disruption, duration of the first relationship, prior fertility (for men only), education, employment, and religion (Wu and Schimmele, 2005).

### PARENTING OTHER PEOPLE'S CHILDREN

The studies reported above suggest that men are more likely to form new committed relationships than women, and therefore there is a greater possibility for a blended family to have a step-father living with them than a step-mother. Some of the most distressing child-abuse and murder cases have been perpetrated by step-parents (or the partner of the child's mother), including the murders of Jasmine Beckford and Maria Colwell discussed in Chapters 6 and 7. Evolutionary psychologists, such as Daly and Wilson, proposed it is the lack of genetic link that has precipitated the cruelty and the manslaughter/murder of step-children. In evolutionary terms, the genetic link suggests lack of conflict between the biological parent and child, while supporting a child who is not genetically one's own might indicate future conflicting interests, particularly that the non-biological child will themselves have offspring who will not be related to the step-parent (Cohen and Fowers, 2004; Ginther and Pollak, 2004).

Most family homicides, Daly and Wilson argue, are spousal homicides, fuelled by male sexual 'proprietariness'. In the case of parent/offspring conflict, an evolutionary model predicts variations in the risk of violence as a function of the ages, sexes and other characteristics of protagonists, and these predictions were upheld in their tests on data involving infanticides, parricides (murder of a relative), and filicides (murder of your own child) (Daly and Wilson, 1988). Daly and Wilson (1996) further argue that, while genetic parents can also kill their children, the motives are different from those of other family members. Genetic parents who kill their children are likely to have mental health problems and may either commit suicide after killing their child/ren or intend to do so.

However, there is likely to be distress for step-parents and children when the new relationship breaks down and ties are broken between the step-parent and their ex-partner's children, particularly if they had lived with them and cared for them over time. The psychologist and expert on the blended family, Kathleen Cox, commenting on several such cases in the media and in lectures, has suggested that, far from being the wicked step-mother (or father), the step-parent can be a stable and unbiased influence on a child, helping them to understand the positions of both of their parents (quoted at www.theguardian.com/books/2002/jun/23/society). But if the new relationship breaks down, even after a long time, unless the children have been adopted by the new (but now ex-)partner there is no legal tie.

The evolutionary psychology argument may be used with equal conviction to apply to foster and adoptive parents and children where, particularly in the former, there have been many recorded as well as anecdotal accounts of incidents of abuse (Hobbs et al., 1999).

There are of, course, many step-parents who transform the lives of children for the better. The evidence from one study suggests that the experience of expecting and then having a child that is not biologically yours may actually be less stressful than the adjustment to biological parenthood (Ceballo et al., 2004). Ceballo and colleagues compared the experiences of gaining a child through birth, adoption or as step-children through marriage/intimate partnerships, extending the focus of this investigation beyond biological parenthood and the transition made by first-time parents. Using a subsample from the *National Survey of Families and Households* (*N* = 204), they compared the reasons for having children, parental well-being, family relationships and work roles of parents who gained a child biologically, through adoption or by becoming a step-parent. Overall, they found there were many similarities in the impact of gaining a child across the three parental groups. However, respondents reported less depressed moods, more disagreements with their spouse and more support from their own parents with the birth of a biological child. The differences across groups overall suggested that the experience of becoming an adoptive parent or a step-parent may be less stressful than the adjustment to biological parenthood.

## PAUSE AND REFLECT

### Adoption

What happens to someone adopting a child?

The stresses overlap but there are other factors to consider – not the least being:

- Trauma, loss and separation anxiety the adopted child might have experienced.
- The potential fits of the child and parental attachment experiences and styles (Howe and Fearnley, 2003).
- The age of adoption (Howe, 1997, 2001).
- The family relationships and parental resilience that pre-existed the adoption (Jones and Hackett, 2012).

Brian and William (who were in their early forties and had been together for more than ten years) had undergone a long forensic process to be accepted as adoptive parents with a local authority in the north of England. They were heartened to find out that the prejudices against them (and arcane stereotyping) had diminished from the cases they had known about ten years previously (Brodzinsky et al., 2002; Hicks, 2006).

They described what happened once they had been accepted and were undergoing the possibility of being matched to a child. They had developed anxieties about whether they had the ability to cope with the child survivors whose lives were described to them. They also felt highly stressed about what the child might think of them and their lifestyle.

However, once they went ahead and met their two-year-old future daughter, all these worries melted and they knew they would be able to do their best for her, even though it was hard sustained work (accompanied with joy). She is now four and they are being introduced to a second child.

This sounds a little like a fairy story but it is a true one.

Pre-placement preparation is a vital factor in the success of the adoption and this needs to include support for the potential adoptive parents. Both Brian and William told me that they had been made to feel that, if they raised anything negative after they had been accepted, they might have had the acceptance withdrawn.

Thus, they kept their growing (and perfectly sensible) anxieties away from the social worker, who should have been the very person with whom to share them.

## CHAPTER SUMMARY

Midlife, far from being a time of stability and latency when nothing much happens, is a time of some turmoil for most people. Positive and negative life events, such as career development or divorce, impose changes some of which are often totally unexpected.

In midlife individuals tend to reflect on their achievements and consider what more they need to do in order to gain a sense of purpose and perhaps peacefulness, all of which can be disrupted by biological and contextual events such as ill health, disability or the outcome of stress, job loss and consequent poverty.

Reading this chapter should enable you to identify the complexities of midlife experiences and expectations and single out potential vulnerabilities for people at this stage of life.

## FURTHER READING

Studies of midlife have increased over recent years, although they tend to focus on negative aspects such as health inequalities and negative life events.

One American study tried to look at the minutiae of events that midlife provides:

Almeida, D.M. (2005) Resilience and Vulnerability to Daily Stressors Assessed via Diary Methods. *Current Directions in Psychological Science*, 14(2), 64–68.

Another study focused on resilience:

Armstrong, A.R., Galligan, R.F. and Critchley, C.R. (2011) Emotional Intelligence and Psychological Resilience to Negative Life Events. *Personality and Individual Differences*, 51(3), 331–336.

Most of the research from Antonia Bifulco and the Lifespan group (now) at Middlesex University is robust and informative, particularly linking how early life impacts upon the ability to deal with life events in adulthood. Some examples are:

Bifulco, A. and Moran, P. (1998) *Wednesday's Child: Research into women's experiences of neglect and abuse in childhood and adult depression*. London: Routledge.

Bifulco, A., Bernazzani, O., Moran, P.M. and Ball, C. (2000) Lifetime Stressors and Recurrent Depression: Preliminary findings of the Adult Life Phase Interview (ALPHI). *Social Psychiatry and Psychiatric Epidemiology*, 35(6): 264–275.

Bifulco, A., Jacobs, C., Bunn, A., Thomas, G. and Irving, K. (2008) The Attachment Interview (ASI) as an Assessment of Support Capacity: Exploring its use for adoption-fostering assessment. *Adoption and Fostering*, 32: 33–45.

Bonanno, G.A. (2004) Loss, Trauma, and Human Resilience: Have we underestimated the human capacity to thrive after extremely aversive events? *American Psychologist*, 59(1), 20–28.

chapter

# 12

# OLDER AGE: INTEGRITY OR DESPAIR?

**LEARNING OBJECTIVES**

- To consider the importance of older age as a stage of lifespan *development*.
- To consider ways in which older individuals reflect on and give meaning to their lives, most of which are in the past.
- To examine the importance of understanding what was learned in earlier chapters about attachment, loss and grief and think about their significance for HGD in older age.

## Introduction

This chapter focuses upon older age – a stage during which Erikson proposed that acceptance of what a person has become enables a sense of *integrity* in his life. That is, the older person looking back consolidates or integrates his experience, and in his present lifespan stage reflects on his life as he is living it, understanding and feeling comfortable with who he has become and has been over the years.

Integrity, however, could be counterbalanced by *despair*. If the individual has left herself without the time and energy to change what she would have wanted to change, and perhaps taken chances to make amends and seek reparation for things she felt bad about, she might regret much of her life which could lead her to despair (Erikson, 1950/1963: 241–242). While there is no doubt that some of the psychosocial elements Erikson identified for older people remain relevant, improved health and longevity for many mean that the experience of being older is *diverse.* Health and social inequalities are deeply embedded in contemporary society, leaving little room for common ground at the last phases of life. Therefore, the everyday experience of being older provides different challenges and opportunities, particularly according to the bio-material and socio-material context of earlier stages of the lifespan (Bowling and Gabriel, 2004; Knight and Poon, 2008).

Older age, however experienced, is the last stage in the lifespan, but not one without development (Reker and Woo, 2011). Studies have shown that, following retirement from work, many people express greater happiness than they might have done earlier in life. This could be because many of the stresses of raising children, employment, career and overall family life have been resolved (Gross et al., 1997; Kupperbusch et al., 2003). Even so, older people are faced with worries related to health status, loss of a partner, the ill health or dependency of a partner, death of their parents and sometimes ill health and death of their adult children and grandchildren. They are also mostly financially disadvantaged compared to earlier periods in their life (Hershey and Mowen, 2000).

Older people are particularly susceptible to mental and physical health vulner-abilities, including Alzheimer's disease which is a major stress factor for partners and families who manage and provide their care. Social isolation is frequent-ly compounded by poor mobility due to health problems, as well as the loss of friends, partners and peers from work (Lane, 2012). Older people have been found to experience abuse from partners and other relatives and carers. This has proven to be a significant social problem in the twenty-first century and graphic CCTV im-ages have made us all witnesses to outstanding examples of abuse (Phelan, 2009; Straka and Montminy, 2006).

## The bio-material context

Older people do become ill and suffer from a range of chronic physical and mental health problems, particularly when over 75 years of age (Williams, 2000). This in-cludes Alzheimer's disease as well as minor cognitive impairment and depression, frequently associated with bereavement and other losses (see below in relation to the intra-psychic context) (Gross et al., 1997).

It is also interesting to note that older adults are less likely to be accurate in interpreting others' emotional responses than younger people, and this could well cause offence to others and further increase isolation without intent to do so (Phil-lips et al., 2002).

There may also be unintentional weight-loss in elderly people. This apparent-ly occurs in 15–20% of those over 65 and is associated with increased morbidity (chronic ill health where the condition is worsening) and the lead-up to mortality. In as many as 25% of cases of such weight loss no identifiable cause can be found, despite extensive clinical investigation (McMinn et al., 2011). Other studies have shown that, in some groups of the elderly, alcohol abuse is the cause of both physi-cal and cognitive impairment (Thomas and Rockwood, 2001). Falls are a frequent cause of physical complications in older people, particularly those with cognitive impairment (Härlein et al., 2009).

On the other hand though, it is important to be aware that cognitive neuroscien-tists have discovered that the older brain is capable of development and learning new skills, which may even result in increased grey matter (Boyke et al., 2008; Grady, 2008). They have also found that memory may hold its own with use, al-though there are some barriers to taking on new memory-related tasks (Burke and Mackay, 1997). This relatively new information about the older brain flies against popular assumptions of deterioration of mental faculties in older age. Further-more, and for some commentators more surprising, older people remain inter-ested in sexual relationships and report missing sexual contact (Gott and Hinchliff, 2003; Uhlenberg et al., 1990).

All this reinforces the view that being older is a biologically diverse experience, and it is likely that socio-material and intra-psychic factors play an important role in outcomes.

## The socio-material context

An insight into the socio-material context of any stage of the lifespan is available through examination of the figures for longevity (the age of death across a popu-lation) and, particularly, how these may have changed over time. In addition to the length of life, the *quality* of the life is also a significant consideration (Bowling and Gabriel, 2004; Knight and Poon, 2008). The quality of life can be understood in broad terms to include physical health, mental faculties and the capacity for devel-oping social and emotional relationships.

---

**PAUSE AND REFLECT**

Asking some of the following questions might help assess quality of life in older people:

- How independent is a person?
- Are they socially isolated?
- What is their mental health status? (Depressed, anxious, suffering from Alzheimer's?)
- Are they able to cope financially?

- Do they eat well (including do they have an appetite)?
- Can they keep themselves warm in winter?
- Do they have any money for 'treats'?
- Are they worried (necessarily or unnecessarily) about money?
- What is their access to, and experience of, health care?

---

Governments around the world (and transnational bodies) regularly compile data figures to describe the average conditions and distribution of population – demography – as we have discussed in earlier chapters. Data for the UK are avail-able at www.statistics.gov.uk/hub/population/.

An American government report indicated a clearly widening gap in life expec-tancy across the socio-economic divide, with white females living the longest and black males having the worst life expectancy. Black women, however, had a simi-lar life expectancy to white men, which was on average four years longer than black men.

In the UK in 2009 the average life expectancy was 80.1 years of age. Women live to 80.4 years (on average) and men 75.7 years, although this does not neces-sarily mean a healthy old age because women's health is generally worse than men's (Hebert, 2004). (UK Government statistics about many topics including life expectancy are available on the website www.statistics.gov.uk/hub/population/.

For detailed international comparisons the World Bank website can be accessed at data.worldbank.org/indicator/SP.DYN.LE00.IN).

There are also disparities in both longevity and health in cities, such as Glasgow and Manchester, and depressed industrial areas, such as South Wales, compared with the Home Counties (Bhui and Dinos, 2011; Harper et al., 2003).

It is also important to think about loneliness and adjustment to being alone, particularly when a person might have had an active social network and long-term partner and family (Carr et al., 2000).

From a different epistemological position, Lund and colleagues followed up a cohort of 911 men and women aged between 70 and 95 years. They wanted to explore the relationship between change and stability in their respondents' lives across three dimensions of social relations (contact frequency with other people, contact diversity, i.e. the range of different people a person saw, cohabitation status, i.e. whether they lived with an intimate partner) and the link with mortality.

For women, continuously living with somebody meant longer survival. In men, they found a significantly increased mortality among those who had lots of contact with different people about different things. In other words, contact with different people, such as social workers and health professionals, rather than steady contact with one or two close or long-term friends (e.g. in the pub) or with a partner may not be conducive to health and well-being. This suggests that, for both men and women, living with someone else (perhaps even more than one familiar person) rather than having endless contact with different people is the healthiest option (Lund et al., 2000).

Lund and colleagues' study provides an important message for those planning social care for older adults. Firstly, social contact is important for lengthening a relatively healthy lifespan and, secondly, living alongside people who are familiar is the most positive lifestyle for older people.

Elder abuse has become increasingly visible over recent years (Biggs and Goergen, 2010; Phelan, 2009; Yan and Tang, 2003). But how far is elder abuse a specific category of mistreatment, violence and neglect by related or unrelated carers or how far does the concept mask male to female domestic violence in older couples (Shemmings, 2006; Straka and Montminy, 2006; Yan and Tang, 2003)? Shemmings has suggested that concentration of the role of the care-givers (particularly the institutional ones constructed as stranger abuse) indicates a series of relationship dysfunctions based on stress as an explanation. Thus, caring for an older person who is unable to carry out basic hygiene and feeding functions for themselves may reduce relatives or professional carers to abusing the older person because of frustrations that might lead them to lose their temper.

It is important, though, to remember that older people are not an homogenous group – diversity prevails throughout the lifespan. Also, remember that characteristics such as laziness, energy, mental well-being, intelligence as well as all the other characteristics that are attributed to younger individuals remain the case throughout life. While the material context impacts upon us in terms of life events of various kinds (see Chapter 11) we are still the same person inside. Someone who was cantankerous, obstructive and unpleasant in their younger days will not change just because they are older.

As this book has demonstrated, we grow and develop, but mostly our identity pulls our whole being together around a core selfhood. The story of Ron in the Pause and Reflect becomes all the more pertinent for these reasons. Despite his age and early onset Alzheimer's, he held on to some of his destructive charac-teristics. He also made a serious suicide attempt, probably because he felt, even as an older man, that things were falling apart for him and his family (Shiner et al., 2009).

## PAUSE AND REFLECT

### Ron's story

Living with a long-term partner may present problems for each one of us faced with supporting the other despite increased mutual frailties. Ron was in his late-sixties, married for many years with grown-up children. No-one knew for certain what Ron had done for a living, not even Deirdre his wife. He was ostensibly a chauffeur, but retired about five years before I met him. He seemed to be very well-off financially, living in a large detached house in south London.

However it turned out later that Ron had always been a keen and apparently successful gambler. He loved his family (two sons now living some distance away) and had always been a good provider, although frequently an absent one. Since his retirement he had maintained the gambling habit, but not the luck that had gone with it, and he had attempted suicide three years previously by walking onto a motorway. Luckily for him, and several drivers, someone managed to take him to safety without causing a major accident.

His wife tried all she could do to make him feel better once she realized the extent of his distress. Eventually, she managed to persuade him to go to the doctor, who indicated the possibility of early onset Alzheimer's and at least some small degree of cognitive impairment.

However, diagnosis and treatment for Ron's condition did not save the couple financially and they had to sell their family home and some of their valuable possessions. There were also anxieties about some previous illegal activities that Ron had either witnessed or, more probably, been party to as well.

Deidre herself had started work as a clerical worker in the offices of a local supermarket shortly after the boys had left home. She was increasingly torn between the need to earn enough for them to live on and caring for Ron whose moods were changeable with the depression. Ironically, she found it a welcome relief that he was depressed, because his other behaviours and moods often made it difficult for her to remain in the office and carry out her work, especially when neighbours or the police phoned her to help contain him.

Deidre sought help for them as a couple as she felt she was at her wits end. She enjoyed her job, loved Ron and their home but realized that everything was slipping away for them both.

In many ways Ron and Deidre were lucky in that they knew each other well and had been through a great deal together. With support, Ron was able to regain some self-esteem even though the Alzheimer's was progressing.

**PAUSE AND REFLECT**

⟶    Working with Ron and Deidre raised issues for reflective-relational practice because of the complex relationships between:

- Mental health social workers, mental health nurses and social care workers who had different agendas for Ron and Deidre and diverse priorities for the care of Ron.
- The criminal legal system.
- Working with Ron and Deidre on how to manage their relationship:

  ◦ As a couple where a previously highly successful (and 'macho') man financially was dependent on his wife's income.
  ◦ As a couple living with a lot less disposable income and trappings of wealth than before.
  ◦ As a couple who were both less physically robust than earlier in their lives.

  ◦ Helping them recognize their own differences from each other and from their earlier selves.

Following Jan Fook's model of reflective practice as with previous cases you might want to think about how you would work with Ron and Deidre:

- What happened?
- What did (or might) you do?
- What stance did you take?
  ◦ What were you thinking might happen?
  ◦ What made you think that?
  ◦ What did you take for granted?
  ◦ What else might you have done or seen differently?
  ◦ What might have been the outcome??

## The discursive context

Aging itself is a biological process, but the way older people's lives are socially constructed is discursive. In other words, older age is constructed to frame the ways in which older people are seen and see themselves. For instance the adage '60 is the new 40' suggests that 60-year-olds have opportunities, challenges and constraints previously prescribed at middle age. You are still relatively young at 60, it is claimed. There is, of course, a degree of physical reality about such a statement because of health improvements. However, mostly it is a rhetorical device which, for both better and ill, ensures that 60-somethings refrain from staying at home by the television or fireside waiting for others to help and care for them. They are still expected to work and earn their living for several years hence.

Getting older always comes as a surprise, however much we are aware of its inevitability. You are still the person you always were and looking in the mirror frequently poses a dilemma: 'Who is that looking at me? It cannot be me with that double chin and grey hair.' You cannot believe you are old, while to another person you are a little old lady or a little old man. A friend reaching 65 recently told me in a light-hearted, but poignant, way that it takes more work to make yourself presentable enough to leave the house in older age – attending to hair colour, being careful how you dress, what you eat, getting rid of unwanted facial hair and disguising liver spots! She had a sense she was aging but she felt able to control the image she was able to present to the world – albeit with some effort. This particular conversation was a telling example of how we think about aging and gender in Western society. As you will have noted, older women need to *do* being attractive and mimicking female attractiveness from a younger stage of the lifespan. As some of the women over 60 in Jill Tunaley's study about body size and the construction of beauty declared, 'I am good for my age', suggesting implicit standards of beauty that apply to the young and the old, and that those relating to the young are the desirable ones (Tunaley et al., 1999).

The post-war baby-boom generation has begun to reach the stage when they can no longer claim midlife, and becoming older requires each of us to construct a sense of who we are as older people (Vincent, 2006). In one study (Paulson and Willig, 2008), ten older women, who exercised regularly or attended the University of the Third Age, were seen to adjust to the aging body in their everyday talk through taking what the researchers called a 'dualist' position. In other words, they held two different ideas about themselves in their heads at the same time, but they kept the ideas separate. They gave a meaning to aging as being biological decline, drawing on the dominant discourse of aging – i.e. time-related aging. However, they also saw *themselves* as being able to control elements of that decline by emphasizing their own specific ability to monitor and manage aging body parts. They did this by exerting the active mind and the busy body through various achievements, or simply by focusing on looking good. As we have seen in earlier chapters, there is some evidence that the way you perform as an aging person can, up to a point, be negotiated (Nelson, 1999).

Individual responsibility for health is a dominant discourse in Westernized countries. This was emphasized by the current generation of older people in a research study in New Zealand. The researchers used discourse analysis to examine 60 adults' uptake of the health promotion discourse in their talk about health and aging. Many participants attempted to defy or manage an aging body through a regime of exercise, food management and other practices. (This is similar to the research work mentioned above, such as Tunaley et al., 1999; Paulson and Willig, 2008.) Being in control of one's health counteracted anxieties about aging and following strictures of health promotion provided a virtuous moral identity. However, there was a danger of feeling individually responsible for ill health or feeling betrayed when health promotion promises contradicted the experience of an aging body (Pond et al., 2010).

Older people taking a discursive position in relation to health and embodiment has been found in other studies too. For example, in one longitudinal, qualitative study the researchers explored the health perceptions of older women with multiple chronic conditions. Guided by a symbolic interactionist perspective (see Chapter 3), they asked how older women with chronic health conditions interpreted their own health in their everyday lives. They also asked the women how they talked about their health with others. The researchers found that women depended on their embodied self, or signs from the body, to interpret their everyday health. The women engaged in identity management to make sense of limitations caused by their chronic health conditions. They did this by regulating how much and with whom they were willing to share issues related to their everyday health. Findings from this study suggested, overall, that everyday health is important in identity construction among older adults (Roberto and McCann, 2011).

### Discourses of sex and older people

Stereotypes of an asexual old age remain pervasive, shaping not only popular images of older people, but also research and policy agendas. However, older people's own attitudes towards the role and value of sex in later life were rarely examined until the early twenty-first century. Gott and Hinchliff (2003), drawing on both quantitative and qualitative data, examined how sex is prioritized in middle age and later life. They discovered that participants in their group of studies who did not consider sex to be of any importance to them neither had a current sexual partner nor felt that they would have another sexual partner in their lifetime. All their participants who had a current sexual partner attributed at least some importance to sex, with many rating sex as 'very' or 'extremely' important. However, experiencing barriers to being sexually active led them to place less importance on sex; this was particularly apparent when health problems and widowhood were experienced. Age was seen as facilitating coping when sex became less frequent or stopped altogether. Participants in this group drew on discourses of sexual desire decreasing with age (for some male participants). They felt that the cessation of sex was easier to cope with in a relationship of long duration and with the expectation that sex will become less possible with normal aging (Gott and Hinchliff, 2003).

The same researchers, this time interviewing participants between the ages of 31 and 91, focused again on the importance and meaning of sexual relationships. Their findings indicated that sexual activity remained an important component of long-term marriage despite the existence of factors that interfered with or prevented sex from taking place. Participants adapted to these barriers and reported little upheaval from them, which was attributed to the mutually supportive context created by long-term marriage (Hinchliff and Gott, 2004).

## Negotiating identity in older life: a bridge between the material, discursive and the intra-psychic

> And what's life, if it isn't invention? Starting with inventing yourself. (Le Carre, 1997)

The most important task across the lifespan is to gain a sense of who you are – your identity. Identity is not just about the moment, but about understanding, and indeed *storying*, your past and making sense of a possible future in the context of what has gone before. These processes constitute the *reflexivity* described by both George Herbert Mead (1934/1967) and Anthony Giddens (1986/2003, 1991) (Chapters 3 and 4).

This means that you have to reflect on, make sense of and remember your earlier life, and tell *yourself* the story of who you are. As will by now be familiar to readers of this book, change and development take place on the three levels of the material, discursive and the intra-psychic, and that process of *inventing yourself* is multi-layered too.

Erikson too, in a clinical context, described identity confusion (1959/1980) which occurs mostly at the stage of adolescence (see Chapter 9), although, at the very heart of Erikson's psychosocial understanding of development, no stage is ever completely behind you, and bits and pieces of earlier crises remain part of our identity. It has been particularly observed that people who experienced disorganized early attachment relations are also likely to retain a sense of identity confusion even into old age (Shemmings, 2006; Shemmings and Shemmings, 2011). That happens when the material, discursive and intra-psychic dimensions clash with potentially damaging results (Dube et al., 2001; Shiner et al., 2009).

The following story by the spy writer, John le Carre, although a work of fiction of course, is a relevant yet sympathetic account of the extreme experience of re-inventing yourself and its psychological consequences.

It is interesting because it combines both discursive and intra-psychic contexts, being about negotiation of selfhood and the unconscious life that takes place – always.

## PAUSE AND REFLECT

**The case of Harry Pendel**

Harry Pendel, le Carre's hero, had re-invented an identity for himself following a childhood of crime, poverty and some unhelpful relationships, followed by a spell in prison. He had trained as a tailor in prison, and on release he invented a mentor who became (in his story) his partner in an old established English firm of Mayfair tailors.

He subsequently moved to Panama where he married a respectable and religious woman and raised a family, all within this fabricated identity that he himself had come to believe. Panama being a town of varying degrees of political turmoil and integrity, its citizens accepted him for who (he said) he was until this identity was challenged by a British secret agent who knew the truth. The agent used this knowledge to force Harry to do some spying (an obvious move to those of you who are attracted to the genre).

However, even though Harry himself had always known the truth (in a conscious sense), at some level he had also become a different person from the petty criminal he had been. Thus, the fact that he was now confronted with his other self ate into his unconscious defence mechanisms (see Chapter 3) and spilled into consciousness, causing distress and confusion that he tried to ignore and push these feelings back into the depths of his mind. But this was now impossible (Smith et al., 2012).

➡ Harry, thus, began slowly to fall apart and experience serious doubt that he knew himself any more. He consequently became scared of how he would be seen by others. The unconscious fear of (self-)discovery was part of his identity. While unconscious and conscious defences were in place and, importantly, the material context supported these (Freud, 1925; Menzies, 1984; Segal and Klein, 1973), he was able to draw on the narrative of the invented life. The invented life was as real to him as anything he had actually lived through before he had arrived in Panama. He was clearly caught in an emotional and intra-psychic trap. This story showed graphically how it is unwise to neglect the unconscious mind.

What is particularly notable is how the destruction of his false identity caused psychological dysfunction. His recovery of a more authentic version of his self caused difficulties, suggesting that he had a highly sophisticated and robust system of defences (particularly denial) in place that enabled him to live largely untroubled as the person he was with the fabricated past that he actually believed in (Smith et al., 2012).

It may be possible to deny or to marginalize parts of your identity in order to manage your role in the world (see the section about the blind eye in Chapter 6), but it takes energy from the task of development so that regrets in later life may, as Erikson proposed, lead to a sense of despair (1950/1963).

Although Harry Pendel is an interesting case that you can read about in detail at your leisure if you enjoy fiction of this kind, Erikson also has fun with his contemporaries, Sigmund Freud and William James. He shows how they, too, demonstrated some degree of blindness to their real selves and invented at least an image of something other – even if not on the scale of le Carre's hero. For both psychologists, though, there was a recognition that identity was emotional and somehow *chosen* by you yourself.

So, identity is forged emotionally, and the sense of being *who you really are* co-exists alongside a sense of *not belonging* (nor, possibly, wanting to belong) to groups who represent either actions or cultures that hold values unlike your own.

Freud and James are positioned by Erikson as struggling to express themselves across all three MDI elements (see *Pause and Reflect* box opposite). James, who came from the background of an upper-class American family influential in society (his brother was the novelist Henry James), grew up in the expectation of development and achievement. Biologically, his appearance fitted into the society in which he lived. This is not to say by any means that achieving the sense of self-knowledge he himself described was untroubled. James had been unsure who was the real me until well into his life.

Freud, on the other hand, was more obviously troubled. Despite his wealth, acute intelligence and family privilege, he was alive in an increasingly hostile and frightening culture. It has been proposed that his life's work of psychoanalysis was actually a Jewish practice. Also, he could not escape his appearance, which demonstrated his difference (Geller, 2007). He did not identify with the Jewish community

## PAUSE AND REFLECT

### Two old men – a true story of identity

Clarifying the concept of identity and its origins in his own thinking, Erikson (1959/1980) also understood that identity could be negotiated, but he drew attention to the psychological problems this brought into play (as with Harry Pendel).

Erikson writes about how he turned to two 'bearded and patriarchal founding fathers of the psychologies on which our thinking on identity is based'. The first is William James (commonly identified as the founding father of psychology), and the second is Sigmund Freud (the founding father of psychoanalysis).

Erikson describes with relish, and at some length, James' ideas that character is a *subjective sense of invigorating sameness and continuity*. James records this in a letter to his wife and describes this as feeling deeply and intensely active and alive because '*this* is the real me'. Erikson considers James is describing here what Erikson himself understands as

identity, with the further implication that James had taken some time before he realized exactly what it was that made him into his real self.

Erikson records too that Freud proposed identity as having both a personal and a cultural component. In 1926 Freud addressed a Jewish organization in Vienna, where he made some important and interesting assertions about himself and how he proposed identity could be experienced. Although he was an unbeliever, and did not like to take what he considered to be a nationalistic position as a Jew, Freud experienced obscure emotional forces which were difficult to express in words but felt like a clear consciousness of inner identity so that he felt that he had a Jewish nature. For Freud, it meant that he was able to take up opposition to many ideas that were seen to be universal and immutable truths which constrained others (i.e. non-Jews). In this speech Freud also contrasted the positive identity of this fearless freedom to a negative trait in the people among whom he lived (i.e. anti-Semitic Austrians).

in Vienna in any overt sense, and struggled to make sense of who he was. However, being who he was, he worked to make sense of his unconscious experiences and expressions of identity. For him too, that took quite some time.

The experiences of James and Freud, described by Erikson as fundamental to making sense of your identity, particularly in older age, is relatively common and, of course, happens to us all to some extent. Janet, a colleague of mine in her mid-50s, had always thought of herself as an ordinary English woman, even though one grandfather had been Spanish. However, this changed for her in a dramatic way when she went to a meeting in Greece with a group of social workers with whom she was planning a research project. None of them had yet met with her face-to-face and when she arrived at the meeting point no-one came up to introduce themselves.

She waited for some time until a woman who had been standing nearby with some others approached her cautiously to see if she were, in fact, Janet. It turned out that they had assumed she was Greek because of her appearance and they had been expecting Janet to be a brown- or blond-haired typical English person.

This became a long-standing joke among her colleagues, but was actually a major disruption to Janet's sense of who she was, and how she believed people saw her and had always seen her. She had not realized previously that she looked different, even as she approached older age and had lived with herself in her body for more than half a century. She then had to renegotiate her identity and, in some ways, her life narrative to take account of her Spanish heritage, as well as the other parts of her that she had lived with and were familiar.

There is currently an increased interest in genealogy – trying to establish your identity through knowledge of your ancestors. This is the stuff of absorbing television and radio broadcasts and individual and family activities and, while intriguing and perhaps even fun, finding out the sources of your DNA can be potentially psychologically destabilizing, as with those who find upsetting evidence of some recent ancestors' behaviours.

## PAUSE AND REFLECT

### Strange tales of loss and change

For some older people, trauma, such as an accident with brain injury or a stroke, may completely wipe out their previous sense of who they are.

The experience of the following two people is neurologically fascinating, although a major cause of distress for both. In the second case, there is a recognized syndrome but, in the first case, it is difficult to find evidence of other examples, although I have no doubt there are some.

In Chapter 2 I described the fashion in psychology for seeing the human mind as a function of brain activity that can be tracked and measured. However, some of the things not explained fully by the brain/mind approach include the psychological consequences of brain damage other than that caused through disease and deterioration.

Talking to people with brain damage sometimes reveals the 'ghost in the machine' that cognitive neuroscientists and some evolutionary psychologists argue is fully explicable in biological terms. But that is not always the case.

Mr Roberts had survived a motor accident that had sadly killed his wife, with bizarre and fascinating consequences for his sense of identity.

The intriguing aspect of Mr Roberts' account was that he told me that he knew who he was

and who he had been, and he now knew he was a different person from the one he had been before the accident – not simply that he had changed the way he looked at things. However he knew now that *he had a totally different past* from the one he knew he had had previously.

In the neurological unit, as he recovered consciousness after some months following the crash, he believed he was a French general captured by the Spanish during the Napoleonic wars. After some time, and after he had returned home and had two young teenagers to care for (although with the support of his late wife's family), he declared that he had yet a different past. He was no longer the French general – he believed he had had that experience because it chimed with the new background he believed was his – he was now a Belgian man with an East European background. He told me he was well aware that he had had the motor accident as a different person. He just said that he had multiple memories about his different pasts – each of which was real – but he had chosen the Belgian man.

Mr Roberts coped well with shopping and looking after his children, who clearly cared deeply for him. Their coping strategy was to see him as the Belgian, while making sure he recognized that they had been the children of a man from Manchester!

The role of the brain in consciousness and self-awareness is clearly indisputable but for the person himself there is an important concern about self in the past, present and future. As

**PAUSE AND REFLECT**

individuals we need to know who we are and, despite the scientific advances in brain science and new discoveries that have accompanied developments in human genetics, these sciences are still unable to show us how we become who we and what it means to be who we are.

Mr Roberts has managed to incorporate the *irrational* into his biographical narrative. But what does it say about the self/mind/body/biology? Because we live in a science culture we try to screen the irrational out – for instance, how often does one hear 'We don't "yet" have an explanation'?, the explicit assumption being there *will* be a scientific advance that will explain.

Similarly, there is a widely reported case of an older woman from Newcastle whose recovery from a stroke was followed by the experience of Foreign Accent Syndrome (FAS). FAS is a rare speech disorder characterized by the emergence of an apparent foreign accent after

an anterior left-hemispheric lesion of the brain (Moonis et al., 1996; Reeves and Norton, 2001). It was first reported in Norway in 1941 when a young woman started to speak with a German accent after being wounded and shocked following an air raid.

In our case, stroke-victim, Linda Walker, aged 60 at the time of the stroke had had a distinctive Geordie accent. However, when she awoke in hospital this accent had been transformed into a mixture of Jamaican, Canadian and Slovakian. This was extremely upsetting for Mrs Walker who was unable to do anything to change these new accents, but it was more distressing because she had no reason in her sense of her own past to have such accents. She was reported to have said: 'I've lost my identity, because I never talked like this before. I'm a very different person and it's strange and I don't like it. It's very hard and I get very upset in my head, but I'm getting better.'

Erikson's idea is that if there is enough emotional credit in a lifespan then older people will feel a sense of integrity that life has run its course and that the older person will go towards their ending with reasonable mental health. He calls it 'integrity', meaning that their experiences will be pulled together and integrated into the meaning of their existence. See the *Pause and Reflect* box overleaf for a surprising example among homeless men. The other side of the equation would be one of despair and the fear of death.

## The intra-psychic context

Getting older is possibly one of the most psychologically disruptive features of psychosocial development through the lifespan, and, despite the exception overleaf relating to the homeless men (Smith and Nicolson, 2011), as a rule securely attached individuals are likely to be resilient and manage the disruptions more easily than those with insecure attachment experiences and styles and disorganized ones.

Being older means that many things are given up, including the identity of being a young or midlife person, and there is a mixed bag of gains as well as losses. Retirement from work means loss of income, status and companionship but it also means being free from the stresses and strains that work brings to many people. Retirement, particularly in reasonable health, means freedom to engage in

## PAUSE AND REFLECT

**An absence of despair**

In the 1990s, Graham Smith conducted a study of older men with histories of extreme alcohol and other substance abuse who were homeless in Scotland. These data were re-analyzed by us both (see Chapter 11) using Erikson's eighth stage as a template (Smith and Nicolson, 2011).

These men all had lived lives during which they were abused physically and sexually, abandoned by parents or bereaved in childhood and in all cases their remaining family had found it difficult to cope. While we were expecting this group to be highly despairing – not least because they were living in an abusive environment even in their old age – this was not what we found.

Most of them believed they had had interesting and adventurous lives and some reported sadness and loss that they had overcome, demonstrating their remarkable resilience in the face of extreme adversity. They all were aware that they had little time to go in their lives at the time of the interview but they were not terrified of death, as we had predicted. We were both struck by the ways in which the men could be reflexive about their experiences, while interpreting and giving meaning to the things they did and the things done to them.

Each case appeared to be one in which early attachment relationships were likely to have been insecure and probably disorganized, and yet they managed to develop a remarkable resilience.

• What do you think might have happened in their lives for them to achieve this ability to reflect on their lives in a peaceful and well thought-out way?

activities that have been denied through lack of time and energy or even conflict of interest in the past (Kupperbusch et al., 2003; Rudman, 2006). Some people have also experienced a freedom from gender role stereotyping as they became older (Greer, 1993).

### Emotion in older people

As people get older, they may experience fewer negative emotions (Mather and Carstensen, 2005) or are less able to process emotions in themselves or others (Phillips et al., 2002). It appears that strategic processes in older adults' emotional attention and memory play a role in this variation with age. Older adults typically recall the good things in their life, more so than some younger people who may not yet have had the chance to process their experiences or indeed see the out-come of particular phases of their lives – such as career success or happy and settled children. Discourses about the golden good old days and endless summers of childhood illustrate this thinking in older people. This thinking, however, masks the anxieties and contradictory experiences that are part of all of our lives, and are just as likely to be part of the older person's past as younger people's. What do we know about this process? It seems there is a positivity effect that takes place in the thinking and emotional experiences of many older people. This may well be a defence against anxiety (Freud, 1923; Klein, 1946).

One experimental study demonstrated that, when shown stimuli that varied in their positive or negative qualities, positive items accounted for a larger proportion of older adults' subsequent memories than those of younger adults. This positivity effect in older adults' memories seemed to be due to their greater focus on emotion regulation and to be implemented by cognitive control mechanisms that enhance positive and diminish negative information. These findings suggested that both cognitive abilities and motivation contribute to older adults' emotion regulation. This may also have relevance in the case of the older homeless men discussed above, whereby a combination of brain activity and the psychosocial processes of development in old age described by Erikson (1959/1980) cause positivity of reminiscence, despite the mostly insecure and disorganized attachments of their childhoods (Smith and Nicolson, 2011).

However, like with every other characteristic, intelligence, emotion and memory reflect the individual ability at least as much if not more than the age of the person (Verhaeghen et al., 1993).

## Bereavement and grief

Loss is the other side of the coin to attachment – the disruption of a close emotional bond. The experience of bereavement, through the loss of a loved one, is universal to humans and to many animals. Even pigeons, who mate for life, have shown grief reactions at the loss of their partner. Grief has been defined as the mental pain, distress and deep violent sorrow that follow such a loss.

---

**PAUSE AND REFLECT**

### Attachment and grief

Steve was a widower of seven years. His family and friends considered that he had managed his grief successfully, eventually having come to terms with the loss of his wife after a happy and long marriage. He was living in the seaside town he and his wife had moved to when they were in their twenties and in the house where he had nursed her and she had eventually died.

Steve and his wife adopted a black Labrador puppy just before she became ill, and they had both been very attached to him. After his wife's death Steve would take him for a walk – which became shorter and slower as the dog grew older. Eventually, it meant Steve would stand near the park by his house while friends and neighbours passing by would stop and pat the dog and chat to Steve.

When the dog died, aged sixteen, Steve fell apart. Caring for the dog had kept him going to

the extent that he had not realized that this dog was also representing for him the last vestige of his married and family life. (See Kaufman and Kaufman, 2006: although this study refers to the loss of a pet in childhood there is resonance with Steve's experience.)

His dog also gave Steve an excuse to be out of his house, passing the time of day with other people. After the dog died, he suddenly felt his age – he was old and could no longer cope living in the big tumbledown house. He went to live near his older son in a new bungalow and sadly developed stomach cancer and died soon afterwards.

Steve had had a secure attachment experience as a child and he and his wife had both achieved satisfaction in their sense of who they were and the contributions they made in life. So, perhaps it was no surprise to those around him that Steve had coped well with his loss. He had loved his wife and had little with which to rebuke himself. However, it seemed

→

→    that in fact Steve had held onto his grief by transferring his feelings about his wife and his attachment to a transitional object (i.e. the dog) (Winnicott, 1971/2001). Winnicott describes these transferrences, which are adopted in infancy – a teddy bear or blanket – as becoming a vitally important defence for the infant against anxiety. The infant will seek the object when distressed, and, importantly for older people,

the need for a transitional object may re-occur at other stages of lives when there are high levels of anxiety and distress. It is important that the object is seen as other, have a vitality of its own and it must survive instinctual loving and hating (in this case, like a lifelong partner might).

For Steve, after the dog's death, he had literally nothing to cling onto any longer and his mental and physical health declined.

Loss, and the disruption of an attachment bond, is a core concept across the lifespan (Parkes et al., 1991), as you know from Chapter 5. Freud (1917) was one of the first thinkers to suggest that the expression of grief following bereavement was not only natural and acceptable, but highly desirable. It was important to cry for what, and who, you have lost. It was also important *not* to maintain the Victorian stiff upper lip. To bury such fundamental feelings of anguish would distort recovery and prevent emotional healing. The loss would be buried in the unconscious and never resolved. Some of the after-effects of unacknowledged loss, Freud believed, would be similar to what we now think of as PTSD (post-traumatic stress disorder) (Bisson, 2007; Busuttil, 2004).

There is a difference between looking back at a period of mourning with sadness, or even shedding a tear for the lost person, and having intrusive thoughts and dreams which cause anxiety. The latter is symptomatic of unresolved grief.

### *Post-traumatic stress disorder*

PTSD is a clinical disorder or a syndrome (see APA (1994)). It is worth thinking about because, as a social worker, you are likely to meet service users who have some or all of these symptoms. Its symptoms are grouped into three types:

1. Re-experiencing the traumatic event, through constantly re-enacting it in your mind and dreaming about it.
2. Numbing or reduced involvement in the external world as if you are at a distance from things that are happening to you.
3. A diverse group of symptoms such as memory impairment, difficulty in concentrating, hyper-alertness (being over-aware of what is going on – 'jumpy').

Some people who have undergone trauma have a few of these symptoms all the time. Others have the symptoms sometimes, while other people have a clearly defined PTSD. That means they experience most of these symptoms all or most of the time. People who have all or any of these symptoms are also likely to feel worse when faced with a situation that reminds them of the trauma. So, if you have survived a train crash, you might be coping well and not thinking about the experience until you have to get on board a train or see a crash on television. That might make you break out in a sweat, tremble and have nightmares. This experience can last for a few hours or a few days. It might go away and then resurface.

It is difficult to predict who will have PTSD or related symptoms, even after a well-recognized traumatic event such as being involved in a car crash, a war, a fire or surviving a personal attack. There is an interaction between personality, emotional history and other life events around the time of the trauma itself. As with depression, the thoughts that depress you depend on personal history and current circumstances.

Almost no studies of PTSD have involved the elderly (Busuttil, 2004) and yet there is a strong possibility that it will frequently impact on old people, particularly, as with Steve above, if a long-term partner dies or a neighbourhood is destroyed or someone is re-housed without their choice (Archer and Hawes, 1988). PTSD was particularly relevant in a burglary study where expectations of security in a long lived-in and trusted home were violated, making some people unable to go on living in the same house (Nicolson, 1994).

### The healthy grief reaction

John Archer (1999), an expert on the evolution of human emotions and behaviour, reviewed the research evidence to identify what he describes as the *typical grief reaction*. Much of what he discovered returns us to thinking about the evidence on attachment and loss that we explored in Chapter 5, although there it was mostly in relation to children (Bowlby, 1982; Field et al., 1999; Freud and Dann, 1951).

Most of the research Archer described was about bereavement and widowhood (Field et al., 1999; Parkes, 1998), but he also looked at studies where a similar kind of response could be found, including loss of a job (Archer and Rhodes, 1987) . He considered from reviewing the evidence that a healthy grief reaction has a pattern.

Firstly, there is the numbness and disbelief, which is seen as a psychological defence against the extreme pain. This is useful and helps us to get through the first painful days and manage formal arrangements such as informing people about the death and planning the funeral. The individual at this point denies they are feeling such grief or represses it, and that is protective of their self. If this stage lasts, however, there is likely to be a psychological repercussion of, for example, unexplained and prolonged depression.

The second response to grief, which sometimes follows the numbness, is also a form of denial: an expression of anger. This may happen when a few weeks have passed and the bereaved person is no longer the focus of concern or attention. This may be followed by guilt and self-blame for the loss, which may mean that some anger is turned inwards upon the bereaved individual themselves.

Fourthly, distress and anxiety often accompany much of the bereaved person's behaviour, which Colin Murray Parkes (Parkes, 1996), in his description of early widowhood, depicted as anxiety verging on panic. This will include sobbing, hyperventilation, inability to sleep, restlessness and psychosomatic problems such as eczema.

Fifthly, bereavement leads to yearning and preoccupation with what has been lost – pining is a word that well describes the aspect of this state. After that, bereaved people sometimes hallucinate or dream about their lost state of being or the person.

The process often ends in a depression, which is an important precursor to the acceptance of the loss. It means that the person is facing and experiencing the pain of grief, having recognized its reality. He no longer tries to avoid the pain and, only once he sees the loss for what it really is, is he able to accept it and rebuild his life.

Archer argues that this process is not only seen in humans living in sophisticated societies. There are many anthropological studies of primitive communities of humans and studies of primates that demonstrate that such grief is a universal, evolutionary and thus an adaptive process (Hrdy, 1997). In other words, it happens whether we like it or not. It is part of the natural way of assisting our emotional healing, and progressing through these stages is the only way to be able to accept the loss and get on with our future life.

Knowledge of the common features of grief reactions, following more frequently recognized experiences of loss, has led psychologists to show that there are, indeed, both successful and pathological outcomes for the process (Hodgkinson, 1982; Moules et al., 2004). Some people continue to grieve for years, which can result in embittered ruined lives. Some people react by expressing their anger, and there are always stories of people who commit murder if they believe someone has been responsible for the break-up of their relationship or the death of their loved one.

There is no clear pathway to getting over loss (Parkes et al., 1991). However, the major factor in psychological adjustment and re-integration is the acceptance of loss and that things have changed for ever. Another major factor in a grief reaction is to help someone recognize where blame (if any) lies and not to take it all upon themselves.

It is not only bereavement relating to a loved one that leads to grief. Peter Marris (1986) has shown that moving away from home or changes in the structure of a community can lead to a grief reaction. My own research on the experience of being burgled (Nicolson, 1994) showed that this experience too can lead to a severe grief reaction, particularly if someone has lost items of great sentimental value or feels their once-loved house has let them down.

The classic community studies of Young and Willmott (1986), for example, described the impact on individuals of clearing away London's old East End. Having your home demolished and being relocated several miles away into flats or other types of new development demonstrated clearly how it was possible to mourn a previous way of life that was about to be lost for ever. Young and Willmott contrasted this traditional life-style of the East End with the impact on family life following that re-housing in suburban or new urban estates. Living alongside strangers influenced the way people related to their own family, community and the State. Relocation in this case had a profound impact on the identity and lifestyle of the people involved.

## CHAPTER SUMMARY

This chapter will have enabled you to link up the stages of the lifespan and review human growth and development for older people. Through doing this, you will also be giving some thought to the ways in which early experiences, particularly the forming of attachment relationships, impact throughout life.

The psychosocial tasks faced in the later stages of life are complex and potentially more disruptive than previous experiences through the lifespan. Older age is discursively constructed and, for the current cohort of post-75-year-olds, the meaning of being elderly and their expectations of themselves are different from those of their parents' generation. Generations to come will have different expectations and experiences yet again – particularly because they are expected to work longer to pay for their retirement.

While older people can on the whole expect greater longevity than their parents it might not necessarily be a healthier life. Poverty, disability and the characteristics of the community will all have an impact on how we experience older age.

For all though, identity needs to be negotiated and managed and, as demonstrated by the study of homeless men in old age, what might from the outside have appeared to others as a destructive and unhappy life could be constructed as one of freedom and survival for those who have lived it.

The major tasks faced by the elderly include being able to overcome the shift in the meaning of their lives caused through losing partners and friends, and taking a role which involves being cared for rather than doing the caring for others.

## FURTHER READING

It is realistic to focus on the losses people experience as older adults because it is likely that these are the people you will be working with as social work practitioners. Much has been written about bereavement and grief, and the following papers provide a variety of approaches, including the classic works of Colin Murray Parkes which remains essential reading.

Castle, J. and Phillips, W.L. (2003) Grief Rituals: Aspects that facilitate adjustment to bereavement. *Journal of Loss and Trauma*, 8(1), 41–71.

Hodgkinson, P.E. (1982) Abnormal Grief – The problem of therapy. *British Journal of Medical Psychology*, 55(1), 29–34.

**FURTHER READING** *continued*

Moules, N.J., Simonson, K., Prins, M., Angus, P. and Bell, J.M. (2004) Making Room for Grief: Walking backwards and living forward. *Nursing Inquiry*, 11(2), 99–107.

Parkes, C.M. (1998) Coping with Loss: Bereavement in adult life. *British Medical Journal*, 316(7134), 856–859.

Vanderwerker, L.C., Jacobs, S.C., Parkes, C.M. and Prigerson, H.G. (2006) An Exploration of Associations Between Separation Anxiety in Childhood and Complicated Grief in Later Life. *Journal of Nervous and Mental Disease*, 194(2), 121–123

Wayment, H.A. and Vierthaler, J. (2002) Attachment Style and Bereavement Reactions. *Journal of Loss and Trauma*, 7(2), 129–149.

John Archer's book on evolutionary aspects of bereavement is also particularly useful because he explores a range of grief reactions:

Archer, J. (1999) *The Nature of Grief: The evolution and psychology of reactions to loss.* London: Brunner Routledge.

chapter

# 13

# AFTERWORD

Becoming human is a major task for us all and we can examine the process from a range of perspectives. As individual human beings, we enter the world without any choice and for much of our lives have a limited say in what happens to us. Those who study HGD academically or clinically do have a choice, and, from what you have read, you will now be aware that our knowledge of the human journey across the lifespan comprises evidence from the viewpoints of biology, psychology, sociology and anthropology. You will also know now that, within those disciplines, there are a number of debates, many of which are not resolved, and that evidence has different value at different periods in history as scientists discover, and sometimes rediscover, core ideas and facts. For example, our understanding of what causes problems with our mental health has gone through many iterations – from explanations giving priority to brain fever, problems in living, the pathologies of the family and society, genetic predisposition and now, for some at least, returning to a predominant psychosocial solution.

In this book I used Erikson's psychosocial development project (1950/1963) as a lens, or organizing device, through which to build the material-discursive-intra-psychic model of human growth and development through the lifespan. I think this model of MDI is effective in bringing together the practices involved in negotiating the lifespan (Sugarman, 2001). The MDI model provides a link to explain the continuity and the sense of lifespan including the biological, societal, familial and emotional contexts with the stages at which our lives unfold. It also allows for transparency of the different perspectives on the same or similar matters. Taking the example of sexual relationships, we can see why biological explanations might be used by both those coming from a feminist standpoint and those coming from an evolutionary psychology.

The bio- and socio-material contexts described in the book have wide implications for who we become, but they are not necessarily the main predictors of our future lives (Bronfenbrenner and Morris, 2007). Lives are negotiated discursively and particular discourses themselves are products of their historical time. History constructs the definitions of what makes a loving and/or good parent (Goodley and Tregaskis, 2006) and what constitutes childhood itself (Ingleby, 1977). Even the apparently tangible concept of madness, notwithstanding its material context (the troubled body and the distressed family, for instance), is also a social construction. Who is mad? Are the demands of contemporary society the problem or is the person who refuses to conform or who cannot meet the demands of others mad (Blackman, 2007; Laing, 1959; Laing and Esterson, 1970)?

The intra-psychic – the emotional and unconscious elements in the life we lead – represents the final part of the equation (Armstrong et al., 2011; Bower, 2005; Fonagy, 2000; Fook and Gardner, 2010). Unfashionable as the unconscious has been of late among hard-pressed social work academics and practitioners, it has always been important to understand that our individual responses are varied, and resilience and the ability to survive a variety of life experiences, have unconscious elements in the mix (Giddens, 1986/2003; Martin, 1920). Ideas about reflective practice, which is vital for social work and increasingly fashionable among social workers, also have clear links to psychoanalytic ideas (Fook and Gardner, 2010).

To make sense of HGD within the complex framework informed by these perspectives we need to ask:

- At what point have we become our self?
- Do we *actually* become our self?
- What are the major influences on our journey through the lifespan?
- How far are innate characteristics essential ingredients in our identities?
- Is nature more influential than nurture, and is nurture necessarily benign (that is, does the context in which we live and grown necessarily *nurture* us)?
- Is there any point during our lifespan that we don't grow or develop?
- How do answers to these questions begin to inform our work with service users?

Each of our lives is complicated and intertwined with others', and this varies at different stages in our own lives (Reavey and Brown, 2007). While we are children we engage with others, many of whom are adults – our early lives are not discrete, pure stages of growth and change, or phenomena that might be examined and explained objectively (McAdams et al., 2001; Moules et al., 2004). Some social workers specialize in child protection – but this work is not only about children, nor is it only about the adults who may fail to care for them, it is also about making sense of the entangled lives of service users (resembling our own, of course) which potentially enhance or destabilize the lives of others.

As adults we are likely to become parents and grandparents and those experiences are intrinsically linked to an inter-generational model of HGD that exemplifies the conundrum of describing development without reference to others at different stages of their lives (Main et al., 1985; Marris, 1986).

Giddens' model of structuration, in which he proposes the different levels of consciousness we operate over time, is particularly helpful in understanding how we relate to the world in which we live (1986/2003). According to Giddens, practical, discursive and unconscious thinking underlies our entire sense of consciousness, and hence our identity. Giddens acknowledges the importance of Freudian thinking about the unconscious and the value of Erikson's ideas about psychosocial development as a framework for grasping hold of the human experience and, particularly, theorizing identity and agency, all of which underpinned the model of structuration (see Chapter 4).

The passing of time, similarly, links this sociological model to the psychoanalytic one (Lieberman, 2004). Time passes us constantly, each minute, each day and across the lifespan. The passing of time enables us to be reflexive, and reflexivity is an essential human quality. By being reflexive, we can construct our sense of who and where we are and plan, or choose not to plan, what we do next. Of course we cannot always move to a position that we choose, but we do have the capacity to make sense of each place we land in, and negotiate how we are going to 'perform' the narrative of our lives at each stage and in each place. Symbolic interactionist thinking, particularly the idea that we are able to reflect and be objective about ourselves, clearly links here to Giddens, Freud and Erikson's work (Mead, 1934/1967). The 'I', the sense we have of being pure experience, the here and now, very quickly passes and we can then, as 'me', evaluate and make sense of how we were and what happened to us (Yip, 2006) (see Chapter 3).

For social workers, it is clear that human vulnerability exists at all ages and stages, but our resilience, strengths and vulnerabilities are all dependent on others of different generations. Social workers are often young, younger than many of the service users they support and challenge. Inter-generational relationships need to be a clear part of the substance of social work education.

But what about social work itself? We are regulated by dominant discourses, and the contemporary discourses in social work are essentially bureaucratic (BASW, 2011). Social workers are not radical, as they were in the 1980s when social workers were seen to be undermining the State in order to support those who were its potential victims (Aymer and Okitikpi, 2000). Nor are they psychoanalytic, as they were in the late 1960s when they were criticized for supporting the status quo to prevent social change. The psychological and the unconscious are not seen to be relevant in understanding oppression in the contemporary climate.

But herein lies the mistake, and the links between Marxism and psychoanalysis need to be reconsidered because traditionally they have offered an effective means of understanding the links between social and behavioural changes that challenged marginalization and oppression (Ferguson, 2001).

For many, the experience of being a social worker is (regretfully) becoming more about being seen to do the right things (box-ticking) than supporting vulnerable people or challenging the system on behalf of service users (Beresford, 2000). What unconscious forces lurk in the area offices? What goes on among those who manage social workers? And among those who formulate policy? The social workers I have taught over the years, and particularly the qualified social workers I work with now, for the most part find themselves alienated from the discourses of regulation, box-ticking and blame. But they find ways around them. They negotiate the system in order to provide the best service they are able to their users.

The *Munro Review of Child Protection* (2011) reiterates that clear thinking, professional training to a high level and awareness of the latest research are paramount. Perhaps we *are* all going round in circles (Dickens, 2011). From the Munro conclusions it seems that social work institutions and social workers themselves are still being held accountable for many social ills. We are led to believe that all that is needed is more rules and guidelines and practice will miraculously improve. That is not how I, nor any of my colleagues, wish to educate professional social work practitioners. They are professionals and can make appropriate judgments, taking responsibility for their own practice and for that of those they supervise. It is so easy to find fault and to dismiss social workers as poorly trained, poorly supervised and overworked. But what goes on beneath the surface for human beings faced with the horrendous truths about child abuse, the abuse of the vulnerable elderly and people with mental health problems (Cooper, 2005; Rustin, 2005)? But what has changed and what will change? This is the challenge for all of you reading this book and practising, managing and forming policy about social work in the twenty-first century.

# REFERENCES

Addington, A.M. and Rapoport, J.L. (2009) The Genetics of Childhood-onset Schizophrenia: When madness strikes the prepubescent. *Current Psychiatry Reports*, 11(2) 156–161.

Ainsworth, M.D. (1962) The Effects of Maternal Deprivation: A review of findings and controversy in the context of research strategy. In *Deprivation of Maternal Care: A reassessment of its effects*, Public Health Papers, No. 14. Geneva: World Health Organization.

Ainsworth, M.D.S., Blehar, M.C., Waters, E. and Wall, S. (1978) *Patterns of Attachment: A psychological study of the strange situation*. London: Lawrence Erlbaum Associates.

Aisenberg Romano, G., Ravid, H., Zaig, I., Schreiber, S., Azem, F., Shachar, I. et al. (2012) The Psychological Profile and Affective Response of Women Diagnosed with Unexplained Infertility Undergoing In Vitro Fertilization. *Archives of Women's Mental Health*, 1–9.

Aldridge, J. and Becker, S. (1993) Punishing Children for Caring: The hidden cost of young carers. *Children & Society*, 7(4), 376–387.

Allen, D.G. (2006) Do Organizational Socialization Tactics Influence Newcomer Embeddedness and Turnover? *Journal of Management*, 32(2), 237–256.

Amato, P.R. (2003) Reconciling Divergent Perspectives: Judith Wallerstein, quantitative family research, and children of divorce. *Family Relations*, 52(4), 332–339.

Andrews, G., Sanderson, K., Slade, T., Issakidis, C. (2000) Why Does the Burden of Disease Persist? Relating the burden of anxiety and depression to effectiveness of treatment. *Bulletin of the World Health Organisation*, 78(4), 446–454.

Andrews, M., Day Sclater, S., Squire, C. and Tamboukou, M. (2007) Narrative Research. In C. Seale, G. Gobo, J. Gubrium and D. Silverman (eds), *Qualitative Research Practice* (pp. 97–112) London: Sage.

APA (American Psychiatric Association) (1994/2010) *Diagnostic and Statistical Manual*, 4th edn. Washington DC: American Psychiatric Association.

Archer, J. (1984) Gender Roles as Developmental Pathways. *British Journal of Social Psychology*, 23(3), 245–256.

Archer, J. (1999) *The Nature of Grief: The evolution and psychology of reactions to loss*. London: Brunner Routledge.

Archer, J. and Hawes, J. (1988) Grief and Rehousing. *British Journal of Medical Psychology*, 61(4), 377–379.

Archer, J. and Rhodes, V. (1987) Bereavement and Reactions to Job Loss: A comparative review. *British Journal of Social Psychology*, 26(3), 211–224.

Archer, J. and Vaughan, A.E. (2001) Evolutionary Theories of Rape. *Psychology, Evolution & Gender*, 3(1), 95–101.

Armstrong, A.R., Galligan, R.F. and Critchley, C.R. (2011) Emotional Intelligence and Psychological Resilience to Negative Life Events. *Personality and Individual Differences*, 51(3), 331–336.

Arnett, J.J. (1995) Adolescents' Uses of Media for Self-socialization. *Journal of Youth and Adolescence*, 24(5), 519–533.

Aron, W.S. and Daily, D.W. (1976) Graduates and Splitees from Therapeutic Community Drug Treatment Programs: A comparison. *Substance Use & Misuse*, 11(1), 1–18.

Arsenio, W.F. and Lemerise, E.A. (2004) Aggression and Moral Development: Integrating social information processing and moral domain models. *Child Development*, 75(4), 987–1002.

Asch, S.E. (1940) Studies in the Principles of Judgments and Attitudes: II. Determination of judgments by group and by ego standards. *Journal of Social Psychology*, 12(2), 433–465.

Aymer, C. and Okitikpi, T. (2000) Epistemology, Ontology and Methodology: What's that got to do with social work? *Social Work Education*, 19(1), 67–75.

Bacchus, L., Mezey, G. and Bewley, S. (2004) Domestic Violence: Prevalence in pregnant women and associations with physical and psychological health. *European Journal of Obstetrics & Gynecology and Reproductive Biology*, 113(1), 6–11.

Bakan, D. (1971) Adolescence in America: From idea to social fact. *Daedalus*, 100(4), 979–995.

Baltes, P.B., Lindenberger, U. and Staudinger, U.M. (2007) *Life Span Theory in Developmental Psychology*. John Wiley & Sons, Inc.

Baltes, P.B., Staudinger, U.M. and Lindenberger, U. (1999) Lifespan Psychology: Theory and application to intellectual functioning. *Annual Review of Psychology*, 50, 471–507.

Bandura, A. (1973) *Aggression: A social learning analysis*. Englewood Cliffs, NJ: Prentice Hall.

Bandura, A. (1977) *Social Learning Theory*. New York: General Learning Press.

Bandura, A. (1978) Social Learning Theory of Aggression. *Journal of Communication*, 28(3), 12–29.

Bandura, A. and McDonald, F.J. (1963) Influence of Social Reinforcement and the Behavior of Models in Shaping Children's Moral Judgment. *Journal of Abnormal and Social Psychology*, 67(3), 274–281.

Banister, E.M. (1999) Women's Midlife Experience of their Changing Bodies. *Qualitative Health Research*, 9(4), 520–537.

Banner, L. (2012) *Marilyn: The passion and the paradox*. New York: Bloomsbury.

Barnett, B. and Parker, G. (1998) The Parentified Child: Early competence or childhood deprivation? *Child and Adolescent Mental Health*, 3(4), 146–155.

Baron-Cohen, S. (2004) *The Essential Difference*. Harmondsworth: Penguin.

BASW (2011) The Code of Ethics in Social Work: Statement of principles (draft). http://cdn.basw.co.uk/upload/basw_125523–5.pdf.

Bateman, A.W. and Fonagy, P. (2000) Effectiveness of Psychotherapeutic Treatment of Personality Disorder. *British Journal of Psychiatry*, 177(2), 138–143.

Bateson, P.P.G. (1966) The Characteristics and Context of Imprinting. *Biological Reviews*, 41(2), 177–217.

Bayer, B. and Malone, K. (1996) Feminism, Psychology and matters of the body. *Theory and Psychology*, 6, 667–692.

Baumeister, R.F., Dale, K. and Sommer, K.L. (1998) Freudian Defense Mechanisms and Empirical Findings in Modern Social Psychology: Reaction formation, projection, displacement, undoing, isolation, sublimation, and denial. *Journal of Personality*, 66(6), 1081–1124.

Baumrind, D. (1966) Effects of Authoritative Parental Control on Child Behavior. *Child Development*, 37(4), 887–907.

Beckett, C. and Taylor, H. (2010) *Human Growth and Development*, 2nd edn. London: Sage.

Bee, H.L. and Mitchell, S.K. (1984) *The Developing Person: A life span approach*, 2nd edn. New York: Harper & Row.

Belsky, J. (1997) Attachment, Mating, and Parenting. *Human Nature*, 8(4), 361–381.

Belsky, J., Steinberg, L. and Draper, P. (1991) Childhood Experience, Interpersonal Development, and Reproductive Strategy: An evolutionary theory of socialization. *Child Development*, 62(4), 647–670.

Bem, S. (1994) *The Lenses of Gender: Transforming the debate on sexual inequality*. Yale: Yale University Press.

Ben-Porath, Y. (1967) The Production of Human Capital and the Life Cycle of Earnings. *Journal of Political Economy*, 75(4), 352–365.

Bentall, R. (2006) Madness Explained: Why we must reject the Kraepelinian paradigm and replace it with a 'complaint-orientated' approach to understanding mental illness. *Medical Hypotheses*, 66(2), 220–233.

Bereczkei, T. and Csanaky, A. (2001) Stressful Family Environment, Mortality, and Child Socialisation: Life-history strategies among adolescents and adults from unfavourable social circumstances. *International Journal of Behavioral Development*, 25(6), 501–508.

Beresford, P. (2000) Service Users' Knowledges and Social Work Theory: Conflict or collaboration? *British Journal of Social Work*, 30(4), 489–503.

Berkowitz, B.P. and Graziano, A.M. (1972) Training Parents as Behavior Therapists: A review. *Behaviour Research and Therapy*, 10(4), 297–317.

Bernazzani, O. and Bifulco, A. (2003) Motherhood as a Vulnerability Factor in Major Depression: The role of negative pregnancy experiences. *Social Science and Medicine*, 56, 1249–1260.

Bernstein, B. (1964) Elaborated and Restricted Codes: Their social origins and some consequences. *American Anthropologist*, 66(6_PART2), 55–69.

Bernstein, B. and Henderson, D. (1969) Social Class Differences in the Relevance of Language to Socialization. *Sociology*, 3(1), 1–20.

Bhui, K. and Dinos, S. (2011) Preventive Psychiatry: A paradigm to improve population mental health and well-being. *British Journal of Psychiatry*, 198(6), 417–419.

Bick, E. (1964) Notes on Infant Observation in Psycho-Analytic Training. *International Journal of Psychoanalysis*, 45, 558–566.

Bifulco, A. (2004) Maternal Attachment Style and Depression Associated with Childbirth: Preliminary results from European/US cross-cultural study. *British Journal of Psychiatry*, 184(suppl 46), s31–s37.

Bifulco, A. and Moran, P. (1998) *Wednesday's Child: Research into women's experiences of neglect and abuse in childhood and adult depression*. London: Routledge.

Bifulco, A., Bernazzani, O., Moran, P.M. and Ball, C. (2000) Lifetime Stressors and Recurrent Depression: Preliminary findings of the Adult Life Phase Interview (ALPHI). *Social Psychiatry and Psychiatric Epidemiology*, 35(6), 264–275.

Bifulco, A., Jacobs, C., Bunn, A., Thomas, G. and Irving, K. (2008) The Attachment Interview (ASI) as an Assessment of Support Capacity: Exploring its use for adoption-fostering assessment. *Adoption and Fostering*, 32, 33–45.

Bifulco, A., Mahon, J., Kwon, J.-H., Moran, P.M. and Jacobs, C. (2003) The Vulnerable Attachment Style Questionnaire (VASQ): An interview-based measure of attachment styles that predict depressive disorder. *Psychological Medicine*, 33(06), 1099–1110.

Biggs, S. and Goergen, T. (2010) Theoretical Development in Elder Abuse and Neglect. *Ageing International*, 35(3), 167–170.

Bion, W.R. (1961) *Experiences in Groups, and Other Papers*. London: Tavistock Publications.

Bion, W.R. (1962) *Learning from Experience*: London: Heinemann Medical.

Bion, W.R. (1963) *Elements of Psycho-Analysis*. London: William Heinemann.

Bion, W.R. (1967) *Second Thoughts: Selected papers on psycho-analysis*. New York and London: Aronson.

Bion, W. (1994) *Clinical Seminars and Other Works*. London: Karnac.

Bird, K. (2007) The Intergenerational Transmission of Poverty: An Overview. *SSRN eLibrary*.

Bisson, J.I. (2007) Post-traumatic Stress Disorder. *Occupational Medicine*, 57(6), 399–403.

Bjorklund, D.F., Yunger, J.L. and Pellegrini, A.D. (2002) The Evolution of Parenting and Evolutionary Approaches to Childrearing. In M. Bornstein (ed.), *Handbook of Parenting, Vol. 1, The Biology of Parenting* (2nd edn). Mahwah, NJ: Erlbaum.

Blackman, L. (2007) Psychiatric Culture and Bodies of Resistance. *Body & Society*, 13(2), 1–23.

Blackmore, S. (2006) *Conversations on Consciousness: What the best minds think about the brain*. Oxford: Oxford University Press.

Blackmore, S. (2012) *Consciousness: An introduction*, 2nd edn. Abingdon: Hodder Education.

Blaxter, M. (1981) *The Health of the Children. A review of research on the place of health in cycles of disadvantage*. London: Heineman.

Block, R.W., Krebs, N.F., (2005) Failure to Thrive as a Manifestation of Child Neglect. *Pediatrics*, 116(5), 1234–1237.

Blom-Cooper, L. (1985) *A Child in Trust: Report of the Panel of Inquiry into the circumstances surrounding the death of Jasmine Beckford*. London: London Borough of Brent.

Blumer, H. (1969) *Symbolic Interactionism: Perspective and method*. Englewood Cliffs, NJ: Prentice Hall.

Bonanno, G.A. (2004) Loss, Trauma, and Human Resilience: Have we underestimated the human capacity to thrive after extremely aversive events? *American Psychologist*, 59(1), 20–28.

Bonanno, G.A., Keltner, D., Holen, A. and Horowitz, M.J. (1994) When Avoiding Unpleasant Emotions Might not be Such a Bad Thing: Verbal-autonomic response dissociation and midlife conjugal bereavement. *Journal of Personality and Social Psychology*, 69(5), 975–989.

Born, L., Shea, A. and Steiner, M. (2002) The Roots of Depression in Adolescent Girls: Is menarche the key? *Current Psychiatry Reports*, 4(6), 449–460.

Boroughs, M. and Thompson, J.K. (2002) Exercise Status and Sexual Orientation as Moderators of Body Image Disturbance and Eating Disorders in Males. *International Journal of Eating Disorders*, 31(3), 307–311.

Bouchard, G.V. (2005) Adult Couples Facing a Planned or an Unplanned Pregnancy. *Journal of Family Issues*, 26(5), 619–637.

Bower, M. (2005) *Psychoanalytic Theory for Social Work Practice*. London: Routledge.

Bowlby, J. (1951/1952) *Maternal Care and Mental Health*. Geneva: World Health Organisation.

Bowlby, J. (1970) Disruption of Affectional Bonds and its Effects on Behavior. *Journal of Contemporary Psychotherapy*, 2(2), 75–86.

Bowlby, J. (1977) The Making and Breaking of Affectional Bonds. II. Some principles of psychotherapy. The fiftieth Maudsley Lecture. *British Journal of Psychiatry*, 130(5), 421–431.

Bowlby, J. (1982) Attachment and Loss: Retrospect and prospect. *American Journal of Orthopsychiatry*, 52(4), 664–678.

Bowlby, J. (1988) *A Secure Base: Clinical applications of attachment theory*. London: Routledge.

Bowling, A. and Gabriel, Z. (2004) An Integrational Model of Quality of Life in Older Age. Results from the ESRC/MRC HSRC Quality of Life Survey in Britain. *Social Indicators Research*, 69(1), 1–36.

Boyer-Pennington, M.E., Pennington, J. and Spink, C. (2001) Students' Expectations and Optimism Toward Marriage as a Function of Parental Divorce. *Journal of Divorce & Remarriage*, 34(3–4), 71–87.

Boyke, J., Driemeyer, J., Gaser, C., Buchel, C. and May, A. (2008) Training-Induced Brain Structure Changes in the Elderly. *Journal of Neuroscience*, 28(28), 7031–7035.

Boyle, M. (1997) *Rethinking Abortion*. London, Routledge.

Boyle, M. (2007) The Problem with Diagnosis. *The Psychologist*, 20(5), 290–292.

Brandt, M. and Hank, K. (2011) *Early and Later Life Experiences of Unemployment Under Different Welfare Regimes*. In A. Börsch-Supan, M. Brandt, K. Hank and M. Schröder (eds), *The Individual and the Welfare State: Life histories in Europe* (pp. 117–124). Heidelberg: Springer Publishing.

Braye, S. and Preston-Shoot, M. (2006) The Role of Law in Welfare Reform: Critical perspectives on the relationship between law and social work practice. *International Journal of Social Welfare*, 15(1), 19–26.

Brewin, C.R. (2007) Autobiographical Memory for Trauma: Update on four controversies. *Memory*, 15(3).

Britton, R. (1994) The Blindness of the Seeing Eye: Inverse symmetry as a defense against reality. *Psychoanalytic Inquiry*, 14(3), 365–378.

Brodzinsky, D.M., Patterson, C.J. and Vaziri, M. (2002) Adoption Agency Perspectives on Lesbian and Gay Prospective Parents – A national study. *Adoption Quarterly*, 5(3), 5–23.

Bronfenbrenner, U. (1977) Toward an Experimental Ecology of Human Development. *American Psychologist*, 32(7), 513–531.

Bronfenbrenner, U. (1999) Environments in Developmental Perspective: Theoretical and operational models. In S.L. Friedman and T.D. Wachs (eds), *Measuring Environment across the Life Span: Emerging methods and concepts*, 1st edn (pp. 3–28). Washington DC: American Psychological Association.

Bronfenbrenner, U. and Condry, J.C., Jr. (1970) *Two Worlds of Childhood: U.S. and U.S.S.R.* New York: Russell Sage Foundation.

Bronfenbrenner, U. and Morris, P.A. (2007) *The Bioecological Model of Human Development.* John Wiley & Sons, Inc.

Brooks-Gunn, J. and Ruble, D.N. (1982) The Development of Menstrual-related Beliefs and Behaviors during Early Adolescence. *Child Development*, 53(6), 1567–1577.

Broughton, J.M. (1981) Piaget and Structural Developmental Psychology. *Human Development*, 24(6), 382–411.

Brown, L.M. and Gilligan, C. (1993) Meeting at the Crossroads: Women's psychology and girls' development. *Feminism & Psychology*, 3(1), 11–35.

Buchanan, A. (1996) *Cycles of Child Maltreatment: Facts, fallacies and interventions.* Chichester: John Wiley & Sons.

Bulik, C.M., Reba, L., Siega-Riz, A. and Reichborn-Kjennerud, T. (2005) Anorexia Nervosa: Definition, epidemiology, and cycle of risk. *International Journal of Eating Disorders*, 37(S1), S2–S9.

Bunnell, T., Yea, S., Peake, L., Skelton, T. and Smith, M. (2012) Geographies of Friendships. *Progress in Human Geography*, 36(4), 490–507.

Bunting, L. and McAuley, C. (2004) Research Review: Teenage pregnancy and motherhood: The contribution of support. *Child & Family Social Work*, 9(2), 207–215.

Burke, D.M. and Mackay, D.G. (1997) Memory, Language, and Ageing. *Philosophical Transactions of the Royal Society of London. Series B: Biological Sciences*, 352(1363), 1845–1856.

Burkitt, I. (1999) *Bodies of Thought: Embodiment, identity and modernity.* London: Sage.

Burman, E. (1997) Telling Stories. *Theory & Psychology*, 7(3), 291–309.

Burnett, S., Gatrell, C., Cooper, C. and Sparrow, P. (2011) Fatherhood and Flexible Working: A contradiction in terms? In S. Kaiser, M.J. Ringlstetter, D.R. Eikhof and M. Pina e Cunha (eds), *Creating Balance?* (pp. 157–171). Berlin, Heidelberg: Springer.

Burney, E. and Gelsthorpe, L. (2008) Do we Need a 'Naughty Step'? Rethinking the parenting order after ten years. *Howard Journal of Criminal Justice*, 47(5), 470–485.

Burr, J. (2001) Women have it. Men want it. What is it?: Constructions of sexuality in rape discourse. *Psychology, Evolution & Gender*, 3(1), 103–105.

Bury, M. (1982) Chronic Illness as Biographical Disruption. *Sociology of Health & Illness*, 4(2), 167–182.

Buss, D.M. (2000) The Evolution of Happiness. *American Psychologist*, 55(1), 15–23.

Buss, D.M., Larsen, R.J., Westen, D. and Semmelroth, J. (1992) Sex Differences in Jealousy: Evolution, physiology, and psychology. *Psychological Science*, 3(4), 251–255.

Busseri, M., Willoughby, T., Chalmers, H. and Bogaert, A. (2006) Same-sex Attraction and Successful Adolescent Development. *Journal of Youth and Adolescence*, 35(4), 561–573.

Busuttil, W. (2004) Presentations and Management of Post Traumatic Stress Disorder and the Elderly: A need for investigation. *International Journal of Geriatric Psychiatry*, 19(5), 429–439.

Butler, J. (1988) Performative Acts and Gender Constitution: An essay in phenomenology and feminist theory. *Theatre Journal*, 40(4) 519–531.

Cadell, S. and Marshall, S. (2007) The (Re)Construction of Self after the Death of a Partner to HIV/AIDS. *Death Studies*, 31(6), 537–548.

Campbell, A. (2004) Female Competition: Causes, constraints, content, and contexts. *Journal of Sex Research*, 41(1), 16–26.

Campos, P., Saguy, A., Ernsberger, P., Oliver, E. and Gaesser, G. (2006) The Epidemiology of Overweight and Obesity: Public health crisis or moral panic? *International Journal of Epidemiology*, 35(1), 55–60.

Canham, H. (1998/2012) Growing up in Residential Care. In A. Briggs (ed.), *Waiting to be Found: Papers on residential care* (pp. 45–60). London: Karnac.

Canter, D. (2012) Challenging Neuroscience and Evolutionary Explanations of Social and Psychological Processes. *Contemporary Social Science*, 7(2), 95–115.

Carlat, D., Camargo, C., Jr and Herzog, D. (1997) Eating Disorders in Males: A report on 135 patients. *American Journal of Psychiatry*, 154(8), 1127–1132.

Carpendale, J.I.M. (2000) Kohlberg and Piaget on Stages and Moral Reasoning. *Developmental Review*, 28(2), 181–205.

Carr, D., House, J.S., Kessler, R.C., Nesse, R.M., Sonnega, J. and Wortman, C. (2000) Marital Quality and Psychological Adjustment to Widowhood Among Older Adults. *Journal of Gerontology Series B: Psychological Sciences and Social Sciences*, 55(4), S197–S207.

Ceballo, R., Lansford, J.E., Abbey, A. and Stewart, A.J. (2004) Gaining a Child: Comparing the experiences of biological parents, adoptive parents, and stepparents. *Family Relations*, 53(1), 38–48.

Chambers, D., Tincknell, E. and Van Loon, J. (2004) Peer Regulation of Teenage Sexual Identities. *Gender and Education*, 16(3), 397–415.

Checkroun, P. and Brauer, M. (2002) The Bystander Effect and Social Control Behavior: The effect of the presence of others on people's reactions to norm violations. *European Journal of Social Psychology*, 32(6), 853–867.

Cherlin, A.J. (2004) The Deinstitutionalization of American Marriage. *Journal of Marriage and Family*, 66(4), 848–861.

Cheung, Y.B. (2000) Marital Status and Mortality in British Women: A longitudinal study. *International Journal of Epidemiology*, 29(1), 93–99.

Chiesa, M., Fonagy, P., Holmes, J. and Drahorad, C. (2004) Residential versus Community Treatment of Personality Disorders: A comparative study of three treatment programs. *American Journal of Psychiatry*, 161, 1463–1470.

Choi, P. and Nicolson, P. (1994) *Female Sexuality: Psychology, biology and social context*. Brighton: Harvester.

Clancy, S.A., McNally, R.J. and Schacter, D.L. (1999) Effects of Guided Imagery on Memory Distortion in Women Reporting Recovered Memories of Childhood Sexual Abuse. *Journal of Traumatic Stress*, 12(4), 559–569.

Clulow, C. (2007) Can Attachment Theory Help Define What is Mutative in Couple Psychoanalytic Psychotherapy? In M. Ludlam and V. Nyberg (eds), *Couple Attachments: Theoretical and Clinical Studies* (pp. 207–220). London: Karnac.

Cohen, J.D. and Fowers, B.J. (2004) Blood, Sweat, and Tears. *Journal of Divorce & Remarriage*, 42(1–2), 39–59.

Cohen, S. (2001) *States of Denial: Knowing about atrocities and suffering*. Cambridge: Polity.

Cohen, S. (2004) The Lies We Tell. *Index on Censorship*, 33(2), 40–47.

Colarusso, C.A. (2006) The Absence of a Future: The effect of past experience and current developmental conflicts on a midlife analysis. *Journal of the American Psychoanalytic Association*, 54(3), 919–943.

Coles, D. and Shaw, H. (2012) Physical Control, Strip Searching and Segregation: Observations on the deaths of children in custody. In A. Briggs (ed.), *Waiting to Be Found: Papers on Children in Care*. London: Karnac.

Collishaw, S., Pickles, A., Messer, J., Rutter, M., Shearer, C. and Maughan, B. (2007) Resilience to Adult Psychopathology following Childhood Maltreatment: Evidence from a community sample. *Child Abuse and Neglect*, 31(3), 211–229.

Conrade, G. and Ho, R. (2001) Differential Parenting Styles for Fathers and Mothers. *Australian Journal of Psychology*, 53(1), 29–35.

Cooley, C.H. (1902/1930/2009) *Human Nature and the Social Order*. Piscataway, NJ: Transaction Books.

Cooney, T.M. and Uhlenberg, P. (1990) The Role of Divorce in Men's Relations with their Adult Children after Mid-life. *Journal of Marriage and Family*, 52(3), 677–688.

Cooper, A. (2005) Surface and Depth in the Victoria Climbié Inquiry Report. *Child & Family Social Work*, 10(1), 1–9.

Cooper, Z. and Fairburn, C.G. (2003) Refining the Definition of Binge Eating Disorder and Nonpurging Bulimia Nervosa. *International Journal of Eating Disorders*, 34(S1), S89–S95.

Cosmides, L. and Tooby, J. (1994) Beyond Intuition and Instinct Blindness: Toward an evolutionarily rigorous cognitive science. *Cognition*, 50(1–3), 41–77.

Coward, R. (1993) *Female Desire*. London: Palladin.

Cozolino, L. (2006) *The Neuroscience of Human Relationships: Attachment and the developing social brain*. New York: W.W. Norton & Co.

Crossley, M.L. (2003) Formulating Narrative Psychology: The limitations of contemporary social constructionism. *Narrative Inquiry*, 13(2), 287–300.

Crowe, M. (2002) Reflexivity and Detachment: A discursive approach to women's depression. *Nursing Inquiry*, 9(2), 126–132.

Currier, J.M., Holland, J.M. and Neimeyer, R.A. (2007) The Effectiveness of Bereavement Interventions with Children: A meta-analytic review of controlled outcome research. *Journal of Clinical Child & Adolescent Psychology*, 36(2), 253–259.

Cushman, F., Young, L. and Hauser, M. (2006) The Role of Conscious Reasoning and Intuition in Moral Judgment. *Psychological Science*, 17(12), 1082–1089.

Daggett, L.M. (1999) *Living with Loss: The lived experience of spousal bereavement in men aged 40 to 60*. Birmingham, AL: University of Alabama at Birmingham, School of Nursing

Dale, F.M.J. (1993) Unconscious Communication of Hatred between Parents and Children. In V. Varma (ed.), *How and Why Children Hate* (pp. 17–30) London: Jessica Kingsley Publishers.

Dale, L.G. (1970) The Growth of Systematic Thinking: Replication and analysis of Piaget's first chemical experiment. *Australian Journal of Psychology*, 22(3), 277–286.

Daly, K.J. (2001) Deconstructing Family Time: From ideology to lived experience. *Journal of Marriage and Family*, 63(2), 283–294.

Daly, M. and Wilson, M. (1988) Evolutionary Social Psychology and Family Homicide. *Science*, 242(4878), 519–524.

Daly, M. and Wilson, M.I. (1996) Violence against Stepchildren. *Current Directions in Psychological Science*, 5(3), 77–81.

Dancet, E.A.F., Van Empel, I.W.H., Rober, P., Nelen, W.L.D.M., Kremer, J.A.M. and D'Hooghe, T.M. (2011) Patient-centred Infertility Care: A qualitative study to listen to the patient's voice. *Human Reproduction*, 26, 827–833.

Danziger, K. (1997) *Naming the Mind: How psychology found its language*. London: Sage.

Dare, J.S. (2011) Transitions in Midlife Women's Lives: Contemporary experiences. *Health Care for Women International*, 32(2), 111–133.

Darley, J.M. and Latane, B. (1968) Bystander Intervention in Emergencies: Diffusion of responsibility. *Journal of Personality and Social Psychology*, 84(4, Pt 1), 377–383.

Dasen, P.R. (2000) Rapid Social Change and the Turmoil of Adolescence: A cross-cultural perspective. *International Journal of Group Tensions*, 29(1), 17–49.

Davey, G.C.L. (1992) Classical Conditioning and the Acquisition of Human Fears and Phobias: A review and synthesis of the literature. *Advances in Behaviour Research and Therapy*, 14(1), 29–66.

Davis, D., Shaver, P.R. and Vernon, M.L. (2004) Attachment Style and Subjective Motivations for Sex. *Personality and Social Psychology Bulletin*, 30(8), 1076–1090.

Dehaene-Lambertz, G., Dehaene, S. and Hertz-Pannier, L. (2002) Functional Neuroimaging of Speech Perception in Infants. *Science*, 298, 2013–2015.

De Jong Gierveld, J. (2004) Remarriage, Unmarried Cohabitation, Living Apart Together: Partner relationships following bereavement or divorce. *Journal of Marriage and Family*, 66(1), 236–243.

Dennis, N., Henriques, F. and Slaughter, C. (1970) *Coal is our Life: An analysis of a Yorkshire mining community*. New York: Barnes & Noble.

Dickens, J. (2011) Social work in England at a Watershed—As Always: From the Seebohm Report to the Social Work Task Force. *British Journal of Social Work,*

Diener, E. (2000) Subjective Well-being: The science of happiness and a proposal for a national index. *American Psychologist*, 55(1), 34–43.

DiLillo, D. and Peterson, L. (2001) Behavior Therapy with Children. In J.S. Neil and B.B. Paul (eds), *International Encyclopedia of the Social and Behavioral Sciences* (pp. 1086–1090). Oxford: Pergamon.

Dingwall, R. (1986) The Jasmine Beckford Affair. *The Modern Law Review*, 49(4), 489–507.

DoH (1974) *Report of the Committee of Inquiry into the Care and Supervision Provided in Relation to Maria Colwell*. London: DoH.

Dore, M.M., Doris, J.M. and Wright, P. (1995) Identifying Substance Abuse in Maltreating Families: A child welfare challenge. *Child Abuse & Neglect*, 19(5), 531–543.

Double, D. (2002) The Limits of Psychiatry. *British Medical Journal*, 324(7342), 900–904.

Dowdney, L. (2000) Childhood Bereavement Following Parental Death. *Journal of Child Psychology and Psychiatry*, 41(7), 819–830.

Driscoll, H., Zinkivskay, A., Evans, K. and Campbell, A. (2006) Gender Differences in Social Representations of Aggression: The phenomenological experience of differences in inhibitory control. *British Journal of Psychology*, 97(2), 139–153.

Dryden, C., Doherty, K. and Nicolson, P. (2010) Accounting for the Hero: A critical psycho-discursive approach to children's experience of domestic violence and the construction of masculinities. *British Journal of Social Psychology*, 49(1), 189–205.

Dub, L.M. (1947) Institutional Treatment of Juvenile Delinquents. *American Journal of Psychiatry*, 103(6), 818–822.

Dube, S.R., Anda, R.F., Felitti, V.J., Chapman, D.P., Williamson, D.F. and Giles, W.H. (2001) Childhood Abuse, Household Dysfunction, and the Risk of Attempted Suicide Throughout the Life Span. *Journal of the American Medical Association*, 286(24), 3089–3096.

Duchaine, B., Cosmides, L. and Tooby, J. (2001) Evolutionary Psychology and the Brain. *Current Opinion in Neurobiology*, 11(2), 225–230.

Duckworth, J.D. and Buzzanell, P.M. (2009) Constructing Work-Life Balance and Fatherhood: Men's framing of the meanings of both work and family. *Communication Studies*, 60(5), 558–573.

Dunbar, R., Knight, C. and Power, C. (1999) *The Evolution of Culture: An interdisciplinary view*. Edinburgh: Edinburgh University Press.

Dunbar, R.I.M. (2003) The Social Brain: Mind, language, and society in evolutionary perspective. *Annual Review of Anthropology*, 32, 163–181.

Einarsen, S. and Skogstad, A. (1996) Bullying at Work: Epidemiological findings in public and private organizations. *European Journal of Work and Organizational Psychology*, 5(2), 185–201.

Ekstrand, M., Tydenn, T., Darj, E. and Larsson, M. (2007) Preventing Pregnancy: A girls' issue. seventeen-year-old Swedish boys' perceptions on abortion, reproduction and use of contraception. *European Journal of Contraception and Reproductive Health Care*, 12(2), 111–118.

Elder, G.H. and Shanahan, M.J. (2007) *The Life Course and Human Development*. John Wiley & Sons, Inc.

Ellis, C. and Flaherty, M.C. (1992) *Investigating Subjectivity: Research on lived experience*. London: Sage.

Emmons, R.A. (1991) Personal Strivings, Daily Life Events, and Psychological and Physical Well-being. *Journal of Personality*, 59(3), 453–472.

Enosh, G. and Buchbinder, E. (2005) The Interactive Construction of Narrative Styles in Sensitive Interviews: The case of domestic violence research. *Qualitative Inquiry*, 11(4), 588–617.

Erikson, E. (1950/1963) *Childhood and Society*. New York: Norton.

Erikson, E. (1959/1980) *Identity, Youth and Crisis*. New York: Norton.

Erlanger, H.S. (1974) Social Class and Corporal Punishment in Childrearing: A reassessment. *American Sociological Review*, 39(1), 68–85.

Fairburn, C.G. and Bohn, K. (2005) Eating disorder NOS (EDNOS): An example of the troublesome 'not otherwise specified' (NOS) category in DSM-IV. *Behaviour Research and Therapy*, 43(6), 691–701.

Faria, G., Barrett, E. and Goodman, L.M. (1985) Women and Abortion: Attitudes, social networks, decision-making. *Social Work in Health Care*, 11(1), 85–99.

Fasick, F.A. (1994) On the 'Invention' of Adolescence. *Journal of Early Adolescence*, 14(1), 6–23.

Featherstone, B. and Trinder, L. (1997) Familiar Subjects? Domestic violence and child welfare. *Child & Family Social Work*, 2(3), 147–159.

Ferguson, C.J. (2009) Research on the Effects of Violent Video Games: A critical analysis. *Social and Personality Psychology Compass*, 3(3), 351–364.

Ferguson, H. (2001) Social Work, Individualization and Life Politics. *British Journal of Social Work*, 31(1), 41–55.

Ferro, A. (2009) *Psychoanalysis as Therapy and Storytelling*. London: Routledge.

Field, N.P., Nichols, C., Holen, A. and Horowitz, M.J. (1999) The Relation of Continuing Attachment to Adjustment in Conjugal Bereavement. *Journal of Consulting and Clinical Psychology*, 67(2), 212–218.

Fine, C. (2010) *Delusions of Gender: The real science behind sex differences*. London: Icon Books.

Finzi, R., Ram, A., Har-Even, D., Shnit, D. and Weizman, A. (2001) Attachment Styles and Aggression in Physically Abused and Neglected Children. *Journal of Youth and Adolescence*, 30(6), 769–786.

Flora, J. and Segrin, C. (2000) Relationship Development in Dating Couples: Implications for relational satisfaction and loneliness. *Journal of Social and Personal Relationships*, 17(6), 811–825.

Floyd, F. and Bakeman, R. (2006) Coming-Out Across the Life Course: Implications of age and historical context. *Archives of Sexual Behavior*, 35(3), 287–296.

Folkman, S. and Lazarus, R.S. (1980) An Analysis of Coping in a Middle-Aged Community Sample. *Journal of Health and Social Behavior*, 21(3), 219–239.

Fonagy, P. (2000) Attachment and Borderline Personality Disorder. *Journal of the American Psychoanalytic Association*, 48(4), 1129–1146.

Fonagy, P. (2001) *Attachment Theory and Psychoanalysis*. Oxford: Blackwell.

Fonagy, P., Target, M., Gergely, G., Allen, J.G. and Bateman, A.W. (2003) The Developmental Roots of Borderline Personality Disorder in Early Attachment Relationships: A theory and some evidence. *Psychoanalytic Inquiry*, 23(3), 412–459.

Fook, J. (2002) *Social Work: Critical theory and practice*. London: Sage.

Fook, J. and Gardner, F. (2010) *Practising Critical Reflection: A resource handbook*. Maidenhead: McGraw Hill/Open University Press.

Foucault, M. (1970) Archaeology of Knowledge. *Social Science Information*, 9(1), 175–185.

Foucault, M. (2001) Technologies of the self. *Filosoficky Casopis*, 49(2), 319–343.

Foucault, M. (2002a). *Archeology of Knowledge*. London: Routledge.

Foucault, M. (2002b) *The Order of Things*. London: Routledge (First published as *Les Mots et les Choses*, 1966, Paris: Editions Gallimard)

Fox, R. and Smith, G. (2011) Sinner Ladies and the Gospel of Good Taste: Geographies of food, class and care. *Health & Place*, 17(2), 403–412.

Fox, R., Heffernan, K. and Nicolson, P. (2009) 'I don't think it was such an issue back then': Changing experiences of pregnancy across two generations of women in south-east England. *Gender, Place & Culture*, 16(5), 553–568.

Fox, R., Platz, D. and Bentley, K. (1995) Maternal Factors Related to Parenting Practices, Developmental Expectations and Perceptions of Child Behavior Problems. *Journal of Genetic Psychology*, 156, 431–441.

Franklin, S. (1997) *Embodied Progress: A cultural account of assisted conception*. New York: Routledge.

Fraser, H. (2004) Doing Narrative Research. *Qualitative Social Work*, 3(2), 179–201.

Freud, A. and Dann, S. (1951) An Experiment in Group Upbringing. *The Psychoanalytic Study of the Child*, 6, 127–168.

Freud, S. (1914) *On Narcissism: An introduction*, Standard edition, vol. 14 (pp. 67–102). London: Hogarth.

Freud, S. (1917) Mourning and Melancholia. *Papers on Metapsychology and Other Works* (Vol. 14).

Freud, S. (1923/2007) The Ego and the Id. In P. Gay (ed.), *The Freud Reader*. London: Vintage.

Freud, S. (1925) Negation. *International Journal of Psycho-Analysis*, 6, 5.

Furby, L. (1971) A Theoretical Analysis of Cross-Cultural Research in Cognitive Development: Piaget's conservation task. *Journal of Cross-Cultural Psychology*, 2(3), 241–256.

Furman, L.D., Benson, P.W., Grimwood, C. and Canda, E. (2004) Religion and Spirituality in Social Work Education and Direct Practice at the Millennium: A survey of UK social workers. *British Journal of Social Work*, 34(6), 767–792.

Galton, F. (1869) *Hereditary Genius*. London and New York: Macmillan & Co.

Gannon, L. (2002) A Critique of Evolutionary Psychology. *Psychology, Evolution & Gender*, 4(2), 173–218.

Gay, P. (1995) *The Freud Reader*. London: Vintage.

Geary, D.C. and Bjorklund, D.F. (2000) Evolutionary Developmental Psychology. *Child Development*, 71(1), 57–65.

Geller, J. (2007) *On Freud's Jewish Body: Mitigating circumcisions*. New York: Fordham University Press.

Gergen, K.J., Lightfoot, C. and Sydow, L. (2004) Social Construction: Vistas in clinical child and adolescent psychology. *Journal of Clinical Child & Adolescent Psychology*, 33(2), 389–399.

Giddens, A. (1986/2003) *The Constitution of Society: Outline of the theory of structuration*. Berkeley and Los Angeles: University of Calfornia Press.

Giddens, A. (1991) *Modernity and Self-identity: Self and society in the late modern age*. San Francisco: Stanford University Press.

Gilbert, M.C. (2000) Spirituality in Social Work Groups: Practitioners speak out. *Social Work With Groups*, 22(4), 67–84.

Gilligan, C. (1983) *In a Different Voice: Psychological theory and women's development*. Cambridge, MA: Harvard University Press.

Ginther, D. and Pollak, R. (2004) Family Structure and Children's Educational Outcomes: Blended families, stylized facts, and descriptive regressions. *Demography*, 41(4), 671–696.

Gladstone, G.L., Parker, G.B. and Malhi, G.S. (2006) Do Bullied Children Become Anxious and Depressed Adults?: A cross-sectional investigation of the correlates of bullying and anxious depression. *Journal of Nervous and Mental Disease*, 194(3), 201–208.

Glew, G., Rivara, F. and Feudtner, C. (2000) Bullying: Children hurting children. *Pediatrics in Review*, 21(6), 183–190.

Goffman, I. (1961) *Asylums: Essays on the social situation of mental patients and other inmates*. New York: Doubleday Anchor.

Gomez, L. (1997) *An Introduction to Object Relations*. London: Free Association Books.

Goleman, D. (2006) *Social Intelligence: The new science of human relationships*. New York: Random House.

Goodley, D. and Tregaskis, C. (2006) Storying Disability and Impairment: Retrospective accounts of disabled family life. *Qualitative Health Research*, 16(5), 630–646.

Goodson, I.F. (1995) The Story So Far: Personal knowledge and the political. *International Journal of Qualitative Studies in Education*, 8(1), 89–98.

Goodstein, L. (1979) Inmate Adjustment to Prison and the Transition to Community Life. *Journal of Research in Crime and Delinquency*, 16(2), 246–272.

Gonsiorek, J.C. (1988) Mental Health Issues of Gay and Lesbian Adolescents. *Journal of Adolescent Health Care*, 9(2), 114–122.

Gott, M. and Hinchliff, S. (2003) How Important is Sex in Later Life? The views of older people. *Social Science and Medicine*, 56(8), 1617–1628.

Gourinchas, P.-O. and Parker, J.A. (2002) Consumption Over the Life Cycle. *Econometrica*, 70(1), 47–89.

Gove, W.R., Hughes, M. and Style, C.B. (1983) Does Marriage Have Positive Effects on the Psychological Well-Being of the Individual? *Journal of Health and Social Behavior*, 24(2), 122–131.

Grady, C.L. (2008) Cognitive Neuroscience of Aging. *Annals of the New York Academy of Sciences*, 1124(1), 127–144.

Green, L. (2010) *Understanding the Life Course: Sociological and psychological perspectives*. Oxford: Polity.

Greene, J.C. and Caracelli, V.J. (1997) Defining and Describing the Paradigm Issue in Mixed-method Evaluation. *New Directions for Evaluation*, 1997(74), 5–17.

Greene, J. and Haidt, J. (2002) How (and Where) does Moral Judgment Work? *Trends in Cognitive Sciences*, 6(12), 517–523.

Greer, G. (1993) *The Change: Women, ageing and the menopause*. London: Hamish Hamilton Ltd.

Griffiths, L.J., Wolke, D., Page, A.S. and Horwood, J.P. (2006) Obesity and Bullying: Different effects for boys and girls. *Archives of Disease in Childhood*, 91(2), 121–125.

Grofman, B. (1974) Helping Behavior and Group Size: Some exploratory stochastic models. *Behavioral Science*, 19(4), 219–224.

Grogan-Kaylor, A. (2004) The Effect of Corporal Punishment on Antisocial Behavior in Children. *Social Work Research*, 28(3), 153–162.

Gross, J., Carstensen, L., Pasupathi, M., Tsai, J., Skorpen, C. and Hsu, A. (1997) Emotion and Aging: Experience, expression, and control. *Psychology and Aging*, 12(4), 590–599.

Grossmann, K.E. (1999) Old and New Internal Working Models of Attachment: The organization of feelings and language. *Attachment & Human Development*, 1(3), 253–269.

Grotstein, J.S. (2007) *A Beam of Intense Darkness*. London: Karnac.

Guerney, L. (2001) Child-centered Play Therapy. *International Journal of Play Therapy*, 10(2), 13–31.

Gustafson, T.B. and Sarwer, D.B. (2004) Childhood Sexual Abuse and Obesity. *Obesity Reviews*, 5(3), 129–135.

Haggerty, K.D. and Ericson, R.V. (2000) The Surveillant Assemblage. *British Journal of Sociology*, 51(4), 605–622.

Hall, T. and Montgomery, H. (2000) Home and Away: 'Childhood', 'Youth' and Young People. *Anthropology Today*, 16(3), 13–15.

Hall, N., Karras, M., Raine, J.D., Carlton, J.M., Kooij, T.W.A., Berriman, M., Sinden, R.E. (2005) A Comprehensive Survey of the Plasmodium Life Cycle by Genomic, Transcriptomic, and Proteomic Analyses. *Science*, 307(5706), 82–86.

Hamre, B.K. and Pianta, R.C. (2001) Early Teacher–Child Relationships and the Trajectory of Children's School Outcomes through Eighth Grade. *Child Development*, 72(2), 625–638.

Hansen, A.M., Hogh, A., Persson, R., Karlson, B., Garde, A.H. and Oerbaek, P. (2006) Bullying at Work: Health outcomes, and physiological stress response. *Journal of Psychosomatic Research*, 60(1), 63072.

Harding, D.J. (2003) Counterfactual Models of Neighborhood Effects: The effect of neighborhood poverty on dropping out and teenage pregnancy. *American Journal of Sociology*, 109(3), 676–719.

Härlein, J., Dassen, T., Halfens, R.J.G. and Heinze, C. (2009) Fall Risk Factors in Older People with Dementia or Cognitive Impairment: A systematic review. *Journal of Advanced Nursing*, 65(5), 922–933.

Harper, C., Marcus, R. and Moore, K. (2003) Enduring Poverty and the Conditions of Childhood: Lifecourse and intergenerational poverty transmissions. *World Development*, 31(3), 535–554.

Harris, P.L. (1999) Individual Differences in Understanding Emotion: The role of attachment status and psychological discourse. *Attachment & Human Development*, 1(3), 307–324.

Harrison, K. (2003) Television Viewers' Ideal Body Proportions: The case of the curvaceously thin woman. *Sex Roles*, 48(5), 255–264.

Hawley, D.R. and DeHaan, L. (1996) Toward a Definition of Family Resilience: Integrating life-span and family perspectives. *Family Process*, 35(3), 283–298.

Hayes, C.L. and Anderson, D. (1993) Psycho-social and Economic Adjustment of Mid-Life Women After Divorce: A national study. *Journal of Women & Aging*, 4(4), 83–99.

Hazan, C. and Shaver, P.R. (1994) Attachment as an Organizational Framework for Research on Close Relationships. *Psychological Inquiry*, 5(1), 1–22.

Hebert, K. (2004) Life Expectancy in Great Britain Rises, but Later Years are Still Spent in Poor Health. *British Medical Journal*, 329(7460), 250.

Henwood, K. and Procter, J. (2003) The 'Good Father': Reading men's accounts of paternal involvement during the transition to first-time fatherhood. *British Journal of Social Psychology*, 42(3), 337–355.

Hershey, D.A. and Mowen, J.C. (2000) Psychological Determinants of Financial Preparedness for Retirement. *The Gerontologist*, 40(6), 687–697.

Hesse, E. and Main, M. (2000) Disorganized Infant, Child, and Adult Attachment: Collapse in behavioral and attentional strategies. *Journal of the American Psychoanalytic Association*, 48(4), 1097–1127.

Hicks, S. (2006) Maternal Men: Perverts and deviants? Making sense of gay men as foster carers and adopters. *Journal of GLBT Family Studies*, 2(1), 93–114.

Hinchliff, S. and Gott, M. (2004) Intimacy, Commitment, and Adaptation: Sexual relationships within long-term marriages. *Journal of Social and Personal Relationships*, 21(5), 595–609.

Hinshelwood, R. (1991) *A Dictionary of Kleinian Thought*. London: Free Associations.

Hobbs, G.F., Hobbs, C.J. and Wynne, J.M. (1999) Abuse of Children in Foster and Residential Care. *Child Abuse & Neglect*, 23(12), 1239–1252.

Hobson, J., Shine, J. and Roberts, R. (2000) How do Psychopaths Behave in a Prison Therapeutic Community? *Psychology, Crime & Law*, 6(2), 139–154.

Hodgkinson, P.E. (1982) Abnormal Grief – The problem of therapy. *British Journal of Medical Psychology*, 55(1), 29–34.

Hollway, W. and Jefferson, T. (2003) *Doing Qualitative Research Differently: Free association, narrative and the interview method*. London: Sage.

Holmes, J. (2010) *Exploring in Security: Towards an attachment-informed psychoanalytic psychotherapy*. London: Routledge.

Holmes, T.H. and Rahe, R.H. (1967) The Social Readjustment Rating Scale. *Journal of Psychosomatic Research*, 11(2), 213–218.

Houston, S. (2001) Beyond Social Constructionism: Critical realism and social work. *British Journal of Social Work*, 31(6), 845–861.

Howe, D. (1996) Surface and Depth in Social Work Practice. In N. Parton (ed.), *Social Theory, Social Change and Social Work*. London: Routledge.

Howe, D. (1997) Parent-reported Problems in 211 Adopted Children: Some risk and protective factors. *Journal of Child Psychology and Psychiatry*, 38(4), 401–411.

Howe, D. (2001) Age at Placement, Adoption Experience and Adult Adopted People's Contact with their Adoptive and Birth Mothers: An attachment perspective. *Attachment & Human Development*, 3(2), 222–237.

Howe, D. (2008) *The Emotionally Intelligent Social Worker*. Basingstoke: Palgrave Macmillan.

Howe, D. (2010) The Safety of Children and the Parent-Worker Relationship in Cases of Child Abuse and Neglect. *Child Abuse Review*, 19(5), 330–341.

Howe, D. and Fearnley, S. (2003) Disorders of Attachment in Adopted and Fostered Children: Recognition and treatment. *Clinical Child Psychology and Psychiatry*, 8(3), 369–387.

Howe, D., Shemmings, D. and Feast, J. (2001) Age at Placement and Adult Adopted People's Experience of being Adopted. *Child & Family Social Work*, 6(4), 337–349.

Hrdy, S. (1997) Raising Darwin's Consciousness. *Human Nature*, 8(1), 1–49.

Hrdy, S.B. (2003) The Optimal Number of Fathers. In S.J. Scher and F. Rauscher (eds), *Evolutionary Psychology* (pp. 111–133). Norwell, MA: Kluwer Academic Publishers.

Hyland, T. (2006) *Swimming Against the Tide: Reductionist behaviourism in the harmonisation of European higher education systems*. Bolton: University of Bolton Institutional Repository.

Ickes, W. (1993) Traditional Gender Roles: Do they make, and then break, our relationships? *Journal of Social Issues*, 49(3), 71–85.

Iliffe, G. and Steed, L.G. (2000) Exploring the Counselor's Experience of Working With Perpetrators and Survivors of Domestic Violence. *Journal of Interpersonal Violence*, 15(4), 393–412.

Ingleby, D. (1977) The Psychology of Child Psychology. In M.P.M. Richards (ed.), *The Integration of a Child into a Social World* (pp. 295–308). Cambridge: Cambridge University Press.

Ingram, R. (2012) Locating Emotional Intelligence at the Heart of Social Work Practice. *British Journal of Social Work*, 43(5), 987–1004.

Jackson, B. and Marsden, D. (1966) *Education and the Working Class*. London: ARK Paperbacks.

James, A. and Jenks, C. (1996) Public Perceptions of Childhood Criminality. *British Journal of Sociology*, 47(2), 315–331.

Janssen, I., Craig, W.M., Boyce, W.F. and Pickett, W. (2004) Associations Between Overweight and Obesity With Bullying Behaviors in School-Aged Children. *Pediatrics*, 113(5), 1187–1194.

Jenkins, R. (2002) *Social Identity*. London: Routledge.

Joffe, H. (1999) *Risk and the Other*. Cambridge: Cambridge University Press.

Jones, C. and Hackett, S. (2012) Redefining Family Relationships Following Adoption: Adoptive parents' perspectives on the changing nature of kinship between adoptees and birth relatives. *British Journal of Social Work*, 42(2), 283–299.

Jones, M. (1956) The Concept of a Therapeutic Community. *American Journal of Psychiatry*, 112, 647–650.

Jones, O. (1999) Tomboy Tales: The rural, nature and the gender of childhood. *Gender, Place & Culture*, 6(2), 117–136.

Jordanova, V., Stewart, R., Goldberg, D., Bebbington, P., Brugha, T., Singleton, N. et al. (2007) Age Variation in Life Events and their Relationship with Common Mental Disorders in a National Survey Population. *Social Psychiatry and Psychiatric Epidemiology*, 42(8), 611–616.

Kanazawa, S. (2010) Evolutionary Psychology and Intelligence Research. *American Psychologist*, 65(4), 279–289.

Kaufman, K.R. and Kaufman, N.D. (2006) And Then the Dog Died. *Death Studies*, 30(1), 61076.

Kawachi, I. and Berkman, L. (2001) Social Ties and Mental Health. *Journal of Urban Health*, 78(3), 458–467.

Kellman, P.J. and Arterberry, M.E. (2000) *The Cradle of Knowledge: Development of perception in infancy*. Boston, MA: MIT Press.

Kendall, T. (2011) The Rise and Fall of the Atypical Antipsychotics. *British Journal of Psychiatry*, 199(4), 266–268.

Kenny, P.J. and Markou, A. (2005) Conditioned Nicotine Withdrawal Profoundly Decreases the Activity of Brain Reward Systems. *Journal of Neuroscience*, 25(26), 6208–6212.

Kenrick, D.T., Sadalla, E.K., Groth, G. and Trost, M.R. (1990) Evolution, Traits, and the Stages of Human Courtship: Qualifying the parental investment model. *Journal of Personality*, 58(1), 97–116.

Kim, J.J. (2001) Classical Conditioning, Neural basis of. In J.S. Neil and B.B. Paul (eds), *International Encyclopedia of the Social & Behavioral Sciences* (pp. 1946–1951). Oxford: Pergamon.

Kissling, E.A. (1996) Bleeding out Loud: Communication about menstruation. *Feminism & Psychology*, 6(4), 481–504.

Klaus, M.H. and Kennell, J.H. (1976) *Maternal-infant Bonding: The impact of early separation or loss on family development*. Saint Louis: Mosby.

Klaus, M.H., Jerauld, R., Kreger, N.C., McAlpine, W., Steffa, M. and Kennell, J.H. (1972) Maternal Attachment. *New England Journal of Medicine*, 286(9), 460–463.

Klein, M. (1946) Notes on Some Schizoid Mechanisms. In H. Segal (ed.), *Envy and Gratitude and Other Works 1946–1963*. London: Virago.

Klein, M. (1953) *Love, Hate and Reparation*. New impression (pp. vii, 119). London: Hogarth Press.

Klein, M. (1959/1975/1993) Our Adult World and its Roots in Infancy. In M. Klein (ed.), *Envy and Gratitude and Other Works 1946–1963* (pp. 247–263). London: Virago.

Klein, M. (1984) *Envy and Gratitude: and Other Works, 1946–1963*. London: Hogarth Press.

Knickmeyer, R., Baron-Cohen, S. Raggatt, P. and Taylor, K. (2005) Foetal Testosterone, Social Cognition, and Restricted Interests in Children. *Journal of Child Psychology and Psychiatry*, 45, 1–13.

Knight, B.G. and Poon, C. (2008) The Socio-Cultural Context in Understanding Older Adults: Contextual adult lifespan theory for adapting psychotherapy. *Handbook of the Clinical Psychology of Ageing* (pp. 437–456). John Wiley & Sons, Ltd.

Knitzer, J. (2000) Promoting Resilience: Helping young children and parents affected by substance abuse, domestic violence, and depression in the context of welfare reform. *Children and Welfare Reform Issue Brief 8*. New York: National Center for Children in Poverty.

Koff, E. and Rierdan, J. (1995) Early Adolescent Girls' Understanding of Menstruation. *Women & Health*, 22(4), 1–19.

Kohlberg, L. (1969) Stage and Sequence: The cognitive developmental approach to socialisation. In D.A. Goslin (ed.), *Handbook of Socialisation: Theory and research*. Chicago: Rand McNally.

Kohlberg, L. (1981) *The Philosophy of Moral Development: Moral stages and the idea of justice*. New York: Harper & Row.

Kondrat, M.E. (2002) Actor-Centered Social Work: Revisioning 'person-in-environment' through a critical theory lens. *Social Work*, 47(4), 435–448.

Koniak-Griffin, D., Lesser, J., Uman, G. and Nyamathi, A. (2003) Teen Pregnancy, Motherhood, and Unprotected Sexual Activity. *Research in Nursing & Health*, 26(1), 4–19.

Kumpulainen, K., Räsänen, E. and Puura, K. (2001) Psychiatric Disorders and the Use of Mental Health Services among Children Involved in Bullying. *Aggressive Behavior*, 27(2), 102–110.

Kupperbusch, C., Levenson, R.W. and Ebling, R. (2003) Predicting Husbands' and Wives' Retirement Satisfaction from the Emotional Qualities of Marital Interaction. *Journal of Social and Personal Relationships*, 20(3), 335–354.

Lachance-Grzela, M. and Bouchard, G. (2010) Why Do Women Do the Lion's Share of Housework? A decade of research. *Sex Roles*, 63(11), 767–780.

Laing, R.D. (1959) *The Divided Self: An existential study in sanity and madness*. London: Tavistock.

Laing, R.D. and Esterson, A. (1970) *Sanity, Madness and the Family*. Harmondsworth: Penguin.

Lampard, R. and Peggs, K. (1999) Repartnering: The relevance of parenthood and gender to cohabitation and remarriage among the formerly married. *British Journal of Sociology*, 50(3), 443–465.

Lane, G. (2012) Caring for Older People: The case in the UK. *Perspectives in Public Health*, 132(4), 158–159.

Laney, C. and Loftus, E.F. (2010) Truth in Emotional Memories. *Emotion and the Law, Nebraska Symposium on Motivation*, 56, 157–183.

Larzelere, R.E. (2000) Child Outcomes of Nonabusive and Customary Physical Punishment by Parents: An updated literature review. *Clinical Child and Family Psychology Review*, 3(4), 199–221.

Leader, D. (2009) *The New Black: Mourning, melancholia and depression*. Harmondsworth: Penguin.

Le Carre, J. (1997) *The Tailor of Panama*. London: Hodder & Stoughton Ltd.

Lee, J. (1994) Menarche and the (Hetero)Sexualization of the Female Body. *Gender & Society*, 8(3), 343–362.

Lee, J. (2009) Bodies at Menarche: Stories of shame, concealment, and sexual maturation. *Sex Roles*, 60(9), 615–627.

Lerner, R.M., Boyd, M.J. and Du, D. (2010) Adolescent Development. *Corsini Encyclopedia of Psychology*. John Wiley & Sons, Inc.

Levinson, D.J. (1986) A Conception of Adult Development. *American Psychologist*, 41(1), 3–13.

Lewis, S., Tarrier, N., Haddock, G., Bentall, R., Kinderman, P., Kingdon, D. and Dunn, G. (2002) Randomised Controlled Trial of Cognitive Behavioural Therapy in Early Schizophrenia: Acute-phase outcomes. *British Journal of Psychiatry*, 181(43), s91–s97.

Lewis, S., Gambles, R. and Rapoport, R. (2007) The Constraints of a Work/Life Balance Approach: An international perspective. *International Journal of Human Resource Management*, 18(3), 360–373.

Leyendecker, B., Lamb, M.E., Harwood, R.L. and Schalmerich, A. (2002) Mothers' Socialisation Goals and Evaluations of Desirable and Undesirable Everyday Situations in Two Diverse Cultural Groups. *International Journal of Behavioral Development*, 26(3), 248–258.

Lieberman, A.F. (2004) Traumatic Stress and Quality of Attachment: Reality and internalization in disorders of infant mental health. *Infant Mental Health Journal*, 25(4), 336–351.

Lindseth, A. and Norberg, A. (2004) A Phenomenological Hermeneutical Method for Researching Lived Experience. *Scandinavian Journal of Caring Sciences*, 18(2), 145–153.

Lobstein, T., Baur, L. and Uauy, R. (2004) Obesity in Children and Young People: A crisis in public health. *Obesity Reviews*, 5, 4–85.

Lorenz, K. (1952/2002) *King Solomon's Ring: New light on animal ways*. London: Routledge.

Lorenz, K. (1966) *On Aggression*. New York: Harcourt.

Loye, D. (2002) The Moral Brain. *Brain and Mind*, 3(1), 133–150.

Ludlam, M. and Nyberg, V. (2007) *Couple Attachments: Theoretical and clinical studies*. London: Karnac.

Lund, R., Modvig, J., Due, P. and Evald Holstein, B. (2000) Stability and Change in Structural Social Relations as Predictor of Mortality Among Elderly Women and Men. *European Journal of Epidemiology*, 16(12), 1087–1097.

Lutfey, K. and Mortimer, J. (2006) Development and Socialization through the Adult Life Course. In J. DeLamater (ed.), *Handbook of Social Psychology* (pp. 183–202). New York: Plenum.

Lyons-Ruth, K. and Jacobvitz, D. (1999) Attachment Disorganization: Unresolved loss, relational violence, and lapses in behavioral and attentional strategies. In J. Cassidy and P.R. Shaver (eds), *Handbook of Attachment: Theory, research, and clinical applications* (pp. 520–554). New York: Guilford Press.

Maguire, M. (1995) *Men, Women, Passion and Power: Gender issues in psychotherapy*. London, Routledge.

Main, M. (1995) Recent Studies in Attachment: Overview with selected implications for clinical work. In S. Goldberg, R. Muir and J. Kerr (eds), *Handbook of Attachment*. Hillsdale, NJ: Analytic Press (pp. 407–474).

Main, M. and Soloman, J. (1990) Procedures for Identifying Infants as Disorganized/Disoriented during the Ainsworth Strange situation. In M.T. Greenberg, D. Cicchetti and E.M. Cummings (eds), *Attachment in the Preschool Years: Theory, research and intervention* (pp. 121–161). Chicago: University of Chicago Press.

Main, M., Kaplan, N. and Cassidy, J. (1985) Security in Infancy, Childhood, and Adulthood: A move to the level of representation. *Monographs of the Society for Research in Child Development*, 50(1/2), 66–104.

Major, B., Appelbaum, Beckman, L., Dutton, M.A., Felipe Russo, N. and West, C. (2008) *Mental Health and Abortion*. Washington: APA.

Malson, H. (1998) *The Thin Woman: Feminism, poststructuarlism and the social psychology of anorexia nervosa*. London: Routledge.

Manstead, A.S.R. and McCulloch, C. (1981) Sex-role Stereotyping in British Television Advertisements. *British Journal of Social Psychology*, 20(3), 171–180.

Marks, J. (2012) The Biological Myth of Human Evolution. *Contemporary Social Science*, 7(2), 139–157.

Marris, P. (1986) *Loss and Change*. London: Routledge.

Martin, C.L. and Ruble, D.N. (2010) Patterns of Gender Development. *Annual Review of Psychology*, 61(1), 353–381.

Martin, E.D. (1920) The Crowd and the Unconscious. In E.D. Martin (ed.),*The Behavior of Crowds: A psychological study*. (pp. 51–72). MacMillan Co.

Martin, G.M. (2007) Modalities of Gene Action Predicted by the Classical Evolutionary Biological Theory of

Aging. *Annals of the New York Academy of Sciences*, 1100(1), 14–20.

Martinez, R.O. and Dukes, R.L. (1997) The Effects of Ethnic Identity, Ethnicity, and Gender on Adolescent Well-Being. *Journal of Youth and Adolescence*, 26(5), 503–516.

Mateas, M. and Sengers, P. (2002) Narrative Intelligence. *Advances in Consciousness Research*, 46, 1–26.

Mather, M. and Carstensen, L.L. (2005) Aging and Motivated Cognition: The positivity effect in attention and memory. *Trends in Cognitive Sciences*, 9(10), 496–502.

Maxwell, G.A. and McDougall, M. (2004) Work/Life Balance. *Public Management Review*, 6(3), 377–393.

McAdams, D.P., Reynolds, J., Lewis, M., Patten, A.H. and Bowman, P.J. (2001) When Bad Things Turn Good and Good Things Turn Bad: Sequences of redemption and contamination in life narrative and their relation to psychosocial adaptation in midlife adults and in students. *Personality and Social Psychology Bulletin*, 27(4), 474–485.

McGuire, J., Langdon, R., Coltheart, M. and Mackenzie, C. (2009) A Reanalysis of the Personal/Impersonal Distinction in Moral Psychology Research. *Journal of Experimental Social Psychology*, 45(3), 577–580.

McLeod, J. and Balamoutsou, S. (1996) Representing Narrative Process in Therapy: Qualitative analysis of a single case. *Counselling Psychology Quarterly*, 9(1), 61–76.

McMinn, J., Steel, C. and Bowman, A. (2011) Investigation and Management of Unintentional Weight Loss in Older Adults. *British Medical Journal*, 342.

Mead, G.H. (1934/1967) *Mind, Self and Society*. Chicago: University of Chicago Press.

Medrano, M.A., Hatch, J.P., Zule, W.A. and Desmond, D.P. (2002) Psychological Distress in Childhood Trauma Survivors who Abuse Drugs. *American Journal of Drug and Alcohol Abuse*, 28(1), 1–13.

Meltzer, B., Petras, J.W. and Reynolds, L.T. (1980) *Symbolic Interactionism: Genesis, varieties and criticism*. London: Routledge & Kegan Paul.

Meltzer, H., Gatwards, R., Corbin, T., Goodman, R. and Ford, T. (2002) *The Mental Health of Young People Looked after by Local Authorities in England*. London: Social Survey Division of the Office for National Statistics and Department of Health.

Meltzoff, A.N. and Decety, J. (2003) What Imitation Tells us about Social Cognition: A rapprochement between developmental psychology and cognitive neuroscience. *Philosophical Transactions of the Royal Society of London. Series B: Biological Sciences*, 358(1431), 491–500.

Menzies, I.E.P. (1984) *The Functioning of Social Systems as a Defence against Anxiety: A report on a study of the nursing service of a general hospital*. London: Tavistock Institute of Human Relations.

Mikkelsen, E.G. e. and Einarsen, S. (2002) Basic Assumptions and Symptoms of Post-traumatic Stress among Victims of Bullying at Work. *European Journal of Work and Organizational Psychology*, 11(1), 87–111.

Milgram, S. (1963) Behavioural Study of Obedience. *Journal of Abnormal and Social Psychology*, 67, 371–378.

Miller, A.M. and Harwood, R.L. (2001) Long-term Socialisation Goals and the Construction of Infants' Social Networks among Middle Class Anglo and Puerto Rican Mothers. *International Journal of Behavioral Development*, 25(5), 450–457.

Model, E. (1986) Summary and Comments on 'A Child in Trust': The Report of the Inquiry into the Death of Jasmine Beckford. *Bulletin of the Anna Freud Centre*, 9(4), 269–282.

Mollon, P. (2006) *Shame and Jealousy: The hidden turmoils*. London: Karnac.

Moonis, M., Swearer, J.M., Blumstein, S.E., Kurowski, K., Licho, R., Kramer, P. et al. (1996) Foreign Accent Syndrome Following a Closed Head Injury: Perfusion deficit on single photon emission tomography with normal magnetic resonance imaging. *Cognitive and Behavioral Neurology*, 9(4), 272–279.

Morrison, T. (2007) Emotional Intelligence, Emotion and Social Work: Context, characteristics, complications and contribution. *British Journal of Social Work*, 37(2), 245–263.

Moules, N.J., Simonson, K., Prins, M., Angus, P. and Bell, J.M. (2004) Making Room for Grief: Walking backwards and living forward. *Nursing Inquiry*, 11(2): 99–107.

Munro, E. (2005) What Tools do we Need to Improve Identification of Child Abuse? *Child Abuse Review*, 14(6), 374–388.

Munro, E. (2011) *Munro Review of Child Protection*. London: London School of Economics.

Murray, C. and Waller, G. (2002) Reported Sexual Abuse and Bulimic Psychopathology among Nonclinical Women: The mediating role of shame. *International Journal of Eating Disorders*, 32(2), 186–191.

Murtagh, J., Dixey, R. and Rudolf, M. (2006) A Qualitative Investigation into the Levers and Barriers to Weight Loss in Children: Opinions of obese children. *Archives of Disease in Childhood*, 91(11), 920–923.

Nelson, E.E., Leibenluft, L.E., McClure, E.B. and Pine, D.S. (2005) The Social Re-orientation of Adolescence: A neuroscience perspective on the process and its relation to psychopathology. *Psychological Medicine*, 35(02), 163–174.

Nelson, L. (1999) Bodies (and Spaces) do Matter: The limits of performativity. *Gender, Place and Culture*, 6, 331–353.

Neumark-Sztainer, D., Story, M., Hannan, P.J., Beuhring, T. and Resnick, M.D. (2000) Disordered Eating among Adolescents: Associations with sexual/physical abuse and other familial/psychosocial factors. *International Journal of Eating Disorders*, 28(3), 249–258.

Newman, T. (2002) 'Young Carers' and Disabled Parents: Time for a change of direction? *Disability & Society*, 17(6), 613–625.

Newson, E. and Newson, J. (1965) *Infant Care in an Urban Community*. Harmondsworth: Penguin.

Newson, J. and Newson, E. (2007) *Four Years Old in an Urban Community*. London: George Allen & Unwin.

Nicholson, N. (2000) *Managing the Human Animal*. London: Texere.

Nicolson, P. (1994) *The Experience of Being Burgled: A psychological study of the impact of domestic burglary on victims*. London: Frizzell Financial Services.

Nicolson, P. (1996) *Gender, Power and Organisation: A psychological perspective*. London: Routledge.

Nicolson, P. (1998) *Post Natal Depression: Psychology, science and the transition to motherhood*. London: Routledge.

Nicolson, P. (2003) *Having it all? Choices for today's Superwoman*. Chichester: Wiley.

Nicolson, P. (2010) *Psychology and Domestic Violence: A critical perspective*. London: Taylor & Francis.

Nicolson, P. and Burr, J. (2003) What is 'Normal' about Women's (Hetero)sexual Desire and Orgasm?: A report of an in-depth interview study. *Social Science & Medicine*, 57(9), 1735–1745.

Nicolson, P., Bayne, R. and Owen, J. (2006) *Applied Psychology for Social Workers*. Basingstoke: Palgrave.

Nicolson, P., Fox, R., Gabriel, Y., Heffernan, K., Howorth, C., Ilan-Clarke, Y. et al. (2011) *Leadership and Better Patient Care: Managing in the NHS*. London: HMSO.

Nishina, A., Juvonen, J. and Witkow, M.R. (2005) Sticks and Stones May Break My Bones, but Names Will Make Me Feel Sick: The psychosocial, somatic, and scholastic consequences of peer harassment. *Journal of Clinical Child & Adolescent Psychology*, 34(1), 37–48.

O'Dea, J.A. (2005) Prevention of Child Obesity: 'First, do no harm'. *Health Education Research*, 20(2), 259–265.

Ogle, J. and Damhorst, M. (2005) Critical Reflections on the Body and Related Sociocultural Discourses at the Midlife Transition: An interpretive study of women's experiences. *Journal of Adult Development*, 12(1), 1–18.

Oliver, M. (1992) Changing the Social Relations of Research Production? *Disability, Handicap & Society*, 7(2), 101–114.

Ontai, L.L. and Thompson, R.A. (2002) Patterns of Attachment and Maternal Discourse Effects on Children's Emotion Understanding from 3 to 5 Years of Age. *Social Development*, 11(4), 433–450.

Orbach, S. (2010) *Bodies*. London: Profile Books Ltd.

Paechter, C. (2006) Reconceptualizing the Gendered Body: Learning and constructing masculinities and femininities in school. *Gender and Education*, 18(2), 121–135.

Parke, R.D. and Buriel, R. (2007) Socialization in the Family: Ethnic and ecological perspectives. *Handbook of Child Psychology*. John Wiley & Sons, Inc.

Parkes, C.M. (1996) *Bereavment: Studies of grief in adult life*. London: Tavistock.

Parkes, C.M. (1998) Coping with Loss: Bereavement in adult life. *British Medical Journal*, 316(7134), 856–859.

Parkes, C.M., Stevenson-Hinde, J. and Marris, P. (1991) *Attachment Across the Life Cycle*. London: Routledge.

Pateman, T. (1972) A Reading of One Case Study in RD Laing and A Esterson, *Sanity Madness and the Family*, Trying to Highlight the Cognitive (Epistemological) Aspects of the Schizophrenic Predicament. *Radical Philosophy*, 1(1).

Paulson, S. and Willig, C. (2008) Older Women and Everyday Talk about the Ageing Body. *Journal of Health Psychology*, 13(1), 106–120.

Pearson, G., Treseder, J. and Yelloly, M. (1988) *Social Work and the Legacy of Freud*. Basingstoke: Macmillan.

Peters, J., Shackelford, T.K. and Buss, D.M. (2002) Understanding Domestic Violence Against Women: Using evolutionary psychology to extend the feminist functional analysis. *Violence and Victims*, 17, 255–264.

Phelan, A. (2009) Elder Abuse and Neglect: The nurse's responsibility in care of the older person. *International Journal of Older People Nursing*, 4(2), 115–119.

Phillips, L.H., MacLean, R.D.J. and Allen, R. (2002) Age and the Understanding of Emotions: Neuropsychological and sociocognitive perspectives. *Journals of Gerontology Series B: Psychological Sciences and Social Sciences*, 57(6), P526–P530.

Piaget, J. (1946/1969) *The Child's Conception of Time*. London: Routledge & Kegan Paul.

Piaget, J. (1965) *The Moral Judgment of the Child*. New York: The Free Press.

Piaget, J. (1990) *The Child's Conception of the World*. New York: Littlefield Adams.

Pomerleau, O.F. (1981) Underlying Mechanisms in Substance Abuse: Examples from research on smoking. *Addictive Behaviors*, 6, 187–196.

Pond, R., Stephens, C. and Alpass, F. (2010) Virtuously Watching One's Health. *Journal of Health Psychology*, 15(5), 734–743.

Pope, K.S. (1996) Memory, Abuse and Science: Questioning claims about the false memory syndrome epidemic. *American Psychologist*, 51(9), 957–974.

Porter, S., Yuille, J.C. and Lehman, D.R. (1999) The Nature of Real, Implanted, and Fabricated Memories for Emotional Childhood Events: Implications for the recovered memory debate. *Law and Human Behavior*, 23(5), 517–537.

Rabbitt, P., Scott, M., Lunn, M., Thacker, N., Lowe, C., Pendleton, N. et al. (2007) White Matter Lesions Account for all Age-related Declines in Speed but not in Intelligence. *Neuropsychology*, 21(3), 363–370.

Radley, A. (1999) The Aesthetics of Illness: Narrative, horror and the sublime. *Sociology of Health & Illness*, 21(6), 778–796.

Raine, A. (2002) Biosocial Studies of Antisocial and Violent Behavior in Children and Adults: A review. *Journal of Abnormal Child Psychology*, 30(4), 311–326.

Ravenscroft, A. (2001) Designing E-Learning Interactions in the 21st Century: Revisiting and rethinking the role of theory. *European Journal of Education*, 36(2), 133–156.

Rayner, E. (1986) *Human Development: An introduction to the psychodynamics of growth, maturity and ageing*. London: Routledge.

Read, J.D. (1999) The Recovered/False Memory Debate: Three steps forward, two steps back? *Expert Evidence*, 7(1), 1–24.

Reavey, P. and Brown, S.D. (2006) Transforming Past Agency and Action in the Present. *Theory and Psychology*, 16(2), 179–202.

Reavey, P. and Brown, S.D. (2007) Rethinking Agency in Memory: Space and embodiment in memories of childhood sexual abuse. *Journal of Social Work Practice: Psychotherapeutic Approaches in Health, Welfare and the Community*, 21(1), 5–21.

Reeves, R.R. and Norton, J.W. (2001) Foreign Accent-Like Syndrome During Psychotic Exacerbations. *Cognitive and Behavioral Neurology*, 14(2), 135–138.

Reimers, E. (2003) A Reasonable Grief: A discursive construction of grief in a public conversation on raising the shipwrecked M/S Estonia. *Mortality*, 8(4), 325–341.

Reiter, E.O. and Lee, P.A. (2001) Have the Onset and Tempo of Puberty Changed? *Archives of Pediatrics & Adolescent Medicine*, 155(9), 988–989.

Reker, G.T. and Woo, L.C. (2011) *Personal Meaning Orientations and Psychosocial Adaptation in Older Adults*. SAGE Open, 1(1).

Rescorla, R.A. (1988) Pavlovian Conditioning: It's not what you think it is. *American Psychologist*, 43(3), 151–160.

Resnick, M.D., Harris, L.J. and Blum, R.W. (1993) The Impact of Caring and Connectedness on Adolescent Health and Well-being. *Journal of Paediatrics and Child Health*, 29, S3–S9.

Revonsuo, A. (2001) Can Functional Brain Imaging Discover Consciousness in the Brain? *Journal of Consciousness Studies*, 8(3), 3–23.

Richards, G. (1987) *Human Evolution: An introduction for the behavioural sciences*. London: Routledge & Kegan Paul.

Richards, G. (2003) Paleopsychology: The road not taken. *Sexualities, Evolution & Gender*, 5(1), 23–30.

Riessman, C.K. and Quinney, L. (2005) Narrative in Social Work. *Qualitative Social Work*, 4(4), 391–412.

Rigby, K. and Slee, P.T. (1991) Bullying among Australian School Children: Reported behavior and attitudes toward victims. *Journal of Social Psychology*, 131(5), 615–627.

Riley, D. (1979) War in the Nursery. *Feminist Review*, 2, 82–108.

Ringrose, J. (2006) A New Universal Mean Girl: Examining the discursive construction and social regulation of a new feminine pathology. *Feminism & Psychology*, 16(4), 405–424.

Ritchie, A. and Woodward, R. (2009) Changing Lives: Critical reflections on the social work change programme for Scotland. *Critical Social Policy*, 29(3), 510–532.

Roberto, K.A. and McCann, B.R. (2011) Everyday Health and Identity Management among Older Women with Chronic Health Conditions. *Journal of Aging Studies*, 25(2), 94–100.

Roberts, R.E., Phinney, J.S., Masse, L.C., Chen, Y.R., Roberts, C.R. and Romero, A. (1999) The Structure of Ethnic Identity of Young Adolescents from Diverse Ethnocultural Groups. *Journal of Early Adolescence*, 19(3), 301–322.

Roosa, M.W., Tein, J.-Y., Reinholtz, C. and Angelini, P.J. (1997) The Relationship of Childhood Sexual Abuse to Teenage Pregnancy. *Journal of Marriage and Family*, 59(1), 119–130.

Rose, H. and Rose, S. (2001) *Alas, Poor Darwin: Arguments against evolutionary psychology*. London: Jonathan Cape.

Rothbart, M.K., Ahadi, S.A., Hershey, K.L. and Fisher, P. (2001) Investigations of Temperament at Three to Seven Years: The children's behavior questionnaire. *Child Development*, 72(5), 1394–1408.

Rotheram-Borus, M.J., Mahler, K.A., Koopman, C. and Langabeer, K. (1996) Sexual Abuse History and Associated Multiple Risk Behavior in Adolescent Runaways. *American Journal of Orthopsychiatry*, 66(3), 390–400.

Rovee-Collier, C. and Hayne, H. (2000) Memory in Infancy and Early Childhood. In E. Tulving and F.I.M. Craik (eds), *The Oxford Handbook of Memory* (pp. 267–282). New York: Oxford University Press.

Rowbotham, J., Stevenson, K. and Pegg, S. (2003) Children of Misfortune: Parallels in the cases of child murderers Thompson and Venables, Barratt and Bradley. *The Howard Journal of Criminal Justice*, 42(2), 107–122.

Ruch, G. (2002) From Triangle to Spiral: Reflective practice in social work education, practice and research. *Social Work Education*, 21(2), 199–216.

Ruch, G. (2005) Relationship-based Practice and Reflective Practice: Holistic approaches to contemporary child care social work. *Child & Family Social Work*, 10(2), 111–123.

Ruch, G., Turney, D. and Ward, A. (2010) *Relationship Based Social Work: Getting to the heart of practice*. London: Jessica Kingsley.

Rudman, D.L. (2006) Shaping the Active, Autonomous and Responsible Modern Retiree: An analysis of discursive technologies and their links with neoliberal political rationality. *Ageing & Society*, 26(02), 181–201.

Rustin, M. (2004) Learning from the Victoria Climbié Inquiry. *Journal of Social Work Practice*, 18(1), 9–18

Rustin, M. (2005) Conceptual Analysis of Critical Moments in Victoria Climbié's Life. *Child & Family Social Work*, 10(1), 11–19.

Rutter, M. (1979) Maternal Deprivation, 1972–1978: New findings, new concepts, new approaches. *Child Development*, 50(2), 283–305.

Rutter, M. and Madge, N. (1977) *Cycles of Disadvantage*. London: Heinemann.

Ryan,V., Malson, H., Clarke, S., Anderson, G. and Kohn, M. (2006) Discursive Constructions of 'Eating Disorders Nursing': An analysis of nurses' accounts of nursing eating disorder patients. *European Eating Disorders Review*, 14(2), 125–135.

Salin, D. (2003a). Bullying and Organisational Politics in Competitive and Rapidly Changing Work Environments. *International Journal of Management and Decision Making*, 4(1), 35–46.

Salin, D. (2003b). Ways of Explaining Workplace Bullying: A review of enabling, motivating and precipitating structures and processes in the work environment. *Human Relations*, 56(10), 1213–1232.

Santosuosso, A. and Bottalico, B. (2009) Neuroscience, Accountability and Individual Boundaries. *Frontiers in Human Neuroscience*, 3, 45.

Savin-Williams, R.C. and Diamond, L.M. (2000) Sexual Identity Trajectories Among Sexual-Minority Youths: Gender comparisons. *Archives of Sexual Behavior*, 29(6), 607–627.

Sayers, J. (1982) *Biological Politics: Feminist and anti-feminist perspectives*. London: Tavistock.

Schaffer, H.R. and Emerson, P.E. (1964a). The Development of Social Attachments in Infancy. *Monographs of the Society for Research in Child Development*, 29(3), 1–77.

Schaffer, H.R. and Emerson, P.E. (1964b). Patterns of Response to Physical Contact in Early Human Development. *Journal of Child Psychology and Psychiatry*, 5(1), 1–13.

Scharlach, A.E. (1991) Factors Associated with Filial Grief Following the Death of an Elderly Parent. *American Journal of Orthopsychiatry*, 61(2).

Scharlach, A. and Fuller-Thomson, E. (1994) Coping Strategies Following the Death of an Elderly Parent. *Journal of Gerontological Social Work*, 21(3), 85–100.

Schmidt, L. (2010) Psychosocial Consequences of Infertility and Treatment. In D.T. Carrell and C.M. Peterson (eds), *Reproductive Endocrinology and Infertility* (pp. 93–100). New York: Springer.

Schmitt, D.P., Shackelford, T.K., Duntley, J., Tooke, W. and Buss, D.M. (2001) The Desire for Sexual Variety as a Key to Understanding Basic Human Mating Strategies. *Personal Relationships*, 8(4), 425–455.

Schoen, R. and Standish, N. (2001) The Retrenchment of Marriage: Results from Marital Status Life Tables for the United States, 1995. *Population and Development Review*, 27(3), 553–563.

Schore, A.N. (2001) Minds in the Making: Attachment, the self-organizing brain, and developmentally-oriented psychoanalytic psychotherapy. *British Journal of Psychotherapy*, 17(3), 299–328.

Schore, A.N. (2005) Back to Basics: Attachment, affect regulation, and the developing right brain: Linking developmental neuroscience to pediatrics. *Pediatrics in Review*, 26(6), 204–217.

Schwartz, H.S. (2010) *Society Against Itself: Political correctness and organizational self-destruction*. London: Karnac.

Schwartz, R.H., Cohen, P., Hoffmann, N.G. and Meeks, J.E. (1989) Self-harm Behaviors (Carving). *Clinical Pediatrics*, 28(8), 340–346.

Schwartz, J.M., Stapp, H.P. and Beauregard, M. (2005) Quantum Physics in Neuroscience and Psychology: A neurophysical model of mind/brain interaction. *Philosophical Transactions of the Royal Society B: Biological Sciences*, 360(1458), 1309–1327.

Scott, J., Paykel, E., Morriss, R., Bentall, R., Kinderman, P., Johnson, T. and Hayhurst, H. (2006) Cognitive Behavioural Therapy for Severe and Recurrent Bipolar Disorders. *British Journal of Psychiatry*, 188(4), 313–320.

Seay, B.L. and Harlow, H.F. (1965) Maternal Separation in the Rhesus Monkey. *Journal of Nervous and Mental Disease*, 140(6), 434–441.

Seay, B., Hansen, E. and Harlow, H.F. (1962) Mother-Infant Separation in Monkeys. *Journal of Child Psychology and Psychiatry*, 3(3–4), 123–132.

Segal, H. (1964) *Introduction to the Work of Melanie Klein*. New York: Basic Books Publishing Co., Inc.

Segal, H. and Klein, M. (1973) *Introduction to the Work of Melanie Klein*, enlarged edn. London: Hogarth Press/Institute of Psycho-analysis.

Segal, J. (1993) *Melanie Klein*. Sage, London.

Segal, L. (2001) Nature's Way?: Inventing the natural history of rape. *Psychology, Evolution & Gender*, 3(1), 87–93.

Segraves, M.M. (2004) Midlife Women's Narratives of Living Alone. *Health Care for Women International*, 25(10), 916–932.

Selman, R.L. (1971) The Relation of Role Taking to the Development of Moral Judgment in Children. *Child Development*, 42(1), 79–91.

Sereny, G. (1995) *Albert Speer: His Battle with Truth*. Basingstoke: Macmillan.

Sereny, G. (1998) *Cries Unheard – Why Children Kill: The story of Mary Bell*. New York: Henry Holt & Co Inc.

Shanahan, M.J. (2000) Pathways to Adulthood in Changing Societies: Variability and mechanisms in life course perspective. *Annual Review of Sociology*, 26: 667–692.

Shaw, I. and Gould, N. (2001) *Qualitative Research in Social Work*. London: Sage.

Shechory, M. and Sommerfeld, E. (2007) Attachment Style, Home-Leaving Age and Behavioral Problems Among Residential Care Children. *Child Psychiatry & Human Development*, 37(4), 361–373.

Sheldon, B. (1987) The Psychology of Incompetence. *After Beckford? Essays on themes related to child abuse*. London: Royal Holloway and Bedford New College.

Shemmings, D. (2006) Using Adult Attachment Theory to Differentiate Adult Children's Internal Working Models of Later Life Filial Relationships. *Journal of Aging Studies*, 20(2), 177–191.

Shemmings, D. and Shemmings, Y. (2011) *Understanding Disorganized Attachment: Theory and Practice for Working with Children and Adults*. London: Jessica Kingsley.

Shiner, M., Scourfield, J., Fincham, B. and Langer, S. (2009) When Things Fall Apart: Gender and suicide across the life-course. *Social Science & Medicine*, 69(5), 738–746.

Shore, R. (1997) Rethinking the Brain: New insights into early development. New York: Families and Work Institute.

Skinner, B.F. (1938) *The Behavior of Organisms*. New York: Appleton-Century.

Skinner, B.F. (1971/2002) *Beyond Freedom and Dignity*. Indianapolis: Hackett Publishing Company, Inc.

Skinner, B.F. (1985) Cognitive Science and Behaviourism. *British Journal of Psychology*, 76(3), 291–301.

Slack, K.S., Holl, J.L., McDaniel, M., Yoo, J. and Bolger, K. (2004) Understanding the Risks of Child Neglect: An exploration of poverty and parenting characteristics. *Child Maltreatment*, 9(4), 395–408.

Slater, M., Antley, A., Davison, A., Swapp, D., Guger, C., Barker, C. et al. (2006) A Virtual Reprise of the Stanley Milgram Obedience Experiments. *PLoS ONE*, 1(1), e39.

Smith, C.A., Ireland, T.O. and Thornberry, T.P. (2005) Adolescent Maltreatment and its Impact on Young Adult Antisocial Behavior. *Child Abuse & Neglect*, 29(10).

Smith, G. and Nicolson, P. (2011) Despair? Older homeless men's accounts of their emotional trajectories. *Oral History*, 30–42.

Smith, V., Collard, P., Nicolson, P. and Bayne, R. (2012) *Key Concepts in Counselling and Psychotherapy: A Critical A–Z Guide to Theory*. Milton Keynes: McGraw-Hill/Open University Press.

Smithson, J. and Stokoe, E.H. (2005) Discourses of Work–Life Balance: Negotiating 'genderblind' terms in organizations. *Gender, Work & Organization*, 12(2), 147–168.

Smolak, L. and Murnen, S.K. (2002) A Meta-analytic Examination of the Relationship between Child Sexual Abuse and Eating Disorders. *International Journal of Eating Disorders*, 31(2), 136–150.

Spitz, R.A. and Wolf, K.M. (1946) Anaclitic Depression— An inquiry into the genesis of psychiatric conditions in early childhood II. *The Psychoanalytic Study of the Child*, 2, 312– 342.

Spock, B. (1946) *The Common Sense Book of Baby and Child Care*. Oxford: Duell, Sloan & Pearce.

Staddon, J.E.R. and Cerutti, D.T. (2003) Operant Conditioning. *Annual Review of Psychology*, 54(1), 115–144.

Stein, J.H. and Reiser, L.W. (1994) A Study of White Middle-Class Adolescent Boys' Responses to 'Semenarche' (The First Ejaculation). *Journal of Youth and Adolescence*, 23(3).

Steiner, J. (1985) Turning a Blind Eye: The Cover up for Oedipus. *International Review of Psycho-Analysis*, 12, 161–172.

Stevenson, O. (1986) Guest editorial on the Jasmine Beckford Inquiry. *British Journal of Social Work*, 16, 501–510.

Straka, S. and Montminy, L. (2006) Responding to the Needs of Older Women Experiencing Domestic Violence. *Violence Against Women*, 12(3), 251–267.

Sudbery, J. (2010) *Human Growth and Development: An introduction for social workers*. London: Routledge.

Sugarman, L. (1986) *Life span Development: Concepts, theories and interventions*. London: Methuen.

Sugarman, L. (2001) *Life-span Development: Frameworks, accounts and strategies*, 2nd edn. Hove: Psychology Press.

Swain, J.E., Lorberbaum, J.P., Kose, S. and Strathearn, L. (2007) Brain Basis of Early Parent–Infant Interactions: Psychology, physiology, and in vivo functional neuroimaging studies. *Journal of Child Psychology and Psychiatry*, 48(3–4), 262–287.

Sylva, K. and Lunt, I. (1983) *Child Development: A First Course*. Oxford: Basil Blackwell.

Symington, N. (1986) *The Analytic Experience: Lectures from the Tavistock*. London: Free Association Books.

Taylor, D. and Bury, M. (2007) Chronic Illness, Expert Patients and Care Transition. *Sociology of Health & Illness*, 29(1), 27–45.

Theron, L., Cameron, C.A., Didkowsky, N., Lau, C., Liebenberg, L. and Ungar, M. (2011) A 'Day in the Lives' of Four Resilient Youths: Cultural roots of resilience. *Youth and Society*, 43(3), 799–818.

Thomas, L.E., McCabe, E. and Berry, J.E. (1980) Unemployment and Family Stress: A reassessment. *Family Relations*, 29(4), 517–524.

Thomas, N., Stainton, T., Jackson, S., Cheung, W.Y., Doubtfire, S. and Webb, A. (2003) 'Your Friends Don't Understand': Invisibility and unmet need in the lives of 'young carers'. *Child & Family Social Work*, 8(1), 35–46.

Thomas, V.S. and Rockwood, K.J. (2001) Alcohol Abuse, Cognitive Impairment, and Mortality Among Older People. *Journal of the American Geriatrics Society*, 49(4), 415–420.

Thompson, S. (1990) Putting a Big Thing into a Little Hole: Teenage girls' accounts of sexual initiation. *Journal of Sex Research*, 27(3), 341–361.

Thornhill, R. and Thornhill, N.W. (1992) The Evolutionary Psychology of Men's Coercive Sexuality. *Behavioral and Brain Sciences*, 15(02), 363–375.

Tischner, I. (2012) *Fat Lives: A feminist psychological exploration*. London: Taylor & Francis.

Tolman, D.L., Striepe, M.I. and Harmon, T. (2003) Gender Matters: Constructing a model of adolescent sexual health. *Journal of Sex Research*, 40(1), 4–12.

Tripp, J. and Viner, R. (2005) Sexual Health, Contraception, and Teenage Pregnancy. *British Medical Journal*, 330(7491).

Tunaley, J.R., Walsh, S. and Nicolson, P. (1999) 'I'm not bad for my age': The meaning of body size and eating in the lives of older women. *Ageing & Society*, 19(06), 741–759.

Tunstill, J. and Allcock, D. (2007) *Understanding the Contribution of Sure Start Local Programmes to the Task of Safeguarding Children's Welfare*. London: DfES.

Turner, M.J., Killian, T.S. and Cain, R. (2004) Life Course Transitions and Depressive Symptoms among Women in Midlife. *International Journal of Aging and Human Development*, 58(4), 241–265.

Tyler, K.A., Hoyt, D.R. and Whitbeck, L.B. (2000) The Effects of Early Sexual Abuse on Later Sexual Victimization Among Female Homeless and Runaway Adolescents. *Journal of Interpersonal Violence*, 15(3), 235–250.

Uhlenberg, P., Cooney, T. and Boyd, R. (1990) Divorce for Women After Midlife. *Journal of Gerontology*, 45(1), S3–S11.

Umaña-Taylor, A.J., Diversi, M. and Fine, M.A. (2002) Ethnic Identity and Self-Esteem of Latino Adolescents. *Journal of Adolescent Research*, 17(3), 303–327.

Ussher, J.M. (1997) *Body Talk: The material and discursive regulation of sexuality, madness and reproduction*. London: Routledge.

Ussher, J.M. (2003) The Ongoing Silencing of Women in Families: An analysis and rethinking of premenstrual syndrome and therapy. *Journal of Family Therapy*, 25(4), 388–405.

Ussher, J.M., Hunter, M. and Cariss, M. (2002) A Woman-centred Psychological Intervention for Premenstrual Symptoms, drawing on cognitive-behavioural and narrative therapy. *Clinical Psychology & Psychotherapy*, 9(5), 319–331.

van der Horst, F. and van der Veer, R. (2008) Loneliness in Infancy: Harry Harlow, John Bowlby and issues of separation. *Integrative Psychological and Behavioral Science*, 42(4), 325–335.

van Heugten, K. (2010) Bullying of Social Workers: Outcomes of a grounded study into impacts and interventions. *British Journal of Social Work*, 40(2), 638–655.

Velmans, M. (2012) The Evolution of Consciousness. *Contemporary Social Science*, 7(2), 117–138.

Verhaak, C.M., Smeenk, J.M.J., Evers, A.W.M., van Minnen, A., Kremer, J.A.M. and Kraaimaat, F.W. (2005) Predicting Emotional Response to Unsuccessful Fertility Treatment: A prospective study. *Journal of Behavioral Medicine*, 28(2), 181–190.

Verhaeghen, P., Marcoen, A. and Goossens, L. (1993) Facts and Fiction About Memory Aging: A quantitative integration of research findings. *Journal of Gerontology*, 48(4), P157–P171.

Vincent, J.A. (2006) Ageing Contested: Anti-ageing science and the cultural construction of old age. *Sociology*, 40(4), 681–698.

Waddell, M. (2005) *Inside Lives: Psychoanalysis and the growth of personality*. London: Karnac.

Waller, G. (1991) Sexual Abuse as a Factor in Eating Disorders. *British Journal of Psychiatry*, 159(5), 664–671.

Wallerstein, J.S. (1986) Women After Divorce: Preliminary report from a ten-year follow-up. *American Journal of Orthopsychiatry*, 56(1), 65–77.

Wallerstein, J.S. and Blakeslee, S. (1995) *The Good Marriage: How and why love lasts*. Boston: Houghton Mifflin.

Warren, C.S., Gleaves, D.H., Cepeda-Benito, A., Fernandez, M. del C. and Rodriguez-Ruiz, S. (2005) Ethnicity as a Protective Factor against Internalization of a Thin Ideal and Body Dissatisfaction. *International Journal of Eating Disorders*, 37(3), 241–249.

Watson, J.B. (2009) *Behaviourism*, 7th edn. New Brunswick, NJ: Transaction.

Webb, S.A. (2010) (Re)Assembling the Left: The politics of redistribution and recognition in social work. *British Journal of Social Work*, 40(8), 2364–2379.

Weidman, J.C., Twale, D.J. and Stein, E.L. (2001) Socialization of Graduate and Professional Students in Higher Education: A perilous passage? *ASHE-ERIC Higher Education Report*, 28(3). San Francisco: Jossey-Bass, Publishers, Inc.

Weinberg, K.M., Olson, K.L., Beeghly, M. and Tronick, E.Z. (2006) Making up is Hard to Do, especially for mothers with high levels of depressive symptoms and their infant sons. *Journal of Child Psychology and Psychiatry*, 47(7), 670–683.

Welch, S. and Fairburn, C. (1994) Sexual Abuse and Bulimia Nervosa: Three integrated case control comparisons. *American Journal of Psychiatry*, 151(3), 402–407.

Werker, J.F. and Tees, R.C. (2005) Speech Perception as a Window for Understanding Plasticity and Commitment in Language Systems of the Brain. *Developmental Psychobiology*, 46(3), 233–251.

Wexler, H.K. and Williams, R. (1986) The Stay 'N Out Therapeutic Community: Prison treatment for substance abusers. *Journal of Psychoactive Drugs*, 18(3), 221–230.

Wiesemann, C., Ude-Koeller, S., Sinnecker, G. and Thyen, U. (2010) Ethical Principles and Recommendations for the Medical Management of Differences of Sex Development (DSD)/Intersex in Children and Adolescents. *European Journal of Pediatrics*, 169(6), 671–679.

Williams, A.W., Ware, J.E., Jr. and Donald, C.A. (1981) A Model of Mental Health, Life Events, and Social Supports Applicable to General Populations. *Journal of Health and Social Behavior*, 22(4), 324–336.

Williams, S. (2000) Chronic Illness as Biographical Disruption or Biographical Disruption as Chronic Illness? Reflections on a core concept. *Sociology of Health & Illness*, 22(1), 40–67.

Winnicott, D.W. (1965) *The Maturational Process and the Facilitating Environment*. New York: International Universities Press.

Winnicott, D.W. (1971/2001) *Playing and Reality*. London: Brunner-Routledge.

Wolock, I. and Horowitz, B. (1984) Child Maltreatment as a Social Problem: The neglect of neglect. *American Journal of Orthopsychiatry*, 54(4), 530–543.

Wonderlich, S.A., Wilsnack, R.W., Wilsnack, S.C. and Harris, T.R. (1996) Childhood Sexual Abuse and Bulimic Behavior in a Nationally Representative Sample. *American Journal of Public Health*, 86(8_Pt_1), 1082–1086.

Wood, J.T. (2001) The Normalization of Violence in Heterosexual Romantic Relationships: Women's narratives of love and violence. *Journal of Social and Personal Relationships*, 18(2), 239–261.

Woodcock, J. (2003) The Social Work Assessment of Parenting: An exploration. *British Journal of Social Work*, 33(1), 87–106.

Workman, L. and Reader, W. (2008) *Evolutionary Psychology: An introduction*. Cambridge: Cambridge University Press.

Wu, Z. and Schimmele, C.M. (2005) Repartnering After First Union Disruption. *Journal of Marriage and Family*, 67(1), 27–36.

Yan, E. and Tang, C.S.-K. (2003) Proclivity to Elder Abuse. *Journal of Interpersonal Violence*, 18(9), 999–1017.

Yardley, L. (1996) Reconciling Discursive and Materialist Perspectives on Health and Illness. *Theory & Psychology*, 6(3), 485–508.

Yip, K. (2006) Self-reflection in Reflective Practice: A note of caution. *British Journal of Social Work*, 36(5), 777–788.

Young, M. and Willmott, P. (1986) *Family and Kinship in East London*. London: Routledge & Kegan Paul.

Zajonc, R.B. (1965) Social Facilitation. *Science*, 149(3681), 269–274.

Zeanah, C.H., Berlin, L. and Boris, N.W. (2011) Practitioner Review: Clinical applications of attachment theory and research for infants and young children. *Journal of Child Psychology and Psychiatry*, 52(8), 819–833.

Zeitlyn, B.B. (1967) The Therapeutic Community: Fact or fantasy? *British Journal of Psychiatry*, 113(503), 1083–1086.

Zucker, K.J. (2005) Gender Identity Disorder in Children and Adolescents. *Annual Review of Clinical Psychology*, 1(1), 467–492.

# INDEX